UNDERSTANDING
ECONOMICS

REVIEWERS

DAVID M. NELSON
*Associate Professor of Economics and
Director, Center for Economic Education
Western Washington University, Bellingham, Washington*

WALTER S. SCHAEFFLER
*Social Studies Teacher
Summit High School, Summit, New Jersey*

SPECIAL ACKNOWLEDGEMENT
We gratefully acknowledge the assistance of Lawrence A. Mayer,
*Director of Publications of the Joint Council
on Economics Education.*

UNDERSTANDING
ECONOMICS

DR. ALLEN W. SMITH

Professor of Economics
Eastern Illinois University

 RANDOM HOUSE SCHOOL DIVISION / NEW YORK

DEDICATION

To my wife, Deanna, and to our children,
Mark, Mike, and Lisa, for their support
and patience during the writing of this book.

Project Editor: Lauren Fedorko
Editor: Janice Lemmo
Manufacturing Supervisor: Lenore Zani
Text Design and Production: Dimensions and Directions Ltd.
Photo Research: Helena Frost / Dana Cooper
Cover Design: Thomas Vroman Associates, Inc.
Cover Photo: © Allen Lee Page, The Stock Market

ISBN 0-676-39629-1

Manufactured in the United States of America

The Features of Your Textbook

Understanding Economics presents the key concepts of economics in a logical and meaningful order. To help you focus on those concepts, each unit and each chapter contain a number of distinctive features. Together, these study aids will help you look at problems in an analytical way so that you can form opinions, make educated decisions, and apply economic concepts.

Chapter Features

- Check Your Understanding. These questions follow the major sections within each chapter and enable you to review important concepts as they occur.

- Chapter Highlights. Each chapter concludes with a helpful summary of key points.

- Important Terms. This is a matching exercise, the first of four exercises at the close of every chapter.

- Extending Your Understanding. The discussion questions in these sections will lead you to look beyond the basic principles presented in a chapter and examine how those principles apply to real-life situations.

- Activities. These special projects and research suggestions take you outside the classroom to investigate real applications of the key concepts introduced in the chapter.

- Building Skills in Economics. The final exercise of each chapter will help you develop an important economic skill that could affect your daily life.

Special Features

- Career Feature. These features profile 18 different economics-related occupations. There is a career feature in each chapter.

- Biography Feature. Several biographical descriptions examine the lives of individuals who have made significant contributions to economics.

- Issues Feature. Each Issue explores the conflicting sides of a topic of economic interest, to give you an opportunity to develop a particular point of view. An Issue is followed by brief questions that will help you analyze the subject.

Throughout the textbook, important economic terms are highlighted in boldface, or darker, type. Terms are defined when introduced and appear again in the Glossary at the back of the book.

The study questions, activities, and special features of your textbook are designed to lead you through the course in a careful and consistent manner. You will find they can be used in a variety of ways, for large- or small-group discussion or as you and your teacher prefer.

Contents

UNIT 2

The American Business Structure

UNIT 3

Economic Performance

UNIT 4

Money, Banking, and Monetary Policy

UNIT 5

Problems on the Home Front

UNIT 6

The International Picture

UNIT 7

Personal Economics

Graphs, Charts and Tables

Issues

Careers

Biographies

Preface

Economics is a broad subject, and it is impossible to cover everything in a single course or textbook. However, by the time you have completed this course, you will know a great deal about the fundamental principles of economics and how they relate to your life. This knowledge will help you make intelligent and well-informed decisions, both as a consumer and as a citizen. For example, your understanding of economics will help you make decisions about earning money and about saving, investing, or spending your money. The decisions you make will affect you, your family, and others around you. Similarly, your understanding of economics will enable you to interpret candidates' positions on economic issues and help you decide on a candidate who, if elected, may someday vote on economic legislation that will affect the lives of many Americans.

This entire book covers the topics that will give you a solid foundation in economics. Let's briefly examine the major topics that will give you a better idea of how economics relates to you personally.

The American Economy

The American economy is quite remarkable. Through our system of free markets, basic economic questions are answered—and answered far more efficiently than they are in a command economy, such as that of the Soviet Union. Even more amazing is the fact that while these questions are being answered, individuals and businesses are allowed a high degree of freedom to pursue their own self-interests. Indeed, it is this economic freedom that makes the American economic system work. As remarkable as it is, the American economy is not without its problems. As you will learn in the chapters ahead, our economy has been plagued with a number of problems in recent years that have seriously affected millions of Americans.

How Prices and Wages Are Determined

Why do some people earn so much more than other people? Why do the prices of some things keep going up, while the prices of other things are coming down? Is there anything that can be done about rising prices? What will determine your future income? Most likely you have asked yourself these questions at one time or another. All of these questions involve the subject of economics, and we will be examining and trying to answer them in the chapters ahead.

Business in the American Economy

In order to examine the role of private enterprise in the American economy, we will consider various types of business organizations and list the advantages and disadvantages of each. We will consider the factors that determine the profits of a business firm and the circumstances under which a firm might be able to take advantage of consumers through excessively high prices.

Labor Unions and Collective Bargaining

Labor unions are, and always have been, very controversial in the United States, and it's difficult to find individuals who are neutral on the subject. As we study labor unions, you will see how and why unions developed as a strong economic force in the United States. We will define and study collective bargaining—the negotiation process between labor and management—and the laws that govern the collective-bargaining process.

Unemployment and Inflation

On a cold January day in 1983, approximately 20,000 applicants stood in line in front of a Milwaukee, Wisconsin, auto frame plant to apply for 200 job openings. The temperature was 17 degrees, and the wind-chill factor was 8 degrees below zero. Yet each job seeker endured the weather for the remote chance that he or she might be one of the lucky ones who would be hired. Similar scenes could be found all across the country in late 1982 and early 1983 as this nation experienced its worst unemployment in nearly half a century. The high unemployment in the early 1980s followed more than a decade of some of the worst inflation in the nation's history. From 1970 to 1980, average prices rose by 112 percent. This means that something that could have been purchased for $100 in 1970 cost $212 in 1980.

Both unemployment and inflation affect nearly every American. Inflation affects all Americans directly in the form of higher prices for the things they buy. Although unemployment does not affect every individual directly, it has an indirect impact on almost everyone. In addition to the millions of Americans who were unemployed during the early 1980s, millions of others—relatives, friends, or acquaintances of the unemployed—were affected indirectly. In addition, millions of other workers who did not actually lose their jobs suffered from the constant fear that they might soon join the ranks of the unemployed.

Whether or not unemployment and inflation will be serious problems for you and your generation depends to a large extent on government economic policies. We will examine the problems of unemployment and inflation in great detail and explore ways to reduce the suffering that results from these two basic economic problems.

Money and Banking

What do gold, seashells, furs, paper, boar tusks, whale teeth, copper, stones, and silver have in common? Each of these items, along with many others, has at some time and place served as money. As you will learn, **money** is anything that is generally accepted and used as a medium of payment. In the United States, money consists of coins, "checkbook" money, and pieces of paper known as Federal Reserve notes. A knowledge of the functions of money, of what constitutes the money supply, and of what the relationship is between the money supply and prices is essential to your understanding of how economics affects your daily life.

We will also look at the organization and functions of banks and the Federal Reserve System, and you will learn how banks can "create" money and how the Federal Reserve attempts to regulate the American economy through a series of actions known as "monetary policy."

Poverty and Urban Problems

Poverty has always existed in the United States to some extent, but the high unemployment of the early 1980s led to a sharp rise in poverty. In early 1983, an estimated two million Americans were homeless. Some were living out of their cars or sleeping in churches or other public shelters. Thousands of others were sleeping in the streets or in abandoned buildings. In addition, hungry individuals stood in long lines in many cities across the nation to receive free food. We will examine the causes and the extent of poverty in this country today. We will also discuss the problems facing the nation's cities, where many of the poor reside, and will include issues of housing, transportation, and the financing of local government.

Energy, Pollution, and the Environment

One of the most crucial factors in determining the health of the American economy is the cost and availability of energy. Much of the high inflation of the 1970s was caused by skyrocketing energy prices, because part of the production cost and much of the transportation cost of all manufactured items and all food products is the cost of energy. From 1973 to 1980, the world market price of crude oil rose from $3 a barrel to about $33 a barrel. This caused a sharp increase in the prices not only of gasoline and home heating oil, but also in the prices of almost everything else.

A secure future involves more than a healthy economy. It involves a healthy and pleasing environment, too. Unfortunately, there is often a basic conflict between economic growth and a clean environment. Governments are often put in the difficult position of having to examine the costs of protecting the environment and of having to choose between a healthy economy and a healthy environment.

The International Picture

How many things do you own and use that were not made in the United States? Probably more than you realize. If you consume either cocoa or bananas, you can be almost certain they were produced in a foreign country. In addition, much of your clothing, many small appliances, and many toys and games are produced outside the United States. In fact, even some "American-made" products are not totally American made. For example, some American automobiles contain parts that were manufactured in foreign countries.

The American economy is an integral part of a much larger and more complex world economy. In addition to the fact that many foreign-made items are sold in the United States, many American jobs depend on sales to foreign nations. We will examine international trade and finance and discuss how many other economic systems differ from our own.

Personal Economics

Finally, this textbook will help you explore how to get the most for your money. We will deal with such topics as whether you should buy your own home or rent; how you can buy furniture and appliances; and how you can spend your money wisely when you buy food, clothing, and other necessities.

We will also cover borrowing and investing money, and explain the importance of establishing and maintaining a good credit rating. You will learn about various types of loans and lenders, and how you can determine the true cost of loans after interest rates are included. In addition, we will examine different investment options, including bank deposits, corporate bonds, government bonds, corporate stocks, and real estate.

By the time you have completed this book, you will have learned that economics is and always will be a part of your life. You also will have learned that a good understanding of economic principles will help you make better decisions about economic matters and will help you live a more productive and enjoyable life.

UNDERSTANDING
ECONOMICS

UNIT 1

An Economic Overview

CHAPTER 1

INTRODUCTION TO ECONOMICS

Jeff and Kate, high school seniors, stare at the stack of books on the coffee table in front of them and then glance back at the TV set. With final exams about to begin, they both know they should finish studying as soon as the show they are watching is over.

An automobile commercial comes on in which a sleek sports car rounds a sharp curve. Jeff and Kate each have dreamed of owning a car, but both admit that the car on TV seems a long way off. After the commercial, a short news capsule is televised. One segment in particular catches Jeff's and Kate's attention. The reporter announces that the unemployment rate is up again. This will mean that summer jobs will be hard to obtain. Jeff and Kate sink slowly into their chairs as they each ponder their futures. They both need summer jobs in order to have enough money to start college in the fall.

Jeff and Kate may not realize it but each of the events just mentioned is directly related to economics. The difficulty of saving enough money to go to college, of getting a summer job, or of purchasing a new car is the result of economic factors. In fact, almost everything Jeff and Kate do—from going out on a date to going to school to choosing their careers—involves economics. Economics affects every individual, every family, every business, and every nation every day.

What Is Economics About?

Economics is the study of choice. It is about people and how they choose to use limited resources in an effort to satisfy unlimited wants. There are two important components to this definition: limited resources and unlimited wants. Together they form what is known as the problem of *scarcity*, which is the most basic of all economic problems. If we stop and think for a moment, we can see why scarcity is such a problem—there are not enough resources on this planet for people to get everything they want. As a result, choices must be made.

Both individuals and nations are faced with the problem of limited resources. Few individuals have enough money or earning power to buy everything they want. No nation in the world has sufficient resources to satisfy the wants of all of its people. A nation has a fixed amount of land, timber, mineral deposits, and other natural resources. At any given point in time, it also has only so many workers, factories, tools, and machines.

Do you have everything you want? Probably not. Very few people ever reach the stage where they have everything they want. In fact, one want often leads to another. It is important to point out, however, that there is a difference between wants and needs. Everyone needs food, clothing, and shelter, but other so-called "needs" are really "wants." For example, you may insist that you need a car, but you may live in an area where you really don't have to have one. You can walk, bicycle, or rely on public transportation to get around. Similarly, you may want new clothes, but whether or not you need them is a value judgment. If you think about it, you probably will agree that most people's needs are limited. In contrast, people's wants are unlimited.

Because of the problem of scarcity, nations, businesses, and individuals all must make choices in an effort to satisfy unlimited wants with limited resources. These choices are not always easy. Suppose you have saved some money and are thinking of buying a new bicycle. Before buying the bicycle, however, you may give some consideration to the possibility of buying something else instead. Would a stereo system give you more pleasure than the bicycle? What about the possibility of buying a used bike so you will have enough money left over to buy the new shoes you need or to put some money aside for college? Or would it be better to save the money toward a down payment on a used car that you can use on your part-time job as well as at college? Because your income is limited and you can buy only a limited number of things, you probably will give considerable thought to the situation before making your purchase.

However you decide to use your money, you will have to give up the opportunity to purchase something else that also may have given you pleasure. If you decide to purchase the second-hand bicycle so that you will have some money to put aside for college, you will have to give up the opportunity to buy the stereo system or to buy the new bicycle. Economists use the term **opportunity cost** to refer to the next best alternative that is given up when a decision is made to use resources in a particular way. In this example, if your second choice would have been the purchase of a stereo system, then the opportunity cost of buying the used bicycle and putting aside the money for college is the stereo system you could have had.

Money is not the only scarce resource that individuals have. Time is also a scarce resource. Suppose that on a particular Saturday night you have the opportunity to go out on a date with a person you like very much. At the same time, you also have the opportunity to go roller skating with several of your friends. Because you can't do both, you must make a choice. No matter which choice you make, you are going to pay a price in terms of the opportunity cost of your decision. If you decide to go out on the date, the opportunity cost of your choice is giving up the opportunity to go roller skating. If you decide to go roller skating, the opportunity cost of that decision is giving up the opportunity to go out on the date.

Nations, too, are constantly faced with the realities of opportunity costs. For example, the federal government must decide how much it will spend for national defense and how much will be spent on nondefense programs, such as education, transportation, and other public services. Since the government has a limited amount of money, a decision to spend more money on national defense usually will require funding for nondefense programs to be cut. Thus, the opportunity cost of the increased defense spending is the reduction in funding of nondefense programs.

Check Your Understanding

1. Define economic How does economics affect your life?

2. Why is scarcity the most basic of all economic problems?

3. What is meant by the term "opportunity cost"? How do opportunity costs affect both individuals and nations?

Satisfying People's Wants

As we have mentioned, economics is the study of how individuals and society choose to use limited resources in an effort to satisfy people's unlimited wants. Satisfying such wants involves the production of economic goods and services. We will first define the terms "economic goods" and "economic services," and then turn our attention to the factors of production needed to produce them. As you will see shortly, deciding which goods and services to produce and how to produce them are two key decisions faced by every society.

Economic Goods and Services

Economic goods are things of value that you can see, touch, and show to others. They are things like bicycles, books, stereos, and clothing. Economic goods also include such things as factories, stores, machines, and tools.

Economic services are intangible things that have value but often cannot be seen, touched, or shown to others. For example, suppose you go bowling on Saturday night. At the bowling alley, you pay for the rental of a pair of bowling shoes and a bowling ball and for the privilege of bowling several games. You enjoy the evening immensely and consider the outing worth the money you spent. However, in terms of tangi-

Individuals, like these customers at a supermarket checkout counter, are constantly making choices about what economic goods and services to buy.

ble purchases, you have nothing to show for your money. This is an example of an economic service. Other examples of economic services are medical care, legal advice, movies, and national defense.

Factors of Production

Factors of production, which are also called **productive resources,** are the basic resources needed for the production of economic goods and services. Economists, traditionally, have divided the factors of production into three basic categories: (1) natural resources; (2) capital goods; (3) labor. In addition, many economists add a fourth factor of production, entrepreneurship, to the list.

Natural resources are things provided by nature. Land, air, water, forests, coal, iron ore, oil, and other minerals are examples of natural resources. Natural resources are the basic materials an economy has to work with. They are the starting point of all production, and they represent the most basic limitation on the productive capacity of an economy. In other words, no matter how much skilled labor and technological knowledge an economy has, it cannot create goods if it lacks natural resources.

Capital goods are human-made resources that are used for the production of other goods and services. Factories, machines, tools, railroads, trucks, and business buildings are all examples of capital goods. Without capital goods, natural resources would not be very useful. For example, timber is a natural resource. No matter how much timber a nation has, however, it is of little use unless capital goods are available to turn it into lumber, firewood, or other usable products. In this instance, possible capital goods might include a simple axe, a chain saw, or a giant sawmill.

It is important to distinguish between capital goods and consumer goods.

Consumer goods—which are not a factor of production—are finished products sold to consumers for their own personal use. They include such things as food, clothing, TV sets, and newspapers. In contrast, *capital goods* are things that are used in the production of consumer goods and services. A factory that manufactures TV sets is a capital good. Some things can be either consumer goods or capital goods, depending on how they are used. For example, an automobile purchased for personal use is a consumer good. However, automobiles purchased for use as taxis or for other business purposes are capital goods.

Labor, sometimes called human resources, is any form of human effort exerted in production. It includes all kinds of work. The work of a janitor, teacher, lawyer, engineer, and the governor of your state are all examples of labor. Labor is essential to production, since natural resources and capital goods are of no value unless they can be put to use.

The three factors of production described above—natural resources, capital goods, and labor—must be combined and organized before production can take place. This is where entrepreneurship, the fourth factor of production, enters the picture. **Entrepreneurship** may be defined as the function of combining and organizing natural resources, capital goods, and labor; assuming the risks of business failure; and providing the creativity and managerial skills necessary for production to take place. An **entrepreneur** is a person who carries out these tasks in the hope of making financial gains from the endeavor.

In order to better understand the important role of entrepreneurship, let us look at the fictitious small community of Rossville. For many years, the Rossville Tile Factory manufactured farm drainage tiles from the high-quality clay soil of the area. Most of the community's labor force was employed by that factory. However, new technology resulted in the development of plastic drainage tiles that could be sold

Lumber is a valuable natural resource that is made useful by capital goods such as this heavy duty tractor.

for a lower price. This caused the company to begin reducing production and laying off workers until the owner of the Rossville Tile Factory finally decided to close the factory permanently. Thus, Rossville is a community with natural resources (high-quality clay), capital goods (the old tile factory), and labor (the unemployed tile workers). The fourth factor of production—entrepreneurship—which had been supplied by the owner of the tile factory for many years, is now missing. As a result, the other resources—the clay, the tile factory, and the unemployed workers—are all idle.

Suppose that Sarah Sharpe, who has just inherited some money from her grandmother, is looking for a business opportunity. Sarah hears about the old tile factory, which is up for sale, and wonders if it might be used for the manufacturing of bricks. She knows that clay can be used for the production of bricks and has also found out that there are no brick factories nearby. Given the situation, Sarah thinks she can earn a profit by producing bricks in Rossville. She decides to convert the old tile factory into a brick factory, and soon the unemployed workers have new jobs. The entrepreneurship provided by Sarah has resulted in the combining of the other factors of production—the clay, the old tile factory, and the unemployed workers—to start a new production unit.

Check Your Understanding

1. What is an economic good? What is an economic service? Give some examples of each.

2. Define each of the four factors of production. How must these factors be combined for the production of goods and services?

3. Why is entrepreneurship such an important factor of production?

The Basic Economic Questions: What? How? For Whom?

Given the problem of scarcity, no nation has sufficient productive resources to produce all the goods and services its people want. Each nation has only a limited supply of natural resources, capital goods, labor, and entrepreneurship. Thus, a nation can produce only so many new factories, houses, automobiles, refrigerators, TV shows, books, movies, and hamburgers in any given year. As a result, the nation must make difficult choices.

There are three basic economic questions that every nation must consider when making these choices. They are (1) What goods and services shall be produced? (2) How shall they be produced? and (3) For whom shall they be produced? Let us briefly examine each of these questions.

Within every nation, people must have some method of deciding what combination of goods and services they should produce with their limited resources. For example, they must decide what portion of total production will be devoted to capital goods and what portion will be devoted to consumer goods. Once this decision is made, it is necessary to decide what kinds of consumer and capital goods will be produced. For example, will the production of consumer goods be restricted to the basic necessities, or will luxury goods, such as stereos and cameras, be produced as well? If luxury goods are to be produced, what kind and how many of each will be produced?

Once the question of what to produce is answered, it is necessary to decide what production methods are to be used. For example, food can be produced by a large number of workers using simple and inexpensive tools, or by a small number of workers using complex

Economic planners make daily decisions about what, how, and for whom goods and services are produced.

and expensive machinery. The same is true of the production of most items you use every day.

Because no nation can produce enough goods and services to satisfy everybody's wants, it is necessary for people to have a method of deciding who gets the goods and services produced. Should everybody get an equal share, or should some people get more goods and services than others? If some people are to get more, how much more should they receive? This second question is perhaps the most difficult question of all because it involves the issue of fairness; and different people have different ideas about what is fair.

In a command economy, the government decides basic questions, such as how much tea is picked on this plantation.

Basic Kinds of Economic Systems

In order to answer the basic economic questions, every society must have some kind of organized set of procedures. This organized set of procedures is called the **economic system.** Although every nation's economic system has some unique characteristics, there are basically three kinds of economic systems in the world. They are (1) traditional economies; (2) command economies; and (3) market economies.

In actuality, although traditional economies exist in various parts of the world today, there never have been any pure command economies or pure market economies. These concepts are simplified representations of the real world, or **economic models.** Economic models are devised by economists to make complex situations more understandable. In this instance, they give economists a basis from which to describe or explain the complex economic situations that today exist in most countries of the world. Economic models will be used at various times in this book to represent similar economic concepts.

Most of the major economies in the world today are actually mixtures of command economies and market economies. Because of their composition, they are known as **mixed economies.** These economies vary greatly in how closely they resemble either the pure command economy or the pure market economy. We will take a look at mixed economies as soon as we examine the three basic kinds of economic systems.

Traditional Economies

Traditional economies are found primarily in the rural, nonindustrial areas of the world. In such areas, there is no national economy. Instead, there are many small segmented economies, each centered around a family or tribal unit. Each unit produces most of its own goods and consumes what it produces. The basic economic questions of "what," "how," and "for whom" are answered directly by the people involved, and the answers are usually based on tradition.

For example, in the East African country of Somalia, more than 75 percent of the people are nomadic. They raise herds of camels, cattle, goats, and sheep, and they live in small, collapsible huts. When the grass and water of an area are used up, these people move on to a new spot, just as their ancestors did for centuries before them. Their life is relatively simple, and their method of answering basic economic questions is based on a tradition passed down from one generation to the next.

Command Economies

In command economies, the basic economic questions are answered by government officials. Government leaders decide what goods and services will be produced, how they will be produced, and how they will be distributed. Individuals have little control or influence over the way the basic economic questions are

answered. They are told what to produce, how to produce it, and what they will receive.

Command economies are often called **planned economies** because the government engages in elaborate, detailed planning in an effort to produce and distribute goods and services in a way that is consistent with the wishes of government leaders. Command economies usually are also characterized by government ownership of the economy's natural resources and capital goods. The economies of China and the Soviet Union are examples of predominantly command economies.

Market Economies

A market economy is the opposite of a command economy. In a command economy, the government answers the basic economic questions. In a market economy, basic economic questions are answered by individual households and businesses through a system of freely operating markets. When we examine the laws of supply and demand, you will learn a great deal about markets. For purposes of our current discussion, however, a **market** can be defined

In a market economy, buyers often have a wide selection of goods from which to choose when they make a purchase.

as the arrangement through which potential buyers and sellers come together to exchange goods and services. A market can be a specific place, such as a local farmers' market, but it usually refers to a much broader geographic area. The area covered by a specific market may be a local community, the entire nation, or, in the case of commodities such as gold and silver, the world.

In market economies, natural resources and capital goods are usually privately owned. In such economies, buyers and sellers have a great deal of economic freedom, and they send signals to one another as they interact through the system. For example, by purchasing more of an item than usual, buyers send a signal to producers to increase production of that item. Similarly, by reducing their purchases of an item, buyers signal producers to reduce production of that item.

The American economy is predominantly a market economy. Other examples of predominantly market economies include the economies of Canada, Japan, and many of the countries of Western Europe.

Mixed Economies

In actual practice, there are no real economies in the world that rely solely on freely operating markets or on government decisions to answer basic economic questions. All major economies are *mixed economies* in the sense that some decisions are made through a system of freely operating, or free, markets, by individual households and businesses, and some are made by the government. In mixed economies, a distinction is usually made between the **private sector,** in which decisions are made primarily by individual households and businesses, and the **public sector,** in which decisions are made by the government.

There are enormous differences in the public–private sector mix among the major economies of the world. In the Soviet Union, most of the economic activity is in the public sector, with the government making most of the economic decisions. In the United States, most of the economic activity is in the private sector, with individual households and businesses making most of the economic decisions through the system of free markets. Thus, it is appropriate to label the Soviet Union as a *predominantly* command economy and the United States as a *predominantly* market economy.

The American and Soviet economies also differ in terms of who owns the means of production: factories, stores, natural resources, and so forth. In the United States, most businesses are privately owned and operated. In the Soviet Union, most businesses are owned and operated by the government. As a result of the differences in the two economies, individuals in the United States have a great deal more personal freedom than their counterparts in the Soviet Union.

Check Your Understanding

1. What are the three basic economic questions that every nation must answer? What are some of the things that nations must consider when answering these questions?

2. What are the three basic kinds of economic systems? What are the characteristics of each?

3. What is a market? How do buyers and sellers send signals to one another in a market economy?

4. What is a mixed economy? How do mixed economies differ from one another?

CAREERS: Economist

Economists study the ways in which individuals and society choose to use limited resources, such as natural resources, labor, factories, and machines, in an effort to satisfy unlimited wants. They are concerned with the production, distribution, and consumption of goods and services and are interested in helping society get as much satisfaction as possible from its limited resources. Economists collect, process, and analyze data to determine the costs and benefits of using resources in various ways.

Economists are employed in a number of different job settings. About half of all economists are employed by government agencies, including a wide range of federal agencies. Government economists collect and analyze information about economic conditions in the nation and about possible changes in government economic policies. Much of this information is published in government bulletins and reports. Private business firms are also a major source of employment for economists, with many economists working for banks, insurance companies, investment companies, manufacturing firms, economic research firms,

and management consulting firms. Some economists operate their own economic consulting businesses. In addition to government and business economists, there are economists who teach and do research at colleges and universities.

The amount of training required to become an economist depends on the type of employment that a potential economist is seeking. A bachelor's degree (four years of college) with a major in economics is sufficient for many entry-level research, management trainee, and business sales jobs. However, most job openings for economists require advanced training. Those college graduates who wish to seek higher level jobs usually enroll in graduate school and obtain either a master's degree or a doctorate in economics. A master's degree requires approximately one year of advanced training, and a doctorate usually requires at least four. Economists must have a thorough understanding of economic theory, mathematical methods of economic analysis, and basic statistical procedures. In addition, training in computer science is becoming increasingly important.

Chapter Highlights

1   Economics is about people and the choices they make. More specifically, economics is the study of how individuals and society choose to use limited resources in an effort to satisfy unlimited wants.

2   Scarcity, the problem of limited resources and unlimited wants, is the most basic economic problem.

3   Because of the problem of scarcity, nations, businesses, and individuals must make difficult choices in an effort to satisfy unlimited wants with limited resources.

4   Any time you decide to use a scarce resource in a particular way, you incur an opportunity cost—the cost of the next best alternative use of that resource.

5   Economic goods are things of value that can be seen, touched, and shown to others. Economic services are intangible things that have value but often cannot be seen, touched, or shown to others.

6   Economists have traditionally divided factors of production into three categories: (1) natural resources; (2) capital goods; and (3) labor. An important fourth factor of production is entrepreneurship. These factors of production are needed to produce goods and services.

7   There are three basic economic questions that every nation of the world must answer. They are (1) What goods and services shall be produced? (2) How shall they be produced? and (3) For whom shall they be produced?

8   There are basically three kinds of economic systems in the world. They are (1) traditional economies; (2) command economies; and (3) market economies. In actual practice, however, most of the major economies of the world are mixed economies in the sense that they have some characteristics of both command and market economies.

9   Traditional economies are found primarily in the rural, nonindustrial areas of the world. The economies of China and the Soviet Union are predominantly command economies. The economies of the United States, Canada, Japan, and many of the countries of Western Europe are predominantly market economies.

10   Mixed economies vary greatly in their private–public sector mix. In the Soviet Union, most of the economic activity is in the public sector. In the United States, most of the economic activity is in the private sector.

Important Terms

Match each of the following terms with the correct definition:

factors of production	scarcity	entrepreneurship
market economies	economic goods	economic services
command economies	economics	natural resources
opportunity cost	capital goods	mixed economies
traditional economies	market	economic model
labor	consumer goods	economic system

1. The study of how individuals and society choose to use limited resources in an effort to satisfy unlimited wants.

2. The function of combining and organizing the natural resources, capital goods, and labor; assuming the risks of business failure; and providing the creativity and managerial skills necessary for production to take place.

3. Things needed for the production of economic goods and services.

4. A simplified representation of the real world.

5. Economies found primarily in the rural, nonindustrial areas of the world, in which the basic economic questions are answered directly by the people involved and the answers are usually based on tradition.

6. Intangible things that have value but often cannot be seen, touched, or shown to others.

7. Finished products that are sold to consumers.

8. Any form of human effort exerted in production.

9. The problem of limited resources and unlimited wants.

10. The next best alternative use of a resource that is given up in order to use the resource for a specific purpose.

11. An organized set of procedures for answering basic economic questions.

12. Productive resources that are provided by nature, such as land, forests, coal, and iron ore.

13. Human-made productive resources, such as factories, tools, and machines, that are necessary for the production of economic goods and services.

14. Economies found in the Soviet Union, China, and other communist countries, in which the basic economic questions are answered by government officials.

15. Economies found in the United States, Canada, Japan, and many of the countries of Western Europe, in which most of the economic questions are answered by a system of free markets.

16. Things of value that can be seen, touched, and shown to others.

17. The arrangement through which potential buyers and sellers come together to exchange goods and services.

18. Economies that have characteristics of both command and market economies.

Extending Your Understanding

1. Imagine a world without the problem of scarcity—a world where nobody had to work and people could have everything they wanted free of charge. Do you think you would enjoy living in such a world? Why or why not?

2. Try to think of several important decisions that you have made recently. What was the opportunity cost of each decision? Do you think that the opportunity cost of any of your decisions was too high?

3. Why is it so important for you and other students to learn about economics?

Activities

1. Over the course of an afternoon, keep a record of your thoughts and activities. Then explain how each is related to economics.

2. Read a newspaper or a news magazine for a week. Then, based on what you read, write a short report called "Economics in the News."

Building Skills in Economics: Interpreting Statistics and Reading a Table

Statistics are numerical facts or data that are assembled, classified, and tabulated. Economists use statistics to measure, compare, contrast, and analyze different aspects of an economy.

One of the common ways in which statistics are presented is in a table. A **table** is a compact arrangement of related facts and figures, arranged sequentially in horizontal rows and vertical columns. Where a row and a column intersect, the data are related. Tables make statistical information easier to read than if the information were presented in paragraph form.

The table that follows presents statistics on how 2,000 suburban residents routinely eat their evening meal. The questions will help you analyze the statistics presented.

Applying Economics Skills

1. What is the most frequent source of the evening meal for the 2,000 suburban residents?
2. What is the least frequent source of the evening meal for these residents?
3. How many of these residents routinely do *not* eat at home?
4. If 725 residents ate at fast-food restaurants and only 20 ate at specialty restaurants two years ago, which type of restaurant is growing faster now?

HOW 2,000 SUBURBAN RESIDENTS ROUTINELY EAT THEIR EVENING MEAL

Source of Evening Meal	Number of Residents	Percentage Distribution
Fast-food restaurants	810	40.5%
Meal prepared at home	600	30.0%
Full-service American-food restaurants	380	19.0%
Specialty restaurants	210	10.5%

CHAPTER 2

THE AMERICAN ECONOMY

As you learned in Chapter 1, the American economic system is predominantly a market economy that relies primarily on a system of free markets to make decisions about what to produce, how to produce, and for whom to produce. The American economic system also is often referred to as "capitalism," or a "capitalist" economy. Basically, **capitalism** is a form of economic organization in which the businesses are privately owned and operated and where free or freely operating markets coordinate most economic activity.

Two of the most important characteristics of capitalism are private ownership of property and the freedom of opportunity to engage in business activities. Therefore, capitalism is sometimes referred to as a "private-enterprise" system or a "free-enterprise" system. However, since most economists use the terms "market economy" and "capitalism" to refer to the American economy, we also will use these two terms. The two terms can be used interchangeably. The word "capitalism" emphasizes the private-ownership aspect of the economy, whereas the term "market economy" emphasizes the fact that a system of free markets makes most of the basic economic decisions. Since we are primarily interested in understanding how the basic economic decisions are made in the American economy, we will use the term "market economy" in most of our discussion.

In a market economy, individuals are free to engage in whatever business and work activities they choose so long as they do not violate any laws. Thus, an individual might become a lawyer, automobile mechanic, shopkeeper, or baseball player, among other things. It is this freedom of choice, accompanied by the profit motive, that makes a market economy work.

In its narrowest and most common definition, the word **profit** refers to the money a business has left over after all costs have been paid. It is the difference between total income and total expenses. However, the word *profit* can be used in a much broader sense to refer to the financial gain or benefit received by any individual or business as a result of work activity. For example, in exchange for working three hours each weekday at Double Dip Ice Cream Parlor, Sandy receives $60 every Friday afternoon. In the broad sense of the word, this represents her profit. For purposes of this chapter, we want to use this broader definition. We also will expand on this definition and define **profit motive** as the desire to maximize financial gains. Thus, the profit motive will lead businesses to attempt to maximize their profits, or to acquire as much profit as possible. It will lead individuals to attempt to maximize their wages and salaries. Of course, there are factors other than profit that motivate businesses in the workplace. The profit motive, however, is a driving force.

It is important to emphasize that the American economy is not and never has been a "pure" market economy or an example of "pure" capitalism. As you learned in Chapter 1, there have never been any "pure" economies in the world—either market or command. All economies are "mixed" in the sense that some decisions are made by individuals and private businesses through a system of free markets and some are made by the government. However, the American economy is *predominantly* a market economy because most economic decisions are made by individuals and businesses. It also is *predominantly* a capitalist economy because most businesses are privately owned and operated.

Because it is predominantly a market economy, the American economy is self-regulating. In other words, there is no "big brother" to tell people which foods to buy, which jobs to take, or which businesses to enter. Let us look at this aspect of the economy more closely.

The Amazing Invisible Hand

Do you ever lie awake at night worrying that the stores in your community won't have your favorite foods the next time you or your parents go shopping? Or, if you are saving your money for a major purchase, such as a motorcycle or a used car, do you worry that when you have saved enough money, the item you want will not be available? Probably not. Most Americans simply take it for granted that the items they want will be in the stores when they are ready to go shopping. If you stop and think about it, though, the fact that most of these items usually are available is truly a remarkable accomplishment.

Consider a major American city, such as New York, Chicago, or Los Angeles. Millions of people in each of these cities would be on the verge of starvation within a week if the tons and tons of food that must arrive daily were to be delayed. Yet millions of people in each of these cities can sleep easily at night without worrying about a breakdown in the complex economic processes upon which the city's existence depends. They may not understand how the economic system works, but they are confident that it will continue to deliver the goods and services they need at precisely the time they need them. Who is responsible for such elaborate planning? The answer may surprise you.

Who Does the Planning?

Suppose you live in Chicago and you get up one morning with a craving for a bowl of cornflakes with a sliced banana on top. Perhaps it has been months since you last purchased either cornflakes or bananas. Yet you can be almost certain that if you go to the nearest supermarket, both the cornflakes and the bananas will be there waiting for you.

Americans expect to find plentiful supplies of whatever goods they need in supermarkets, produce markets, and department stores.

The cornflakes may have been manufactured from corn grown in Iowa, and the bananas were grown in a foreign country. How did the corn farmers decide to grow enough corn, and how did the manufacturer of cornflakes and your local supermarket manager know to have the box of cornflakes on the store shelf when you arrived? They didn't know you would awaken that particular morning with a craving for cornflakes. What's even more amazing is that the highly perishable bananas had to be grown in a foreign country and shipped to your local supermarket at just the right time, so they would be neither green nor overripe on the very morning that you decided you wanted them.

Who do you think makes sure that each city has the proper amount of each of the thousands of goods and services that the people need and want? Does the government of each city have a master plan for seeing that the needs of its citizens are met? Or do the state and federal governments plan to have the right amounts of goods and services delivered at the proper times to each geographic area?

The answer to these questions is that no government determines either the production or the distribution of goods and services in the United States. If the government doesn't do the planning, then who does? As amazing as it may seem, the answer is, "Nobody." No government agency, no business firm, and no individual is responsible for seeing that all of the economic needs of the people of Chicago, or of any other city, are met. Yet most of the needs are, in fact, met. Goods and services are produced and made available to the people in the right amounts at the proper time and in the correct locations.

The Invisible-Hand Principle

It is the American economic system itself that determines the production and distribution of economic goods and services. Some economists say that the economic system works like an "invisible hand" in determining what should be produced, how it should be produced, and for whom it should be produced. This invisible-hand principle was first identified by Adam Smith, a Scottish professor who is generally considered to be the founder of economics. In 1776, the same year that our Declaration of Independence was signed, Adam Smith published a monumental work entitled *The Wealth of Nations*.

In this book, Smith argued that in a market economy, if individuals were allowed to pursue their own self-interests without interference by the government, they would be led, as if by an invisible hand, to achieve what is best for society. Although the American economy is very different from the type of economy that Adam Smith described more than two hundred years ago, the principle of the invisible hand still applies to our economy in a modified way.

With some exceptions, individuals are generally motivated by economic forces. Most individuals tend to act in such a way as to obtain the greatest amount of satisfaction for the least amount of sacrifice or cost. Thus, businesses

BIOGRAPHY   Adam Smith: Founder of Economics

1723—1790

Adam Smith, who was affectionately called "a shy and absent-minded scholar" by his contemporaries, revolutionized the economic world with the publication of his book *The Wealth of Nations* in 1776. Because of the ideas expounded in this book, Smith is generally credited with championing the economic freedom, industrialization, and prosperity that characterized the Western world during the nineteenth century.

At the age of 28, the Scottish-born Smith became a professor of logic and moral philosophy at the University of Glasgow. His studies led him to believe that people always act in their own best interests. Individual self-interest, he contended, was not a curse but a powerful vehicle for economic progress. He argued that if individuals were allowed to pursue their own interests free from government interference, they would be led as if by an "invisible hand" to promote what was best for society as a whole.

Smith also promoted other revolutionary ideas. He argued that the wealth of a nation did not lie with gold and silver, as was commonly thought, but rather was determined by the goods and services available to the people. In addition, he recognized the advantages of the division of labor. To Smith, it was more productive for a worker to become skilled at and complete a particular task in a job than it was for the worker to do the entire job alone. Such greater productivity would in turn lead to greater wealth for individuals.

Smith's ideas paved the way for the systematic study of economics. Later economists were to build on Smith's foundation. Because of his approach to economic questions, his organization of the discipline, and his substantive theory, Adam Smith is generally regarded as the founder of economics.

will attempt to maximize their profits, workers will seek higher wages and/or increased leisure time, and consumers will attempt to get the maximum pleasure from goods and services purchased at the lowest price.

If businesses wish to maximize profits, they must produce the goods and services that consumers wish to buy and make them available to consumers at the right time and in the right places. This partially explains why cornflakes and bananas are available in local supermarkets when individuals wish to buy them. Producers and sellers of cornflakes and bananas do not know which individual consumers are going to want these products on any given day, but they do know that a substantial number of people probably will want to purchase these items each day. If these producers and sellers want to maximize their profits, they must make sure that these commodities are available when and where the consumers want them. In this way, the American economy operates as if an invisible hand were regulating it.

Check Your Understanding

1. What is meant by the invisible-hand principle?

2. How does this principle operate to make sure that the proper combination and quantity of goods and services are available at the right place and time?

Competing fast-food restaurants often line roads leading in and out of American towns and cities.

The Importance of Competition

For the invisible-hand principle to work, there must be a great deal of **competition.** This means a substantial degree of economic rivalry among sellers, buyers, workers, and employers. It is competition that keeps sellers of goods and services from charging excessively high prices. In order to gain a better understanding of how competition keeps prices down, let us look at a specific example.

The Hamburger Price War

Suppose that in your community Burger is the only place where you can buy hamburgers. Taking advantage of the situation, the owner of Burger decides to raise his price. At first he may experiment with only a small price increase, perhaps ten cents per hamburger. Soon, though, he discovers that he can sell just as many hamburgers after the ten-cent price increase as before. As a result, he raises his price even higher—an additional ten cents. This second price increase results in a small decline in sales, and the Burger owner realizes that people may substitute hotdogs from another restaurant if he raises his price again. So he confines his increase to 20 cents a burger and continues to attract many customers.

Observing the situation closely, the owner of Heloise's Hamburgers, in a neighboring community, decides to open a new restaurant right across the street from Burger. She thinks she can sell her hamburgers for a much higher price than what she could charge at her other location. At first, Heloise's Hamburgers may charge almost as much as Burger has been charging. However, both the new seller and the old seller soon learn an important lesson. There are not enough consumers in the community to buy all the hamburgers that the two restaurants want to sell at the current high prices. If each restaurant wants to stay in business, it must try to attract more customers.

In an effort to take customers away from Burger, the owner of Heloise's Hamburgers probably will lower her price. As customers abandon Burger to buy less expensive hamburgers across the street, however, the owner of Burger will be forced to reduce his price even further than that of his new competitor. The two sellers may continue their price war until the price of hamburgers in your community drops to a record low.

What have you just learned? You have learned that competition is necessary for the invisible-hand principle to work. The two hamburger sellers were each pursuing their own self-interests of trying to maximize their profits. At the same time, the consumers were also following their own self-interests by patronizing the seller with the lower price. In order to keep their customers and/or attract new customers, the sellers found it necessary to lower their prices. Thus, in this case, when both the sellers and buyers of hamburgers pursued their own self-interests, what was best for the community was achieved just as if an invisible hand were at work.

As we have just seen, though, this is not always true. When there was only one seller, the pursuit of personal interests had a negative effect on the community. Thus, sometimes the pursuit of one's self-interests does not result in the common good.

Competition in the Job Market

Competition is also essential if workers are to receive the highest possible wages and if employers are to be able to hire the most qualified workers. Suppose you go to college and study to become an electrical engineer. When you graduate and begin looking for a job, how do you know you will be paid as much as you are worth? Again, the answer is competition. If you have earned high grades in college, there probably will be a substantial number of employers

interested in hiring you. These employers will compete with one another, and as a result, you may be offered a much higher salary and better working conditions than would be the case if only one firm had an interest in you.

Just as employers compete with one another in their efforts to hire the very best job candidates, potential employees compete with one another to get the best jobs. The competition between job seekers begins long before they are actually ready to accept jobs. Many of you are already engaged in competition for the jobs that you hope to get in the future. You know that if you don't go on to college, your high school performance will be considered the best measure of your potential job performance by some employers. If you do plan to attend college, your academic performance in high school will play an important role in determining which colleges will accept you. Once you get to college, you will be competing with other students who also want to get a top job after graduation.

Competition for jobs tends to provide employers with better qualified employees. Similarly, competition among employers for new employees tends to provide the employees with higher earnings and better working conditions.

Check Your Understanding

1. How does competition enable the invisible-hand principle to work?

2. How does competition in the job market benefit both employers and employees?

The Price System

You have just learned that competition controls a market economy. It prevents individuals and businesses from taking advantage of one another when they pursue their own self-interests. Yet competition alone is not sufficient to enable an economy to operate properly. An economy must also have a coordination and communication system through which the various sectors can interact with one another. The basic coordination and communication system of a market economy is the **price system.**

The price system operates on the principle that everything bought and sold has a price. Every good and service produced has a price, and every form of labor has a price. The price of labor is the wage a worker receives.

Through the price system, producers and consumers transmit valuable information to each other that helps keep the economy in balance. Such information helps producers decide whether to increase or decrease production of their various products. Similarly, it helps employees decide which careers to choose. Let us see how the price system maintains balance in a market economy.

Communicating Messages Between Buyers and Sellers

Suppose consumers decide they want more tea and less coffee. How would they inform the coffee and tea producers of their preferences? They would send a message through the price system by buying more tea and less coffee. As consumers start to buy more tea, there will be a temporary shortage, causing the price of tea to rise. As the price of tea rises, producers will increase their production of tea. When the additional tea reaches the market, the price will tend to fall back toward the original level. Consumers then will have the extra tea they want.

At the same time that the quantity of tea produced is being adjusted upward to meet the wishes of consumers, a downward adjustment also will be taking place in the production of coffee. As consumers reduce their purchases of coffee, there will be a temporary surplus, which will lead to a reduction in price. At the lower price, coffee production will be less profitable for producers, and they will reduce production until the surplus has been eliminated. Once this happens, the price of coffee will tend to return toward its original level. The net result of the above action is that, with both consumers and producers following their own self-interests, the desired adjustment in the production of tea and coffee was accomplished efficiently with messages communicated through the price system.

Communicating Messages Between Employers and Employees

In a market economy, employers and employees also send messages to each other through the price system, and the net result is the proper allocation of workers among the various job categories. Suppose, for example, that there was a surplus of electricians and a shortage of

Through the classified, or help wanted ads, employers communicate with potential employees about job opportunities.

plumbers. How would the price system restore balance to these two occupations? Competition among electricians for the scarce jobs in that field would result in a decline in the wage rate of electricians. In the meantime, plumbers' wages would be increasing because potential employers would be competing with each other to hire the scarce plumbers.

The net result of these actions will mean falling wages for electricians and rising wages for plumbers. Young people contemplating a career in one of these two fields will be more likely to enter the higher paying field of plumbing. As more young people train to become plumbers and fewer train to become electricians, balance will be restored between these two occupations. The shortage of plumbers will be eliminated, and wages may decline.

At the same time, the surplus of electricians will be eliminated, and wages in that occupation will tend to rise toward their original level. Once again, the price system has communicated messages between employers and employees and eliminated the problems of shortages and surpluses.

The Price System in the American Economy

The previous examples of the price system correcting problems of shortages and surpluses were based on the assumption of a theoretical "pure" market economy. In such an economy, the price system would serve as an almost perfect communications system in which producers and consumers would continually be sending messages to each other. Prices would rise and fall in response to these messages, and no other factors, such as advertising or labor unions, would have any effect on prices. Such an economy also presupposes pure competition, which is characterized by the following four factors:

1. *Many sellers:* There would be many sellers in each market, and each firm would be so small relative to the entire market that it would be unable to have any effect on the price of its product. Instead, it would have to accept the going market price, which would be identical to the price received by each of it competitors.

2. *Standardized product:* The products of the various firms in each market would be so nearly identical that buyers would not prefer the product of any one firm over that of any other firm. For example, it wouldn't make any difference to consumers whether they had a Big Mac, a Whopper, or a Wendy's hamburger. These products would be so similar that consumers couldn't distinguish among them.

3. *Easy entry and exit:* Sellers would be free to enter and leave any business field at will, and new firms would be able to sell their products just as easily as long-established firms. This would mean that there could be no patent laws, no brand-name trademarks, and no exclusive possession of needed raw materials, skilled workers, or technical knowledge. It also would mean no advertising.

4. *No artificial restrictions:* There would be no artificial restrictions on the free movement of prices and wages up and down. This would mean no government wage and price controls, no minimum wage laws, no labor unions, and so forth.

The American economy is very different from the theoretical "pure" market economy. In the American economy, many areas of production are controlled by a few giant business firms. For example, most of the gasoline and home heating fuel available in the United States is produced by a relatively small number of large firms. The same is true of the production of many crucial, life-maintaining drugs. Similarly, your electricity is purchased from a single company that has been given the exclusive right by the government to supply electricity to your community.

In addition to the inadequate competition that often exists in these fields, it also is often difficult, if not impossible, for new competitors to enter these fields. Patent laws prevent firms from producing and selling medicines or other products that have been developed or invented by specific companies. It is difficult for new firms to enter the gasoline and home heating fuel industry when most of the known crude oil reserves are already owned or leased by the existing companies. New firms are prohibited from attempting to generate and sell electricity in an area where another company has already been given the exclusive right by government to supply electrical power.

Despite the differences between the American economy and a pure market economy, the price system still plays a major role in coordinating economic activity in the United States. However, because of these differences, we cannot rely totally on the price system to answer the basic economic questions of "what," "how," and "for whom" to produce. As is true of all modern economies, government must play a role in the American economy.

Check Your Understanding

1. What is the price system? Why is it referred to as the basic coordination and communication system of a market economy?

2. How are messages communicated between buyers and sellers in a pure market economy? Between employers and employees?

3. Can you describe the four characteristics of pure competition?

4. How does the American economy differ from a pure market economy?

Government Intervention

A certain amount of government involvement is necessary in any economy to ensure an orderly and equitable society. The government of the United States—a government of the people, by the people, and for the people—serves as rule maker, protector, and referee in the American economy.

Enforcement of Rules

Did you ever wonder what a tennis match or a basketball game would be like if there were no rules or referees? Would players play fairly? Probably not, because different individuals have different ideas about what playing fairly means. Suppose, for example, a tall basketball player knocks an opponent to the floor to prevent him from making a basket. Would that be fair? Most people would say no. In a game without rules, however, the tall player might insist that this was the best way of preventing his opponent from making points. Thus, to the tall player, this action was perfectly fair.

Now let us assume that we have established rules for tennis matches and basketball games but we don't have any referees to enforce them. Would all the players abide by the rules on their own? If you believe they would, then a lot of money is wasted each year on referees.

Most people probably would agree that in any athletic contest it is necessary to have both rules and officials in order to have a fair and orderly game. The same holds true for any society. Rules are necessary if a society is to be orderly and equitable.

In the United States, the government reflects the will of the people. Government officials get their power from the people, and in order to stay in office, they must pursue policies that have widespread support. If they pursue policies that don't have the support of the majority, they risk losing their jobs in the next

Through gasoline and other taxes, the government has built and maintained a complex highway system that allows for transportation of goods as well as travel of individual motorists.

election. This is quite different from the situation in certain other nations where government leaders gain and maintain power through military force. Policies often do not reflect the will of the people, and leaders use military force to eliminate any resistance. In order to better understand the role of the government in the American economy, let us briefly examine some of the areas in which the government gets involved.

Collective Goods and Services

One area in which there is general agreement that the government must play a major role is in the production and distribution of collective goods and services. **Collective goods and services** (also known as **public goods and services**) are items that tend to benefit large numbers of people collectively and would not be available to everyone if each individual had to provide them. National defense, the public schools, and highways are examples of collective goods and

services. Let us look at the role of government in the production and distribution of these items.

It would be impossible for private enterprise to provide for the nation's defense. Businesses and individuals might arm themselves in an effort to protect themselves and their property, but there is no way they could provide adequate defense for the nation as a whole. Americans have generally agreed that the government should collect taxes from everyone to provide for the nation's defense.

In the case of highways, some people benefit more than others. Some people use the highways extensively, driving thousands of miles each month. Others use the highways only occasionally, and still others do not use the highways at all. Taxes used to finance the cost of building and maintaining the nation's highways are based on the theory that those people who benefit the most should be the ones to pay the most. Thus, every time a motorist fills his or her tank with gasoline, part of the price of each gal-

ISSUE: How Much Government Involvement?

A controversial topic in economics is the question of how much government involvement in the economy is appropriate. Some believe that the government should be limited solely to providing for the nation's defense, and they would eliminate such programs as Social Security, public welfare, public transportation, and consumer protection. Others support these programs and argue that the government should play a definite role in the economy. Most arguments for and against government involvement center around three basic goals: (1) economic efficiency; (2) equity; and (3) consumer protection.

Economic efficiency involves producing the maximum amount and proper combination of goods and services from the nation's limited productive resources. Except for general policies aimed at improving the economy's overall performance and reducing unemployment, it is difficult to make a strong argument in favor of government involvement on the basis of economic efficiency. Most economists agree that in the production of goods and services, private enterprise is usually more efficient than government, and that government involvement should be kept to a bare minimum.

Equity is a second area around which arguments focusing on the issue of government involvement center. **Equity** involves the question of fairness, of making sure that all people get the same opportunity to obtain the goods and services produced by the economy, regardless of their ability to pay for them. Some people argue that because income and wealth distribution are unequal in the United States, government programs are necessary to make sure that the needs of the poor are met. Others argue that well-intentioned government programs often result in wasted tax dollars without solving the problems of the poor. Although most people probably would agree that the government should play some role in seeing that the basic needs of the poor are met, there is much disagreement over how large that role should be.

The appropriate government role in the area of consumer protection is also very controversial. **Consumer protection** includes government efforts to protect consumers from unsafe products, unsafe working conditions, and an unsafe environment. Some who subscribe to the philosophy "let the buyer beware" believe that government policies aimed at protecting consumers from potentially unsafe products constitute an inappropriate intrusion into the affairs of private firms and lead to reduced economic efficiency. Others argue that this is a small price to pay for policies that might save lives.

Why might some people want to *limit* the government's role in the economy? What arguments might they give? Why might others want to *increase* government intervention? What arguments might they offer to support their views? The class might make a chart showing the pros and cons of government intervention. Keep updating the chart as new thoughts come to mind.

lon of fuel goes to the state and federal governments. This money goes into a special fund for the building and maintenance of highways.

In the early days of our nation, only the children of wealthy parents had the opportunity to get an education. There were no public schools, and parents who valued education had to hire a private tutor or enroll their children in private schools, where a tuition fee was charged. Eventually, however, our society decided that it was in the nation's best interests to make education available to all. As a result, our public school system was born. Although tuition is not charged, the public schools are not free. To pay for the cost of public education, the government uses a portion of the money it collects from all taxpayers in the community.

Regulating Prices and the Quality of Services

In addition to national defense, highways, and public education, there are other areas of the economy in which the government intervenes. One such area involves portions of the public utilities that provide electricity or water. In this area, there is little or no competition, partly because competition is seen as less efficient than government intervention. Let us examine why this is thought to be true.

Suppose that three competing firms were to attempt to supply the electrical needs of a community that had previously been served by a single company. Each firm would have to run electrical wires throughout the entire community in an effort to obtain as many customers as possible. Since each of the three competing firms would attract fewer customers than the single firm had served previously, there would be fewer people among whom to divide the fixed costs of each company. As a result, the cost per customer would rise. Thus, in this case competition would lead to higher prices.

Because of this problem, the government grants a single company the exclusive right to supply the electrical needs of each community. In exchange for this right, the company must

Only a single electrical utility company that is subject to government regulation serves each community.

accept government regulation. A government agency determines the prices firms can charge and makes sure that consumers receive good service. Of course, not all people agree with this arrangement, but it is still regarded by many as the most efficient way to provide necessary services to the public.

It is important to point out that not all areas of the public utilities are subject to such government regulation. For example, vigorous competition exists today in some areas of telephone service. Although consumers must deal with a single company when making local calls, they may choose among competing companies

In the 1800s, there were no laws regarding child labor. Children like these worked long hours for a few cents a day.

when making long distance calls or when purchasing telephone equipment.

Other areas of government involvement in the economy include laws that regulate the amount of pollution that companies may put into the air or waterways; laws designed to make factories, mines, and other places of employment safer; and child labor laws that attempt to prevent employers from hiring children below certain ages for certain types of work.

In summary, government serves as rule maker, protector, and referee in the American economy. However, despite this substantial government involvement in the economy, the American economy is still predominantly a market economy in which most basic economic decisions are made by the price system.

Check Your Understanding

1. In what ways does the government intervene in the American economy?

2. What are collective goods and services? What role does the government play in the production and distribution of national defense, highways, and the public schools?

3. Why does the government regulate the services and prices in some areas of the economy?

Answering the Basic Questions

You learned in Chapter 1 that there are three basic economic questions that must be answered by every economic system. They are (1) What goods and services shall be produced? (2) How shall they be produced? and (3) For whom shall they be produced? Let us see how the American economy answers these basic economic questions.

What Shall Be Produced?

The question of what goods and services shall be produced in the United States is answered by the people partly through government and partly through consumer spending. A portion of the nation's limited resources must be used for national defense and other government services. Through their elected representatives in government, the American people determine what portion of the nation's resources will be used to provide these services. The remaining productive resources are available for private production. Of those resources used for private production, some will be used to produce capital goods, and the remainder will be available for the production of consumer goods and services.

As you learned in Chapter 1, capital goods include such things as factories, tools, and machines that are necessary for the production of consumer goods and services. *Consumer goods and services* are things produced for direct use by consumers, such as food, clothing, bicycles, automobiles, basketballs, movies, and medical care. In general, the more capital goods and consumer goods and services a country produces, the higher that country's standard of living will be.

Consumer sovereignty In many nations, the government decides how many and what kinds of consumer goods and services shall be produced. But in the United States, consumers decide what shall be produced. The process of allowing the people to make this decision is called **consumer sovereignty.** It means that people vote with their dollars for the goods and services they want most. Those items that receive the most votes are produced in large quantities. Those that receive few votes are discontinued or produced in minimal amounts.

The rise and fall of the convertible automobile is an example of how the buying habits of consumers affect production. During the 1950s and 1960s, the convertible was extremely popular in this nation. However, during the 1970s there was a substantial decline in the number of convertibles sold. This decline in sales was probably due partly to the production of hardtop automobiles with air-conditioning units and partly to the increased concerns about the safety of convertibles. In any case, by the late 1970s sales had fallen so low that for a short period of time, no new American convertibles were being produced. Not all Americans were pleased with this development, though. To demonstrate their preferences, some individuals hired shops to custom-make convertibles from hardtop cars. As a result of this "voting pattern," automobile manufacturers began producing convertibles again.

The kinds of songs recorded, the types of books published, the styles of clothing manufactured, and the kinds of new products produced are all determined by consumer tastes. When a new product is introduced to the American public, its success or failure will be determined by whether or not consumers vote for the item with their dollars in the marketplace. If not enough consumers purchase a new product to make it profitable, it will soon be withdrawn from the market.

The Edsel experiment In the late 1950s, the Ford Motor Company learned a very expensive lesson about consumer sovereignty. The company spent hundreds of millions of dollars to

Consumers spurned the much-publicized Edsel, forcing the Ford Motor Company to stop making the car after only two years.

design, produce, and promote a new car called the Edsel. A fortune was spent on a public relations campaign intended to create an aura of suspense and mystery about the new car. Ads showed the car as a shapeless bulk beneath canvas, and Edsel buildings were fitted with special locks to prevent anyone other than company employees from seeing the new car before it was scheduled to be presented to the American public. Some called the launching of the Edsel the most expensive such venture in the history of commerce. Ford's Edsel division had its own plant with 800 executives and 15,000 workers.

Nearly 1,200 automobile dealers across the United States surrendered profitable franchises for other makes of cars in order to sell Edsels. If the Edsel proved as popular as they hoped, they would become rich.

The Edsel was formally introduced to the American public in September 1957. The Ford Motor Company had left little to chance. Extensive market research had been conducted, and the new car was launched with a massive advertising campaign. Yet, the Edsel flopped miserably. In November 1959, the Ford Motor Company discontinued manufacture of the Edsel.

During its two years on the market, the Edsel accounted for less than 1 percent of all cars sold, and it lost its manufacturer hundreds of millions of dollars.

Why was the Edsel such a failure? The answer can be given in just two words: consumer sovereignty. The American consumers simply did not vote for it with their dollars. Historians and industry analysts have given a variety of explanations as to why the Edsel failed. Some say the design was wrong, and others say the time was wrong for such a car. *Consumer Reports* said it represented "the many excesses" with which Detroit was "repulsing more and more potential car buyers." *Time* reported that it was a "classic case of the wrong car for the wrong market at the wrong time" and "a prime example of the limitations of market research."

Nobody will ever know for sure why the Edsel was not accepted by the American public. Yet, one thing can be said with absolute certainty about the Edsel experiment: It demonstrated the enormous power of consumer sovereignty. The spending of hundreds of millions of dollars was not sufficient to make consumers accept a product they did not want.

In addition to determining the production of consumer goods and services, consumers also indirectly determine the production of capital goods (factories, tools, and machines). If people won't buy Edsels, there is no need for Edsel factories. If large numbers of people want to buy personal computers, then factories, tools, and machines for the production of personal computers will be built.

How Shall Goods and Services Be Produced?

The question of how goods and services shall be produced is determined by competition through the price system. Basically, the least costly, most efficient method of production must be used by those businesses faced with a substantial degree of competition.

Suppose a number of business firms located in the same geographic area and experiencing similar production costs are producing an item using the traditional methods of production. Also assume that each firm is able to earn a modest profit by selling the item at a price of $100 each. Now suppose that a new technology is developed that will reduce the cost of producing the item so much that it can now be sold for $80 and still earn the producer a similar profit.

If one of the producers decides to use the new technology and begins selling the item for $80, the remaining producers must also adopt the new method or, probably, be forced out of business. They cannot continue to use the old method of production which requires them to charge a price of $100 if one of their competitors is selling the item for $80.

Of course, a firm in another part of the country where other costs, such as labor and land, are lower may still be able to use the old, less efficient method of production and still earn a profit by selling the item for $80. Yet it will be just a matter of time until new firms using the new technology move into the area with lower labor and land costs and begin selling the item for less than $80. At that time, the firm that had resisted using the new technology will be forced to use it in order to stay in business.

In a competitive market economy, efficiency is the price of survival. Market forces are continually at work pressuring firms to find more efficient, lower cost methods of production. This is generally good for consumers because it usually means that they will pay lower prices for the goods and services they buy.

For Whom Shall Goods and Services Be Produced?

Goods and services are distributed by the American economic system on the basis of dollar votes. Those people with the most dollars are the ones who receive the most goods and services. However, although this may be an efficient way to decide who gets the goods and services that are produced, it is not necessarily a fair way. Those people with the most dollars are not necessarily the most deserving or the most in need of the goods and services. Indeed, those people with the greatest need may have few, if any, dollars with which to vote.

There is, of course, an important relationship between what people produce and what they are entitled to receive in terms of goods and services. Economic incentives are crucial to the functioning of the American economy. Individuals and businesses must be able to see potential rewards for their work and the risks they take. If people who did little or no work received the same income as those who worked hard, there would be little incentive for anyone to work.

Those people with the most money are not necessarily those who work the hardest, and some people who work very hard earn very small incomes. Conversely, many wealthy people received their wealth through inheritance rather than from hard work. Also, people who are poor and unemployed are not necessarily lazy. The fact that a person is able and willing to work does not guarantee that he or she will be able to find a job. At certain times and in certain geographic areas, large numbers of individuals are unable to find jobs no matter how hard they try. In addition, some people are so disabled that they are unable to work even if a job were available. Yet these people still have a need for goods and services.

If the American economy were left free to distribute goods and services entirely on the basis of dollar votes, some very needy people would be without sufficient food, clothing, shelter, and medical care through no fault of their own. Fortunately, our society is a compassionate society; and thus a number of government and private charity programs have been developed to help the very poor obtain at least some goods and services. Many argue that these programs are inadequate. They believe that in a society as affluent as ours, everyone should have sufficient food, clothing, shelter, and other

basic necessities; and they advocate additional government efforts to reduce poverty. Others argue that the government already has too many social programs, and they believe private charity should be responsible for meeting the needs of the poor.

Of course, one of the most attractive ways to solve the problems of the poor is to manage the economy in such a way as to create maximum economic opportunity for all, rich and poor alike. In later chapters, you will learn about the problems of inadequate economic growth and high unemployment, and we will examine ways to solve these problems. Regardless of what economic policies are followed, however, there will always be a need for some programs to help those who through no fault of their own find themselves without the basic necessities of life.

Check Your Understanding

1. How is the question "What shall be produced?" answered in the American economy?

2. What is meant by the term "consumer sovereignty"? How was consumer sovereignty responsible for the failure of the Edsel?

3. How is the question "How shall goods and services be produced?" answered in the American economy?

4. How is the question "For whom shall goods and services be produced?" answered?

CAREERS: Real Estate Agent

If you like a challenge, enjoy meeting people, and like variety in your work, you might be well suited for a career as a real estate agent. Real estate agents rent or sell homes and other property for clients. To be successful, an agent must have a thorough knowledge of the housing market, be familiar with each piece of real estate listed with his or her agency, and recognize what potential buyers are looking for. The real estate agent must be a skilled salesperson who can emphasize favorable qualities of a home, such as the soundness of construction, the convenient floor plan, and the proximity to schools and shopping facilities.

In addition to selling real estate, agents assist in closing, or finalizing, sales; often arrange for loans to help clients finance the real estate; serve as mediators between buyers and sellers during price negotiations; and seek out additional real estate to sell.

Real estate agents receive a percentage of the sale price of each home or piece of property they sell, and the income of most agents depends on the volume of sales made. Although many people earn a good living selling real estate, the work of a real estate agent is seldom easy. An agent may have to meet several times with prospective buyers and show them several different homes before a sale is made. Moreover, there is never a guarantee that a sale will take place—no matter how much effort the agent puts forth. Also, factors such as the health of the economy and the availability of loans at low interest rates play a major role in how well the agent does. In addition, real estate agents often have to work evenings and weekends in order to accommodate the schedules of potential buyers.

Real estate agents must be licensed; and a prospective agent must be a high school graduate, be at least 18 years old, and pass a written examination. Most states also require the completion of a specified number of hours of classroom instruction. A college education is not required for a license, but some large real estate firms seek college graduates to fill job vacancies. Personality traits are very important, too. A pleasant personality, a neat appearance, maturity, tact, and enthusiasm for the job are generally considered essential qualities for success as a real estate agent.

Chapter Highlights

1 The American economic system is predominantly a market economy that relies primarily on a system of free markets to make basic economic decisions. It is also an example of capitalism. Capitalism is a form of economic organization in which businesses are privately owned and operated and where free markets coordinate most economic activity.

2 According to the invisible-hand principle, if individuals were allowed to pursue their own self-interests without interference by government, they would be led, as if by an "invisible hand," to achieve what is best for society.

3 Although the American economy is very different from the type of economy that Adam Smith described in *The Wealth of Nations*, the principle of the invisible hand still applies to our economy in a modified way.

4 For the invisible-hand principle to work, there must be a great deal of competition.

5 Competition is the controlling mechanism of capitalism. It prevents individuals and businesses from taking advantage of one another when they pursue their own self-interests.

6 The price system is the coordination and communication system of capitalism. It communicates messages between buyers and sellers and between employers and employees.

7 The government serves as rule maker, protector, and referee in the American economy. Government produces collective goods and services, regulates prices and the quality of services of public utility companies, and enacts laws designed to regulate pollution, make the workplace safer, and prevent employers from hiring children below certain ages for certain types of work.

8 American consumers determine what will be produced by voting in the marketplace with their dollars.

9 The question of how goods and services shall be produced is determined by competition through the price system. Basically, the least costly, most efficient method of production must be used.

10 Goods and services are distributed by the American economic system on the basis of dollar votes. However, a number of government and private charity programs help to ensure that the very poor obtain some goods and services.

Important Terms

Match each of the following terms with the correct definition:

capitalism   price system   collective goods and
competition   consumer sovereignty   services
profit motive   invisible-hand principle   profit

1. The concept that in a market economy if individuals were allowed to pursue their own self-interests without interference by government, their actions would lead to what is best for society.

2. The economic rivalry that controls a market economy.

3. The coordination and communication system of a market economy.

4. Things that tend to benefit large numbers of people collectively and that would not be available to everyone if each individual had to provide them.

5. The process of allowing the people to decide what shall be produced by voting with their dollars for the goods and services they want most.

6. An economic system in which the businesses are privately owned and operated for profit and where free markets coordinate most economic activity.

7. The desire to maximize financial gains.

8. Financial gain or benefit received by an individual as a result of work activity.

Extending Your Understanding

1. Why is competition so important in the American economy? Give some examples of businesses in your community that have little or no competition. Would the interests of your community be better served if these businesses had more competitors?

2. Do you think American consumers always make wise decisions when they vote in the marketplace with their dollars? Why or why not?

3. Some people have argued that in order to protect the American automobile industry, the government should restrict the import of foreign cars. What arguments can be made for and against such government intervention?

Activities

1. Suppose you are the manager of a new clothing boutique that has just opened in your neighborhood. Prepare a strategy on how you would try to ensure the store's success.

2. With one student playing the role of a career counselor and another playing the role of a college student, prepare a short skit on factors to consider when choosing a career and looking for a job.

Building Skills in Economics: Reading a Line Graph

In this chapter, you saw how sales of Burger dropped when Heloise's Hamburgers initially moved across the street. Sometimes it is easier to present such relationships in the form of a **line graph.** A line graph is useful for making comparisons and for seeing how a particular item changes over a period of time. The line graph at right shows the number of ice cream cones sold each week at three competing businesses during the months of April through September.

The bottom line of this graph is called the **horizontal axis.** It always shows units of time, in this case months of the year. The line on the side is called the **vertical axis.** It always presents numerical data. The following questions will help you interpret the information shown on this line graph.

Applying Economics Skills

1. In general, how did the sales of all three businesses progress from April through July? Which company had the highest weekly sales in July? How many cones did it sell each week?

2. At the beginning of August, Fun Cones decided to raise its price ten cents a cone. Did sales increase or decrease during August? Did sales of the other two businesses increase or decrease during this same period? What effect did Fun Cones's price increase appear to have on sales?

3. What kind of a change in sales did all three businesses experience between August and September? What might account for this change?

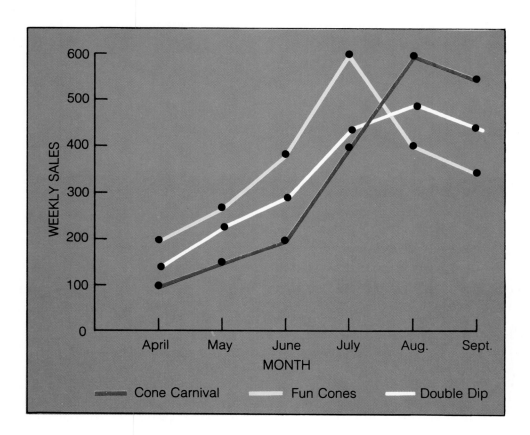

CHAPTER 3

DEMAND, SUPPLY, AND THE INTERACTION OF MARKETS

It has been said that a parrot could be taught to answer most economic questions by simply teaching it three words: "supply and demand." This, of course, is an exaggeration, but there is some truth to the statement. The answer to many economic questions is "supply and demand." Take the following questions, for example: (1) Why is the price of gold so high? (2) Why is the price of salt so low? (3) Why are the incomes of doctors so high? (4) Why are the wages of unskilled workers so low? Each of these questions could be answered with the words "supply and demand."

Of course, knowing that the answer to a particular question is "supply and demand" won't be of much help unless you know what these words mean. In this chapter, you will learn the meaning of these words, and why they are so important in the study of economics.

What Is Demand?

The word "demand" has a different meaning in economics than in everyday life. Many people use the word "demand" to give an order or a command. For example, a bank robber might say, "I demand all your money!" In economics, however, the word "demand" refers to the ability and willingness of people to buy things. Both the *ability* to buy something and the *willingness* to make the purchase must be present for demand to occur. It is not enough to say that you want something very much. You must have the money to pay for it and be willing to pay the seller's asking price. For example, although you may want a new sports car, you may not have or be willing to spend the $15,000 the seller is asking. In this case, you do not have a "demand" for the car.

The Law of Demand

What would happen if the seller in the above example lowered the price of the car to $12,000? Most likely, assuming people had the money, there would be more people willing to buy the car. Moreover, if the price were dropped to $10,000, there would be an even greater number of prospective buyers. This inverse relationship between price and quantity demanded is known as the **law of demand.**

The law of demand says simply that as the price of an item rises and other factors remain unchanged, the quantity demanded by buyers will fall; as the price of an item falls and other factors remain unchanged, the quantity demanded by buyers will rise. In other words, people will buy more of an item if the price is low than they will if the price is high. The law of demand is little more than common sense. Most people would agree that consumers will usually buy more of an item at low prices than they will at high prices. But do you know why this is so? There are a couple of economic concepts that help to explain the law of demand. They are (1) the income and substitution effects; and (2) the principle of diminishing marginal utility. Let us briefly examine each of these concepts.

The income and substitution effects As the price of an item declines, people can buy more of it out of a given income. For example, suppose a family has $10 per week to spend on chicken. If the price of chicken were $2 per pound, the family could buy 5 pounds of chicken. If the price dropped to $1 per pound, they could then buy 10 pounds. The family can buy twice as much chicken at the lower price than they can at the higher price. Put another way, when the price of chicken is $1 per pound, the family can get twice as much without spending more money. This is known as the **income effect.**

As the price of an item falls, it becomes more attractive to buyers relative to other items they might spend their money on. For example, suppose a family normally spends $10 on chicken and $10 on fish each week. Now suppose the price of chicken declines substantially while the price of fish remains unchanged. In addition to being able to buy more chicken than normal out of the $10 chicken allowance, the family also may decide to spend some of the $10 fish allowance on chicken. Compared to fish, chicken is now considered a better buy. This tendency for consumers to substitute lower priced items for more expensive items is the **substitution effect.**

The principle of diminishing marginal utility also helps to explain the law of demand. According to this principle, as an individual obtains more and more units of an item during a specified time period, he or she will obtain less and less additional utility (or satisfaction) from each additional unit. To illustrate this point, let us look at a hypothetical situation.

Suppose you have a summer job doing heavy construction work in a local park. Because you burn up so many calories on the job, each morning you eat a large breakfast and pack a generous lunch to take to work. Now suppose that one morning you awaken too late to eat breakfast or make your lunch. By eleven that morning, you are so famished that you walk over to a vendor in the park who sells fruit cups for 50 cents each. You eagerly hand the vendor 50 cents and wolf down the fruit cup. You find, however, that while that fruit cup relieves your hunger somewhat, you are not completely full. As a result, you buy a second fruit cup and are now satisfied. How would you feel about a third fruit cup? Would it taste as good as the previous two? Perhaps if the vendor lowered the price to 35 cents, you might decide to purchase a third fruit cup. After finishing that one, however, you probably wouldn't want a fourth one even if the vendor lowered the price to ten cents.

You are experiencing the principle of diminishing marginal utility. You obtained 50 cents worth of utility (satisfaction) from each of the first two fruit cups. However, you would receive only 35 cents worth of utility from a third fruit cup, and less then ten cents worth from a fourth. Since individuals obtain less and less additional utility, or satisfaction, as they obtain more units of an item, they will buy larger quantities of the item only at lower prices.

The Demand Schedule

In the previous example of marginal utility, we considered the relationship between the price of an item and the quantity demanded. Economists, too, are interested in seeing how the quantity demanded of an item changes as the price rises or falls. As a result, they often construct **demand schedules,** which are listings that show the various amounts of an item that buyers are willing and able to buy at various prices during some stated time period. Demand schedules illustrate demand in table form. They list the quantity of an item demanded per period alongside the price of the item. Table 3–1 depicts a demand schedule, which we will explain by way of an example.

Suppose there is a restaurant named Fear-less Fred's Fast Foods near your school where students can buy fish sandwiches, among other things, for lunch. How many fish sandwiches do you think students would buy each day? The answer to this question depends on several factors, such as the number of students in your school who like fish sandwiches, the amount of money the students have, whether or not there are other fast-food restaurants nearby, and whether or not your school has a cafeteria.

One of the most important determining factors, however, is the price of the fish sandwiches. As you can see in Table 3–1, students will buy fewer fish sandwiches at higher prices than at lower prices. At the hypothetical low price of 50 cents per fish sandwich, students will be willing to buy 550 fish sandwiches per day. When the price rises to 80 cents per fish sandwich, they will buy only 400 fish sandwiches per day. This number drops to 250 at the high price of $1.10. Thus, as the law of demand states, as the price of an item rises, the quantity demanded by buyers will fall.

TABLE 3–1 DEMAND SCHEDULE FOR FISH SANDWICHES AT FEARLESS FRED'S FAST FOODS

Price per Fish Sandwich	Quantity of Fish Sandwiches Demanded per Day
$1.10	250
1.00	300
.90	350
.80	400
.70	450
.60	500
.50	550

It is important to make a distinction here between the terms "demand" and "quantity demanded." The term "demand" refers to the entire demand schedule, or the whole schedule of possible prices and quantities demanded. It is not correct to use the term "demand" to refer to a specific quantity demanded at a specific price. For example, it is incorrect to say that at a price of 60 cents, the demand for fish sandwiches is 500. When we refer to a specific quantity at a specific price, we must use the term "quantity demanded." When referring to the number of fish sandwiches demanded at a price of 60 cents, we can correctly say, "The *quantity demanded* at a price of 60 cents per fish sandwich is 500 fish sandwiches per day." The terms "demand" and "quantity demanded" probably sound almost identical to you. However, there is an important difference between the two terms. You will learn why it is important to make this distinction when we examine changes in demand.

The Demand Curve

The demand schedule in Table 3–1 has a serious limitation. For example, how many fish sandwiches would be demanded at a price of 85 cents per sandwich? We know the answer lies somewhere between 350 and 400, but we cannot be any more specific. Because of this limitation, as well as for other reasons, economists often construct demand curves. **A demand**

curve is a graphical representation of a demand schedule. Such curves take into consideration all the in-between points. Figure 3–1 is an example of a demand curve using the data from Table 3–1.

Note that in Figure 3–1, the price of fish sandwiches is measured on the vertical line, and the quantity of fish sandwiches demanded at the various prices is measured on the horizontal line. Each dot along the demand curve represents a single price and quantity relationship from Table 3–1. Thus, at a price of $1.10 per fish sandwich, we can see that 250 fish sandwiches per day will be demanded. At a $1 price, 300 fish sandwiches per day will be demanded, and so on. The rest of the line that is not marked by dots represents the in-between points. For example, 375 fish sandwiches would be demanded each day if the price were 85 cents per sandwich.

In the real world, supply and demand curves usually have some curvature to them. That is why they are called supply and demand curves instead of supply and demand lines. However, for the purpose of demonstration, we will use straight lines in the examples.

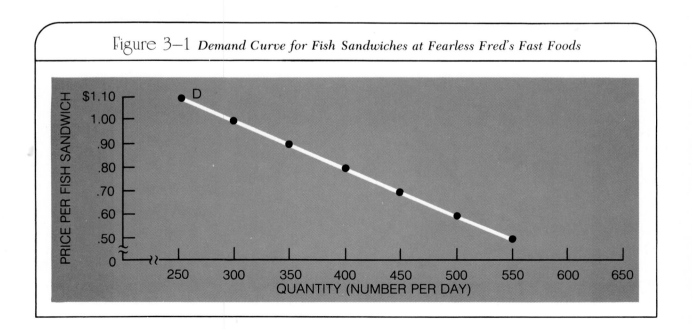

Figure 3–1 *Demand Curve for Fish Sandwiches at Fearless Fred's Fast Foods*

Changes in Demand

Sometimes consumers decide to buy more, or less, of an item at all possible prices. When this happens, a change in demand takes place. Unlike a simple change in quantity demanded, which results from a change in the price of the product in question, a change in demand involves a change in the entire demand schedule and the demand curve. Changes in demand can result from a number of factors. If the income of consumers rises substantially, they may be willing to buy more of many items at each possible price. Likewise, if income falls, consumers may buy less at each possible price. Changes in the general attitude and tastes of consumers also may result in changes in demand. For example, when consumers expressed a preference for small cars, the demand for such cars soared.

Changes in the availability and prices of substitute items may result in a change in the demand for a specific item. For example, suppose there is a shortage of chicken and the price of chicken rises substantially. This could cause an increase in the demand for fish, a relatively good substitute. Changes in the availability and prices of complementary items also may affect the demand for a specific item. **Complementary items** are items that are often used together. Thus, if the price of gasoline rises dramatically, the demand for new cars will decline.

TABLE 3–2 NEW DEMAND SCHEDULE FOR FISH SANDWICHES AT FEARLESS FRED'S FAST FOODS AFTER AN INCREASE IN DEMAND

Price per Fish Sandwich	Quantity of Fish Sandwiches Demanded per Day
$1.10	350
1.00	400
.90	450
.80	500
.70	550
.60	600
.50	650

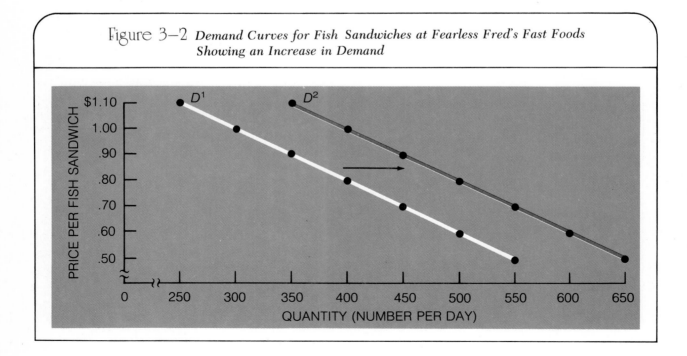

Figure 3–2 *Demand Curves for Fish Sandwiches at Fearless Fred's Fast Foods Showing an Increase in Demand*

How do we show a change in demand graphically? Let us take an example. Suppose that because of an increase in income or a change in tastes, there is an increase in the demand for fish sandwiches at Fearless Fred's. This increase in demand results in a new demand schedule, which is shown in Table 3–2. When we plot these figures on a graph along with the original demand curve (D^1), as in Figure 3–2, we find that the demand curve shifts to the right. Whenever there is an increase in demand for any item, the entire demand curve shifts to the right. Note that the new demand curve, D^2, shows that buyers are now willing to buy more fish sandwiches at all of the possible prices.

A decrease in demand has just the opposite effect. If Fearless Fred's customers should decide to buy fewer fish sandwiches at each possible price, the demand curve would shift to the left.

Check Your Understanding

1. How is the word "demand" used in economics?

2. State the law of demand.

3. What is meant by the income and substitution effects? Give examples to show how these two principles operate.

4. Explain the principle of diminishing marginal utility. Give an example of this principle.

5. What is the difference between demand and quantity demanded?

6. What factors can lead to a change in demand?

What Is Supply?

The law of demand only partially explains the relationship between price and the quantity of goods and services bought and sold. The other part of the explanation lies in the concept of supply. Like the word "demand," the word "supply" also has a very specific meaning in economics. It refers to the ability and willingness of sellers to make things available for sale. The fact that there are many houses in your community does not mean that the supply of houses in your community is large. There is a large supply of houses only if the owners are both willing and able to make the houses available for sale.

The Law of Supply

An important influence on potential sellers in the example just mentioned is the price of houses. At higher prices they would be more willing to sell their houses than at lower prices. This relationship between price and quantity supplied is known as the **law of supply.** According to the law of supply, as the price of an item rises and other factors remain unchanged, the quantity supplied by suppliers will rise; as the price of an item falls and other factors remain unchanged, the quantity supplied by suppliers will fall. Like the law of demand, this law is largely common sense. It is only natural that as prices rise, suppliers will be willing to supply larger quantities of their goods and services.

The Supply Schedule

Like demand, supply can be expressed in the form of a schedule. A **supply schedule** is a listing that shows the various amounts of an item that sellers are willing to sell at various prices during some stated time period. As before, it is important to understand the difference between the terms "supply" and "quantity supplied." The term "supply" refers to the whole schedule of possible prices and quantities supplied. When we want to refer to a specific quantity supplied at a specific price, we must use the term "quantity supplied." For example, we would say that the quantity supplied at a price of 80 cents per fish sandwich is 400 fish sandwiches per day. Table 3–3 is an example of a possible supply schedule for fish sandwiches at Fearless Fred's Fast Foods.

TABLE 3–3 SUPPLY SCHEDULE FOR FISH SANDWICHES AT FEARLESS FRED'S FAST FOODS

Price per Fish Sandwich	Quantity of Fish Sandwiches Supplied per Day
$1.10	550
1.00	500
.90	450
.80	400
.70	350
.60	300
.50	250

Study Table 3–3 for a moment. Note that in this table the relationship between the price of fish sandwiches and the quantity supplied is just the opposite of the relationship between the price and quantity demanded that you observed in Table 3–1. In Table 3–3, as the

price of fish sandwiches rises, Fred is willing to supply more and more fish sandwiches. At the low price of 50 cents per fish sandwich, Fred is willing to sell only 250 fish sandwiches per day. At a price of 80 cents, he is willing to supply 400 fish sandwiches per day. If the price rises to $1.10, Fred would be willing to increase his quantity supplied to 550 fish sandwiches each day.

As prices keep getting higher, Fred sees that he can make greater profits. This profit motive prompts Fred to want to supply more and more fish sandwiches. In contrast, at lower prices Fred's costs of supplying fish sandwiches may well exceed the price of the sandwiches. As a result, he would lose money on each fish sandwich sold and would not want to sell the fish sandwiches at such low prices. Production costs are an important factor in determining supply. We will examine production costs in detail in Chapter 5.

The Supply Curve

The supply schedule has the same limitations as the demand schedule. Economists usually present the data from such schedules graphically in the form of **supply curves.** In Figure 3–3, the data from Table 3–3 are plotted to produce a supply curve. The price of fish sandwiches is measured on the vertical line, and the quantity

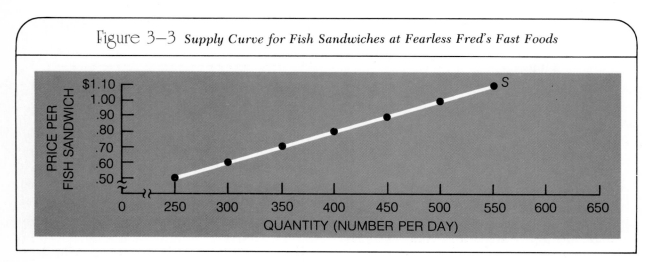

Figure 3–3 *Supply Curve for Fish Sandwiches at Fearless Fred's Fast Foods*

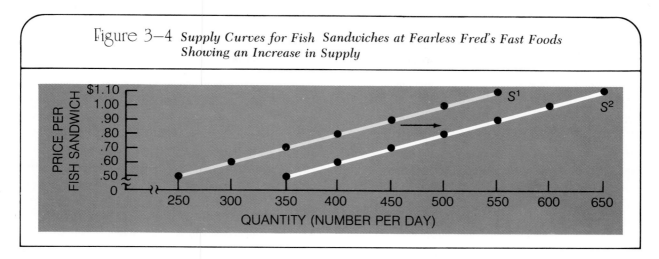

Figure 3—4 *Supply Curves for Fish Sandwiches at Fearless Fred's Fast Foods Showing an Increase in Supply*

of fish sandwiches supplied at the various prices is measured on the horizontal line. Each dot along the supply curve represents a single price and quantity relationship from Table 3–3. For example, the bottom dot on the supply curve tells us that at a price of 50 cents per fish sandwich, the quantity of fish sandwiches supplied will be 250 per day. The lines between the dots represent the in-between points. Thus, at a price of 85 cents, the quantity of fish sandwiches supplied will be 425 fish sandwiches each day.

Changes in Supply

Just as demand can change, supply can change as well. Changes in supply can result from a number of factors. In the case of farm products, weather conditions can have a big impact on supply. For example, unusually good growing conditions can result in an increase in supply. On the other hand, too much or too little rain or a severe frost can cause a substantial decrease in supply. Also, changes in the costs of producing an item can cause a change in the supply of that item. Any change in supply causes the supply curve to shift. An increase in supply causes the entire supply curve to shift to the right, and a decrease in supply causes the entire curve to shift to the left.

Suppose Fearless Fred's costs decline because of a decrease in his rent. As a result, Fred is now willing to sell more fish sandwiches than before at each possible price. This fact is reflected in the new supply curve, S^2, shown in Figure 3–4. Note that the new supply curve is to the right of the old supply curve, showing that more fish sandwiches will be supplied at each possible price.

A decrease in supply has just the opposite effect. If Fearless Fred's costs increase, he may be willing to supply fewer fish sandwiches at each possible price. In this case, the supply curve would shift to the left.

Check Your Understanding

1. How is the word "supply" used in economics?

2. State the law of supply.

3. Describe the difference between supply and quantity supplied.

4. What factors can cause a change in supply?

Supply and Demand Together Make a Market

Supply and demand together make a market. We defined markets in Chapter 1, and we discussed the role that markets play in the American economy in Chapter 2. However, let us define market again so the idea will be fresh in your mind as we continue with this chapter. A market is the arrangement through which potential buyers and sellers come together to exchange goods and services. A market exists whenever and wherever the decisions of buyers and sellers interact through the laws of supply and demand. A market can be a specific place, such as a local farmers' market where sellers and buyers come together to exchange goods. However, markets are usually much broader in scope and may extend over an entire nation or the world.

The market for college presidents is an example of a national market. When a college— the buyer—needs to hire a new president, it usually makes a nationwide search before narrowing down the choices. At the same time, once the vacancy is announced, many hopeful candidates throughout the nation—the sellers—probably will submit applications for the position. The same interaction between buyers and sellers takes place in the market for professional coaches and athletes. If you follow the sports news, you know that professional athletes and coaches transfer to new jobs in other sections of the nation on a regular basis. The markets for gold, silver, crude oil, and many other commodities, or items, are worldwide. In these markets, buyers and sellers from all over the world interact with one another through the laws of supply and demand.

The exchange of goods between buyers and sellers can take place on a small scale, such as at this store, or on a large, national scale.

Supply and Demand Determine Prices

One of the most important aspects of the transactions between buyers and sellers in a market is the determination of price. Price is determined by supply and demand. In order to understand how supply and demand determine price, let us put together the demand and supply schedules and the demand and supply curves for fish sandwiches at Fearless Fred's Fast Foods. Table 3–4 and Figure 3–5 show both the quantity of fish sandwiches demanded and the quantity supplied at various prices.

Equilibrium Price

Note that in Table 3–4 at the price of 80 cents per fish sandwich, the quantity demanded and the quantity supplied are exactly equal. At 80 cents per fish sandwich, Fred is willing to sell 400 fish sandwiches per day and buyers are willing to buy 400 fish sandwiches per day. In this example, the price of 80 cents per fish sandwich is the equilibrium price. The *equilibrium price* of any item is that price at which the quantity demanded is exactly equal to the quantity supplied.

Figure 3–5 depicts the same thing graphically. Note that in Figure 3–5, the equilibrium price is where the two curves cross. At that point, at the price of 80 cents per fish sandwich, both the quantity demanded and the quantity supplied are 400 fish sandwiches per day. The equilibrium price is a point of balance. If the price of any item is at the equilibrium price, it will tend to remain there until something causes a change in demand and/or supply. If the price of any item is not at the equilibrium price, it will continue to move toward that price until that price is reached. Let us see why this is so by looking at what happens when prices are higher or lower than the equilibrium price.

Prices Too High for Equilibrium Cause a Surplus

When prices are higher than the equilibrium price of 80 cents, the quantity supplied exceeds the quantity demanded. For example, at a price of $1.10 per fish sandwich, the quantity that Fred is willing to supply is 550 fish sandwiches per day. At a price of $1.10, however, buyers are willing to buy only 250 fish sandwiches per day. The amount of fish sandwiches left over is known as a **surplus**. In this example, there is a surplus of 300 fish sandwiches when the price is

TABLE 3–4 DEMAND AND SUPPLY FOR FISH SANDWICHES AT FEARLESS FRED'S FAST FOODS

Price per Fish Sandwich	Quantity of Fish Sandwiches Demanded per Day	Quantity of Fish Sandwiches Supplied per Day
$1.10	250	550
1.00	300	500
.90	350	450
.80	400	400
.70	450	350
.60	500	300
.50	550	250

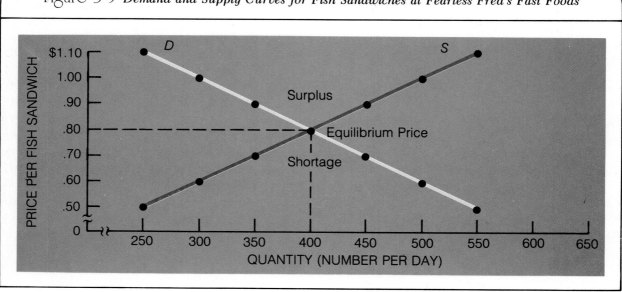

Figure 3-5 *Demand and Supply Curves for Fish Sandwiches at Fearless Fred's Fast Foods*

$1.10. Given this situation, Fred will lower his price, thus causing an increase in the quantity of fish sandwiches demanded. Common sense tells us that this will happen whenever there is a surplus of any item. Prices will fall, and they will continue to fall until the surplus has been eliminated. Figure 3–5 shows the range in which a surplus will occur.

Prices Too Low for Equilibrium Cause a Shortage

Just as prices above 80 cents are too high for equilibrium to be attained, prices below 80 cents are too low to permit equilibrium. At a price of 60 cents per fish sandwich, buyers will want to buy 500 fish sandwiches per day. At a price of 60 cents, however, only 300 fish sandwiches per day will be available. Thus, at a price of 60 cents, there will be a shortage of fish sandwiches. As you already know, when there is a shortage of anything, the price will tend to rise until the shortage is eliminated. Figure 3–5 shows the range in which there is a shortage.

In summary, supply and demand work together to determine prices. The price of any item will tend to move toward the equilibrium price at which the quantity demanded is equal to the quantity supplied.

Check Your Understanding

1. What is a market? Give examples of local, national, and worldwide markets.

2. How do supply and demand determine prices?

3. What is an equilibrium price? How is it achieved?

4. What happens when prices are too high for equilibrium?

5. What happens when prices are too low for equilibrium?

How Changes in Demand Affect Price

As you already know, changes in the demand for an item can result from a number of factors, including changes in consumer income, changes in tastes, and changes in the cost and availability of related items. How do these changes in demand affect price? Let us first examine the effect of an increase in demand. Figure 3–6 shows what happens to the price of fish sandwiches at Fearless Fred's when there is an increase in demand. Note that the new demand curve, D^2, intersects the supply curve at a price of 90 cents. Thus, the equilibrium price for fish sandwiches has risen from 80 cents to 90 cents. At the new equilibrium price, the quantity demanded is exactly equal to the quantity supplied.

A decrease in demand has just the opposite effect on price. A decrease in demand would cause the demand curve to shift to the left, thus resulting in a decline in the equilibrium price. In short, an increase in the demand for an item will usually cause the price of the item to rise, and a decrease in demand will usually lead to a decline in price.

How Changes in Supply Affect Price

Like changes in demand, changes in supply also affect price. Figure 3–7 shows an increase in the supply of fish sandwiches at Fearless Fred's. As you can see, the new supply curve, S^2, intersects the demand curve at a price of 70 cents per fish sandwich. Thus, the equilibrium price has declined from 80 cents to 70 cents.

A decrease in supply has the opposite effect on price. A decrease in supply would cause the supply curve to shift to the left, resulting in a price increase.

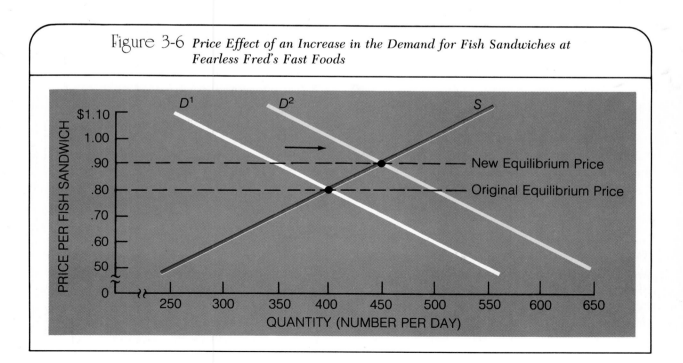

Figure 3-6 *Price Effect of an Increase in the Demand for Fish Sandwiches at Fearless Fred's Fast Foods*

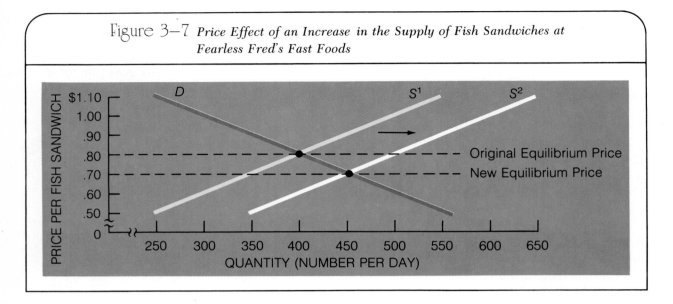

Figure 3–7 *Price Effect of an Increase in the Supply of Fish Sandwiches at Fearless Fred's Fast Foods*

Government Interference and the Laws of Supply and Demand

If the forces of supply and demand are allowed to operate freely, they will determine market prices and eliminate both shortages and surpluses. However, when the government thinks prices are rising too quickly or that they are not high enough, it can intervene and establish prices that are either above or below the prices set by the free market. This intervention has taken the form of either **price ceilings** or **price floors.** Let us briefly examine each of these concepts.

Price Ceilings

Price ceilings are government-imposed regulations that prevent prices from rising above a certain maximum level. During periods of rapidly rising prices, the government has at times attempted to halt the price increases by making it illegal for prices to rise above a level it has

established. Let us use an example to illustrate the effects of price ceilings. During the 1970s, Americans saw the price of gasoline rise at an alarming rate. When the price reached $1 per gallon, many people demanded that the government halt further rises by imposing a price ceiling. The government decided to allow the forces of supply and demand to interact and did not impose the ceiling. Prices continued to rise, ultimately topping the $1.50 per gallon mark in some areas before leveling off.

Suppose the government had imposed a price ceiling of $1 per gallon. How would such a ceiling have affected buyers and sellers of gasoline? The effects can easily be seen by examining Figure 3–8, which shows hypothetical supply and demand curves for gasoline. When the market was allowed to operate freely, it established an equilibrium price of approximately $1.50 per gallon. Consumers reacted to the rising prices by buying smaller cars and by driving less. Thus, at a price of $1.50 per gallon, the quantity of gasoline demanded by consumers was less than at $1 per gallon. Also, the quantity supplied at $1.50 per gallon was larger than it would have been at $1. The net effect was that at $1.50 per gallon, the quantity of gasoline

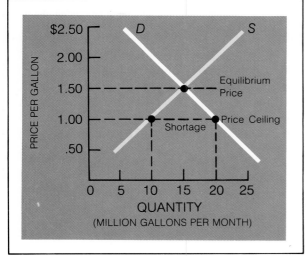

Figure 3–8 *Hypothetical Supply and Demand Curves for Gasoline Showing the Effect of a Price Ceiling*

Price Floors

Price floors are government-imposed regulations that prevent prices from falling below a certain minimum level. The government often establishes price floors for agricultural products to prevent the prices of these products from falling below the cost of production. In other words, the government guarantees farmers a certain minimum price.

Figure 3–9 presents hypothetical supply and demand curves for wheat. Note that if the forces of supply and demand are allowed to operate freely, they will establish an equilibrium price of $3 per bushel. However, suppose the government establishes a legal price floor of $4 per bushel. At this price, the quantity of wheat supplied exceeds the quantity demanded, resulting in a surplus. Thus, if the government maintains a price floor of $4, it will have to devise some plan for dealing with the surplus wheat. Over the years, the government has used a number of plans to deal with agricultural surpluses resulting from price floors. In all of the plans, however, either the government buys up the surplus or it encourages farmers to reduce the quantity supplied by planting fewer acres.

demanded was approximately equal to the quantity supplied.

If a legal ceiling of $1 per gallon had been established, there would have been a shortage of gasoline because the quantity demanded at that price would have exceeded the quantity supplied. Thus, it would have been necessary for the government to develop some form of rationing program in an effort to distribute the scarce gasoline equitably. In fact, the government did have a standby rationing plan. Rationing coupons were printed, and had the government decided to ration gasoline, each motorist's weekly allotment would have depended on the number of coupons issued to that motorist by the government.

Under normal circumstances, most economists do not favor price ceilings and government rationing programs. They prefer instead to allow the market to do the rationing through the forces of supply and demand. Because gasoline prices were allowed to rise to the equilibrium level during the 1970s, market forces were allowed to prevail and rationing was avoided.

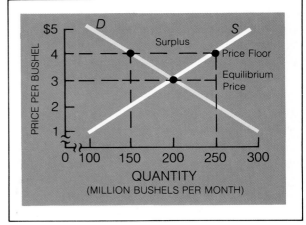

Figure 3–9 *Hypothetical Supply and Demand Curves for Wheat Showing the Effect of a Price Floor*

Elasticity of Demand and Supply

You have learned that a change in the price of a product will cause the quantity demanded and the quantity supplied to change. But how much of a change in quantity demanded or quantity supplied will result from a given change in price? The answer to this question involves the concepts of elasticity of demand and elasticity of supply. Let us introduce these concepts by looking at some examples.

Suppose a box of table salt that normally sells for 40 cents is now selling for 80 cents. How big of an impact on quantity demanded will this doubling of price have? If you said very little, you would be correct because many people consider salt a necessity that has no substitutes. In addition, because the price of salt is so low to begin with, salt would still be considered inexpensive even after doubling in price. Moreover, people use only a limited amount of salt, and thus the cost of an entire year's supply, even at the higher price, would seem insignificant to most people.

If a doubling in the price of salt would have very little impact on the quantity of salt demanded, does this mean that the doubling in price of any other item would have a similar effect? No. In some cases, a doubling in price would result in a drastic change in quantity demanded. For example, suppose all car manufacturers suddenly raised their prices from $10,000 to $20,000. Many people would then turn to used cars or rely on other methods of transportation. The action of these car manufacturers would cause the quantity demanded to decrease dramatically.

The change in quantity demanded resulting from any given change in price will depend on the elasticity of demand for the commodity in question. **Elasticity of demand** is a measure of the responsiveness of quantity demanded to a change in price. If a change in the price of an item will have little effect on the quantity demanded, we say the demand is very *inelastic*. Salt, milk, and sugar are some commodities with a very inelastic demand.

On the other hand, if a change in the price of an item will have a very big effect on the quantity demanded, we say the demand is very *elastic*. In this case, the responsiveness of quantity demanded to a change in price is very large. A particular brand of orange juice is a commodity whose demand is very elastic. If one producer raises orange juice prices substantially, most consumers will just switch to another brand.

What Determines Elasticity

The elasticity of demand for any given good or service depends on a number of factors, the most important of which is the degree to which the item is a necessity. For example, the demand for a life-maintaining medication, such as insulin for diabetics, is very inelastic. If the buyer has to have the medication in order to live, he or she probably will continue to buy the same amount no matter how high the price goes. On the other hand, an item that is strictly a luxury probably will have a very elastic demand. For example, if the price of bubble bath doubled, the quantity demanded probably would fall off dramatically. Other determining factors include how expensive the item is relative to consumers' total expenditures and the availability and cost of good substitutes for the item. As we have seen, salt is relatively inexpensive and without many substitutes. As a result, the demand for it is inelastic. In contrast, a new car is very expensive, and one make of car can easily be substituted for another. Therefore, the demand for a particular new car is very elastic.

A change in the price of an item affects not only the quantity demanded, but also the quantity supplied. **Elasticity of supply** is a measure of the responsiveness of quantity supplied to a change in price. If a change in price will have a very large effect on the quantity supplied, we say that the supply is very *elastic*. In contrast, if a change in price will have very little effect on the quantity supplied, we say the supply is very *inelastic*.

Elasticity of supply depends largely on the time period under consideration. For example, an increase in the price of corn probably will cause farmers to raise more corn during the next growing season. In this case, there will be an increase in the quantity of corn supplied within the next year and so the supply is elastic. However, in some cases it may take years for the quantity supplied to respond to a change in price. For example, suppose there is a substantial increase in the price of apples. Will apple growers produce many more apples the following year? No. Apple growers may plant more apple trees, but it will be several years before the new trees will be mature enough to bear fruit. In this example, the supply of apples is inelastic.

Check Your Understanding

1. How does an increase in demand affect price? A decrease?

2. How does an increase in supply affect price? A decrease?

3. What is a price ceiling? A price floor? When are such forms of government intervention used?

4. What is meant by elasticity of demand and elasticity of supply? Give examples of very elastic and very inelastic commodities.

5. What determines elasticity of demand and supply?

ECONOMY

Drawing by Roy Doty

When economics goes wild, the economist is called upon to cage it.

Economists have defined a series of laws such as the law of supply and demand to explain changes in the economy.

The Interaction of Markets

Now that we've learned how the forces of supply and demand determine prices in markets, we want to see how various markets interact with one another. The hundreds of thousands of individual markets in the United States are interwoven into a highly complex system of markets that makes up the price system that we examined in Chapter 2. Every time there is a change in any one market, it will affect many other markets. In this section, we want to examine (1) the ripple effect that occurs in the market system whenever there is a change in any one market and (2) the circular flow of economic activity.

The Ripple Effect

Whenever there is a change in demand or supply in one market, it sets off a series of changes in supply and demand that will affect many other markets. This tendency for changes in a single market to cause changes in many other markets is called the **ripple effect.** In order to better understand the ripple effect, let us look at a specific example.

Suppose there is a substantial increase in the demand for new houses in the United States. What will be the effects of this occurrence? The first and most obvious effect will be an increase in the price of new houses. However, that is only the beginning. There will be an increased demand for carpenters, bricklayers, plumbers, and electricians. There also will be an increased demand for lumber, concrete, bricks, glass, electrical and plumbing supplies, furniture, appliances, and carpeting. In addition, there will be an increased demand for electricity, gas, home heating oil, and homeowners' insurance.

All these changes will result from the simple fact that there is an increase in the demand for houses. Furthermore, the changes in each of these markets will themselves cause many other changes in still other markets. For example, the increased demand for lumber, bricks, and other building supplies will result in an increased demand for workers, natural resources, and capital goods with which to produce the additional building supplies. Similarly, the increased demand for furniture and appliances will result in an increased demand for workers and other resources in these industries.

All of these changes result from an initial change in demand in a single market: housing. In actual practice, there will be initial changes taking place simultaneously in many other markets. For example, if the increased demand for housing is the result of an increase in the number of young families in the nation, there probably also will be an increase in the demand for automobiles. In addition, there might be an increase in the demand for pediatricians, schools, and daycare centers.

It should now be clear to you how interdependent the various markets are. Changes in supply and/or demand in any one market will have far-reaching effects throughout the entire economy. In the following section, we will group markets into two categories and examine the circular flow of economic activity.

The Circular Flow of Economic Activity

The many individual markets in the economy may be grouped into two categories: markets for consumer products and markets for productive resources. The **markets for consumer products** are those markets in which households are the buyers and businesses are the sellers of the many consumer goods and services. The interaction of households and businesses in these markets determines the prices and the quantities exchanged of everything from ice cream cones to TV sets to automobiles. In contrast, the **markets for productive resources** are those markets in which businesses are the buyers and, to a large extent, households are the sellers of productive resources. The interaction of businesses and households in these markets determines the prices and the quantities exchanged of the factors of production: natural resources, capital goods, and labor.

The interrelationship between the markets for consumer products and the markets for productive resources can be seen in the circular flow diagram presented in Figure 3–10. The circular flow diagram is a simplified model of a market economy and, thus, is not totally representative of the complex American economy. Nevertheless, it can be very useful in gaining insight into how the product and resource markets interact. Let us examine this diagram.

First of all, let us focus our attention on the two complete circles. Note that the outer circle represents a continuous flow of money between households and businesses. Households pay money to businesses for goods and services, and businesses pay money to households for factors of production. The money continues to flow around the circle, from households to businesses and then back to households again. At the same time that money is flowing around the outside circle, goods and services and factors of production are flowing in the opposite direction around the inside circle. Note that households buy goods and services from businesses, and

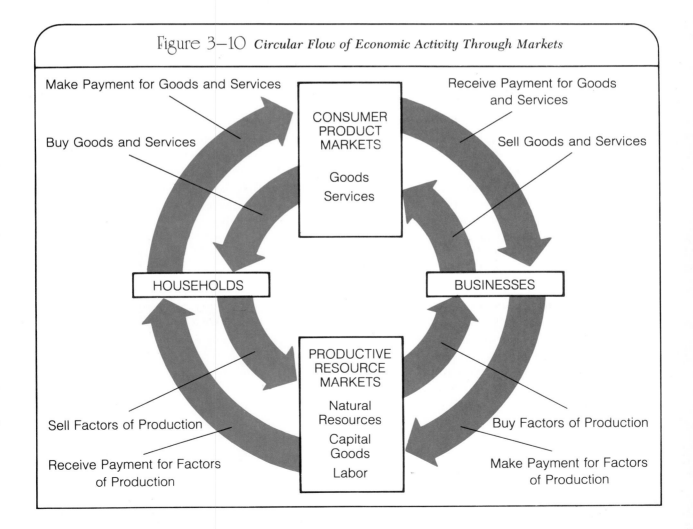

Figure 3–10 *Circular Flow of Economic Activity Through Markets*

Make Payment for Goods and Services

Buy Goods and Services

CONSUMER PRODUCT MARKETS

Goods
Services

Receive Payment for Goods and Services

Sell Goods and Services

HOUSEHOLDS

BUSINESSES

PRODUCTIVE RESOURCE MARKETS

Natural Resources

Capital Goods

Labor

Sell Factors of Production

Receive Payment for Factors of Production

Buy Factors of Production

Make Payment for Factors of Production

businesses buy factors of production from households. Study the diagram carefully and make sure you can see the two circular flows before reading any further.

Now let us focus our attention on only one half of the diagram at a time. Begin by looking at the top half, which involves only the market for consumer products. Note that businesses sell and households buy goods and services through the consumer product markets. In addition, households make payment and businesses receive payment for these goods and services through the same markets. Can you see the two opposite flows in the top half of the diagram? Money is flowing from households to businesses through the consumer product markets. In return for that money, goods and services are flowing from businesses to households. The amount of money flowing to businesses and the quantity of goods and services flowing to consumers through the consumer product markets are determined by the forces of supply and demand within those markets. The stronger the demand for consumer products, the higher the prices and, thus, the larger the flow of money.

Now let us look at the bottom half of the diagram, which involves the markets for productive resources. Households sell and businesses buy factors of production through these markets. At the same time, businesses make payment and households receive payment for factors of production through these same markets. In the bottom half of the diagram, money is flowing from businesses to households. In return for that money, factors of production are flowing from households to businesses. The amount of money flowing to households and the quantity of factors of production flowing to businesses through the productive resource markets are also determined by the forces of supply and demand.

The circular flow of economic activity in the American economy is similar to that of our simple model except for two major differences. In the American economy, labor is the only factor of production owned entirely by house-holds. Most of the natural resources and capital goods in the United States are owned by businesses. The other major shortcoming is that our simple model does not include government. In the American economy, government collects money from both businesses and households in the form of taxes and buys both goods and services and factors of production. In spite of these shortcomings, our simple model is useful as an aid to understanding the circular flow of economic activity in the American economy.

In summary, the American economy is made up of hundreds of thousands of individual markets that interact with one another. A change in supply or demand in any one market affects supply and demand in many other markets. Furthermore, the supply and demand conditions in the various individual markets help to determine the overall performance of the American economy. At the same time, the overall performance of the total economy is a major determinant of the supply and demand conditions in the various individual markets. After we've studied economic performance in Unit 3, you'll be better able to understand this interrelationship between individual markets and the economy as a whole. Until then, just remember that the many individual markets are the building blocks that make up the total American economy.

Check Your Understanding

1. How does the "ripple effect" affect markets in the American economy?

2. Distinguish between markets for consumer products and markets for productive resources.

3. Explain the circular flow of economic activity.

CAREERS: Statistician

Do you ever keep track of the batting averages of your favorite baseball players? Do you enjoy trying to analyze the results of an election? If your answer to either question is yes, you might be interested in a career as a statistician.

Statisticians collect and analyze numerical data to make predictions, to help make decisions, or to evaluate results. For example, they may try to find out how many people watch a particular television program to help the network decide whether to take it off the air. Or they may try to predict population growth in the suburbs to help

officials make sure that the school system is adequate.

In many cases, statisticians do not work with the population as a whole. In other words, they do not obtain information from every television viewer or suburban resident. Rather, they use a sample, or a small portion of the population, that is representative of the entire population. This sample will consist of the same proportion of males, females, old people, young people, blacks, whites, Hispanics, and so forth, as is found in the general population. A statistician will then survey, or question, this sample and apply certain techniques to make predictions for the population as a whole.

Very often statisticians do not collect the data themselves. Instead, they analyze data that have been collected by people who are trained in data-gathering techniques. For example, statisticians who work for the Bureau of the Census rely on data that have been collected by thousands of census takers.

Statisticians often work in a specific field, such as economics, psychology, education, physics, or engineering. They also may work for a government agency, a private company, a large university, or a public opinion research organization. However, despite these differences, all statisticians must have a college degree. Some jobs require a bachelor's degree in statistics, while others accept a degree in a related area, such as economics, or in the area in which the person plans to work. In addition, some jobs require a doctorate. In any case, the prospective statistician will have to take several mathematics courses, as well as some courses in computer programming.

Chapter Highlights

1   The words "supply" and "demand" are two of the most important words in economics. A sound understanding of the principles of supply and demand will help you to understand both specific economic issues and the operation of the entire economic system.

2   It is important to make a distinction between the terms "demand" and "quantity demanded." "Demand" refers to the whole schedule of possible prices and quantities demanded. "Quantity demanded" refers to a specific quantity demanded at a specific price.

3   "Supply" refers to the whole schedule of possible prices and quantities supplied. "Quantity supplied" refers to a specific quantity supplied at a specific price.

4   Supply and demand together create markets and establish prices within these markets. A market is the organized action through which potential buyers and sellers come together to exchange goods and services. A market exists whenever and wherever the decisions of buyers and sellers interact through the forces of supply and demand to determine prices.

5   The equilibrium price is that price at which the quantity demanded is exactly equal to the quantity supplied. When the equilibrium price has been achieved, it usually will not change unless some external force causes a change in demand and/or supply.

6   When allowed to operate freely, the price system tends to eliminate both shortages and surpluses through the forces of supply and demand. If the government interferes with the price system through the use of price ceilings or price floors, then the government will have to establish policies for coping with the resulting shortages and/or surpluses.

7   When there is an increase in demand, the entire demand curve shifts to the right, causing the price to rise. When there is a decrease in demand, the entire demand curve shifts to the left, causing the price to fall.

8   An increase in supply causes the entire supply curve to shift to the right, resulting in a decline in price. A decrease in supply causes the entire supply curve to shift to the left, causing the price to rise.

9   The change in quantity demanded resulting from any given change in price will depend on the elasticity of demand for the item. The change in quantity supplied resulting from any given change in price will depend on the elasticity of supply for the item.

10 The hundreds of thousands of individual markets in the United States are interwoven into a highly complex system of markets that make up the price system. When there is a change in any one market, there will be a ripple effect that will result in changes in many other markets.

11 Markets for consumer products are those markets in which households are the buyers and businesses are the sellers of goods and services. Markets for productive resources are markets in which the interaction of the decisions of businesses and households determine the prices and the quantities exchanged of natural resources, capital goods, and labor.

Important Terms

Match each of the following terms with the correct definition:

equilibrium price	supply curve	supply schedule
elasticity of demand	demand	law of demand
substitution effect	market	law of supply
elasticity of supply	price ceiling	quantity demanded
income effect	price floor	quantity supplied
principle of diminishing	supply	demand curve
marginal utility	demand schedule	ripple effect

1. A listing showing the various amounts of an item that sellers are willing to sell at various possible prices.

2. A law stating that as the price of an item rises and other things remain unchanged, the quantity demanded by buyers will fall; as the price of an item falls and other things remain unchanged, the quantity demanded by buyers will rise.

3. A listing showing the various amounts of an item that buyers are willing and able to buy at various possible prices during some stated time period.

4. A law stating that as the price of an item rises and other things remain unchanged, the quantity supplied by sellers will rise; as the price of an item falls and other things remain unchanged, the quantity supplied by sellers will fall.

5. The arrangement through which potential buyers and sellers come together to exchange goods and services.

6. The ability and willingness of people to buy things.

7. The ability to purchase more or less of an item without spending any more or less money.

8. A graphical representation of a demand schedule.

9. The ability and willingness of sellers to make things available for sale.

10. The price at which the quantity demanded is exactly equal to the quantity supplied.

11. A government-imposed upper price limit that prevents market forces from establishing a price above this limit.

12. A government-imposed lower price limit that prevents market forces from establishing a price below this limit.

13. A specific quantity that will be demanded at a specific price.

14. A specific quantity that will be supplied at a specific price.

15. A measure of the responsiveness of quantity demanded to a change in price.

16. A measure of the responsiveness of quantity supplied to a change in price.

17. The tendency for individuals to receive less and less additional satisfaction from an item as they obtain more and more units of the item during a specified time period.

18. The tendency for consumers to substitute lower priced items for more expensive items.

19. A graphical representation of a supply schedule.

20. The tendency for a change in one market to cause changes in many other markets.

Extending Your Understanding

1. Under what circumstances do you think the government might be justified in imposing price controls on the American economy? What kinds of problems would be created by price controls?

2. Suppose an increase in the birth rate leads to a substantial increase in the number of students enrolled in the nation's schools. What markets would be affected by this development? How would they be affected?

Activities

1. To explore how the laws of supply and demand operate, ask several merchants in your community how they decide which items to order, how many of the items to order, what prices to charge, and which of these items they generally put on sale and why. Summarize your findings in a short report.

2. Bring in several recent newspaper or news magazine clippings that describe a change in the demand or supply of some commodity. Discuss these clippings in class.

Building Skills in Economics: Understanding Supply and Demand Curves

As you learned in this chapter, the term "supply" refers to the entire schedule of possible prices and quantities supplied for a particular item. The term "demand" refers to the entire schedule of possible prices and quantities demanded for a particular item. Supply and demand are often represented graphically.

   The graph that follows shows supply and demand curves for rock music records and tapes bought during a recent year. The questions will help you interpret the graph.

Applying Economics Skills

1. At a price of $5.50, how many rock music records and tapes would be supplied? How many would be demanded?
2. At what price are the quantity supplied and the quantity demanded exactly equal? What is this price called?
3. Within what price range will a shortage exist? Within what price range will there be a surplus?
4. What will happen to the supply curve if the supply of records and tapes increases? Will the equilibrium price be higher or lower?
5. What will happen if the demand suddenly increases? How will an increase in demand be reflected in the equilibrium price?

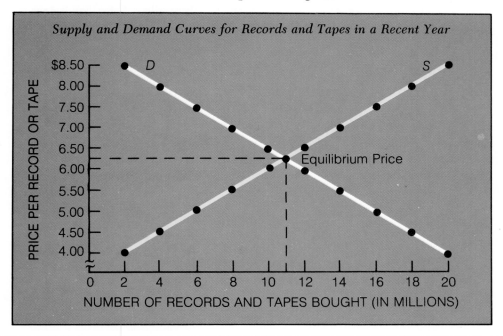

Supply and Demand Curves for Records and Tapes in a Recent Year

UNIT 2

The American Business Structure

CHAPTER 4

BUSINESS ORGANIZATION AND MARKET STRUCTURES

Carol Chin owns and operates a furniture store. Gary Parker is a sales representative for a large national company. Manuel Gonzalez is a high school senior who plans to attend college. What do these three people have in common? Their futures all depend on the success or failure of businesses.

Carol has invested all her savings, plus a substantial amount of borrowed money, in her business. She has high hopes for her furniture store and dreams of expanding it in the future. She knows, however, that she could lose everything if her business fails. Gary's income depends on how many sales he makes, and he, too, knows that his success is tied to the success of his company. If his company has several bad years, one outstanding sales record cannot keep it from folding. Manuel has not yet decided on a career, but whether he eventually goes into business for himself, starts a business with a friend, or works for a business owned by someone else, his livelihood probably will depend on the success of a business.

Businesses play a vital role in our lives. We depend on them not only for our livelihood, but also for the goods and services we use in our daily lives. Nearly everything we own and use—from our food and clothing to our automobiles and homes—is produced by businesses.

In this chapter, we will examine business organization and market structures in the United States. We will examine the various ways in which a business can be organized and consider the advantages and disadvantages of each. We also will explore the various types of market structures under which businesses in this nation operate and examine government efforts to promote and maintain competition. Let us begin by examining the characteristics of business firms.

Characteristics of Business Firms

A **business firm** is an organization that brings together the factors of production—natural resources, capital goods, and labor—for the purpose of producing and/or distributing goods and services. Business firms purchase the factors of production, transform them into goods and services, and sell the goods and services to consumers and other firms. For example, a furniture-manufacturing firm purchases lumber and equipment from other firms and labor in the form of its employees. It then uses these resources to produce furniture, which is sold to consumers and to other business firms.

One of the major characteristics of business firms is specialization and division of labor. Workers are trained in specific tasks and perform only a small part of the production process. For centuries, people have been aware of the advantages of specialization and division of labor. Even when early households produced many of their own basic necessities, at least some goods and services were produced by specialized workers outside the household. Today, most commodities are produced by outside business firms.

Specialization and division of labor result in increased efficiency in the production process. Economists refer to the savings resulting from this increased efficiency as economies of scale. **Economies of scale** occur when a large volume of output can be produced at a lower cost per unit than can a small volume of output. In other words, whereas it might cost Cindy Leonard $5 to produce each of five toys if she worked alone, a business firm that utilized mass production techniques, including specialization and the division of labor, might be able to produce 5,000 of the same toys for 25 cents each.

Another important characteristic of the business firm centers around risk. There is

A small business employs only a few workers and has a low volume of output.

always the possibility that a business will fail and the money invested in it will be lost. Despite this possibility, the owners of business firms are willing to invest substantial sums of money in the hope that their business ventures will be profitable. If the businesses fail, of course, the owners suffer the consequences. Needless to say, not all people are willing or able to take such risks, so many instead choose what they consider to be more secure ways of earning a living.

Check Your Understanding

1. What is a business firm? What are some of its characteristics?

2. What is meant by economies of scale? Give an example of how economies of scale work.

Forms of Business Organization

Business firms may be classified in various ways. One way is to group them according to the products they produce. Firms that produce identical or similar products are said to be in the same **industry.** For example, General Motors, Ford, and Chrysler are all part of the automobile industry. Similarly, General Electric, Whirlpool, and Westinghouse are all part of the home appliance industry. However, many major companies produce products in more than one industry. In addition to producing automobiles, General Motors also produces trucks, buses, diesel locomotives, and home appliances. Therefore, it would be correct to say that General Motors is also in the truck industry, the bus industry, the diesel locomotive industry, and the home appliance industry.

Another way to classify firms is by their legal form of organization. There are three basic forms of business organization that we will consider: (1) the individual proprietorship; (2) the partnership; and (3) the corporation. Let us briefly examine the special characteristics of each.

Individual Proprietorships

An **individual proprietorship** is a form of business organization in which the business firm is owned by a single individual (the individual proprietor) who makes all the business decisions, receives all the profits earned by the firm, and is responsible for any losses incurred by the firm. It is the simplest, oldest, and most common type of business organization in the United States. More than 75 percent of all business firms are individual proprietorships as Figure 4-1 shows. Most, however, are very small. Individual proprietorships account for only 7 percent of all **business receipts,** or the money business firms take in. Typical individual proprietorships include neighborhood grocery stores, barbershops, auto repair shops, and farms.

Individual proprietorships have both advantages and disadvantages. We already have mentioned the risks involved when considering

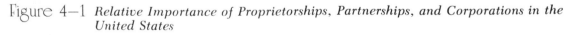

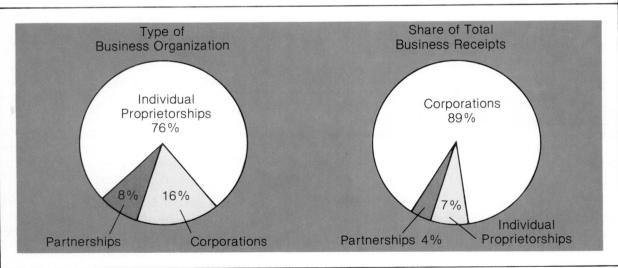

Figure 4—1 *Relative Importance of Proprietorships, Partnerships, and Corporations in the United States*

The individual owner of this dairy farm makes all the decisions for the business. However, the farm owner faces such risks as disease in the herd or low prices in the market.

a business venture. Let us now further examine the pros and cons of starting an individual proprietorship.

One of the major advantages of an individual proprietorship is the ease with which it can be started. There are few formalities, relatively little red tape, and few fees to pay. Anyone who wants to start an individual proprietorship can do so as long as he or she has the money. These factors are especially significant when the business to be started is very small and has limited profit potential.

A second advantage of an individual proprietorship is that the owner gets all the profits, assuming the business is successful. This is especially appealing to people who believe that the chance of phenomenal success is worth the risk of failure. Although the odds of turning a very small investment into a business empire are small, there have been enough amazing success stories to entice others to try.

A third advantage of this form of business organization is that an individual proprietor is

his or her own boss. Although individual proprietors may hire salaried employees to help them operate the business, they are still the final decision makers. They decide such things as what items to stock, the hours of operation, and how the business should be run. For people who dislike working for and having to take orders from someone else, the prospect of owning their own business is very attractive.

Despite these advantages, there are also some important disadvantages of the individual proprietorship. One of the most serious disadvantages involves **unlimited liability,** the potential for a business owner to incur and have to pay unlimited business debts. Every potential proprietor should give serious consideration to this problem before going into business. Let us take a hypothetical example.

Suppose a person who has had a successful career as an employee decides to quit his or her job to launch a small business with $20,000 worth of savings. This person has a mortgage-free home worth $100,000 and a new car worth

$12,000, in addition to the $20,000 in cash. How much can this person lose if the business venture fails? The answer is almost everything, including the home and the car, depending on the bankruptcy laws in his or her state. In short, people who launch individual proprietorships are liable for far more than the amount of money they invest.

A second disadvantage centers around the limited fund-raising ability of individual proprietorships. Individual proprietors themselves are unlikely to have sufficient funds with which to start or expand a business. They are also less likely than a group of people to get substantial bank loans. Therefore, it is often difficult for individual proprietors to raise enough money to experience the economies of scale that result from increased size. If the individual proprietor is competing with larger firms that, because of economies of scale, are able to produce goods and/or services for a lower cost per unit, he or she ultimately may be forced out of business.

A third disadvantage of individual proprietorships involves a limited life. When the proprietor dies or decides that he or she no longer wants to remain in business, it is possible that the business firm will cease to exist. This limited life feature may result in the loss of potential

The owner of a small business such as this lunch wagon has limited ability to raise funds to expand.

customers who are concerned about service for the products they buy. For example, suppose you are buying a microwave oven with a ten-year warranty. Would you rather buy it from a firm that is likely to be in business for years or from an individual proprietor who may go out of business in the near future? Chances are you'll deal with the more permanent firm.

Partnerships

A **partnership** is a form of business organization that is collectively owned by two or more people (called partners) who jointly make the business decisions, share the profits of the business, and bear the financial responsibility for any losses. Partnerships are the least common form of business organization in the United States, accounting for only 8 percent of all business firms and 4 percent of all business receipts. Essentially, partnerships are expanded proprietorships in which all decisions and responsibilities are shared by the partners. Because of their structure, they have the same advantages and disadvantages as individual proprietorships, except on a different scale. Let us examine these advantages and disadvantages.

Like the individual proprietorship, a partnership also is relatively easy and inexpensive to start up, with the owners collectively getting all the profits and making all the decisions. In addition, in a partnership there is the opportunity for some specialization in management. For example, one partner might concentrate most of his or her efforts on sales while another partner specializes in production. The partnership also has better fund-raising abilities than an individual proprietorship, although the ability of the business to raise cash is still very limited.

On the negative side, a partnership has limited life, lasting only as long as the partnership agreement is in force. There are many things that can put an end to the agreement. For example, suppose a senior partner who owns a substantial portion of the business decides to leave the business over a disagree-

Corporations dominate the American business scene. Large department stores such as this one are usually owned by corporations.

ment. In order to remain in business, the other partners must buy this person's share of the business or find a new partner willing to do so. If they cannot do either, the partnership has to be dissolved. Other factors that might cause a partnership to end are changing interests and the death of a partner.

In addition, partnerships face unlimited liability of a far more serious nature than for an individual proprietorship. In a partnership, a business debt incurred by any of the partners becomes the responsibility of the partnership. As a result, each partner stands to lose substantial personal wealth if the business fails.

To take an extreme example, suppose that an individual decides to invest $90,000 in a partnership with a friend who is investing only $10,000. The first individual owns 90 percent of the business, and the second individual owns 10 percent. As long as the business succeeds, there is no problem. The first individual reaps 90 percent of the profits, while the other reaps 10 percent. However, suppose that the partner with only 10 percent ownership incurs $150,000 of business debts. If this partner has no other assets, the other partner could end up liable for

the entire $150,000. This problem of unlimited liability justifiably causes many people to think long and hard before entering a partnership.

Corporations

Corporations are the third basic form of business organization. A **corporation** is a form of business organization that is collectively owned by a number of individuals but has the legal status to act as a single fictitious person. The corporation is by far the most important form of business organization in the United States. Although corporations make up only 16 percent of all business firms in this country, they employ more than 60 percent of the labor force and account for 89 percent of all receipts. Corporations completely dominate many major industries, including manufacturing, transportation, and public utilities. In manufacturing, for example, corporations account for approximately 98 percent of all business receipts; in the transportation and public utilities industries, this figure exceeds 90 percent.

Unlike the minimal paperwork required to establish individual proprietorships and partnerships, setting up a corporation requires obtaining a corporate charter. **A corporate charter** is a legal document granted by a state government that gives a business the authority to operate in that state. Each state has its own set of rules and regulations governing the establishment of corporations. However, obtaining a charter is usually relatively easy and inexpensive.

The corporate charter establishes the corporation as a "legal person," separate from the actual owners of the corporation. As a legal person, the corporation can enter into contracts and make commitments in its own name for which the corporation alone is responsible. Thus, the corporation as a whole can be sued, although the individual owners cannot.

A corporate charter also authorizes the corporation to issue and sell shares of **stock,** or ownership in the corporation, to enable the corporation to raise money. The people who buy the stock are called **stockholders.** There are two major types of stock that people may buy: preferred stock and common stock. **Preferred stock** gives the stockholder a prior claim on dividends but no voting privileges. **Dividends** are cash payments made to stockholders out of a corporation's profits. Thus, assuming a corporation is profitable, owners of preferred stock are the first to receive dividends after all interest obligations are paid. This dividend payment is always a fixed amount, regardless of how profitable the corporation is. However, should the corporation fail, preferred stockholders are the first to receive payment for their investment after all creditors have been paid.

Common stock gives stockholders voting privileges but no prior claim on dividends. In addition, common stockholders are the last to be paid if the corporation fails. However, there is a potential for greater earnings over the long run if the corporation is successful because the dividends paid can be increased in a good year. Also, common stock gives investors some voice in the operation of the corporation through their voting privileges.

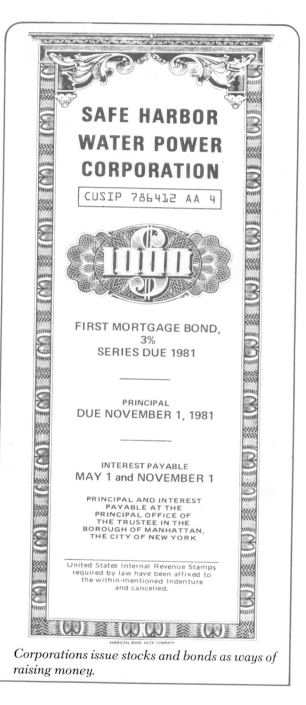

Corporations issue stocks and bonds as ways of raising money.

In addition to issuing shares of stock, corporations can raise money by selling bonds to investors. Corporate **bonds** are IOUs of the corporation that bind the corporation to pay a fixed sum of money when the bonds reach maturity.

The corporation must also pay a fixed sum of money to bondholders annually until the maturity date. This fixed annual payment is called the **interest** or the **coupon payment.** Unlike stockholders, bond owners do not own shares in the corporation. When people buy bonds, they are simply lending money to the corporation for which they will receive interest payments.

The stockholders of a corporation elect a board of directors who is responsible for the mangagement of the corporation. Each stockholder gets one vote for each share of common stock owned. In large corporations, the board of directors hires a president and other officers to carry out the corporation's day-to-day management operations. The employed officers are responsible to the board of directors, who is in turn responsible to the stockholders. In smaller corporations, one or more members of the board of directors may also serve as officers of the corporation.

In addition to voting for the board of directors, stockholders also have the right to vote on other matters affecting the corporation, such as proposed mergers with other companies. They do this at an annual stockholders meeting, where they may cast their votes in person or vote by **proxy** (sign over their voting privileges to the current management or to some other group). In the United States, most stockholders in large corporations choose the latter option and play little or no role in corporate decision making. They often live far from the meeting place and are too involved with their own lives to devote much attention to corporate affairs. Moreover, few stockholders own enough shares to have an influence on corporate policies.

As with the other forms of business organization, corporations have both advantages and disadvantages. The advantages include limited liability, ability to raise large sums of money, and unlimited life. The drawbacks include separation of ownership and management and double taxation. Let us look at each of these.

Perhaps the most important advantage of the corporation from the standpoint of potential investors is that of limited liability. Unlike individual proprietorships and partnerships, investors in a corporation can lose no more than the amount of money they invest. The stockholders of a corporation cannot be held personally liable for the debts of the corporation. If a corporation is successful, the stockholders may reap large profits. If the corporation fails and goes bankrupt, the stockholders' loss is limited to the value of the shares of stock owned.

The limited liability feature of corporations contributes significantly to the second advantage of the corporation form of organization— the ability to raise large sums of money. Since potential stockholders will share in large profits if the corporation succeeds and face only limited losses if the corporation fails, they are more willing to invest in stocks than in other more risky ventures. Corporations can raise large sums of money by issuing stock, by selling corporate bonds, and by borrowing from lending institutions. This ability to raise large sums of money is the primary reason that almost all large business firms are corporations.

Another important advantage of corporations is the fact that they have an unlimited life. Unlike individual proprietorships and partnerships, the death or resignation of the current president does not alter the legal status of the corporation. Similarly, when owners (stockholders) die, their heirs simply inherit the shares of stock and the corporation is unaffected. Few major corporations today have the same owners and officers they had when they were founded. Many corporations, in fact, are over a hundred years old. This unlimited life feature contributes to a corporation's ability to raise money. Banks and other lending institutions are willing to make long-term loans to corporations because they know the corporations will outlive their current owners and officers. Also, new stockholders can more easily be brought into a corporation because they know that the existence of the corporation does not depend on the individuals who currently run it.

The first corporations set up in the United

States were small firms whose founders had simply chosen the corporate form of business organization over that of the proprietorship or partnership. The people who set up the corporation owned most or all of the stock and they managed the firm. However, as corporations grew larger and larger, ownership passed from the hands of the founding owner–managers into the hands of millions of stockholders. Management was turned over to salaried officers who were hired to manage the day-to-day operations of the corporation. Only a very few of the large corporations today are privately owned by those who are responsible for their management.

This separation of ownership and management may pose some problems. Since the owners and managers of many large corporations are two separate groups of people, their views of what is best for the company may not always coincide. Most hired managers have been trained in business administration, and they are likely to feel that their training and their familiarity with day-to-day operations put them in a better position than the stockholders to know what is best for the corporation.

Generally, both groups are interested in maximizing profits, but they may not agree on the best way to do so. For example, there is the question of short-term profits versus long-term profits. Managers who are only five years away from retirement may be most interested in maximizing profits during that five-year period. Their personal income may be linked to the annual profit of the corporation, and certainly their status will be enhanced if their corporation shows relatively large profits. Maximizing profits during that five-year period, however, may not be in the best interests of either the corporation or the stockholders. It might be better to forgo large profits during that period in order to invest in new technology that will enable the company to earn even greater profits over a longer period of time.

The problem of double taxation is considered by some to be a disadvantage of the corporate form of business organization. **Double taxation** refers to the fact that corporations have to pay taxes on their profits even though stockholders later pay a tax on some of these same profits when they are distributed as dividends. However, there is considerable disagreement over just how much of a disadvantage this problem of double taxation really is. Some argue that many large corporations with substantial market power are able to pass the corporate income tax on to their customers in the form of higher prices. When this happens, it is the consumer, not the corporation or the stockholders, who is actually paying the corporate income tax.

Other Forms of Business Organization

In addition to individual proprietorships, partnerships, and corporations, there are two other forms of business organization that provide goods and services: nonprofit organizations and cooperatives. Let us briefly examine each of these forms of business organization.

Nonprofit organizations are dedicated to providing public services. They may not and do not earn a profit. Any revenue in excess of operating costs is used to further the purposes of the organization. Churches and many other private charity organizations, as well as cultural organizations such as opera or museum associations, are nonprofit organizations.

Some nonprofit organizations are engaged in production in much the same way as are other business firms. For example, Goodwill Industries, which is devoted to helping the handicapped, employs handicapped workers who repair clothing, furniture, and other household items that have been donated. The repaired items are then sold to the public through stores operated by the organization. The earnings of the organization are used to pay the workers and to help train them for jobs in the private sector.

A **cooperative** is a voluntary association of people formed for the purpose of providing economic benefits for its members. The three most common types of cooperatives are consumer

The owners of these cranberry bogs formed a producer cooperative to obtain higher prices for their cranberries.

cooperatives, producer cooperatives, and credit unions.

Consumer cooperatives are formed for the purpose of collectively buying consumer products in large quantities at low prices. The objective of consumer co-ops is to offer their members lower prices than those charged by regular businesses. Members usually pay regular prices to the co-op at the time they make their purchases but receive rebates at the end of each year.

Producer cooperatives are voluntary associations of producers of certain products that attempt to obtain higher prices than the members could get by selling individually. Most producer co-ops in the United States are made up of farmers. Some farm co-ops have meat-processing plants or facilities for processing grain, and they often help transport and advertise their members' products. The primary objective of producer cooperatives is to eliminate middleman charges and pass the savings on to their members in the form of higher prices.

Credit unions, which are very common in large cities, are often created by employees of a large company or by other large groups of people. They accept deposits and make loans. Their purpose is to help their members buy goods instead of making a profit. Thus, compared to other financial institutions, they usually pay higher interest rates on members' savings and charge lower interest rates on members' loans.

Check Your Understanding

1. What is an industry? Give examples of firms that produce products in more than one industry.

2. What are the advantages and disadvantages of the individual proprietorship as a form of business organization?

3. What are the advantages and disadvantages of the partnership as a form of business organization?

4. How do the advantages and disadvantages of the corporation compare with those of individual proprietorships and partnerships?

Market Structures

In the preceding section, we examined the ways in which business firms can be organized. In this section, we want to examine the various ways that the markets in which business firms sell their products are structured. Market structure is determined primarily by (1) the number of firms selling in the market; (2) the extent to which the products of the different firms in the market are the same or different; and (3) the ease with which firms can enter into or exit from the market. Based on these three criteria, economists usually group market structures into four basic categories: (1) pure competition; (2) monopoly; (3) oligopoly; and (4) monopolistic competition. Let us examine each of these market structures.

Pure Competition

In our discussion of the theoretical "pure" market economy in Chapter 2, we listed the characteristics of pure competition. So that they will be fresh in your mind, let us again review them here:

1. *Many sellers:* There are many sellers, and each firm is so small relative to the entire market that its actions will have no effect on the price of its product. Instead, it must accept the going market price, established by the forces of supply and demand, just like all the other firms in the market.

2. *Standardized product:* The products of the various firms in the market are so nearly identical that buyers do not prefer the product of any one firm over that of any other firm.

3. *Easy entry and exit:* There are no significant financial, legal, technological, or other barriers to prevent new firms from entering the market or to prevent existing firms from leaving the market. Firms are free to enter and leave the market at will.

4. *No artificial restrictions:* There are no wage and price controls, minimum wage laws, labor unions, or other artificial restrictions on the free movement of prices and wages up and down.

Given these characteristics and what you know about the American economy, an obvious question should come to mind. Does pure competition actually exist? Let us consider this question.

In the American economy, many markets are dominated by a few giant firms, and the products of different firms are usually not identical. Also, it is very difficult for new firms to enter certain markets. In addition, labor unions, minimum wage laws, and other artificial restrictions prevent the free movement of prices and wages. Given this situation, we can safely conclude that pure competition does not exist in the American economy. Does it exist anywhere? The answer is probably not.

Why, then, are we devoting space and time to pure competition? There are two reasons. First, a pure competition model gives us a useful standard against which to compare other market structures. It is regarded by some economists as the ideal model that, if it actually existed, would result in maximum freedom and the most efficient allocation of scarce resources. It would also make it difficult for any firm to take advantage of its customers.

The second reason for studying pure competition is that some industries do, in fact, come quite close to this market structure. American agriculture is the best example. There are hundreds of thousands of small farmers in the United States, and each one produces only a small percentage of the national farm output. No one farmer is able to influence the prices of farm products. In addition, the products produced are almost identical. A bushel of corn from one farmer is very similar to a bushel of corn from any other farmer. Moreover, entry into an agricultural market is easier than in most other industries. It is true that the high cost of land and machinery have made it increasingly difficult in recent years for new farmers to enter agriculture. However, existing farmers can enter new agricultural markets with relative ease because they already have machinery and land. For example, farmers who normally produce only corn and soybeans could easily plant wheat if it became more profitable to do so.

An evaluation of pure competition Because American agriculture approximates pure competition, consumers get a better buy on food than just about anything else. Farmers cannot take advantage of consumers by raising their prices. The prices farmers receive for their products are determined by the forces of supply and demand, and there is little that any single farmer can do to change these prices. If a farmer wants to charge $4 per bushel for corn when the market price is $3.50, he or she will be left with a lot of unsold corn.

Would Americans be better off, then, if all markets were purely competitive? The answer to this question is not nearly as simple as it might seem. On the positive side, a purely competitive economy would be an economy without big business, big labor, and big government. No individual would have any economic power over any other individual. All power would rest in the hands of the impersonal market forces of supply and demand. Each business firm would simply adjust its level of output according to market conditions since it would have no control over the prices of its products. There would be no need for unions because market forces would determine wages. Finally, there would be freedom of opportunity that would allow anyone who wanted to enter a business the freedom to do so.

This is only one side of the coin, however. A purely competitive economy also has serious shortcomings. First of all, most people would not be content to have all products standardized. They would not want to wear clothes or drive automobiles that were identical to those of everyone else. Life wouldn't be very exciting under such conditions.

A second major problem that would result

from pure competition is that firms would lack incentives to conduct research and develop new and improved products. Because there could be no patent laws in a purely competitive market, any time a firm developed a new product, all other firms would be free to produce the new product immediately. This would cut down dramatically on a firm's potential profits, and as a result firms would be reluctant to produce new products for consumers.

A third problem in a society in which all markets are purely competitive is that in many industries, a few large firms can produce the total quantity demanded of a product at much lower cost than could many small producers. These economies of scale result from specialization and the division of labor in the production process. The automobile industry is a good example. Suppose that instead of three major automobile manufacturers in the United States, there were 1,000 small firms producing cars. Each firm would be too small to take advantage of the economies of scale that are available to the existing "Big Three." As a result, the production costs of these firms would be much higher, and these costs would be reflected in the prices of automobiles. Also, with pure competition firms would be free to enter and leave the market at will. How would you like to buy a new automobile from a firm that might not be in business a year from now?

As you can see, pure competition has its limitations. Although it works well in an industry such as agriculture, it is not practical for all markets and all industries. Nevertheless, since competition is the controlling mechanism of a market economy, a high degree of competition is usually desirable in most markets.

Monopoly

Monopoly is the extreme opposite of pure competition and has the following characteristics: (1) the market consists of a single seller; (2) the seller sells a product for which there are no close substitutes; (3) there are barriers to entry that prevent competitors from entering the market; and (4) the seller can control the price of his or her product.

Cases of pure monopoly are rare in the United States today because there are few products for which there are no close substitutes. Also, permanent barriers to entry generally are not permitted. There are, however, numerous markets that approximate pure monopoly because the available substitutes are not considered adequate by many people, and certain barriers restrict the entry of firms into the market. Let us briefly examine each of these factors.

Availability of adequate substitutes In the broadest sense of the word, the Ford Motor Company has a monopoly on Ford automobiles. No other company is permitted to produce cars that look exactly like Fords or carry the Ford name. However, since most people consider automobiles manufactured by General Motors and Chrysler Corporation adequate substitutes for Fords, there is little market power in such a monopoly. To have real monopoly power, Ford would need to have a monopoly on all automobiles produced and sold, and even then some people would substitute motorcycles or public transportation for automobiles. Even companies that have monopoly control of public utilities, such as a local supplier of electricity, have some competition. Gas, heating oil, and wood can be substituted for electricity as a source of heat. In extreme cases, candles, kerosene lamps, and battery-powered lights can be used for lighting. However, because many people may not consider them adequate substitutes, the electric company can be thought of as a monopoly.

Barriers to entry For a monopoly to exist for any extended period of time, it must have strong barriers to entry that prevent potential competitors from entering the market. In the case of the electric company, the barriers to entry are provided by the government. As you learned in Chapter 2, competition in the market for local electrical power would result in duplication of facilities that would increase costs of supplying electricity to local communities. Thus, the government grants a single company the exclusive right to serve a specific community. In return for this right, the company must accept government regulation of rates and the quality of service. Because competition is not considered practical in the case of the electric company and many other public utilities, economists usually refer to the public utilities as **natural monopolies.**

Control of essential raw materials needed for the production of a product also can be an important barrier to entry. For example, until 1945 the Aluminum Company of America (ALCOA) manufactured more than 90 percent of the aluminum produced in this country. ALCOA was able to maintain its monopoly power because it owned most of the nation's bauxite—the ore from which aluminum is made—and refused to sell bauxite to potential competitors. In 1945, however, ALCOA's monopoly power was broken when the government intervened.

Another important barrier to entry occurs when a seller develops a new product and obtains a patent on it. Patents are granted by the government and prohibit potential competitors from producing or selling the patented product without the permission of the patent owner. Patents encourage potential inventors to create new products by assuring them the profits from their inventions. Monopolies that result from patents are called **technological monopolies.** For many years, Xerox Corporation had a technological monopoly on photocopying equipment in the United States because of patents it owned. However, in 1975 the government required Xerox to make some of its patents available to competitors in an effort to increase competition in the market.

The size of a potential market is another barrier to entry. Many small communities have only one drugstore, hardware store, barbershop, bank, and so forth because the local market is too small for two firms to operate success-

In recent years, a government monopoly, the United States Postal Service, has faced competition from express mail companies that charge high rates but promise fast service.

Oligopoly

Although few industries are controlled by a single firm, many industries in the United States are dominated by a few giant firms. Such a market structure is known as **oligopoly,** and it is the market structure under which most large corporations operate. Oligopoly has the following characteristics: (1) a few sellers; (2) substantial barriers to entry; (3) standardized or differentiated products; and (4) substantial nonprice competition. Let us examine each of these characteristics briefly.

A few sellers When we say oligopoly is characterized by a few sellers, what do we mean? Economists usually define oligopoly as few enough firms so that there is mutual interdependence among the firms. This means that the actions of any one firm in the market will affect the other firms in the market and vice versa. Thus, a firm operating in a market characterized by oligopoly would not change the price of its product, the quality of its product, or its advertising without first taking into consideration the possible reaction of its competitors.

Let us look at a specific example. The American automobile industry is certainly an example of oligopoly. It is dominated by three giant companies: General Motors, Ford, and Chrysler. Suppose Ford is contemplating a substantial price increase for its cars. One of the most important considerations in making such a decision is the likely response of GM and Chrysler. If Ford believes that its two chief competitors will match the increase, then it probably will go ahead and implement the planned price change. If, however, GM and Chrysler do not match the price increase, then Ford will be forced to either roll back its price or risk losing many of its customers.

In contrast, if Chrysler is considering doubling its advertising expenditure in an effort to win new customers from Ford and GM, it will take into consideration whether or not its chief competitors will react by also doubling their advertising expenditures. If they do, each firm

fully. If a second firm tried to enter the market, neither firm would have enough business to earn a satisfactory profit. Such monopolies that occur because of the seller's location are called **geographic monopolies.**

In some monopoly situations, known as **government monopolies,** the government itself is the sole producer of a product and serves as the barrier to entry. Examples of government monopolies are the United States Postal Service, the interstate highway system, and the manufacture of coins and paper currency.

may end up spending a great deal more for advertising without obtaining many new customers.

Any time there are few enough sellers in a market that each one worries about the actions and reactions of its competitors, the market is characterized by oligopoly. Economists consider this mutual interdependence to be the most important feature of oligopoly. In addition, not all oligopolies are national in scope. There are many examples of local and regional oligopolies. For example, if there are only three gas stations in a small community, the actions of the owner of any one of the stations will have an effect on the owners of the other two stations. Thus, all three are operating in an oligopolistic market structure.

Barriers to entry Although the barriers to entry in an oligopolistic market are not as strong as in a monopolistic market, they are usually substantial. In the case of national oligopolies, such as the automobile and steel industries, the primary barriers may be the high cost of acquiring the resources necessary to establish a new firm and the inability to begin producing on a sufficiently large scale to take advantage of the economies of scale that the established firms are experiencing. For example, it would be extremely difficult for a new firm to raise enough money to enter the automobile industry. Furthermore, a new firm would be unlikely to experience large enough sales in its first few years of existence to enable it to take advantage of the economies of scale that result from mass production. As a result, its production costs will be higher than that of its competitors, and it will be unable to compete successfully. Because of these barriers, few new firms can enter such industries as the automobile and steel industries. In recent years, only foreign manufacturers, such as the Japanese automobile manufacturers, have successfully entered these fields.

Also, as in the case of monopoly, control of important raw materials can be a strong barrier to entry. If a small number of large firms control most of the supply of a necessary ingredient for the production of a product, potential new competitors will be prevented from entering the market.

In the case of local oligopolies, market size may be the primary barrier to entry. If the existing three gas stations are able to supply all the gasoline needs of a community, it is unlikely that a fourth station would be very profitable. Also, customer loyalty to established firms may be a very difficult obstacle for new firms to overcome, in the case of both local and national oligopolies.

Standardized or differentiated products The products sold in oligopolistic markets may be either standardized or differentiated, depending on the industry. In industries such as steel, aluminum, and light bulbs, the products are almost identical. However, in other industries—such as breakfast cereals, laundry detergents, and automobiles—the products are differentiated.

Nonprice competition In those oligopolistic industries where the products are differentiated, sellers engage in vigorous nonprice competition. Nonprice competition involves efforts to persuade consumers to buy a particular product for reasons other than price. How many breakfast cereal commercials have you seen on TV in which viewers are asked to buy the product because it is less expensive than that of competitors? How about soap and laundry detergent commercials? Commercials for all these products attempt to convince consumers that the product is better, not less expensive, than that of competitors. According to most commercials, the breakfast cereal they are advertising is tastier or more nutritious, or their detergent gets clothes cleaner than competing brands. Firms operating in oligopolistic markets seldom engage in price wars. If a firm operating in an oligopolistic market lowers its price, its competitors will be forced to match the price cut. As a result, all firms will suffer a reduction in profits.

Therefore, prices tend to remain relatively stable in oligopolistic markets, with most of the competition being of a nonprice nature.

Monopolistic Competition

Monopolistic competition is a market structure that is characterized by (1) many sellers; (2) differentiated products; (3) nonprice competition; (4) relatively easy entry and exit. It has similarities to both pure competition and oligopoly.

Monopolistic competition is similar to pure competition in the sense that there are many sellers and no strong barriers to entry. Firms can enter and leave markets on a regular basis and, indeed, do so. The amount of money required to go into business is relatively small, and there are few government regulations restricting those wishing to enter a market. In addition, each seller controls such a small share of the market that each believes that his or her actions will bring no reactions from competitors.

Unlike pure competition, however, monopolistic competition is characterized by product differentiation and nonprice competition. In fact, product differentiation and nonprice competition are the most important characteristics that distinguish monopolistic competition from pure competition. Firms operating in markets characterized by monopolistic competition do extensive advertising in an effort to convince consumers that their products are better than those of their competitors. Often there is little or no actual difference in the products, but advertising campaigns lead at least some consumers to believe otherwise. A good example of this is the market for aspirin. All brands of aspirin contain very similar ingredients that are stipulated by federal law. Yet, many consumers believe that some highly advertised brands are better than others, and they are willing to pay a premium price for them.

Most retail stores in medium-to-large-sized cities fall into the category of monopolistic competition. They advertise heavily and try to convince consumers that their products and services are superior to those of their competitors. A store may emphasize such things as convenient location, ample parking space, courteous service, and a large selection of merchandise.

Although gasoline service stations operating in small communities where there are only two or three competitors fall into the category of oligopoly, in larger cities where there are many gas stations, the market structure in which they operate is monopolistic competition. These stations attempt to differentiate themselves from their competitors in numerous ways, such as convenient location, the availability of auto repair service and an automatic car wash, and long hours of operation.

Check Your Understanding

1. What are the four characteristics of pure competition? Does pure competition exist?

2. What problems would exist in a purely competitive economy?

3. Describe four characteristics of monopoly. What are the two key factors that determine the market power of a single seller?

4. Identify four characteristics of oligopoly. What is meant by "mutual interdependence"? Describe nonprice competition.

5. What are the four characteristics of monopolistic competition? In what ways is monopolistic competition similar to oligopoly? In what ways is it similar to pure competition?

Government Efforts to Promote and Maintain Competition

Since competition is so essential to the proper functioning of a market economy, the promotion and maintenance of competition have long been important goals of American government. Business firms, though, sometimes have tried to reduce competition in an effort to increase their profits.

One way that firms operating in an oligopolistic market have avoided competition among themselves is by entering into secret agreements in which each firm agrees to charge a certain fixed price. Through such "price-fixing" agreements, the firms have achieved almost as much market power as if they were one giant monopoly. Although price-fixing agreements are illegal in the United States, they have occurred in the past and probably will occur in the future. The larger the number of firms in an industry, the more difficult it is for them to engage in price-fixing agreements. It is much easier to convince two competitors to enter into such an agreement than it is to convince ten.

Another obvious way for firms to decrease competition among themselves is to buy up one another or in some other way to join together to produce a smaller number of firms in the market. During the late 1800s, some firms were able to eliminate competition almost completely by entering into a formal arrangement known as a **trust**—a device that for all practical purposes converted a group of firms into a single monopoly. For example, during the 1880s and 1890s, John D. Rockefeller organized more than 40 oil companies into the Standard Oil Trust, which nearly monopolized the entire crude and refined oil market in the United States. In response to the public outcry over the monopolization that was taking place in the oil industry and other industries, both state and federal governments began enacting antitrust laws. In all, five major antitrust laws were enacted by the federal government during the period 1890 to 1950. Let us briefly examine each of these laws.

Sherman Antitrust Act (1890)

The Sherman Antitrust Act was the first significant law against monopolies passed in this country. This law prohibited "every contract, combination in the form of a trust or otherwise, or conspiracy" that limited competition. In short, this law made it illegal to monopolize or even to attempt to monopolize trade. For those who violated the law, the penalties of imprisonment and/or fines were clearly prescribed.

'Now the big ones are eating the big ones'

Federal laws prevent unfair business practices such as trusts. However, many kinds of mergers and acquisitions are still allowed under the law.

Unfortunately, the language of the Sherman Act was vague, and it was not clear which specific acts constituted violation of the law. Furthermore, since the act did not establish any government agency for enforcing its provisions, it was poorly administered in its early years.

Clayton Antitrust Act (1914)

In order to clarify the intent of the Sherman Antitrust Act, Congress passed the Clayton Antitrust Act in 1914. This act explicitly prohibited the following four specific practices if their "effect was to substantially lessen competition or tend to create a monopoly": (1) price discrimination (selling the same good to different buyers at different prices); (2) exclusive dealing arrangements (requiring a buyer to agree not to purchase goods from competitors); (3) interlocking directorates (a practice in which the same person serves on the board of directors of two or more competing companies); and (4) the acquisition of the stock of one company by competing companies.

Federal Trade Commission Act (1914)

To make sure that the Clayton Antitrust Act was properly enforced, Congress passed the Federal Trade Commission Act in the same year. This act created the Federal Trade Commission (FTC) to administer the Clayton Act and to investigate, hold hearings, and issue cease and desist orders in cases of "unfair methods of competition" and "unfair acts or practices." The Federal Trade Commission Act was later amended to extend protection to consumers as well as competitors. By broadening the FTC's power, the government made it a major force in policing deceptive advertising practices.

Robinson–Patman Act (1936)

The Robinson–Patman Act was passed in response to complaints by small retailers that large chain stores and mass distributors were getting quantity discounts from suppliers that enabled them to undersell the small retailers.

This law made it illegal for suppliers to sell "at unreasonably low prices" when such practices reduced competition. In addition, it prohibited them from giving rebates and discounts to large buyers unless the rebates and discounts were available to all.

Celler–Kefauver Antimerger Act (1950)

Whereas the Clayton Act prohibited one firm from acquiring shares of stock of another if this lessened competition, it said nothing about purchasing outright the assets (plant, equipment, and so forth) of another firm. As a result, a number of companies got around the intent of the Clayton Act by purchasing competing firms' assets. To curtail this practice and to strengthen the prohibition against firms joining together to control too large a part of the market, Congress passed the Celler–Kefauver Antimerger Act. This act, which was an amendment to the Clayton Act, specifically prohibited firms from purchasing either the assets or stock of other firms where "the effect of such acquisition may be substantially to lessen competition, or to tend to create a monopoly." Together with the other antitrust legislation, the Celler–Kefauver Act tried to curb monopolistic practices and to promote competition.

Check Your Understanding

1. Why is the promotion and maintenance of competition such an important goal of the American government?

2. How have firms tried to reduce competition among themselves?

3. Describe the five major antitrust laws that were enacted between 1890 and 1950.

CAREERS: Purchasing Agent

Having the right materials, supplies, and equipment when they are needed is crucial to the efficient operation of any business or government agency. It is the responsibility of the purchasing agent to see to it that these items are purchased in sufficient quantity and quality and at the right prices. Purchasing agents in industry and government buy raw materials, machinery, parts and components, furniture, business machines, vehicles, and office supplies for use by the business or government agency.

In their efforts to select suppliers who offer the best values, purchasing agents compare listings in catalogs, meet with salespersons, examine samples, and attend demonstrations of products and equipment. Purchasing agents must thoroughly understand the characteristics and functions of the items they purchase. In the case of some items, such as computer equipment, this means that the agent must have considerable technical knowledge. Purchasing agents also must work closely with other employees. For example, they often discuss the design of products with company engineers.

More than half of all purchasing agents work for manufacturing firms. Other major employers of purchasing agents are construction companies, hospitals, schools, advertising firms, and the government. The Department of Defense employs about 70 percent of all purchasing agents working for the federal government. The Department of Agriculture, the General Services Administration, and the Veterans Administra-

tion also employ a substantial number of purchasing agents.

Most large companies and government agencies seek college graduates to fill job openings in this field. Companies that manufacture products such as machinery or chemicals may prefer backgrounds in engineering, science, and other technical fields, while other companies prefer business administration majors. Courses in purchasing, economics, and accounting are useful, and familiarity with computers is becoming increasingly important. Regardless of their educational background, most new purchasing agents must enroll in company-sponsored training programs and spend considerable time learning about company operations and purchasing procedures.

Chapter Highlights

1 A business firm is an organization that brings together the factors of production for the purpose of producing goods and services.

2 Businesses are characterized by specialization and the division of labor, as well as by a certain amount of risk.

3 Firms that produce identical or similar products are said to be in the same industry. Many major companies produce products in more than one industry.

4 The three basic forms of business organization are (1) the individual proprietorship; (2) the partnership; and (3) the corporation.

5 Advantages of the individual proprietorship are (1) it is easy and relatively inexpensive to start up; (2) the owner gets all the profits; and (3) the owner is the sole decision maker. Disadvantages are (1) unlimited liability; (2) limited ability to raise financial capital; and (3) limited life.

6 Advantages and disadvantages of the partnership as a form of business organization are essentially the same as those for an individual proprietorship, except on a different scale.

7 A corporation is a form of business organization that is collectively owned by a number of individuals called stockholders, and that has the legal status of a single fictitious individual.

8 Corporations raise money by selling stocks and bonds. There are two kinds of stock: preferred stock and common stock. Common stock may yield higher income than preferred stock in the long run.

9 Advantages of the corporation as a form of business organization are (1) limited liability; (2) ability to raise large sums of money; (3) unlimited life. Disadvantages are (1) separation of ownership and management and (2) double taxation.

10 In addition to individual proprietorships, partnerships, and corporations, nonprofit organizations and cooperatives also provide goods and services.

11   The four basic categories of market structure are (1) pure competition; (2) monopoly; (3) oligopoly; and (4) monopolistic competition.

12   There are few actual examples of either pure competition or monopoly in the American economy. Most firms operate under market structures of either oligopoly or monopolistic competition.

13   Oligopoly is characterized by (1) a few sellers; (2) substantial barriers to entry; (3) standardized or differentiated products; and (4) substantial nonprice competition. Monopolistic competition is characterized by (1) many sellers; (2) differentiated products; (3) nonprice competition; and (4) relatively easy entry and exit.

14   The promotion and maintenance of competition have long been important goals of government in the United States. During the period 1890 to 1950, five major antitrust laws were enacted by the federal government in order to eliminate business practices developed to limit competition.

Important Terms

Match each of the following terms with the correct definition:

monopolistic competition	oligopoly	common stock
proxy	corporation	business firm
cooperative	partnership	pure competition
nonprofit organization	industry	preferred stock
economies of scale	bonds	antitrust laws
individual proprietorship	monopoly	

1. An organization that brings together the factors of production for the purpose of producing goods and services.

2. Laws designed to promote and maintain competition by prohibiting practices that tend to lead to the creation of monopoly power.

3. A market structure characterized by a few sellers, substantial barriers to entry, standardized or differentiated products, and substantial nonprice competition.

4. The increased efficiency resulting from specialization and the division of labor that makes possible the production of a large volume of output at a lower cost per unit than a small volume of output.

5. IOUs of corporations.

6. An organization that provides a service and whose revenue is used to further the purposes of the organization.

7. Turning over voting privileges to the current management of a corporation or to some other group.

8. A voluntary organization formed for the purpose of providing economic benefits for its members.

9. A form of business organization that is collectively owned by two or more people who jointly make the business decisions, share the profits, and bear the financial responsibility for any losses.

10. A type of corporate stock that gives shareholders a prior claim on dividends but no voting privileges.

11. A market structure characterized by a single seller, a product for which there are no close substitutes, and strong barriers to entry that prevent potential competitors from entering into the market.

12. A group of firms producing the same or similar products.

13. A form of business organization that is owned by a single individual who makes all the business decisions, receives all the profits, and is responsible for any losses of the firm.

14. A market structure characterized by many sellers, standardized products, easy entry and exit, and no artificial restrictions on the free movement of prices and wages up and down.

15. A type of corporate stock that gives shareholders voting privileges but no prior claim on dividends.

16. A form of business organization that is collectively owned by a number of individuals called stockholders, and that has the legal status of a single fictitious individual.

17. A market structure characterized by many sellers, differentiated products, nonprice competition, and relatively easy entry and exit.

Extending Your Understanding

1. If you were starting up a new business, which form of business organization would you choose? Why?

2. If you could choose the market structure under which your business would operate, which structure would you choose? Why?

3. Why does the government enact and enforce antitrust laws and other measures designed to prevent monopoly power? What do you think would happen if the government repealed all antitrust laws and abandoned all efforts to control monopoly power?

Activities

1. Try to find out about your state's requirements for setting up a corporation. You may be able to obtain this information in your local library or by writing to your state's Chamber of Commerce. Present your findings to the class.

2. Suppose you have just been hired as an employment counselor. Your first client is a young woman who cannot decide whether to go into business for herself, start a business with a friend, or take a job with a large corporation. How would you advise this person, based on what you learned in this chapter?

Building Skills in Economics: Reading a Pie Graph

A **pie,** or **circle, graph** shows the relationship of the parts of a structure to the whole structure. It enables the student, the businessperson, and the economist to compare, at a glance, the relative sizes of each part of a structure. Whereas tables and lists of figures often take lengthy analysis, pie graphs usually can be interpreted quickly and easily.

A pie graph is based on the fact that there are 360 degrees in a circle. Each percentage that a person wishes to represent is converted to degrees and transferred to the graph. This is done by multiplying by 360 and then using a protractor to mark off an appropriate wedge of the pie. For example, suppose 75 percent of all businesses in your state are corporations. If you multiply 75 percent by 360 (.75 × 360), you get 270. The resulting wedge—270 degrees—will be three quarters of the pie. Because the pie represents the whole and all wedges must be accounted for, all percentages must add up to 100.

The pie graph that follows represents the market structure in the fictitious small town of Prairieville. The questions will help you interpret the graph.

Applying Economics Skills

1. Under which market structure do the majority of all businesses in Prairieville operate? Which structure is least common?

2. What is the relationship between the percentage of firms engaged in pure competition and those engaged in monopolistic competition? Between the percentage engaged in oligopoly and those engaged in pure competition?

3. Assuming that farming totally accounts for the percentage of firms engaged in pure competition, what percentage of purely competitive businesses would remain if the number of farms were reduced by 50 percent?

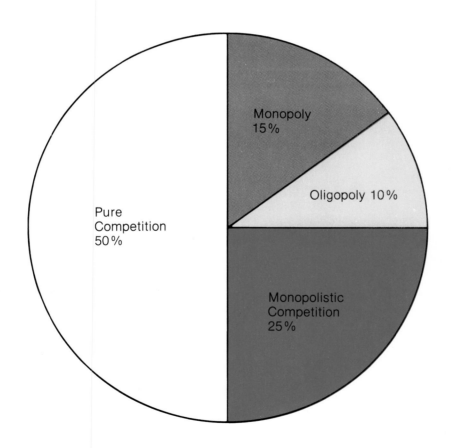

CHAPTER 5

THE ECONOMICS OF THE FIRM: HOW OUTPUT AND PROFITS ARE DETERMINED

Regina Wozek is in the computer software business. It started out as a hobby when Regina was a high school senior and she started to develop computer games for a few of her friends. She soon discovered that there was a market for her software, so she started her own business. Sales boomed at first but they soon tapered off, and Regina realized that the market for computer games is not a very steady one. Regina then decided to try her hand at educational software. To her amazement, the sales of her word processing and math programs took off just like her computer games had done earlier. Regina really wasn't surprised, however, when her educational program sales also tapered off.

It's been five years now since Regina entered the computer software business, and she has seen sales of her software rise and fall several times. There are times when many people want to buy her products and other times when very few people want to buy them.

Because of the ups and downs in Regina's business, she is constantly having to make decisions about how many computer games and educational programs to produce. Her goal is to operate her small business at the output level that will produce as much profit as possible. Not all firms experience as much fluctuation in the demand for their products as does Regina's firm, but most firms do share Regina's desire to operate at the profit-maximizing level. This level is determined by two key factors: production costs and revenues. In this chapter, we will examine both of these concepts, which are equally important in determining a firm's profit-maximizing level of output.

Five Important Cost Concepts

Does the following dialogue sound familiar?

CUSTOMER: The last time I was in here to buy plumbing fixtures, I paid a fraction of this price!

STORE OWNER: I'm sorry, sir, but my costs have gone up.

Similar dialogue may have taken place in stores ranging from camera shops to pizzerias. In fact, if you ask business owners to list the most serious problems they face, a majority probably will include rising costs.

Production costs are a major factor in determining a firm's profit-maximizing level of output. This holds true regardless of whether the firm is a corner lemonade stand or a giant automobile manufacturer. If costs rise, firms must constantly adjust their output so that they continue to earn the greatest profits. Costs can be classified in a number of ways, but for purposes of determining how costs affect output, we need to be able to observe how costs change as output changes. In this section, we will examine the following five important cost concepts: fixed costs, variable costs, total cost, average total cost, and marginal cost.

Fixed Costs

Fixed costs are those costs that do not vary with changes in output. Fixed costs, sometimes called "overhead costs," include such things as rent, interest on borrowed money, insurance premiums, and property taxes. Fixed costs are the same whether a firm is operating at full capacity, half capacity, or zero capacity. Even if a firm produces nothing at all during a given day, week, or month, it still must pay its rent, insurance, and other fixed costs.

Paul Henderson operates a small firm that manufactures picnic tables. We'll use Paul's firm throughout this chapter as an example to illustrate the various costs that all firms incur. Paul's production costs are presented in Table 5–1. Note that Paul's fixed costs (column 2) are $100 per day no matter how many tables he produces. He must pay the $100 of fixed cost whether he produces one, five, or ten tables per day. He must pay it even if he doesn't produce any tables at all.

Variable Costs

Variable costs are those costs that change as the level of output changes. Variable costs rise as output increases and fall as output decreases. Variable costs include such things as labor, raw materials, and power to operate machines.

Column 3 in Table 5–1 shows how Paul Henderson's variable costs change with the level of output. When Paul produces only one picnic table per day, his variable costs are $120. However, these costs rise to $220 when he produces two tables per day ($425 when he produces five picnic tables per day, and $1,300 when he produces ten tables per day). They would continue to rise even further if Paul

Business owner Paul Henderson must calculate both fixed and variable costs in manufacturing picnic tables.

increased his output beyond ten tables per day.

Note, though, that these costs do not rise by the same amount each time. They rise by $100 when Paul increases his output from one to two tables, by $80 when he increases his output from two to three tables, and by only $60 when output is increased from three to four tables. In contrast, they rise by $220 when Paul's daily output is increased from nine tables to ten. This variation is the result of how efficiently all resources are being used. When resources are being used most efficiently, the increase in variable costs is at its lowest point. Your understanding of this variation will be important when we examine marginal costs.

Note also that when Paul does not produce any picnic tables, he does not have any variable costs. Variable costs depend on the level of output, and any time a firm closes down temporarily and produces nothing, it will have no variable costs. This is because the firm's owner will not have to pay such costs as workers' salaries and the cost of power to run idle machinery.

Total Cost

Total cost is the sum of fixed and variable costs at each level of output. Paul Henderson's total

cost at each level of production is shown in column 4 of Table 5–1. You can see that when Paul produces one table per day, his total cost is $220. This is calculated by adding the $100 of fixed cost to the $120 of variable cost at that output. Notice, though, that Paul's total cost is $100 even when he does not produce any tables at all. Since Paul has no variable costs when he has an output level of zero, the entire $100 is fixed cost. This fixed cost remains constant regardless of the level of output. Thus, each time Paul increases his production by one picnic table per day, his total cost will increase by only the amount of the additional variable cost of producing one more unit.

Average Total Cost

Average total cost is calculated by dividing the total cost at each output level by the number of units being produced. Average total cost declines as output is increased up to a certain level, and then average total cost begins to rise and continues to rise as output is increased beyond that level. Note in Table 5–1 that Paul Henderson's average total cost declines from $220 when he is producing only one table per day to a minimum of $105 at an output of five

TABLE 5–1 COST DATA FOR THE PRODUCTION OF PAUL'S PICNIC TABLES

Output (Tables per Day)	Total Fixed Costs	Total Variable Costs	Total Cost	Average Total Cost	Marginal Cost
0	$100	0	$100	—	—
1	100	$120	220	$220.00	$120
2	100	220	320	160.00	100
3	100	300	400	133.33	80
4	100	360	460	115.00	60
5	100	425	525	105.00	65
6	100	540	640	106.67	115
7	100	700	800	114.29	160
8	100	880	980	122.50	180
9	100	1,080	1,180	131.11	200
10	100	1,300	1,400	140.00	220

tables per day. However, increases in production beyond the level of five tables per day will result in higher and higher average total costs. If Paul produces ten tables per day, his average total cost will be $140 per table.

Marginal Cost

Marginal cost is the additional cost of producing one more unit of output. As you learned earlier, variable costs do not change by the same amount each time output is increased. The same holds true for marginal cost. It is calculated by computing the increase in total cost that results from increasing production by one additional unit. Let us look again at Table 5–1 to further examine this concept.

Paul Henderson's marginal cost schedule is presented in column 6 of this table. When Paul goes from zero production to the production of one table per day, his total cost per day rises from $100 to $220. Thus, Paul's marginal cost of producing one picnic table per day is $120 ($220 − $100). If Paul increases production from one table per day to two tables per day, his total cost will rise from $220 to $320. Therefore, the marginal cost of producing the second picnic table is $100 ($320 − $220). Each time Paul increases production by one more picnic table per day, the marginal cost of producing that table is determined by calculating the increase in total cost that results from producing it.

If you examine Table 5–1 closely, you will notice that, like average total cost, marginal cost decreases to a certain point and then rises again. In this case, the lowest marginal cost is $60, and that occurs when Paul produces four picnic tables daily. This variation in marginal cost is the result of the efficiency with which resources are being used. Resources are being used most efficiently when the marginal cost is $60 and least efficiently when the marginal cost is $220. Marginal cost is used to determine the level of output that will yield the maximum profit for a firm. We will examine this relationship later in this chapter.

Law of Diminishing Returns

You have just learned that Paul Henderson's average total cost and marginal cost both decrease until they reach a minimum level. They then begin to rise and continue to rise as Paul produces more and more tables per day. The minimum average total cost of $105 is reached at an output level of five picnic tables per day. As Paul increases production beyond that level, his average total cost becomes larger and larger. Why do his costs behave in this way? Because of an economic principle known as the **law of diminishing returns.** This law states that increasing the quantity of one factor of production while quantities of the other factors of production remain fixed will result in smaller and smaller increases in total output.

The size of Paul's small manufacturing plant is fixed for the present, and he has a fixed number of tools and machines in the plant with which to turn lumber into picnic tables. However, Paul can increase or decrease the amount of labor he uses. Thus, labor is Paul's variable factor of production. Table 5–2 shows what happens when Paul adds workers to his fixed-size plant in order to increase output. If Paul uses only one worker, himself, he alone will have to perform all the tasks of producing a table—saw the lumber, assemble the table, paint it, and so forth. As a result, he will be able to produce only one picnic table per day. This would be a very inefficient use of Paul's plant because much of its capacity would be unused. If Paul uses two workers, himself and one employee, each worker can specialize in certain tasks; and the two of them will be able to produce two and one-half tables per day. If Paul uses three workers, they can be still more efficient and produce five tables per day.

As Paul increases production from one table per day to five tables per day, he is experiencing what economists call **increasing returns** from the additional labor used. That is, each additional unit of labor causes the total product to rise by a greater amount than was caused by the previous unit. In other words, the additional units of labor enable Paul to make more efficient use of his fixed-size plant. These increasing returns can be seen in column 3 of Table 5–2, which shows the increased output, or **marginal product,** resulting from each additional worker. Note that the marginal product of the first worker is one picnic table per day, the marginal product of the second worker is one and one-half tables per day, and the marginal product of the third worker is two and one-half tables per day. As long as the marginal product is rising, Paul's firm is experiencing increasing returns.

Note that the marginal product is at its maximum (two and one-half tables per day) when three workers are used and five tables per day are produced. This is the level at which Paul's small plant was designed to operate, and thus it is the most efficient level of production. Paul can use additional workers and produce more tables per day; but if he does, he will experience **diminishing returns.** In other words, each additional worker will add less and less additional output. For example, the marginal product of the fourth worker is two tables per day as compared to two and one half for the

third worker. The marginal product of the seventh worker is only one-half table per day.

Like Paul Henderson's manufacturing plant, all business firms experience diminishing returns if they continue to increase the quantity of one factor of production while quantities of the other factors of production remain fixed. For example, if a shoe store has only one salesperson, that salesperson may be unable to wait on all potential customers, resulting in some loss of sales. By adding a second salesperson, the store can increase its total sales. The store might even be able to increase sales further by adding a third salesclerk, but the chances are good that this third salesperson will not add as much to total sales as the second one did. A fourth salesperson would not increase sales at all if three clerks are capable of serving all the customers that enter the store. This shoe store is experiencing diminishing returns as soon as it increases the quantity of labor beyond the level at which this store of fixed size was designed to operate.

Diminishing returns also can occur when one of the other factors of production is varied while the quantity of labor remains fixed. For example, suppose Henry Simmons owns and operates a 500-acre corn farm. Henry has a fixed amount of farm equipment, and he uses no

TABLE 5–2: PRODUCTION SCHEDULE FOR PAUL'S PICNIC TABLES

Number of Workers	Total Product (Number of Tables Produced per Day)	Marginal Product (Additional Tables Produced per Day)	
0	0	0	
1	1	1	
2	2½	1½	Increasing
3	5	2½	Returns
4	7	2	Diminishing
5	8½	1½	Returns
6	9½	1	
7	10	½	

Owners of businesses such as this farm must calculate how varying one factor of production can affect the level of output.

hired workers. If Henry increases his acreage of land (natural resources) from 500 acres to 600 acres, he can increase his production by making more efficient use of his time and machinery. However, if Henry increases his acreage to 700 acres, he will have difficulty getting all the work done with his fixed equipment and labor. As a result, the addition of the second 100 acres will result in less increase in total corn production than did the first 100 additional acres. Henry is experiencing diminishing returns—little or no increase in production—because his fixed equipment and labor will not allow him to handle the additional land. Similarly, if Henry increases the quantity of machinery (capital goods) while his labor and acreage of land remain fixed, he will soon experience diminishing returns because he already has adequate machinery to farm his 500 acres of land.

However, you cannot yet conclude that Henry's most profitable level of output is 600 acres. Similarly, you cannot yet conclude that Paul Henderson's most profitable level of output is five tables per day just because that is his

least-cost level of production. In order to determine a firm's most profitable level of production, you also need revenue data. Revenue data will be discussed in the next section.

Check Your Understanding

1. Define fixed costs and variable costs and give examples of each.

2. How are total cost and average total cost calculated?

3. What is marginal cost? Why is it such an important cost concept?

4. State the law of diminishing returns. Why do most firms experience diminishing returns as output is expanded beyond a certain level?

Revenue

Revenue is the money a firm receives for the products it sells. It is the money Regina Wozek gets for her computer software and Paul Henderson gets for his picnic tables. If a firm's revenue is greater than its costs, it earns a profit. If costs exceed revenue, the firm suffers a loss. Let us examine three revenue concepts: revenue per unit, total revenue, and marginal revenue.

Revenue Per Unit

The **revenue per unit** of any product is simply the selling price. For some firms, the revenue per unit may remain constant no matter how much is sold. For example, if the market price of corn is $3 per bushel, a farmer will receive that price whether he sells 10 bushels or 10,000 bushels. However, some firms can sell different amounts at different prices. For example, a firm might find that at a price of $100 it could sell 600 units of a product per month; but if it lowered the price to $90, it could sell 700 units per month.

Firms operating in a market structure of, or approximating, pure competition are faced with a constant selling price no matter how much they sell. If they tried to raise this price, they would be left with most of their goods unsold. Thus, if the farmer in the example just mentioned was asking $3.50 for a bushel of corn, he or she probably couldn't sell any corn at all. In contrast, firms operating under market structures of monopoly, oligopoly, and monopolistic competition have varying degrees of control over their selling prices. For example, an automobile firm that can sell a given number of cars at a price of $10,000 each can raise or lower its price and still sell cars. It might sell fewer cars at $11,000 than at $10,000, but it still could sell some cars at the higher price.

Total Revenue

Total revenue is the selling price of an item times the quantity sold. For example, if a farmer sells 10,000 bushels of corn at a price of $3 per bushel, his or her total revenue is $30,000. Since firms operating under monopoly and oligopoly have some control over their prices, they must calculate the potential total revenue at various price and quantity combinations. For example, if a firm finds that it can sell 600 units at a price of $100, its total revenue will be $60,000 ($100 × 600 units). If it establishes a price of $90 per unit and can sell 700 units, its total revenue will be $63,000 ($90 × 700 units). In this case, should the firm set the price at $90 per unit since it will receive a larger total revenue at that price? Not necessarily. The most profitable price and output combination depends on both revenue and cost data, which we will see later.

Marginal Revenue

Marginal revenue is the additional revenue that results from producing and selling one more unit of output. It is calculated by computing the increase in total revenue that results from the production and sale of this additional unit. Like marginal cost, marginal revenue is a very important concept because it too is used to determine the level of output that will yield the maximum profit for a firm.

For firms operating under pure competition, marginal revenue is the same as price. This is because the price of each additional unit of output is the same as that for all the other units of output. When a farmer who is selling corn at the market price of $3 per bushel decides to sell one more bushel of corn, his or her marginal revenue will be $3, the same as the selling price. However, for firms operating in markets characterized by monopoly, oligopoly, and monopolistic competition, marginal revenue and price are not equal. When such a firm lowers its price to sell more units of its product, it will have to lower the price on all units sold, including those units that it was selling at a higher price. Thus, its marginal revenue will be lower than its price. For our discussion, we are using an example in which marginal revenue and price are equal. Keep in mind, however, that in market structures other than pure competition, marginal revenue will be less than the price.

Check Your Understanding

1. What is revenue?

2. Define revenue per unit. Does it always remain constant? Explain.

3. How is total revenue calculated?

4. Define marginal revenue. How is it calculated? Why is it such an important concept?

Determining the Profit-Maximizing Level of Output

Regina Wozek wants to make as much profit as possible from her computer software, and Paul Henderson wants to do the same with his picnic tables. It is reasonable to assume that most business firms want to maximize their profits. How do they accomplish their objective? They accomplish it by continuing to expand production so long as the revenue brought in by each additional unit of output exceeds the cost of producing that additional unit. If the production of one more computer game or educational program will add more to Regina's revenue than to her costs, it is profitable for her to produce that game or program. However, when Regina reaches the point where the production of one more computer disk will add more to her costs than to her revenue, she should not expand production any further. She has reached her profit-

The computer industry has seen tremendous expansion in recent years. Here, as in other businesses, owners must determine the maximum-profit level of output.

maximizing level of output, and any additional production beyond that point will result in a reduction of her total profit.

As you have already learned, the additional cost of producing one more unit of an item is the marginal cost. The additional revenue resulting from the production and sale of one more unit is the marginal revenue. Therefore, in order to maximize profit, a firm will continue to expand production so long as marginal revenue exceeds marginal cost.

In Table 5–3, selected portions of Paul Henderson's cost, revenue, and profit data are presented so that we can see how Paul determines his profit-maximizing level of output. Paul is able to sell all the picnic tables he produces at a price of $175 each, so he has no reason to lower his price. On the other hand, Paul knows that if he raises his price by very much, people may buy picnic tables made elsewhere, and he will have some left over. Thus, Paul's price is fixed at $175 per table whether he produces one, five, or ten tables per day.

Since Paul's price remains constant at $175 per table no matter how many tables he produces, his marginal revenue will be equal to the price. Every time he produces and sells one more table, he will add $175 to his total revenue. Thus, Paul's marginal revenue is $175 at all levels of production. This is shown in column 7 of Table 5–3.

Unlike marginal revenue, marginal cost is not the same at each level of output. Paul's marginal cost starts at $120 with the production of one table per day and then declines until it reaches a minimum of $60 at an output of four tables per day. Beyond that point, marginal cost increases with each additional table produced. Remember that marginal cost is simply the increase in total cost that results from the production of one more table. Why does marginal cost decline up to a certain level of production and then begin to increase? Because of the *law of diminishing returns*.

As you will recall from our discussion of average total cost, when Paul is producing only one or two tables per day, he is not using his plant very efficiently. Therefore, as he expands production, the additional cost of producing each extra table will decline at first. However, as Paul adds more and more units of labor while the size of his plant and the number of tools and

TABLE 5–3: COST, REVENUE, AND PROFIT DATA FOR THE PRODUCTION OF PAUL'S PICNIC TABLES

Output (Tables per Day)	Total Cost	Marginal Cost	Average Total Cost	Price	Total Revenue	Marginal Revenue	Profit or Loss
0	$100	—	—	—	0	—	$100 loss
1	220	$120	$220.00	$175	$175	$175	45 loss
2	320	100	160.00	175	350	175	30 profit
3	400	80	133.33	175	525	175	125 profit
4	460	60	115.00	175	700	175	240 profit
5	525	65	105.00	175	875	175	350 profit
6	640	115	106.67	175	1,050	175	410 profit
7	800	160	114.29	175	1,225	175	425 profit
8	980	180	122.50	175	1,400	175	420 profit
9	1,180	200	131.11	175	1,575	175	395 profit
10	1,400	220	140.00	175	1,750	175	350 profit

machines remain constant, he will get less and less additional production from each extra unit of labor, and the cost of producing each additional table will rise.

At what level of output should Paul operate in order to maximize his profit? You can easily find the answer to this question by looking at the last column of Table 5–3. As you can see from studying this profit or loss column, Paul will earn a maximum total profit of $425 if he produces seven picnic tables per day. This is more profit than he could earn at any other level of output. At an output of seven tables per day, Paul's total revenue will be $1,225 per day and his total cost will be $800 per day. As you already know, total profit is the difference between total revenue and total cost.

Suppose Table 5–3 did not present either profit and loss data or total revenue and total cost data. Could we still determine Paul's maximum-profit level of output? The answer to this question is yes. As long as we knew the marginal revenue and marginal cost for each level of output, we could determine the maximum-profit level of output without any of the other data. Let us closely examine the relationship between marginal revenue and marginal cost at four different levels of output in Table 5–3. Remember, the rule for maximizing profit is to continue to expand production so long as marginal revenue exceeds marginal cost.

We will begin by observing the cost and revenue data at an output of five tables per day. Note that at this level the marginal cost of producing the fifth table is only $65 while the marginal revenue of the fifth table is $175. Therefore, Paul adds $110 more to his total revenue than he adds to his total cost when he produces the fifth unit. This means that his profit at five tables per day is $110 higher than at four tables per day.

Now let us examine the marginal cost and the marginal revenue of producing the sixth table. Note that the marginal cost of producing the sixth table is $115 while the marginal revenue of the sixth table is $175. Thus, Paul adds

$60 more to his total revenue than he adds to his total cost when he produces the sixth table. His profit, therefore, is $60 higher for six tables than for five tables.

Now let us see what happens when Paul increases production from six tables to seven tables per day. The additional cost (marginal cost) of the seventh table is $160, while the additional revenue (marginal revenue) of that table is $175. Thus, by producing the seventh table, Paul adds $15 more to total revenue than he adds to total cost and increases his profit from $410 to $425. This is Paul's maximum profit.

Just to make sure that Paul couldn't increase his profit still more by producing eight tables per day, let us see what happens to total cost and total revenue when production is expanded to that level. The marginal cost of the eighth table is $180, while the marginal revenue is only $175. Thus, when Paul produces the eighth table, he adds $5 more to total cost than he adds to total revenue. As a result, Paul's total profit declines by $5, from $425 to $420.

Note that Paul's profit-maximizing level of output is not his least-cost level of output. Paul's average total cost is at its lowest level at an output of five tables per day. Although Paul could earn a profit by operating at that level, it would not be his maximum profit. By using marginal cost and marginal revenue to determine the most profitable level of output, Paul is able to earn considerably more profit than he would if he operated at the point where his average total cost is at a minimum.

Can you see why the concepts of marginal cost and marginal revenue are so important in economic analysis? Do you have a clear understanding of how marginal cost and marginal revenue are related to total cost and total revenue? If you don't, study the data in Table 5–3 until you understand these relationships. To test your understanding of the concepts, suppose that as a result of increased competition Paul suddenly finds that he must lower the price of his tables from $175 to $150 per table. If Paul's

In a market structure with competition, business owners have little control over the prices of their products. To compete, they must sometimes offer products at special sale prices.

price and marginal revenue were $150 instead of $175, would his maximum-profit level of output still be seven tables per day? If not, what would it be?

Profit Maximization Under Other Market Structures

Paul Henderson operates under a market structure very similar to that of pure competition. Since there are many other producers of picnic tables and since there are no significant barriers to prevent additional firms from entering the market, Paul has little or no control over the price of his product. However, as you have already learned, most firms in the United States operate under market structures other than pure competition.

How do firms operating under monopoly, oligopoly, and monopolistic competition maximize their profits? They do so in the same way that Paul Henderson does: by expanding production up to but not beyond the point where marginal cost equals marginal revenue. There is

an important difference, however. As you learned earlier, under market structures other than pure competition, marginal revenue is not equal to price. A monopolistic firm has some control over its price and output. If it lowers its price, it will be able to sell more of its product; and if it raises its price, it will sell less. But when a monopolistic firm lowers its price in order to sell more units, it will have to do so on all units, including those that were selling for a higher price. For this reason, the marginal revenue of a monopolistic firm will be lower than its price.

When monopolists attempt to maximize profits, the results may be less desirable from the standpoint of society than when firms operating under pure competition seek to do so. Because monopolists often restrict output in order to obtain higher prices, they produce less and receive higher prices than firms operating under pure competition. The same is true, but to a lesser extent, in the cases of oligopoly and monopolistic competition.

Check Your Understanding

1. Why should a firm continue to expand production so long as marginal revenue exceeds marginal cost?

2. What happens to profit when a firm expands production to the extent that marginal cost exceeds marginal revenue?

3. What is the rule for maximizing profit?

4. How do the results of profit maximization under monopoly compare to the results of profit maximization under pure competition?

Other Cost Concepts

In our discussion so far, we have delayed the introduction of certain other important cost concepts. Let us examine these other concepts.

Explicit and Implicit Costs

Production costs can be classified on the basis of whether they are explicit costs or implicit costs. **Explicit costs** are those costs that involve an actual payment of money to "outsiders" who supply labor, raw materials, fuel, the use of buildings and equipment, and so forth to the firm. Wages and salaries, rent, insurance premiums, utility bills, and payment for raw materials are all examples of explicit costs.

In addition to costs that involve a direct cash payment, most firms have other costs in which a regular direct cash outlay is not involved. For example, if a firm owns its own building, it does not have to make a monthly rent payment. Yet there is a cost in this case, too. If the firm did not use the building for its own operations, it could rent the building to another firm and receive a monthly rental payment. As you learned in Chapter 1, this type of cost is called opportunity cost. If the building could be rented for $1,000 per month, the firm's opportunity cost of using the building for its own business operations is that amount.

The opportunity costs resulting from a firm's use of the resources that it owns are called **implicit costs.** The opportunity cost of managerial labor contributed to a business is an implicit cost. Since Paul Henderson contributes his time and managerial skills to his business, he must include as part of his production costs an amount equal to what he could earn if he were employed by another firm. Also, the opportunity cost of funds invested in a business must be included as implicit costs. If a person has $100,000 of his or her own money invested in a business, he or she must include as an implicit cost an amount equal to what could have been earned if the $100,000 had been invested elsewhere. Even if the money just sat in the bank, there would be an implicit cost involved. If it were placed in a bank account, the $100,000 would earn substantial interest.

Short-Run and Long-Run Costs

Economists usually distinguish between the "short run" and the "long run" when analyzing production costs. The **short run** is a time period too short to allow a firm to alter the size of its plant yet long enough to allow the firm to change the level at which the fixed plant is used. There is no definite time period affixed to the term "short run." Rather, short run is determined more by a firm's ability to make major changes in the size of its plant than by the calendar. All of our analysis of Paul Henderson's firm involved the short run. Paul was able to vary the amount of labor used, but he was not able to alter the size of his plant. Because a firm's plant is fixed in the short run, it can expand output only by adding more units of variable inputs, such as labor. As the firm adds more and more units of variable inputs to a fixed-size plant, it is able to get less and less additional output from these additional inputs. As you have learned, this tendency for output to taper off is called the law of diminishing returns.

In contrast, the **long run** is a time period long enough to allow a firm to vary all of its factors of production, including the size of its plant. In the long run, everything is variable. For example, in the long run, Paul Henderson would be able to double or triple the size of his plant or make any other adjustment in plant size that would enable him to reduce production costs. Because it is based on the assumption of a fixed-size plant, the law of diminishing returns does not apply in the long run. However, two other important concepts that affect cost do exist in the long run. They are economies and diseconomies of scale. Let us examine each of these concepts briefly.

Expensive, electronically programmed robots are helping to revolutionize the auto industry. A large expenditure of capital is needed to add this modern machinery to the assembly line.

Economies of scale As you learned in Chapter 4, economies of scale occur when a large volume of output can be produced at a lower cost per unit than can a small volume of output. As a firm expands its capacity over the long run, a number of factors will contribute to its economies of scale, including labor specialization, managerial specialization, and more efficient use of capital goods (machines, tools, and so forth).

As the number of workers hired increases, jobs can be divided and subdivided so that each worker performs and becomes proficient at only one or a few tasks. Management also can become more specialized as each member of the management team performs and becomes more proficient at his or her specific duties. One of the greatest sources of economies of scale, however, is the increased efficiency with which capital goods can be utilized. In many industries, the most efficient machinery is available only in very large and expensive units, and efficient utilization of this equipment requires a high volume of production. For example, a machine capable of producing ten times the output of a smaller machine will not cost nearly ten times as much as the smaller machine. Yet it is affordable only by firms that can use it at or near its full capacity.

Diseconomies of scale In some industries, it is possible for firms to grow so large that they experience **diseconomies of scale.** This means that costs per unit begin to rise as the firm becomes larger and larger. The major cause of diseconomies of scale appears to be the inability of management to control and coordinate all of a large firm's operations efficiently. In a giant firm, top management may be so far removed from the actual production operations of the plant that communication and coordination problems occur. However, economists do not agree on the extent to which diseconomies of scale are a problem in the American economy. Some economists argue that the success and continued growth of giant corporations indicate that diseconomies of scale are not a serious problem for American firms.

Check Your Understanding

1. What is the difference between explicit costs and implicit costs? Give examples of each.

2. What is meant by the terms "short run" and "long run"? How do short run costs differ from long run costs?

3. What factors contribute to economies of scale as a firm gets larger? What can lead to diseconomies of scale?

CAREERS: Mathematician

Do you enjoy working with numbers? If so, you might want to consider a career as a mathematician. Mathematicians work in a wide variety of job settings, depending on their area of interest.

There are two broad areas of work in the field of mathematics: theoretical mathematics and applied mathematics. Theoretical mathematicians attempt to develop new mathematical principles and to discover new relationships between existing principles of mathematics in an effort to advance mathematical science. Applied mathematicians use existing principles of mathematics to develop solutions to practical problems in business, government, engineering, and the sciences. Their work ranges from the mathematical analysis of launching satellites to the study of the effects of various business practices on productivity. Many mathematicians work in jobs that involve both theoretical and applied aspects of mathematics.

Mathematicians work for various kinds of businesses, including research and development laboratories, engineering and architectural firms, aircraft manufacturers, and firms that manufacture communications equipment, guided missiles, and space vehicles. Mathematicians also are employed by many government agencies, but almost three fourths of the mathematicians working for the federal government are employed by the Department of Defense and the National Aeronautics and Space Administration. In addition to employment in business and government, many mathematicians teach at colleges and universities.

A bachelor's degree in mathematics is adequate for many beginning jobs in business and government. However, a master's degree or a doctorate degree is usually required for college or university teaching positions and for most research positions. For work in applied mathematics, training in the field in which the mathematics will be used is also very important. Fields in which applied mathematics is used extensively include physics, chemistry, engineering, operations research, computer science, business and industrial management, economics, statistics, life sciences, and behavioral sciences. To succeed in mathematics, the prospective mathematician should have good reasoning ability, intellectual curiosity, persistence, and the ability to apply basic principles to new types of problems. Mathematicians also must be able to communicate well with words as well as with mathematical terms and symbols because they often need to discuss problems with nonmathematicians.

Chapter Highlights

1   Firms maximize profits by adjusting output to the profit-maximizing level, which is determined primarily by production costs and revenue.

2   Fixed costs are those costs that do not vary with changes in output. They include such things as rent, interest on borrowed money, insurance premiums, and property taxes.

3   Variable costs are those costs that change as the level of output changes. They include such things as labor, raw materials, and power to operate machines.

4   Total cost is the sum of fixed and variable costs at each level of output. Because fixed costs remain constant at all levels of output, any change in total cost can be attributed to a change in variable costs.

5   Average total cost is calculated by dividing the total cost at each output level by the number of units being produced. Average total cost declines as output is increased up to the point where it reaches its minimum level. As output is expanded beyond that point, average total cost begins to rise again.

6   Marginal cost is the cost of producing each additional unit of output. Like average total cost, marginal cost decreases to a certain point and then rises again.

7   The behavior of marginal cost and average total cost can be explained by the law of diminishing returns. This law states that increasing the quantity of one factor of production while quantities of the other factors of production remain fixed will result in smaller and smaller increases in total output.

8   The money a firm receives for the products it sells is its revenue. The revenue per unit is simply the selling price. The total revenue is the selling price times the quantity sold. Marginal revenue is the additional revenue that results from producing and selling one more unit of output.

9   A firm maximizes its profit by continuing to expand production so long as marginal revenue exceeds marginal cost.

10 Explicit costs are those costs that involve an actual payment of money. Implicit costs are the opportunity costs resulting from a firm's use of resources that it owns.

11   The short run is a time period too short to allow a firm to alter the size of its plant yet long enough to allow the firm to change the level at which the fixed plant is used.

12   The long run is a time period long enough to allow a firm to vary all of its factors of production, including the size of its plant. In the long run, everything is variable.

13   Economies of scale occur when a large volume of output can be produced at a lower cost per unit than can a small volume. In some industries, it is possible for firms to grow so large that they begin to experience diseconomies of scale in which costs per unit begin to rise as the firm becomes larger and larger.

Important Terms

Match each of the following terms with the correct definition:

economies of scale   long run   variable costs
revenue per unit   total revenue   explicit costs
diseconomies of scale   total cost   marginal cost
marginal revenue   fixed costs   implicit costs
law of diminishing returns short run   average total cost
                           revenue

1. The cost that is calculated by dividing the total cost at each output level by the number of units being produced.

2. A law stating that if one factor of production is increased while the others remain fixed, after a certain point each additional unit of the variable factor of production will result in smaller and smaller increases in total output.

3. A time period long enough to allow a firm to vary all of its factors of production, including the size of its plant.

4. The additional revenue that results from producing and selling one more unit of output.

5. Those costs that do not vary with changes in output.

6. Those costs that involve an actual payment of money.

7. Reduction in efficiency and increased cost per unit that sometimes result from a firm's becoming too large.

8. The opportunity costs resulting from a firm's use of resources that it owns.

9. The additional cost of producing one more unit of output.

10. The selling price times the quantity sold.

11. The increased efficiency resulting from specialization and the division of labor that makes possible the production of a large volume of output at a lower cost per unit than a small volume of output.

12. The money a firm receives for the products it sells.

13. The selling price of a product.

14. Those costs that change as the level of output changes.

15. The sum of fixed and variable costs.

16. A time period too short to allow a firm to alter the size of its plant yet long enough to allow the firm to change the level at which the fixed plant is used.

Extending Your Understanding

1. Do you think that all firms attempt to maximize profit at all times? Why or why not?

2. What is the effect on society when firms operating under conditions similar to pure competition attempt to maximize profit? How does this effect differ from the effect that would result from a monopolist's attempting to maximize his or her profit?

Activities

1. Suppose you have just been placed in charge of a sporting goods store. List all the fixed costs and variable costs that you might incur. What explicit and implicit costs might become part of your business expenses?

2. Draw a cartoon showing how the law of diminishing returns might be applied to your school.

Building Skills in Economics: Computing Profit or Loss

In this chapter you learned that both costs and revenue determine a firm's most profitable level of output. Where costs exceed revenue, a firm suffers a loss. Where revenue is greater than costs, a firm makes a profit. In order to maximize its profit, a firm keeps expanding production so long as the revenue brought in by each additional unit of output exceeds the costs of producing that additional unit.

The table that follows represents cost and revenue data for Lucinda Washington's lamp factory. On a separate sheet of paper, copy the table and insert the correct figure whenever a question mark appears. The questions will help you better understand how a company computes profit or loss and decides when to stop expanding production.

Applying Economics Skills

1. How were you able to compute Lucinda's average total cost? Marginal cost? At what level of output is Lucinda's marginal cost the lowest?
2. How were you able to compute Lucinda's total revenue? Marginal revenue?
3. At what level of output does Lucinda's total revenue begin exceeding her total cost? Should she stop expanding production there? Explain.
4. At what level of output does Lucinda reach her maximum profit level? Should she expand production any further? Explain.

COST, REVENUE, AND PROFIT DATA FOR LUCINDA WASHINGTON'S LAMP FACTORY

Output (Lamps per Day)	Total Cost	Average Total Cost	Marginal Cost	Price	Total Revenue	Marginal Revenue	Profit or Loss
0	$ 75	—	—	—	0	—	$ 75 loss
1	220	$220	$145	$150	$150	$150	70 loss
2	305	152.50	?	150	300	150	?
3	370	122.33	?	150	?	150	80 profit
4	400	?	?	150	?	?	200 profit
5	440	?	40	150	?	?	?
6	520	86.87	?	150	?	?	?
7	630	?	?	150	?	?	420 profit
8	810	101.25	?	150	?	?	?
9	1,100	?	290	150	?	?	200 profit

CHAPTER 6

LABOR UNIONS, COLLECTIVE BARGAINING, AND WAGE DETERMINATION

Labor unions are an important force in the United States. They have a substantial influence on the nation's economy, and they also play an important role in American politics. Whether you eventually become a union member, an employer, or neither, you can be sure that labor unions will play a role in your future. In this chapter, we will examine the history of American labor unions, the important role that unions and collective bargaining play in today's economy, and the factors that determine wages in the American economy. Let us begin by examining union history.

The History of American Unions

The history of union activity in the United States dates back almost as far as the history of the nation itself. As early as 1636, a group of fishermen in what is now Maine organized a protest against having their wages withheld. In 1741, bakers in New York City called a strike to protest a municipal regulation on the price of bread. It was not until the closing years of the eighteenth century, however, that unions as we know them today appeared on the American scene. We will begin our study of union history with a look at these unions.

The First Unions

The first labor unions—or *societies* as they were called at the time—were formed around 1790 in response to changing economic conditions. Prior to this time, many of the essential products that could not be made in the home, such as shoes, were produced by local craftspeople who hired a small number of local workers to help them complete certain jobs. Employers and their employees were often good friends, and since production was on a custom-work basis, prices could be manipulated so that both the employer and the employees earned a good income.

By the late 1700s, however, improved transportation facilities and reduced transportation costs helped to change the relationship between employer and employee. Gradually, markets in different regions came into competition with one another as shoes and other commodities from some regions began to appear in other regions many miles away. As local employers faced increasing competition from outside areas, they were forced to become more cost conscious. Since labor was the major source of production costs, employers were forced to restrain wage increases and in some cases actually to cut wages. This caused a conflict between employer and employee and set the stage for the organization of the first unions.

The early unions were local organizations of skilled craftspeople such as shoemakers, tailors, and printers. They sought higher wages, improved working conditions, and a shorter workday. Employers resisted the demands of these early unions; and in some instances, the unions engaged in strikes against the employers. Although a few of these unions achieved their goals, the overall success of early unions was very limited.

The economic hard times and high unemployment of the early 1800s brought an end to most of these early unions. As economic conditions improved, new unions were formed, but many of them lasted only until the next economic downturn. The period 1837 to 1852, which some historians describe as the "long depression," wasn't very conducive to sustained union growth, but increased industrialization during the 1840s and 1850s did enable unions to make some small gains. The most significant development during this period was the gradual decline in the length of the average workday in most factories to 10 or 11 hours. Prior to this development, workers often had to work 72 hours a week (six 12-hour days) for very low wages.

The Knights of Labor

Following the Civil War, the nation experienced phenomenal industrial growth. As the railroad lines from the East and West merged to form a transcontinental transportation system, a national market came into being. Industrial growth was accompanied by growth in union membership and by increased efforts to combine local unions across the country into national organizations. One of the first labor organizations to be formed on a national level was the Noble Order of the Knights of Labor. Founded in 1869 as a secret society by seven Philadelphia tailors, the organization was characterized by an

Frank Farrell introduces Terence Powderly to a meeting of the Knights of Labor. Powderly led the union, during its peak years in the mid-1880s.

The American Federation of Labor

In 1886, the same year that the Knights of Labor reached its peak, a group of national unions held a meeting in Columbus, Ohio. Each of these unions was a **craft union,** a union composed of workers in a particular trade or craft, such as carpenters, electricians, or plumbers. The purpose of their meeting was to form a new labor organization, which was called the American Federation of Labor (AFL). This organization was itself not a union but a collection of unions under a central leadership that was to promote and coordinate an overall labor movement. Each member union was to make all of its own internal decisions, with the new organization serving to maintain general harmony. Samuel Gompers, an official of the cigarmakers' union, was elected president of the AFL; and he held that post continuously, except for one year, until his death in 1924.

The early history of the AFL is largely a history of the efforts of Samuel Gompers, who more than any other individual is responsible for the success of the American labor movement. Born in London, Gompers's formal education ended when he was 10; and when he was 13, he and his family immigrated to the United States. The following year, Gompers became involved with union work and thereafter devoted his entire life to the union movement. For the first few years of the AFL, Gompers was the only full-time officer, and at first his office was the front room of his apartment. The AFL was so poor that even the purchase of a used typewriter was a major financial decision.

From such modest beginnings, the AFL grew into a giant federation, and its success can be attributed primarily to Gompers's determination to promote a specific type of unionism. Instead of trying to bring about reform through direct involvement in party politics, as earlier labor organizations had done, Gompers advocated "economic unionism"—a practical policy of seeking basic improvements in wages and working conditions by bargaining directly with

elaborate system of rituals, secret handshakes, and passwords. Ten years later, however, the secrecy was dropped, and the Knights became a national labor organization with the goal of bringing together workers of all types—both skilled and unskilled—into one giant organization.

Membership in the Knights of Labor, which had grown from 9,000 in 1879 to 100,000 in 1885, suddenly increased sevenfold to a peak of 700,000 members in 1886, following an important strike victory against a major railroad company. However, the success of the Knights was short-lived. A series of unsuccessful strikes, internal squabbling, and inept leadership led to a rapid decline in membership after 1886. By 1893, membership had fallen to 75,000, and by the early 1900s, the organization was virtually extinct.

employers. Through Gompers's leadership, the AFL and its member unions were able to achieve higher wages, shorter hours, and a better working environment for their members.

Antiunion Policies

From the time of the formation of the first unions in the late 1700s until the 1930s, there were no federal or state laws governing union activities. Without legal protection, unions faced a losing battle in their attempts to organize American workers. Employers resisted unions every step of the way, and the nation's courts provided employers with the legal power they needed to block unionization through the conspiracy doctrine and court injunctions.

The conspiracy doctrine Since there were no state or federal laws governing union activities, judges made their decisions on the basis of common law. **Common law,** which was a concept inherited from the British, consists of the accumulation of judicial decisions over time that have the force of law in the absence of specific statutes enacted by legislatures. Common law may be thought of as law by tradition. An example of how common law affected union activity occurred in 1806 when a Philadelphia court ruled that a group of workers who had banded together in an effort to obtain higher pay were guilty of a criminal conspiracy. The court based its decision on the common law doctrine that it is illegal for two or more people to conspire to commit an illegal act. The implication of this ruling was that it was illegal for workers to organize for the purpose of obtaining higher wages. Many other courts handed down similar rulings against unions, and the **conspiracy doctrine** posed a major obstacle to union organization for many years.

The court injunction When later court decisions made the conspiracy doctrine ineffective as a legal barrier to unionization, the courts began to issue injunctions. An **injunction** is a court order issued by a judge requiring a party to do or to cease doing specific activities. For example, a judge could issue an injunction ordering striking workers to return to work, and failure to obey the injunction could result in a jail sentence. The injunction became the standard remedy for employers who wished to stop various union practices. If employers wanted to stop a specific union activity, they would ask a judge to issue an injunction against it. The judge usually did so, and the activity became illegal. Union members who failed to obey the injunction could go to jail.

Other antiunion activities In addition to the court injunction, employers used a number of other devices to combat the efforts of employees to form unions. Some hired **labor spies** to infiltrate unions and provide the employers with names of workers who were union members or union sympathizers. These workers were then fired, and their names were added to an industry-wide list of "union activists" that was circulated among employers. This made it difficult, if not impossible, for these workers to find jobs elsewhere. Some employers also forced employees to sign agreements known as **yellow-dog contracts.** Such contracts required the employees to promise as a condition of employment not to join a union. In addition, some imposed **lockouts**—the temporary closing of plants by employers—to persuade workers to abandon their union efforts.

Prolabor Legislation and Mass Unionization

After nearly a century and a half of government hostility toward unions, the fortunes of organized labor underwent a dramatic reversal during the 1930s. During that decade, the United States Congress passed a series of laws that were designed to reverse past government policies and encourage the growth of unions. Workers were guaranteed the right to organize and engage in union activities, and employers were prohibited from engaging in certain practices that had long been used to oppose unionism. Two of the most important laws passed during this period are the Norris–LaGuardia

FROM "HARPER'S WEEKLY" FOR JULY 28, 1894.

In the late 1800s, strikes often ended in violence in part because employers hired strikebreakers to take the jobs of union workers. Here, federal troops guard trains near Chicago during the Pullman Strike of 1894.

Anti-Injunction Act (1932) and the National Labor Relations Act (1935). Both will be discussed later in this chapter.

This prounion legislation set the stage for unprecedented growth in union membership in the United States. Millions of previously unorganized workers in the automobile, steel, and other mass-production industries became interested in joining unions. (See Figure 6-1.)

The Congress of Industrial Organizations

Most of the new unions formed in the 1930s were industrial unions. An **industrial union** is a union composed of workers from a particular industry regardless of the kind of jobs they hold. Examples of industrial unions include unions of coal miners, steel workers, or auto workers. Unlike craft unions, industrial unions included many unskilled workers. Because of

their composition, these new industrial unions posed a problem for the AFL, which had a long history of admitting only skilled craftspeople. A controversy arose within the AFL leadership over the admission of industrial unions. Finally, in 1938 the industrial unions banded together and formed a rival organization called the **Congress of Industrial Organizations** (CIO). These two giant organizations competed for union members for many years, with both experiencing substantial growth. In 1955, however, the two giants merged into a single organization known as the **American Federation of Labor–Congress of Industrial Organizations** (AFL–CIO).

The Present Status of Unions

Union membership as a percentage of the total labor force peaked at 25 percent in the mid-

1950s and then began a gradual decline. Today, union members account for only about 20 percent of the labor force. This figure, however, is somewhat misleading because union membership is concentrated in certain key industries and geographic areas. For example, in many steel and automobile plants, nearly 100 percent of the production workers are union members. Their dominance in these industries gives unions substantially more economic power than their 20 percent overall membership would suggest.

The Structure of Organized Labor

The structure of organized labor in the United States today involves three levels of organization; the local union, the national union, and the federation.

Local unions The most basic level of organization is the local union. Some local unions have only a few dozen members, while others have thousands of members. A local **craft union** would consist of all the plumbers or all the electricians in a specific community. A local **industrial union** would usually consist of all the production workers in a given factory. There are approximately 70,000 local unions in the United States. The local union enrolls members, collects dues, holds meetings to discuss problems, and negotiates contracts.

National unions The next level of organization is the national or international union. (If a union has some local branches in Canada, it is considered to be an international union.) Most local unions are branches of national unions, and they must pay a portion of their dues to the national union. The national union determines the broad policies within which the locals must operate and provides assistance in the organization of new locals. The staff of the national union usually includes expert lawyers and negotiators, who often assist local officials during contract talks with employers.

The federation The third level of organization is the federation. Most national unions are affiliated with the AFL–CIO, which is a giant federation of American unions. The AFL–CIO depends on the national unions for funds, and its primary role is to promote the cause of all unionized workers by lobbying for prolabor legislation at the state and federal government levels and by soliciting public support for organized labor. Although most national unions are affiliated with the AFL–CIO, a few important national unions—including the Teamsters, the International Longshoremen, and the United Mine Workers—are **independent unions** that do not belong to the AFL–CIO.

Figure 6-1 *Labor Union Membership in the United States, 1897-1984*

Sources: National Bureau of Economic Research, 1936; U.S. Bureau of Labor Statistics, 1984; A.F.L.–C.I.O., 1985

Check Your Understanding

1. What changing economic conditions led to the formation of the first unions? What led to the downfall of these early unions?

2. What was the primary goal of the Knights of Labor? What led to the decline of the Knights?

3. Describe the structure of the American Federation of Labor. How did the AFL accomplish its goals?

4. What were the major antiunion policies used against labor unions prior to the 1930s?

5. Describe the composition of the Congress of Industrial Organizations. Why was this organization formed?

6. Describe the three levels of organizational structure of American labor unions.

Collective Bargaining

The primary way in which unions attempt to improve the status of their members is through collective bargaining. **Collective bargaining** is the process by which a union negotiates with management (an employer) in an attempt to reach a mutually acceptable agreement with regard to wages, hours, and other terms and conditions of employment. The union negotiates collectively on behalf of all union members,

regardless of the length of time they've been on the job, their financial status, or their individual personalities. Through collective bargaining, the workers gain power. Whereas management is not likely to listen if one worker tries to bargain alone, it is very likely to pay attention when workers bargain as a group. In this section, we want to examine the various aspects of collective bargaining. We will examine the legal framework under which collective bargaining takes place, union security arrangements, major bargaining issues, and methods of settling labor–management disputes. Let us begin with an examination of the legal framework of collective bargaining.

The Legal Framework

Like any other process, effective and orderly collective bargaining requires a set of rules and procedures that both parties must follow during the negotiations. The legal framework of collective bargaining is based on four major labor-relations laws that were enacted by the federal government during the period 1932 to 1959. Let us examine the major provisions of each of these laws.

Norris–LaGuardia Anti-Injunction Act (1932) The Norris–LaGuardia Act, the first piece of prolabor legislation passed by Congress, was enacted at a time when the fortunes of unions were at their lowest point. It marked a significant change in public policy—from strong repression to strong encouragement of union activity. This law greatly restricted the power of the courts to issue injunctions against union activities, and it made yellow-dog contracts illegal.

National Labor Relations Act (1935) This law, also known as the **Wagner Act,** is the cornerstone of modern labor relations law. It guaranteed workers the right to organize unions and to engage in collective bargaining; and it required employers to bargain in good faith with unions. This law also made it illegal for employers to interfere with legitimate union activities or to discriminate against workers who form unions or engage in union activities. In addition, the act established the **National Labor Relations Board** (NLRB). The Board's job was to enforce the act and to conduct and supervise free elections among a company's employees to determine which union, if any, shall represent the workers.

Labor–Management Relations Act (1947) This law, which is usually called the **Taft-Hartley Act,** amended the National Labor Relations Act. It came at a time when antiunion sentiment was strong, and one of its most important provisions was to prohibit mandatory union membership as a precondition for employment. Prior to this law, many unions forced employers to hire only union members. When this law took effect, both union and nonunion workers could be hired for a job.

Another important provision of the act gave power to the President to temporarily halt strikes that threaten to "imperil the national health or safety." The President has the power to order an 80-day "cooling-off period" in the case of such strikes, to give management and labor the opportunity to reconsider their positions and to resolve their differences under calmer circumstances. A long-lasting national trucking strike could fall under this category. If such crucial items as food and medicine were unable to reach their destinations, life-threatening situations could result. In addition, factories that depend on trucks to deliver their raw materials and to haul their finished products to customers might decide to lay off their employees until the strike was over. Under such circumstances, the President might use the provisions of the Taft–Hartley Act to order the workers back to work.

Even strikes of a less crucial nature can lead to serious problems for the nation if they last long enough. In 1959, a national steel strike that had lasted for 116 days came to an end only when the President used the powers of the Taft–Hartley Act to order the strikers back to work.

Labor–Management Reporting and Disclosure Act (1959) This law, better known as the **Landrum–Griffin Act,** regulated union activities even further. Specifically, the law required all union officers to submit detailed financial reports to the Secretary of Labor and to hold periodic secret-ballot elections of union officers.

Union Security Arrangements

When a group of employees wishes to form a union, the group submits a petition (signed by at least 30 percent of the employees) to the National Labor Relations Board, requesting a representation election. The NLRB then will conduct a secret-ballot election. If a majority of the employees vote for the union, the NLRB will certify the union as the exclusive bargaining agent for all the employees. This means that the union must represent all employees equally, and any gains made by the union will go to all the employees, including those who are not union members. Because nonunion members receive the benefits of the union, too, some workers choose not to join and, thus, avoid paying union dues. Most unions are against this practice and attempt to negotiate a union security arrangement with the employer. A **union security arrangement** is an agreement between the union and the employer that requires employees to join the union or, at least, pay union dues. Let us examine the most common union security arrangements.

The closed shop Under this arrangement, the employer agrees to hire only union members. This means a potential employee must join the union before he or she can get a job. The closed shop was common in the United States during the late 1930s and early 1940s. However, the Taft–Hartley Act of 1947 made the closed shop illegal. Despite the legal ban, arrangements very similar to the closed shop still exist today. For example, many building contractors hire most or all of their construction workers through union hiring halls. In practice, this means that workers must join the unions in order to have access to these jobs.

The union shop Under this arrangement, employers can hire nonunion workers. However, employees must join the union within a specified time period (usually 30 to 60 days) as a condition of continued employment. The union shop is the most common form of union security arrangement today, although many states have passed **right-to-work laws,** which make mandatory union membership illegal.

The modified union shop Union-shop arrangements are sometimes modified to exempt certain employees. For example, a provision might stipulate that workers hired before a specified date are not required to join the union. However, all employees hired after that date must join the union if they wish to keep their jobs.

The agency shop Under an agency-shop arrangement, employees are not required to join the union but they are required to pay union dues. Agency shops exist primarily in states where the union shop has been outlawed. This arrangement represents a compromise between those who argue that workers should not have to join the union against their will and those who say that workers should have to pay for any benefits of union representation they receive. States can make the agency shop illegal if their right-to-work laws specifically prohibit the collection of fees as a condition of employment.

Maintenance of membership Under this arrangement, employees are not required to join a union. However, those employees who belong to the union at the time a contract is negotiated and those who join at a later date must maintain their union membership for the rest of the contract period as a condition of employment.

Open shop The open shop is one in which none of the above arrangements exists. In an open shop, union membership is optional, and nonunion members are not required to pay union dues. Although unions oppose the open-shop

arrangement, it continues to exist, especially in those states with right-to-work laws.

Major Bargaining Issues

The primary purpose of collective bargaining from the union's point of view is to improve the economic status and working conditions of the employees. The union tries to negotiate the most favorable contract possible; and there are many issues that come up during the negotiations. Let us briefly examine some of the most important bargaining issues.

Wages and fringe benefits Perhaps the most important issue from the standpoint of both the union and management is that of wages and fringe benefits. Fringe benefits include such things as paid holidays and vacations, sick pay, retirement programs, and employer-financed insurance coverage. Because wages and fringe benefits are, in effect, income to employees and costs to employers, there is a natural conflict of interests. Unions push hard for higher wages and improved fringe benefits, and employers push just as hard to keep worker compensation as low as possible.

There are many wage-related issues. In addition to the question of basic hourly wages, there is the question of differential pay for workers with different skill levels and different lengths of service with the company. For example, should skilled workers get a bigger pay increase than unskilled workers? If so, how much bigger? Similarly, how much more should employees with ten years of service to the company earn than employees with only five years of service? There is also the question of overtime pay. Federal law requires employers to pay workers time and one half for any work over 40 hours per week. Unions, however, often attempt to negotiate overtime pay rates above those established by law. For example, a union may attempt to negotiate a provision that would require the employer to pay double time for work on Saturdays and triple time for work on Sundays and holidays.

Job security Another very important issue is job security. High wages are of no value to workers if they lose their jobs, so unions push hard to negotiate contract provisions that will provide the maximum job security for their members. A typical collective bargaining contract will include provisions stipulating the conditions under which an employer legally can fire employees, as well as guidelines for determining which employees will be laid off during periods of declining employment.

A major goal of unions is to obtain contract provisions that guarantee seniority rights. **Seniority rights** grant certain privileges to employees on the basis of length of service with the company. Those who have the most seniority (who have been with the company the longest) are given preferential treatment over those with less seniority. For example, most contracts state that when layoffs are necessary, those employees with the most seniority will be laid off last and those employees with the least seniority must be the first to go. Seniority rights provide a great deal of job security for employees who have held their jobs for several years. Seniority also is often an important factor in determining which employees will be promoted to higher paying jobs.

Working conditions Improved working conditions are an important goal of most unions. There are many topics that fall under this category. Shorter hours, longer rest periods, safer working conditions, and well-defined job descriptions are just a few of the issues involving working conditions that are regularly negotiated by unions.

Grievance procedures No matter how careful the union and employer are in negotiating and writing a collective bargaining contract, there will almost always be later disagreements over its interpretation. Such disagreements often take the form of **grievances,** which are formal complaints accusing one of the parties of violating the collective bargaining agreement. Because grievances are common, it is important that the provisions of the contract include a good grievance procedure, which is used to settle disagreements over the implementation of the contract without strikes.

A typical grievance procedure will call for a series of meetings at different levels of authority between union and management representatives. If a grievance cannot be satisfactorily resolved at these meetings, it usually will move on to binding arbitration. **Binding arbitration** involves submitting the grievance to a neutral third party acceptable to both the union and the employer who will listen to the arguments of both parties and then issue a decision. This decision is binding on both the union and the employer, in that both parties agree in advance to accept the decision as the final settlement of the grievance.

Settling Labor–Management Disputes

Collective bargaining is a power relationship in which both sides make threats to back up their demands. The union's major weapons are the boycott and the strike. A **boycott** is a campaign by workers to discourage people from buying the employer's product in an effort to put economic pressure on the employer. In the late 1960s, for example, farm workers called for a nationwide boycott of grapes to pressure grape growers to make concessions to workers. A **strike** is a mutual agreement by the employees to stop working until their demands are met. During a strike, workers also usually engage in **picketing,** which involves standing or walking in front of the employer's place of business with signs that spell out the workers' complaints against the employer. Picketing can sometimes prove embarrassing to the employer, and it can also discourage nonstriking workers from entering the place of employment.

The employer's major weapon is the lockout, which is just the opposite of the strike. In a **lockout,** the employer closes down the place of employment, depriving workers of their jobs in

Many labor contracts are negotiated each year without strikes. When a strike does occur, union members like these UAW workers picket outside the affected company.

an effort to put pressure on them to accept the employer's contract demands. In actual practice, the lockout is not used nearly as frequently as the strike.

Because strikes make the news and peaceful settlements do not, there is an exaggerated notion of the amount of work time lost each year because of strikes. In actuality, studies have shown that since 1935 the amount of work time lost each year from strikes has averaged less than one percent of total work time. This is far less than the amount lost because of the common cold. Yet those strikes that do occur are costly to both employer and employees, and every effort is usually made to resolve disputes peacefully before resorting to a strike. Two procedures often used are mediation and advisory arbitration.

Mediation When negotiations break down between a union and an employer, sometimes a strike can be avoided by the use of **mediation.** This process, which is also sometimes called **conciliation,** is a means by which a third party,

the mediator, tries to resolve the differences between the two parties. The mediator tries to keep the parties talking and may suggest compromises that might lead to a peaceful resolution of the dispute. However, unlike an arbitrator, a mediator does not make a specific recommendation for settling the dispute. The federal government, most states, and some larger cities provide mediation and conciliation services.

Advisory arbitration Advisory arbitration, which is sometimes used when collective bargaining talks break down, should not be confused with the binding grievance arbitration discussed earlier. In grievance arbitration, both parties agree in advance to accept the arbitrator's decision with regard to a specific grievance. However, usually the stakes are too high in the negotiation of an entire collective bargaining contract for either party to agree to a binding settlement. Instead, they agree to **advisory arbitration,** which is a procedure giving either or both parties the right to reject an arbitrator's decision.

Check Your Understanding

1. Name the four labor-relations laws that were enacted between 1932 and 1959. What were the major provisions of each law?

2. What is the difference between a union shop and a closed shop? Between a union shop and an agency shop?

3. What are "right-to-work" laws?

4. What are some of the most important collective bargaining issues?

5. What is a grievance procedure? Why is it so important that collective bargaining contracts include good grievance procedures?

6. What are the most common methods of settling labor–management disputes?

Wage Determination

What determines wages? Basically, the answer to this question is supply and demand. As you learned in earlier chapters, the price of almost everything is determined by these two forces, and labor is no exception. However, simply stating that wages are determined by supply and demand is not very enlightening. Moreover, it raises many other important questions. For example, what determines the supply and demand for labor? The answer to this question is not so simple, because many factors, such as unions and minimum wage laws, prevent the forces of supply and demand from operating freely in labor markets.

There are many different occupations and labor markets in the United States, and each has its own unique characteristics. For purposes of analysis, however, let us group all occupations into two categories: those that involve primarily unskilled and semiskilled workers and those that involve primarily skilled and professional workers.

Highly trained managers fall into the category of skilled, professional workers. Because of their training, they can command high wages.

Wage Determination for Unskilled and Semiskilled Workers

Unskilled and semiskilled workers are people who have few special work skills. They include maids, janitors, certain factory production workers, and so forth. Most unskilled and semiskilled workers usually attempt to find employment in or near their home community. Thus, there are literally thousands of local labor markets for such workers, and the supply and demand conditions will vary from one area to another. However, the demand for such workers is usually low relative to the supply. With the increasing use of mechanical robots and other labor-saving technology, this gap between the supply and demand for such workers is likely to widen even further.

Because of supply and demand conditions, unskilled and semiskilled workers often have difficulty finding employment, and their pay is usually low relative to that of other groups. They have almost no individual bargaining power with employers because they can easily be replaced. For this reason, such employees often benefit greatly from unionization. Whereas an employer can easily replace one or a few individual workers, it is not so easy to replace a thousand unionized workers who have banded together to call a strike.

Wage Determination for Skilled and Professional Workers

Skilled workers include such groups as carpenters, plumbers, electricians, typists, and computer programmers; whereas professional workers include doctors, lawyers, entertainers, professional athletes, and so forth. Both skilled and professional workers have special skills and training, and they can be replaced only by other workers with similar attributes. As is the case for any group, the wages and salaries of skilled and professional workers are determined by supply and demand. And because the demand is often strong relative to the supply, such workers frequently experience high earnings compared to other groups of employees.

In the case of some skilled workers such as electricians and plumbers, the supply may be kept artificially low by unions. To become a plumber or an electrician, workers usually must obtain special training through apprenticeship programs that are controlled at least partially by craft unions. Some critics argue that these craft unions deliberately restrict the supply of such labor and keep wages artificially high by limiting the number of apprentices accepted into these training programs. However, union supporters argue that some restriction is necessary to protect the job security of those who have already gone through the apprenticeship programs. Moreover, craft unions are not the only organizations accused of restricting entry into their occupations. Some critics charge that the American Bar Association and the American Medical Association act like unions and attempt to restrict the supply of lawyers and doctors.

In the case of some professional employees, there will always be a relatively small supply. It's not possible to mass-produce highly talented entertainers and professional athletes. Although there are millions of people who would love to enter these fields, most of them do not have the talent necessary to achieve stardom. Thus, the demand for such "stars" will always be high relative to the supply, and those who make it to the top will be rewarded highly, both financially and otherwise.

The Effects of Minimum Wage Laws

Minimum wage laws set a lower limit on the wage that can be paid to most workers. The first national minimum wage was enacted by Congress in 1938 and established a minimum wage of 25 cents per hour. Approximately 43 percent of American business firms were covered by this law. Today, the federal minimum wage has been set at $3.35 per hour and affects approximately 84 percent of all employers. In addition to the federal minimum wage requirement, 40

Workers in fast-food chains are protected by the federal minimum wage law.

states have state minimum wage laws. The state laws cover most of the employers not covered by the federal law, so most workers in the nation have some minimum wage protection.

Most workers in the United States earn wages above the minimum wage and, as a result, are not directly affected by the minimum wage laws. However, a substantial number of younger and older workers are directly affected. In 1980, less than 8 percent of employees aged 25 to 64 years earned the minimum wage or less. In contrast, in the same year, 44 percent of all teenagers and 38 percent of all workers aged 65 years and over earned the minimum or less. Most of these workers were employed at unskilled, and often part-time, jobs.

Minimum wage laws have long been a source of controversy among economists and others. Some argue that minimum wage laws do more harm than good by reducing employment opportunities. They argue that many teenagers who are unable to find jobs at the current minimum wage could find employment at a wage of $2 per hour. Their reasoning is based on the belief that employers would find it more profitable to hire teenagers at this lower wage. These critics advocate a lower minimum wage for teenagers than for older workers. However, others argue that a dual minimum wage would encourage employers to discharge older workers in order to employ teenagers.

Check Your Understanding

1. What determines the wages of unskilled and semiskilled workers? Why is unionization especially beneficial for such workers?

2. Why do skilled and professional workers earn so much more than unskilled and semiskilled workers? What actions might skilled workers take in order to keep their supply artificially low?

3. What are minimum wage laws? In what way might minimum wage laws hurt the very people they were intended to help?

ISSUE: Should There Be a Lower Minimum Wage for Teenagers?

Minimum wage laws have been controversial ever since the first law was passed in 1938. Proponents of such laws have argued that these laws help to ensure that disadvantaged, unskilled workers receive a decent wage. Critics have argued that minimum wage laws hurt the very workers that they are intended to help, by reducing employment opportunities. They contend that minimum wage laws push the wages of some unskilled workers—especially teenagers—above that level at which it is profitable for employers to hire them.

The high unemployment rates of teenagers in recent years have led many people to advocate a lower minimum wage for teenagers than for adults. Such a change, they argue, would create additional employment opportunities for young people. However, not all people agree, and the issue of a lower minimum wage for teenagers is the subject of extreme controversy.

Proponents of a lower minimum wage for teenagers argue that the current minimum wage law is the principal cause of high teenage unemployment. They believe that if the current law would be amended to allow employers to pay teenagers a lower minimum wage than they pay to adults, more teenagers would be able to find jobs. This, in turn, would help teenagers by giving them a source of income, and it would help the economy by creating more jobs.

Opponents of a lower minimum wage for teenagers argue that the high unemployment rates of teenagers are caused by many other factors besides the current minimum wage law. They believe that a reduction in the minimum wage for teenagers would increase the total number of unskilled jobs available to them only slightly. These opponents also contend that any gains in teenage employment resulting from such a change would be offset by an increase in the unemployment rates of older workers. If employers legally could pay teenagers a lower wage than adults, many older adults holding unskilled jobs would be laid off, and a transfer of jobs from older workers to teenagers would not be in the public interest. For one thing, they contend, older workers who earn the minimum wage are far more likely than teenagers to have families to support. Furthermore, the employment prospects of most teenagers are likely to improve as they mature and acquire skills. In contrast, they argue that older workers currently earning the minimum wage are likely to have less favorable futures.

Would you favor a lower minimum wage for teenagers? Why or why not? How do you think older adults would feel about such a change? As a class, you might want to hold a debate on whether or not the minimum wage for teenagers should be lowered.

CAREERS: Labor Relations Specialist

Do you like working with people? Are you good at settling disputes? If your answers are yes, you may have the talent to become a successful labor relations specialist—a person who deals with union–management relations. As a labor relations specialist working for a private company, you will help company officials prepare for collective bargaining sessions, participate in contract negotiations, handle routine labor relations problems, and advise management on all aspects of union–management relations. In order to perform your duties successfully, you will need to be familiar with economic and wage data as they relate to your company and with labor law and collective bargaining trends. You must also be able to work well with union officials because you will have frequent meetings with them about grievances and other labor relations matters. In addition, you will have to keep up with current developments in labor law, including arbitration decisions.

Instead of working for a private business, you might work for a unit of government that engages in collective bargaining with its employees. If you do, your duties will be very similar to those of a labor rela-

tions specialist working for a private business. You might also find employment with a union, in which case you will help union officials prepare for collective bargaining and handle other labor relations matters. In whatever capacity you work, you will need to be able to speak and write effectively and to be able to work with people at all levels of education and experience. You will need patience to cope with conflicting viewpoints, and you should be able to function under pressure, be fairminded, and have a persuasive and congenial personality.

If you plan to become a labor relations specialist, you will need a college education. However, because of the diverse nature of the job, there is no one single college major that is best. Some employers prefer applicants who have majored in personnel administration or labor relations, while others prefer applicants with majors in business, psychology, or counseling. Still others feel that a well-rounded liberal arts education is most suitable for the job. Another possible preparation might be a major in labor relations, with elective courses taken in such related fields as psychology, business, and counseling.

Chapter Highlights

1   Organized activity among workers in the United States was recorded as early as 1636, but unions as we know them today first appeared during the late 1700s. These first unions were formed in response to changing economic conditions that caused a conflict to develop between employer and employees.

2   The strong industrial growth that followed the Civil War led to growth in union membership and increased efforts to combine local unions into national organizations. The Knights of Labor was founded in 1869, and by 1886 it had 700,000 members. However, a series of unsuccessful strikes, internal squabbling, and inept leadership led to a rapid decline after 1886.

3   The American Federation of Labor (AFL) was founded in 1886 by Samuel Gompers. Gompers emphasized "economic unionism" instead of trying to bring about reform through direct involvement in political parties. The AFL attempted to make basic gains in wages and working conditions by bargaining directly with employers.

4   Prior to the 1930s, there were no federal or state laws governing union activities or collective bargaining. Without legal protection, labor unions faced opposition from the courts in the form of the conspiracy doctrine and injunctions and from employers, who used labor spies, yellow-dog contracts, and lockouts.

5   Following the enactment of prolabor legislation in the 1930s, many new unions were formed. Many of the new industrial unions banded together and formed the Congress of Industrial Organizations (CIO).

6   The structure of organized labor in the United States involves three levels of organization: the local union, the national union, and the federation.

7   Collective bargaining is the process by which unions negotiate with management in an attempt to reach a mutually acceptable agreement with regard to wages, hours, and other terms and conditions of employment. It is the primary way in which unions try to improve the economic status of their members.

8   The legal framework of collective bargaining is based on four labor relations laws: the Norris–LaGuardia Anti-Injunction Act (1932); the National Labor Relations Act (1935); the Labor–Management Relations Act (1947); and the Labor–Management Reporting and Disclosure Act (1959).

9   A union security arrangement is an agreement between the union and the employer that requires employees to join the union or, at least, to pay union dues. Examples of union security arrangements include the closed shop, the union shop, and the agency shop.

10 Wages and fringe benefits, job security, working conditions, and grievance procedures are some of the most important collective bargaining issues.

11 Mediation and advisory arbitration are often used in an effort to settle labor–management disputes and avoid a work stoppage. The union's major weapons for pressuring management to agree to its terms are the strike and the boycott. A lockout is a work stoppage called by management.

12 Unskilled and semiskilled workers often have difficulty finding employment, and their pay is usually low relative to other groups. Since they have almost no individual bargaining power, unionization is often especially beneficial to such workers.

13 Skilled and professional workers have special skills and training, and they can be replaced only by other workers with similar skills and training. Because the demand is often very strong relative to the supply, such workers frequently experience high earnings compared to other groups of employees.

14 Minimum wage laws set a lower limit on the wage that can be paid to most workers. Such laws are controversial because some critics believe they do more harm than good by reducing employment opportunities.

Important Terms

Match each of the following terms with the correct definition:

yellow-dog contract   lockout   craft union
collective bargaining   closed shop   conspiracy doctrine
advisory arbitration   union shop   court injunction
minimum wage laws   agency shop   labor spy
right-to-work laws   boycott   industrial union
grievance procedure   strike   seniority rights
binding arbitration   picketing   mediation

1. A union composed of workers in a particular trade or craft.

2. The common law doctrine that the organization of workers for the purpose of obtaining higher wages was a violation of property rights and, thus, illegal.

3. A union composed of workers from a particular industry.

4. An arrangement under which employers are free to hire nonunion workers but the new employees are required to join the union within a specified time period as a condition of continued employment.

5. A person hired by management to infiltrate unions and provide management with the names of union members and supporters.

6. State laws that make it illegal to require workers to join a union as a condition of employment.

7. Standing or walking in front of an employer's place of business with signs that spell out the worker's complaints against the employer.

8. A process under which grievances are submitted to a neutral third party acceptable to both the union and management who issues a decision that is binding on both parties.

9. The temporary closing of the place of employment by management in an effort to pressure unions to agree to management's terms.

10. An arrangement under which employees are not required to join the union but they are required to pay union dues.

11. Laws that set a lower limit on the wage that can be paid to most workers.

12. A campaign by workers to discourage people from buying the employer's product in an effort to put economic pressure on the employer.

13. Rights that give certain privileges to employees on the basis of length of service with the employer.

14. The process by which a union negotiates with management in an attempt to reach a mutually acceptable agreement with regard to wages, hours, and other terms and conditions of employment.

15. A court order issued by a judge requiring a party to do or to cease doing specific activities.

16. An arrangement under which employers agree to hire only union members.

17. A procedure for settling disagreements over the implementation of the collective bargaining contract without resorting to strikes.

18. A process in which a neutral third party's recommended settlement for a labor–management dispute can be refused by either party.

19. A mutual agreement by employees to stop working until their demands are met.

20. A process under which a neutral third party tries to keep the union and management talking in an effort to reach a peaceful settlement to a labor–management dispute.

21. An agreement under which employees promise not to join a union as a condition of employment.

Extending Your Understanding

1. Why was it so difficult for unions to organize American workers prior to the 1930s?

2. Do you think it is fair to require workers to join a union as a condition of employment?

3. Suppose unions and collective bargaining were made illegal in the United States. How do you think disagreements between employers and employees would be settled in the absence of collective bargaining?

Activities

1. With some students acting as union leaders and others playing the role of management, conduct a collective bargaining session. Some of the issues to be negotiated might include higher wages, better fringe benefits, and job security. If necessary, call in a mediator or an arbitrator.

   To get an idea of the impact of labor unions in your community, conduct some research on their number and size. How many unions are there? How many members do they have? What percentage of the community's labor force does this comprise? What kinds of jobs do these workers have? In what industries are they employed? Summarize your findings in a table or chart. You may need to contact your local library and Chamber of Commerce, as well as some of the unions themselves, to get the information you need.

Building Skills in Economics: Understanding Cause and Effect

Cause and effect is an important relationship in economics. It helps to explain why things occur. Simply stated, in a cause and effect relationship, one event—the cause—leads to another event—the effect. Put another way, an effect is the result of a cause.

Certain key words and phrases often indicate the presence of a cause and effect relationshiop. Among the most commonly used are *therefore, because, as a result of, since, if . . . then, in response to,* and *in turn.* Sometimes, however, cause and effect relationships are not stated directly. In such cases, you have to infer them.

This chapter contains several cause and effect relationships. The following questions will help you identify some of them.

Applying Economics Skills

1. Why were the first labor unions formed? Would the first unions be considered the cause or the effect?
2. During the late 1700s, what caused employers to cut the wages of employees? Why did some of these employees strike? Can an effect in one situation be a cause in another? Explain.
3. What caused the decline of the Knights of Labor?
4. What was the effect of the conspiracy doctrine? What was the effect of court injunctions?

CHAPTER 7

GOVERNMENT AND THE ECONOMY

No study of the American economy would be complete without an examination of the important role of government. As you already know, the government is involved in the American economy in many ways. It enacts and enforces laws designed to promote an orderly and equitable society, regulates public utility companies, promotes competition, and provides many other services. However, government's biggest impact on the economy results from the collection and spending of hundreds of billions of dollars each year. Any change in the amount of taxes the government collects affects the spending power of millions of American taxpayers, and changes in government spending affect thousands of private business firms as well as millions of individuals.

In this chapter, we want to focus our attention on what economists call public finance. **Public finance** is the study of government expenditures and revenues at all levels of government; local, state, and federal. We will examine government expenditures, taxes, and the American tax system.

Government Expenditures

How much government spends and the taxes necessary to finance that spending are two of the most controversial of all economic topics. Most election campaigns, at all levels—from local government to the presidency of the United States—are dominated by the issues of government spending and taxes. Election after election, candidates for public office have pledged to adjust government spending and to lower taxes. Yet, despite campaign promises, government spending and taxes have continued to grow year after year, decade after decade. Government spending for all levels of government (local, state, and federal) in 1983 amounted to more than $1.2 trillion. That's more than $5,100 for every man, woman, and child in the nation! Let us examine the reasons for long-term rise in government spending.

Reasons for Long-Term Rise in Government Spending

A number of factors have contributed to the long-term rise in government spending. Three of the most important are the increased demand for collective goods and services, the rising cost of national defense, and the urbanization of the population. Let us examine each of them.

Increased demand for collective goods and services In any nation as the standard of living increases to the point where a majority of citizens have adequate food, shelter, and clothing, the people increasingly turn their attention toward collective goods and services. As you learned in Chapter 2, collective goods and services are items that tend to benefit large numbers of people collectively and would not be available to everyone if each individual had to provide them.

The United States is no exception to this statement. Over the years, Americans have increasingly demanded the various collective goods and services that are typically produced by government. Education is a prime example. During the colonial period, only about one child out of ten attended school, and the few schools that existed were supported by churches or private tuition fees. During the early 1800s, however, an increasing number of Americans began to advocate free, tax-supported elementary schools. In 1852, Massachusetts became the first state to enact a compulsory school-attendance law, and other states soon followed suit. Public high schools, however, did not become commonplace until the late 1800s. As late as 1890, only about 10 percent of high-school-aged young people were enrolled in high schools.

Today, students in every state attend public, tax-supported elementary schools and high schools, as well as public, partially tax-supported colleges. Modern schools are very expensive to build and maintain compared to the schools of the past. Thus, the increasing cost of public education has been a major factor contributing to the long-term rise in government spending.

A portion of annual government spending is devoted to the support of public schools that offer an education to all young Americans.

Federal, state, and local governments spend tax money on the maintenance of the nation's highway system.

Education is only one of a number of collective goods and services that have led to increased government spending. Another major area responsible for this spending pattern is the nation's highway system. Prior to the invention of automobiles and trucks, government expenditures on roads were minimal. Horse-drawn vehicles did not require expensive roads, and railroad companies built their own railbeds. However, the development of automobiles and trucks was accompanied by a public demand for good roads and highways. Today, the United States has a modern nationwide system of interstate highways that probably exceeds the wildest dreams of early motorists. These highways were built at great cost, and their continued maintenance and improvement represent a major area of continued government spending.

Another area of increased collective services spending is health and income security. **Income security** is the assurance that people will not be deprived of all income as a result of unemployment, illness, disability, old age, and so forth. Prior to the Great Depression of the 1930s, the individual was responsible for pro-

viding for family health, income, and retirement needs. The care of the needy was generally left to private charity. However when the Social Security Act of 1935 was enacted into law, some of the responsibility for the health, income security, and welfare needs of the nation was transferred from the family and private charitable organizations to the government. Although both workers and employers pay into Social Security, this new responsibility requires large government expenditures.

Rising cost of national defense The United States has always spent money on national defense. However as technology has led to the development of increasingly complex and sophisticated weapons, the cost of national defense has soared. During the Civil War, military spending was less than $1 billion per year. By 1960, the government was spending about $44 billion per year for defense. By 1984, this figure had soared to more than $230 billion. Part of the increase is due to the general rise in prices. However, defense spending has been rising much faster than the general price level.

During the period 1960–84, average prices in the United States rose by approximately 250 percent. During the same period, defense spending rose by more than 420 percent.

The urbanization of the population In 1800, only 5 percent of all Americans lived in urban areas. Today, more than 70 percent of the American people are urban dwellers. This mass movement from rural to urban areas over the past 150 years has been an important factor in the long-term growth of government spending.

In the early 1800s when most Americans lived in rural areas, people provided for most of their own needs. They had to dig wells or to find other ways of supplying their own water. They had to dispose of their own garbage and to provide for their own sanitation. They usually had little or no police and fire protection. As large numbers of people began to move into cities, it was no longer possible for each family to provide for its own needs. Water supply, sewage treatment, and garbage removal had to become the responsibility of the city government. As cities became congested, there was an increased need for police protection, fire protection, street lighting, and paved streets. As a result, government spending and taxes increased to pay for these services.

As cities continued to grow, their problems became more complex and more expensive to solve. Sections of many cities began to decay because sufficient funds could not be raised through taxation to provide the degree of services necessary. Today, government expenditures are still being used to try to revitalize some cities and to stem the tide of deterioration in others.

How Government Spends Its Money

Tables 7–1 and 7–2 provide a breakdown of how government spends its money. As you can see, at the federal level, national defense and income security (Social Security and related programs) account for more than 60 percent of government spending. Interest on the federal debt, which is the amount of money the federal government owes, is the next largest category. This is followed by health; education, training, employment, and social services; veterans benefits and services; and transportation.

At the state and local level, education is the largest single area of spending, accounting for approximately 30 percent of the total government expenditures. Public welfare, highways, health and hospitals, and police and fire protection are other important areas of spending for state and local governments. Sanitation and sewage, housing and urban renewal, parks and recreation, and natural resources round out the list.

TABLE 7–1: FEDERAL GOVERNMENT EXPENDITURES FOR 1983

Item	Billions of Dollars	Percent
National Defense	$209.9	26.4
Social Security and Other Income Security Programs	292.9	36.8
Health	81.3	10.2
Veterans Benefits and Services	24.8	3.1
Education, Training, Employment, and Social Services	26.6	3.3
Interest	89.8	11.3
Transportation	21.4	2.7
All Others	49.3	6.2
Totals	$796.0	100.0

Source: *Statistical Abstract of the United States,* 1985

TABLE 7–2: STATE AND LOCAL GOVERNMENT EXPENDITURES FOR 1982

Item	Billions of Dollars	Percent
Education	$154.6	29.7
Public Welfare	56.3	10.8
Highways	34.5	6.6
Health and Hospitals	40.3	7.7
Police and Fire Protection	23.4	4.5
Sanitation and Sewage	14.9	2.9
Housing and Urban Renewal	8.1	1.6
Parks and Recreation	7.4	1.4
Natural Resources	6.5	1.2
All Others	175.0	33.6
Totals	521.0	100.0

Source: *Statistical Abstract of the United States*, 1985

As you can see, the money spent by the different levels of government amounts to hundreds of billions of dollars. Where does all this money come from? To a great extent, the answer is you. By paying taxes, you help to finance various government programs. In the next section, we will examine the principles of taxation and the ways in which taxes are classified.

Check Your Understanding

1. Define "public finance."

2. Give three important reasons for the long-term rise in government spending. How has each contributed to this spending pattern?

3. How does the federal government spend its money?

4. How do state and local governments spend their money?

Taxes

Few words in the English language are more disliked than the word "taxes". From colonial times to the present, Americans have complained more about the collection of taxes than almost any other thing the government does. Yet, taxes are probably inevitable and unavoidable because the government must have money with which to operate.

Principles of Taxation

Since taxes are both unpopular and inevitable, certain guidelines must be established to make sure the collection procedure goes as smoothly as possible. First, the tax should be easy and inexpensive to collect. Second, the tax must be difficult to avoid. If people can easily get around paying the tax, the tax will raise very little revenue. Third, the tax must be clear. People are more willing to pay a tax they understand than one that is incomprehensible to them. Finally, every effort should be made to make the tax as fair as possible. Of course, it is impossible to get everyone to agree on what is fair. What appears to be fair to some people may seem very unfair to others. As a result, there probably is no such thing as a tax on which everyone would agree. However, efforts to devise a fair tax system have resulted in two fundamental principles of fairness in taxation. They are the benefit principle and the ability-to-pay principle. Let us examine each of these principles.

The benefit principle According to the **benefit principle** of taxation, those people who benefit from any government program or project should pay the taxes to finance that government program or project. The best example of the benefit principle of taxation is the financing of the American highway system. Those people who drive on the nation's highways are the ones who pay for highway construction and maintenance. They may pay either directly or indirectly. In the case of toll roads and bridges, motorists may pay a direct fee for the use of these public facilities. In most cases, however, motorists pay indirectly. Whenever they stop to fill up their gas tanks, a portion of the money spent for each gallon of gas is a tax that funds the entire highway system. Those people who benefit the most from the system pay the most to keep it operating. The more a person drives, the more gasoline is bought, and, thus, the more taxes paid.

Although the benefit principle of taxation works very well for financing the nation's highway system, it is not a practical way to finance most other government programs and projects. There are two major reasons the benefit principle cannot serve as a general guide for all taxes: (1) it is impossible to determine exactly how much each citizen benefits from most government programs and projects and (2) in some cases, those who benefit from a program are least able to pay for it. Let us examine each of these problems.

In the case of such government services as public education, health and sanitation facilities, police and fire protection, and national defense, everybody benefits, but not all citizens benefit equally. For example, in addition to protecting lives, police officers and firefighters

Every time motorists fill their automobile tanks with gas, they pay an indirect—gasoline—tax, which helps to maintain the national highway system.

also protect property. Because some people have more property to protect than others, they benefit more from police and firefighting services. Exactly how much more? It is impossible to answer this question. Therefore, it is also impossible to determine the amount of taxes that each citizen should pay based on the benefit principle.

The other problem with the benefit principle results from the fact that such programs as public welfare assistance and food stamps are designed to help people who are financially unable to provide for their own current needs. Thus, it would be impossible for these people to pay for the cost of such programs.

The ability-to-pay principle Since the benefit principle of taxation is not a feasible guide for the financing of most government activities, policy makers have tended to base most taxes on the **ability-to-pay principle.** According to this principle, the fairest tax is one that is based on the ability of taxpayers to pay it, regardless of the amount of benefits they receive. Thus, the more wealth a person has or the higher his or her income, the more taxes the person should pay. This principle is based on the assumption that each dollar of taxes paid by a wealthy person "hurts" less than each dollar paid by a poor person. The individual income tax is an example of a tax based on the ability-to-pay principle.

Classification of Taxes

Taxes are often classified on the basis of how they affect a taxpayer as the person's income rises. There are three possible classifications. A tax can be (1) a proportional tax; (2) a progressive tax; or (3) a regressive tax.

A **proportional tax** is one where the percentage of income paid as taxes remains constant as income rises. For example, suppose a taxpayer pays $100 in taxes on an income of $1,000, $1,000 in taxes on an income of $10,000, and $10,000 in taxes on an income of $100,000. In each case, the person is paying a

tax of 10 percent. Although the *amount* of tax paid increases as income rises, the *rate* remains the same. Thus, even if the person earned $1 million, he or she would still be paying taxes at the rate of 10 percent.

A **progressive tax** is one where the percentage of income paid as taxes increases as income rises. For example, suppose a taxpayer is required to pay a tax of $100 on an income of $1,000, $1,500 on an income of $10,000, and $20,000 on an income of $100,000. In this case, the tax rate is 10 percent on $1,000, 15 percent on $10,000, and 20 percent on $100,000. With a progressive tax, both the *rate* and the *amount* of taxes increase as income rises.

A **regressive tax** is one where the percentage of income paid as taxes decreases as income rises. An example of a regressive tax would be one where a taxpayer pays $100 in taxes on an income of $1,000, $900 in taxes on an income of $10,000, and $8,000 in taxes on an income of $100,000. In this case, the tax rate is 10 percent on $1,000, 9 percent on $10,000, and 8 percent on $100,000. With a regressive tax, the *amount* of tax paid may actually increase as income rises but it increases at a decreasing rate.

Check Your Understanding

1. What is meant by the benefit principle of taxation? Give an example of a tax based on this principle.

2. What is meant by the ability-to-pay principle? Give an example of a tax based on this principle.

3. How do proportional, progressive, and regressive taxes differ from one another?

The American Tax System

Americans pay many different kinds of taxes, and they must pay taxes to all levels of government. Some of these taxes, such as the federal individual income tax, are well known, and individuals are aware of the amount they pay each year. However, some taxes (often referred to as "hidden" taxes) are added to the price of items that consumers buy, and many Americans are not even aware that they are paying these taxes. Let us examine the most important kinds of taxes in the American tax system.

Federal Taxes

Most federal revenue comes from taxes that are based on income. The three major sources of federal revenue are the individual income tax, Social Security taxes, and the corporate income tax. In addition to these major taxes, the federal government receives small amounts of revenue from a number of other kinds of taxes. The various sources of federal revenue and the relative importance of each are shown in Table 7–3.

The federal individual income tax The individual income tax is the most important source of revenue for the federal government, accounting for more than 44 percent of all federal revenue. This tax is sometimes referred to as the "gradu-

ated" federal income tax because it is a progressive tax that takes an increasing percentage of income as income rises. Let us see what we mean.

In 1984, a married couple filing a joint return would not have owed any taxes on a taxable income below $3,400. On a taxable income between $3,400 and $5,500, they would have paid taxes at a rate of 11 percent; and on a taxable income between $5,500 and $7,600, they would have paid at a rate of 12 percent. The tax rate would continue to increase as income rose, until the maximum rate of 50 percent was reached at an income in excess of $162,400.

There is a common misconception about the federal individual income tax. Many people believe that if they were to receive a pay raise that put them into a higher tax bracket (that is, a bracket that was taxed at a higher rate), they might be worse off than before. This is generally not true. Under certain circumstances, a person receiving a very small pay raise of less than $50 per year might end up a few dollars worse off because the tax tables used for calculating the individual income tax are based on income increases of $50. Aside from this technical problem, however, an increase in a taxpayer's income that puts the taxpayer into a higher tax bracket cannot leave the taxpayer with less after-tax income. The reason for this is that only the additional income is taxed at the higher rate. The amount of the taxpayer's income

TABLE 7–3: FEDERAL GOVERNMENT RECEIPTS FOR 1984

Source	Billions of Dollars	Percent
Individual Income Taxes	$296.2	44.4
Social Insurance Taxes and Contributions (Social Security)	241.6	36.3
Corporate Income Taxes	56.9	8.5
Excise Taxes	37.4	5.6
Customs Duties	11.4	1.7
Estate and Gift Taxes	6.0	0.9
Miscellaneous	17.0	2.6
Totals	$666.5	100.0

Source: Economic Report of the President, 1985

before the increase continues to be taxed at the same rate that was appropriate before the increase.

For example, suppose a married couple filing a joint return in 1984 with a taxable income of $162,400 receives $100 of additional income. This will put them in the maximum bracket of 50 percent. However, this couple would still be better off by $50 than before they received the additional $100 because only this $100 would be taxed at the 50 percent rate. The first $3,400 of their income would be taxed at zero tax rate, income between $3,400 and $5,500 would be taxed at a rate of 11 percent, income between $5,500 and $7,600 would be taxed at 12 percent, and so forth on up the tax schedule. The taxes on their previous income of $162,400 would not be affected by the $100 increase in income. As a result, after the $100 is taxed at a rate of 50 percent, the couple will have $50 left over.

Similarly, if a single individual with a taxable income of $10,800 received $100 of additional income, this person would still be better off by $82 after taxes. The first $2,300 of the person's income would be taxed at zero tax rate; income between $2,300 and $3,400 would be taxed at a rate of 11 percent; income between $3,400 and $4,400 would be taxed at 12 percent; and so forth. Only the last $100 would be taxed at a rate of 18 percent.

Social Security taxes Since the Social Security system was founded in 1935, it has been financed by payroll taxes. In the case of people who are not self-employed, half of these taxes are paid by employers and half are paid by employees. (Self-employed people pay a tax higher than the share paid by people working for someone else but lower than the combined shares of employees and employers.) These payroll taxes finance the various Social Security programs, including old age, survivors, disability, and health insurance benefits.

Unlike the individual income tax where individuals and families with very low income are exempt from paying the tax, Social Security payroll taxes are paid starting with the first dollar of earnings, except for individuals earning less than $400 per year. Also, there is a limit to the amount of earnings subject to the tax. In 1985, the payroll tax for those not self-employed was 14.1 percent of the first $39,600 of earnings, with the employer paying one half of the tax and the employee paying the other half. All earnings above $39,600 in 1985 were exempt from Social Security taxes. Because the Social Security payroll tax is imposed only on earnings up to $39,600, it is a regressive tax. In 1985, a person earning $39,600 would pay a Social Security tax on 100 percent of his or her income. However, a person earning $390,000 would pay Social Security taxes on $39,600, or only on about 10 percent of his or her income.

Corporate income taxes Corporations must pay a federal tax on their profits. The tax is based on the net profit (the difference between total income and total expenses) of corporations. The tax rate for corporations has varied over the years, and small corporations with profits of less than $100,000 pay a smaller rate than larger corporations. During recent decades, the tax rate for corporations with profits above $100,000 has averaged approximately 50 percent. In 1985, it was 46 percent.

The corporate income tax has always been a source of controversy. Some people argue that the corporate income tax rate should be lower so that corporations would have more profits to use for expanding their operations. This, they argue, would then lead to the creation of more jobs. However, others argue that corporations should pay higher taxes so that other taxes, such as the individual income tax, could be lowered.

There is a great deal of disagreement over who really bears the burden of corporate income taxes. Some economists believe that many corporations are able to pass the tax burden on to consumers by simply raising the prices of their products. Others believe that many corporations shift much of the tax burden back to their employees in the form of lower wages. Still others argue that the tax burden falls on the stockholders of the corporation in the form of lower dividend payments.

Another source of controversy involving the corporate income tax is the fact that corporate profits that are distributed to stockholders as dividends are taxed twice. The corporation pays a tax on its profits, and then the stockholder pays an individual income tax on the dividends received from those profits. Many argue that this **double taxation** is unfair.

Excise taxes A small proportion of federal revenue comes from excise taxes. Excise taxes are taxes levied on the production or sale of specific goods or services. The federal government imposes taxes on various goods and services, including alcoholic beverages, cigarettes, gasoline, tires, firearms, and telephone service. These taxes are often referred to as "hidden" taxes because many people are not even aware that they are paying an excise tax as part of the price of these items.

Other taxes The federal government receives a very small amount of revenue from estate taxes, gift taxes, and customs duties. **Estate taxes** are taxes levied on the estates—property or possessions—of people who have died. The size of the estate must exceed a minimum level established by the government before a tax is due. **Gift taxes** are taxes on gifts of money or other forms of wealth. **Customs duties** are taxes on goods brought into the United States from other countries.

State and Local Taxes

Like the federal government, states impose both individual and corporate income taxes on their residents. However, as you can see from Table 7–4, state and local governments obtain only about 11 percent of their total revenue from individual income taxes and about 3 percent from corporate income taxes. The revenue received from excise taxes and other minor taxes also comes to a relatively small amount, comprising only a fraction of the other sources of revenue. State and local governments obtain a substantial amount of their revenue from the federal government. In addition, there are two major sources of state and local tax revenue that are not used by the federal government—sales taxes and property taxes. Let us examine each of these taxes.

Sales taxes are similar to excise taxes except that they apply to a wide range of goods and services instead of just specific items. Some state and local governments impose a flat general sales tax on the retail prices of all goods and services purchased, while others exempt such items as food and medicine from the tax. The sales tax is the major source of revenue for most states, and some local governments also derive a substantial amount of their revenue from sales taxes.

TABLE 7–4: STATE AND LOCAL GOVERNMENT RECEIPTS FOR 1983

Source	Billions of Dollars	Percent
Sales and Gross Receipts Taxes	$100.2	20.6
Property Taxes	89.3	18.3
Individual Income Taxes	55.1	11.3
Corporate Income Taxes	14.3	2.9
Revenue from Federal Government	90.0	18.5
All Others	138.0	28.4
Totals	$486.9	100.0

Source: *Economic Report of the President,* 1985

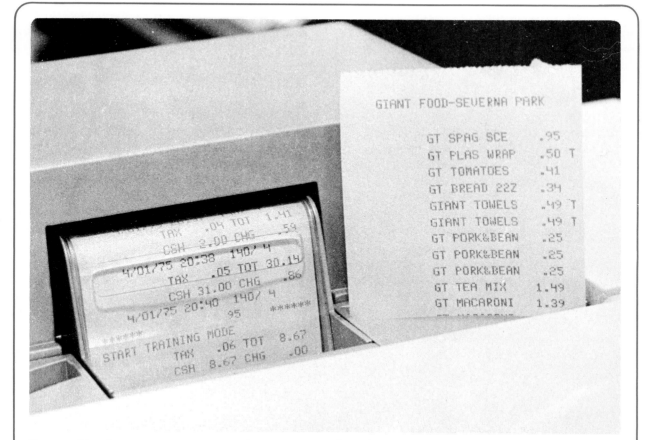

State and local governments impose sales taxes on goods and services ranging from meals served in restaurants to light bulbs sold in supermarkets.

Like all other taxes, the sales tax is controversial. The main source of controversy comes from the fact that the sales tax tends to be regressive. As you have already learned, a regressive tax is one in which the percentage of income paid in taxes decreases as income rises. Let us examine why the sales tax falls under this category.

Suppose a state imposes a flat-rate general sales tax of 5 percent on all items. This means that for every $100 spent, a consumer must pay $5 in sales tax to the state. An individual with an income of $10,000 would probably need to spend almost his or her entire income for living expenses, and thus he or she would pay a sales tax on almost 100 percent of his or her income. However, an individual with an income of $100,000 is likely to save part of his or her paycheck. Therefore, even if this person spent $50,000 on taxable items, he or she would pay a sales tax on less than 100 percent of what he or she earns. In this case, the person would pay a sales tax on 50 percent of his or her income, with the remaining 50 percent exempt from the tax.

The above example is based on a general sales tax levied against all items. Some states exempt such basic necessities as food, shelter, and medical care from the sales tax. In such cases, the sales tax is far less regressive than in the above example.

Probably the most disliked tax in this country is the property tax. Yet, it is the tax that generates most of the revenue for public education and other local government expenditures. **Property taxes** are levied primarily on land and buildings. Homeowners must pay property taxes on their homes, farmers must pay taxes on their land and farm buildings, and businesses must pay taxes on their business property.

The property tax is unpopular for a number of reasons, but most of them center around the fact that many people believe it is a very unfair tax. In the early days of American history, many wealthy people held their wealth in the form of real estate, and thus the property tax was usually levied against those people most able to pay. Today, however, many wealthy individuals hold much of their wealth in the form of bank accounts, stocks, bonds, and other investments that are not subject to the property tax. In contrast, many low-income homeowners spend a larger proportion of their income for housing than do those with higher incomes. Because of this situation, the property tax tends to be regressive.

Another factor contributing to the property tax's unpopularity is that it is very difficult to administer equitably. This tax is based on an assessed valuation of the property, which is calculated by a tax assessor. Since human value judgments are involved in determining this assessed valuation, there is much room for error. Some properties probably are assessed too high, while others are assessed too low. Every taxing district in the nation is contacted each year by angry property owners who complain about the high assessed valuation of their property.

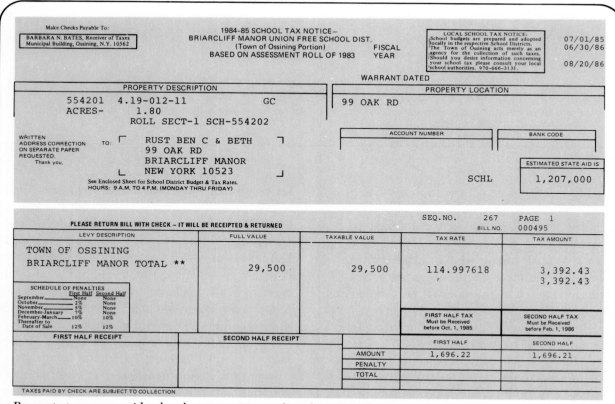

Property taxes are paid to local communities and are based on the assessed value of individual properties. Such taxes support the local school system and pay for local government.

Tax rates vary from one community to the next. Some poor communities, however, have a higher tax rate than wealthier ones.

Still another problem with the property tax is that the rates vary so much from community to community. The property tax on a home valued at $50,000 in one community might be twice as high as the tax on a similar home in another community because the rate of taxation might be 10 percent of the assessed valuation in the first area and only 5 percent in the second area. The tax rate is determined both by how much revenue the local government needs and by the total value of all property in the community. In a community with many expensive homes and highly valued industrial property, a relatively low tax rate may yield all the revenue the local government needs. However, in a poverty-stricken area where there is little industrial property and few valuable homes, even a very high tax rate may be insufficient to provide adequate revenue for local government. It is the wide disparity in the amount of tax paid by different homeowners on homes of similar value that is the source of much of the controversy surrounding the property tax.

Check Your Understanding

1. What are the three major sources of federal revenue?

2. Could a pay raise cause a person to have less take-home pay than the person had before the raise? Explain.

3. Why has the corporate income tax been a source of controversy?

4. What are the two major sources of state and local government tax revenue not used by the federal government?

5. Why is the property tax so unpopular?

Fiscal Policy

As you will learn in the next three chapters, government spending and taxing powers can be used to influence the performance of the American economy. The deliberate use of the government's spending and taxing powers to accomplish desired economic objectives is called **fiscal policy,** which can be used to help combat basic economic problems such as inflation and unemployment.

Issues in Public Finance

There are many controversial issues involving public finance. As you already know, taxation and the amount of government spending have always been important sources of controversy at all levels of government. Another important area of disagreement is the basic question of which levels of government should provide which services. Certainly, the federal government must assume the responsibility for national defense, and local governments must provide police and fire protection. However, other areas of public finance are not so clear-cut.

Public education is a good example of a public service that could be funded at any or all levels of government. In fact, public education does receive some funding from all three levels of government: local, state, and federal. However, most of the funding for public education comes from local government in the form of revenue generated by the property tax.

Use of the local property tax as the primary source of school funding results in substantial variation in the quality of public education from one area to another. The reason for this is that affluent areas with a great deal of valuable real estate can raise a lot more money from the local property tax than can poverty-stricken areas. Some critics argue that as a result, some students are being denied a quality education because of where they live. These critics argue that the tax base for public education should be much broader than the local level. They argue that increased state and federal funding for public education would result in greater opportunity for all students to receive a good education.

Opponents of increased state and federal funding of education argue that such increased funding would also result in increased state and federal control of education, and they believe local communities should retain as much control over their educational systems as possible. Also, residents of affluent communities fear that a broadening of the tax base would result in more dollars leaving their communities in the form of taxes than would be coming back for the funding of their local schools. As a result, they fear that improving the quality of education for the state or the nation as a whole would result in a reduction in the quality of education in their local communities.

Other important issues involving public finance include the problems of deficit spending, the large federal debt, and methods of balancing the federal budget. We will examine these issues in depth in Chapter 10.

Check Your Understanding

1. What is fiscal policy? What is its purpose?

2. Why does reliance on the local property tax as the primary source of school funding result in substantial variation in the quality of public education from one area to another?

3. Why do critics of the current system of school funding advocate increased state and federal funding for public education? Why is there strong opposition to increased state and federal funding?

CAREERS: Accountant

Accurate and up-to-date financial information is absolutely essential to the efficient operation of any business or government agency. Accountants keep financial records and develop, analyze, and interpret financial reports that furnish managers with the up-to-date financial information they need to make important decisions.

The three major fields of employment for accountants are public accounting, private accounting, and government accounting. Public accountants have their own business or work for accounting firms. They provide accounting services to private businesses and individuals for a fee. These accountants often specialize in one or more areas, such as preparing income tax forms, advising clients on tax matters, or helping businesses to set up new accounting systems or to revise current systems. Private accountants, sometimes called management or industrial accountants, work as salaried employees of private business firms. They handle the financial records of their company and provide the financial information that management needs to make sound business decisions. Government accountants are employed in a variety of positions. Some handle the financial records of government agencies in much the same way that private accountants handle the records of private business firms. Others, however, work in such capacities as bank examiners and Internal Revenue Service agents.

To become an accountant, you need at least a bachelor's degree in accounting, and you probably will want to become certified. Certified public accountants (CPAs) must pass a rigorous, comprehensive examination after which they receive a certificate and a license issued by a state board of accountancy. In most states, some experience as a public accountant is also required.

In addition to academic training, you must be good at mathematics, be able to analyze, compare, and interpret facts and figures quickly, and be able to communicate the results of your work clearly, both orally and in writing. You should be able to concentrate for long periods of time and be good at working with people as well as with systems and computers.

Chapter Highlights

1   Government's biggest impact on the economy results from the collection and spending of hundreds of billions of dollars each year. The study of government expenditures and revenues at all levels of government is called public finance.

2   Despite the fact that government spending and taxes have always been controversial, both have continued to increase year after year, decade after decade.

3   Three of the most important reasons for the long-term rise in government spending are the rising cost of national defense, the increased demand for collective goods and services, and the urbanization of the population.

4   National defense and income security are the two biggest areas of federal government spending, while education and public welfare are the two largest categories of spending for state and local governments.

5   According to the benefit principle of taxation, those people who benefit from a government program or project should pay the taxes to finance the program or project. The funding of the American highway system is based on the benefit principle.

6   The benefit principle is not practical for funding most government programs because it is often impossible to determine how much each citizen benefits from them and because many government programs are aimed at helping people who are unable to pay for the cost of these programs.

7   The ability-to-pay principle of taxation is based on the assumption that those people best able to pay taxes should pay the most taxes. An example of a tax based on this principle is the individual income tax.

8   Taxes are often classified on the basis of how they affect a taxpayer as his or her income rises. With a proportional tax, the percentage of income paid as tax remains constant as income rises. With a progressive tax, the percentage of income paid as tax increases as income rises. And with a regressive tax, the percentage of income paid as taxes decreases as income rises.

9   The three major sources of federal revenue are the individual income tax, Social Security taxes, and the corporate income tax. The two most important sources of state and local government tax revenue are the sales tax and property taxes.

10   The property tax generates most of the revenue for public education and other local government expenditures. It is a very unpopular tax primarily because many people believe it is not assessed fairly.

Important Terms

Match each of the following terms with the correct definition:

ability-to-pay principle	public finance	proportional tax
individual income tax	property taxes	regressive tax
Social Security taxes	excise taxes	benefit principle
corporate income taxes	sales taxes	progressive tax

1. The principle that those who benefit from a government program should pay the taxes to finance the program.

2. The study of government expenditures and revenues at all levels of government.

3. A tax that takes a decreasing percentage of income as income rises.

4. Taxes levied primarily on land and buildings.

5. Taxes based on the net profits of corporations.

6. A principle of taxation based on the assumption that those most able to pay taxes should pay the most taxes.

7. A tax that takes a constant percentage of income as income rises.

8. Taxes levied on the production or sale of specific goods or services.

9. Taxes levied on the sale of a wide range of goods and services instead of just specific items.

10. The most important source of revenue for the federal government.

11. A tax that takes an increasing percentage of income as income rises.

12. Payroll taxes, half of which are paid by employers and half of which are paid by employees.

Extending Your Understanding

1. Why has government spending grown so much over the years? Do you think government spending will continue to grow in the future at about the same rate, faster, or slower than in the past? Why?

2. Which taxes do you think are the most equitable? Which are the least equitable? Why?

3. Suppose you were given the task of devising the most equitable tax possible. What kind of tax would it be?

Activities

1. Find out how property taxes are assessed and how this money is used in your community. Then prepare a graph or a table showing how this money is spent. What is the largest expenditure?

2. Obtain a copy of the latest federal income tax form from your local Internal Revenue Service office. Following the instructions carefully, calculate the amount of tax paid by a single person earning $20,000. (Assume the person has one exemption and takes the standard deduction.)

Building Skills in Economics: Understanding Payroll Deductions

Every pay period, millions of Americans must contribute a portion of their salaries to payroll deductions. As you learned in this chapter, personal income taxes and Social Security taxes are among those taxes paid in this manner. On most pay stubs or earnings statements, Social Security deductions are labeled "FICA." This stands for Federal Insurance Contributions Act. Other payroll deductions include the federal withholding tax and, depending on where you live and work, state and city withholding taxes. Withholding taxes enable workers to pay their income taxes over a yearly period. Any difference between the amount paid during the year and the amount owed at the end of the year is settled when the person files his or her annual tax returns.

Some people also choose to have an additional portion of their income deducted for various purposes, such as union dues, pension contributions, insurance policies, and savings bonds. Unlike FICA and tax deductions, these are voluntary deductions.

The earnings statement that follows illustrates various payroll deductions. The questions will help you understand these deductions.

Applying Economics Skills

1. How much money did this person earn before any taxes or voluntary contributions were made (gross pay)? How much did he or she earn after all deductions were taken (net pay)?
2. What portion of this person's income went toward the federal withholding tax? FICA? The state withholding tax? The city withholding tax?
3. What voluntary deductions did this person authorize? How much was deducted for each?

EARNINGS STATEMENT	X Y Z Corporation (Please detach and retain for your records)		
EMPLOYEE NAME	DEPT.	PERIOD ENDING	DATE
John Doe	2366	12/31/85	12/28/85

DEDUCTIONS THIS PERIOD

Federal Withholding Tax	FICA	State Withholding Tax	City Withholding Tax
72.40	28.80	9.60	4.30

OTHER DEDUCTIONS

Union Dues	Pension	Insurance	Savings Bonds
10.00	12.00	5.00	10.00

Gross Pay	Net Pay
480.00	317.90

Quality
MEANS BUSINESS
BUSINESS
MEANS YOUR JOB

UNIT 3

Economic Performance

CHAPTER 8

GROSS NATIONAL PRODUCT: A MEASURE OF THE NATION'S ECONOMIC HEALTH

How well is the American economy performing today? Is it operating at full capacity or are some of the nation's productive resources idle? Are the nation's productive capacity and actual production growing? If so, is production growing at a faster rate than the population? These are the kinds of questions that economic policy makers are constantly asking themselves. The answers to these questions directly affect your life because the level of total production determines both the quantity of goods and services available for distribution to the American people and the number of jobs available in the nation.

In order for policy makers to formulate sound economic policies for maintaining the nation's economic health, it is necessary to have accurate measures of the economy's performance. There are a number of such measures, the most basic and comprehensive of which is the gross national product. We will examine this vital indicator here. In the next chapter, we will take a look at two other important measures: the unemployment rate and the inflation rate.

The Concept of GNP

The gross national product, usually called GNP, is a yardstick of the economy's performance. It tells how much has been produced in a given year and gives economists a basis from which to compare the economy from one year to the next. By using the GNP, economists can judge the nation's economic well-being.

The GNP is calculated by adding up the dollar value of all goods and services produced in a year's time. Why do we use the dollar value and not just the actual numbers of goods and services produced? The answer is relatively simple. If we added up the physical number of automobiles, apples, oranges, and so forth, the numbers would be meaningless. For example, suppose this year we produce more apples and automobiles but fewer oranges and airplanes than we produced last year. Is this year's pro-duction better or worse than last year's production? We can't tell unless we have a common measure for each item. That common measure is the market value, or the dollar value, of all these items.

By using the market value of all goods and services instead of the physical numbers, we can get an accurate measure of the economy's overall performance. Specifically, the **gross national product** is defined as the total dollar value of all goods and services produced in a year's time measured in terms of their market prices.

Measuring the GNP

The U.S. Department of Commerce is responsible for measuring and reporting the nation's GNP. The GNP is calculated by adding up the market value of all the goods and services produced by all business firms and by all levels of government. In addition to the value of these

The dollar value of the thousands of new helicopters made at this plant each year represents only a fraction of a percentage of the GNP.

goods and services, the Commerce Department estimates and adds to the GNP the value of certain other types of production that have value but do not enter the marketplace. Examples of types of production that must be estimated are the rental value of all owner-occupied houses in the nation, the room and board that some workers are given as a part of their pay, and the value of home-grown, home-consumed food.

In measuring the GNP, the Commerce Department uses certain guidelines. Three of the most important are excluding certain items, avoiding double counting, and adjusting for inflation.

Certain items are excluded from the GNP because it is difficult to get accurate estimates of their market value. Among these items are do-it-yourself activities for which individuals do not get paid. For example, if Jan and Peter Carrero decide to tune up their own car rather than take it to a local garage, the value of their services is not computed in the GNP. The same holds true for the services done by people who mow their own lawns, paint their own homes, and do their own housecleaning. If these people paid others to perform these same activities, a dollar amount (market value) could easily be placed on these services. If individuals perform these services themselves, however, it is difficult to calculate their value in monetary terms.

In addition to excluding certain items, the Commerce Department makes sure that all items are counted only once. To do this, it includes the value of all *final* products. In other words, it does not compute the value of intermediate products that go into making goods. If such intermediate items were included, many items would be counted twice. For example, if both the total value of steel produced and the total value of automobiles produced were entered into the GNP, the value of the steel would be counted twice because a substantial portion of the value of an automobile is the steel used to produce it. Similarly, the Commerce Department would not include the value of the flour that goes into making bread, the wool that

goes into making sweaters, and the wood that goes into making baseball bats. Each of these items will be taken into account when the value of the final product is computed.

Another way of avoiding double counting is to include the value only of new goods. If secondhand goods were counted, many items might be counted two or three times. For example, suppose Ellen Tang buys a new car for $10,000 and sells it that same year for $9,000. If both the initial sale and the later sale were included, the reported value of the car would be $19,000 instead of the actual value of $10,000.

A third procedure that the government follows is adjusting for inflation. Inflation will be discussed in detail in the following chapter, but for our purposes here we will define it as a general rise in prices. Since GNP is a measure of the "dollar value" of goods and services produced, rising prices can cause an icrease in the GNP even when there is no actual increase in the goods and services produced. For example, if the inflation rate were 10 percent, a car that cost $10,000 last year would cost $11,000 this year. For each new car produced, an extra $1,000 would be added to the GNP, and the GNP would rise. However, this rise does not represent a rise in production and does not present a true picture of the economy. In fact, there actually could have been fewer cars produced this year than last year.

To compensate for distortions in the GNP caused by inflation, a special price index called the **GNP deflator** is used. GNP figures are usually presented in two forms. One set of figures is called "money GNP." These figures are based on current prices and are not adjusted for inflation. The other set is called "real GNP," or "GNP in constant dollars." These figures have been adjusted for inflation—that is, the increased dollar values that resulted from price increases and not from increases in production have been removed. This second set of figures is the one used in evaluating the economy's performance.

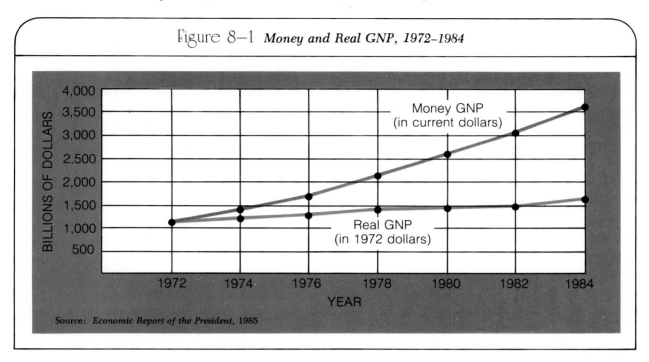

Figure 8–1 *Money and Real GNP, 1972–1984*

Source: *Economic Report of the President*, 1985

Figure 8–1 shows the two ways of presenting GNP figures. As you can see from this graph, money GNP increased at a much faster rate than did real GNP. If real GNP figures were not presented, we would get a very distorted view of the economy.

Check Your Understanding

1. What is the GNP? How is it calculated?

2. What are the three guidelines that the Commerce Department uses to measure the GNP?

3. Why is it necessary to adjust the GNP for inflation?

Other Measures of the Economy

Gross national product is the broadest and most widely used measure of the economy's performance. However, there are four other related measures—all derived from the GNP—that government officials and economists find very useful. They are net national product, national income, personal income, and disposable personal income. Let us briefly examine each of these related measures.

The **net national product** (NNP) is simply a refined measure of gross national product (GNP). It takes into account **depreciation,** or the "wear and tear," on the nation's capital goods—factories, tools, and machines. Depreciation calculations are based on the useful life of capital goods. For example, suppose a $10,000 machine has a useful life of ten years. This means that after a ten-year period the machine will be worn out and will have to be replaced. Assuming that the machine wears out at a steady rate, the depreciation will be $1,000 for each of the ten years.

The net national product is computed by subtracting from the gross national product the total value of the depreciation of all of the nation's capital goods during the year. In a sense, this gives a more realistic picture of the nation's economy since depreciation is a considerable production expense.

National income is an estimate of the total income earned in the economy in a year's time. It is calculated by subtracting a variety of sales taxes—called **indirect business taxes**—from the net national product. These taxes go to the government and not to the individuals and are therefore not considered income. For example, a part of the price of every gallon of gasoline sold goes to the federal and state governments in the form of excise taxes. Other indirect business taxes include property taxes and customs duties.

Income earned sometimes differs from income received. **Personal income** is the total income received by all persons in the nation before personal taxes are paid. In order to get from national income to personal income, we must subtract that portion of national income that does not go to households and add income that is received by households but is not a part of the current year's national income. Three categories of income that must be subtracted are undistributed corporate profits, corporate income taxes, and Social Security contributions. **Undistributed corporate profits** are those profits of corporations that are kept and reinvested in new plants and equipment. Since these funds are not distributed to stockholders, no individuals receive them as income. Also, both corporate income taxes and Social Security contributions go to the government instead of to individuals.

The one category of income that must be added to national income in order to get personal income is called transfer payments. **Transfer payments** include all sources of income to individuals that do not represent current income earned by them for producing goods and services. Examples of transfer payments are Social Security benefits, private pension benefits, unemployment compensation, and welfare payments.

Disposable personal income is the amount of money that individuals have available for spending after personal taxes are paid. It is the amount left over when taxes are subtracted from personal income. Most of disposable per-

Americans spend their disposable personal income on necessities such as food, clothing, and shelter as well as on luxuries such as vacations, VCRs, and new cars.

sonal income is spent for personal consumption. That portion not spent for consumption is called personal savings.

TABLE 8–1: GROSS NATIONAL PRODUCT AND RELATED MEASURES

GROSS NATIONAL PRODUCT
    Minus: Depreciation
            Equals

NET NATIONAL PRODUCT
    Minus: Indirect Business Taxes
            Equals

NATIONAL INCOME
    Minus: Undistributed Corporate Profits
               Corporate Income Taxes
               Social Security Contributions
    Plus: Transfer Payments
            Equals

PERSONAL INCOME
    Minus: Personal Taxes
            Equals

DISPOSABLE PERSONAL INCOME

Table 8–1 summarizes the relationship between gross national product, net national product, national income, personal income, and disposable personal income. Each of these measures is important. However, gross national product is the most basic measure, and we want to devote the remainder of the chapter to this vital economic indicator.

Check Your Understanding

1. How does GNP differ from NNP?

2. How is national income determined?

3. What are the four adjustments that must be made in order to get from national income to personal income?

4. What is disposable personal income?

Uses of GNP

GNP figures are used to make comparisons over time and among countries. Let us examine the nature of such comparisons.

Comparisons Over Time

GNP is a measure of the speed of the economy. Just as a speedometer on a car can tell the driver whether he or she is driving at, below, or above the speed limit, the annual rate of growth of the GNP adjusted for inflation can tell policy makers whether the GNP is growing too fast, too slowly, or at the proper level.

GNP figures are calculated and reported each quarter, or three-month period, of the year, to enable economists to project economic growth for the entire year. In other words, based on the figures for a particular quarter, economists can calculate how much production would take place in a year's time if the economy were to continue producing for the entire year at that same rate. For example, the Commerce Department might report that during the first quarter, January through March, the GNP was growing at a real annual rate of 4 percent. This means that if the economy continues to operate for the rest of the year at the first-quarter rate, the gross national product for the entire year, adjusted for inflation, will increase by 4 percent.

The rate of growth of the GNP is used by policy makers to determine what kinds of economic policies are needed. As you will learn later in this chapter and in the next chapter, if the GNP grows too slowly, or actually declines, there will be an increase in the number of workers unemployed. Similarly, if the GNP grows too rapidly, there may be an increase in inflation. Economists watch the rate of growth of the GNP very closely in an effort to forecast the future performance of the economy. If they think the GNP is growing too slowly, they recommend economic policies that will contribute to increased growth. If the GNP seems to be growing too rapidly, economists will recommend policies to slow it down.

GNP statistics are also sometimes used to make comparisons over longer periods of time in an effort to measure economic welfare. However, this is a questionable use of the GNP because GNP statistics used for this purpose can be misleading. For example, real GNP adjusted for inflation in 1980 was approximately double that of 1960. Does this mean that Americans were living twice as well in 1980 as they were 20 years earlier? Not necessarily, because the negative effects of production were not taken into account. As economic production increases, there are many social costs that don't show up in the GNP statistics. For example, air, water, and land pollution, the defacing of beautiful landscapes, and the crowded conditions of cities and towns are all by-products of industrial production. Many people believe that these and many other social costs should be subtracted from the GNP if it is to be used as a measure of economic welfare.

Furthermore, a substantial portion of the GNP includes the production of things that many people believe have a negative effect on life. The production of cigarettes, pornography, and nuclear weapons counts the same in GNP calculation as does the production of education, medical care, and food. Most people probably would agree that each of these items does not contribute equally to national welfare per dollar's worth of production. Yet, in GNP calculation they are all equal. Therefore, using the GNP to measure economic welfare is questionable at best.

Comparisons Between Countries

Although GNP figures are frequently used to make comparisons between countries, there are problems with making such comparisons. First of all, it is impossible to get comparable statistics for any two coutnries because each country has its own monetary unit and its own way of calculating production. In addition, there is the problem of different lifestyles in different countries. The lifestyle of a traditional economy is so different from that of the United States that GNP comparisons between the United States and such a country would not be very meaningful. For example, there are places in the world where nomadic tribes move from place to place, carrying their total worldly possessions with them. They have little or no cash but their environment provides them with everything they need. Given the lifestyle of these people, it would be difficult to prove that they are only one twentieth as well off as Americans just because the GNP of their nation is lower than that of the United States. In some nations with low GNPs there is widespread poverty and sometimes starvation. In such nations the GNP does reflect prevailing economic conditions.

Despite the above-mentioned problems, GNP comparisons between countries sometimes can provide useful information. For example, by comparing the rate of growth of the GNP in the United States with that of other major industrial nations, we can get some idea as to how well our economy is performing in relation to the other major economies of the world. If we find that our economy is not performing as well as another major industrial economy—Japan, for example—we might want to analyze it in an effort to find out why the other economy is outperforming our own.

Furthermore, we can get some idea of the economic well-being of various nations if we make GNP comparisons between countries with similar characteristics. For example, we might compare the GNPs of the various rural nonindustrial nations of the world. Of course, in making such comparisons we must take into consideration the differences in population of the various countries or we might jump to the wrong conclusions. For example, suppose we are told that two countries have the same GNP. Initially, we might conclude that both are equally well off. However, if we find out that

In a country where many people live in a traditional economy, the GNP is likely to be much lower than in an industrialized nation. However, making comparisons between developing and industrial nations must take into account the differing lifestyles of the people.

one country has a population of 20 million while the other has a population of 200 million, we would probably revise our conclusions. Therefore, for comparison purposes we divide each nation's GNP by its population in order to calculate the GNP per person.

Generally, if we select two nations with similar overall characteristics and find that one nation has a much larger GNP per person than the other, we can conclude that the nation with the larger GNP per person probably is better off economically. However, as we already have mentioned, such comparisons will hold true only for countries with similar lifestyles. Making comparisons between countries with very different lifestyles is not very meaningful.

Check Your Understanding

1. What are the most important uses of GNP?

2. Why is GNP not a good measure of economic welfare? Give some examples.

3. Can meaningful GNP comparisons be made between countries? Explain.

Determining the Level of GNP

The rate of growth of the GNP is very important. If the GNP grows too rapidly, it may cause increased inflation. If it grows too slowly or actually declines, there will be an increase in the number of people unemployed. What determines the level of GNP? The answer to this question is very simple. The level of total spending determines the level of GNP. What determines the level of total spending? We will examine the answer to this question in detail in this chapter and in the chapters that follow.

Before beginning our analysis of the factors that determine the gross national product, let us look at the factors that determine production in a single factory. Understanding production on such a small scale will help you to understand how the production of the entire economy is determined.

Suppose the Pedal-Power Bicycle Company normally sells 100 bicycles per week. Since the company does not want to produce more bicycles than it can sell, it also produces approximately 100 bicycles per week. The company knows that sales can fluctuate up or down, and it doesn't want to be caught in the position of losing sales because it has not produced enough bicycles. Therefore, the company maintains an inventory of 300 bicycles in a warehouse. If there should be a sudden temporary increase in the demand for its bicycles, the company could sell its warehouse reserves.

With a reserve inventory of 300 bicycles, there is no reason for the company to produce more bicycles than it is currently selling. Thus, if sales of bicycles should decline from 100 per week to 80 per week, the company would probably lay off some of its workers and reduce its production accordingly. If sales should further decline to 60 bicycles per week, the company would lay off still more workers and reduce its production to 60 bicycles per week.

On the other hand, if sales of bicycles should increase from 100 per week to 130 per week and continue at that level for several weeks, the company probably would hire additional workers and attempt to increase its production to 130 per week. The company could temporarily get the additional 30 bicycles per week from its warehouse. If sales continued at 130 per week, however, the warehouse supply would be depleted in just ten weeks. Long before that happened, the company would increase its production to meet the increased demand for its bicycles.

In summary, the Pedal-Power Bicycle Company's production of bicycles will be determined by its sales. Over the long run, it will produce just as many bicycles as it can sell at a profitable price. If customers increase their spending on bicycles, the company will increase its production of bicycles. If customers decrease their spending on bicycles, the Pedal-Power Bicycle Company will lay off workers and reduce its production.

What is true of the Pedal-Power Bicycle Company is also true of the economy as a whole. Just as the Pedal-Power Bicycle Company will increase or decrease production and the size of its work force depending on the relationship of sales to the level of production, the nation, too, will adjust production and the number of workers employed when total spending rises or falls compared to the production level. In other words, if total spending in the economy increases, total production (GNP) also will increase. If total spending decreases, total production (GNP) also will decrease.

The total spending in the American economy can be calculated by adding up the spending in three different sectors of the economy. These are consumption, investment, and government. There is also a foreign sector, but for purposes of our current analysis we will assume that the amount of goods and services Americans purchase from foreign countries (imports) is offset by an equal amount of American goods and services sold to foreign nations (exports). This assumption allows us also to assume that the total production of goods and services (GNP) will be available for consumption, investment, and government.

Because these three sectors are so important, we will examine each carefully. We will look at the factors that determine each, as well as the effects that each has on GNP.

Consumption

Consumption spending involves the purchase of consumer goods and services. As you learned in Chapter 1, consumer goods and services are things that consumers buy for their own personal use, such as food, clothing, medical care, and entertainment. The purchase of stocks and bonds by consumers is *not* consumption spending. Consumption spending includes only those purchases that consumers make for their own personal use.

Consumption is the largest component of the GNP, with nearly two thirds of the GNP going for consumption each year (see Figure 8–2). Because of the relative size of consumption, changes in consumption have the biggest effect on the level of GNP. Let us examine some factors that determine consumption spending.

Income The most important determinant of consumption, both for an individual and for the nation as a whole, is the amount of income that the individual or the population as a whole receives. When a person receives income, he or she must first pay taxes. After all tax obligations have been paid, the amount of remaining income (disposable personal income) may be spent or saved, and most people do some of both. The larger the percentage of income saved, the smaller the amount left for consumption spending.

If individuals decide to save more or to save less than they usually do, a change in consumption can take place even when there is no change in income. However, the major factor that causes changes in consumption is a change in income. If the GNP is declining and large

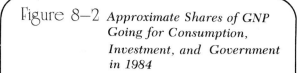

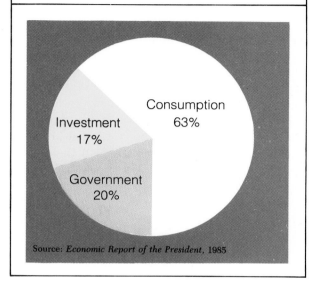

Figure 8–2 *Approximate Shares of GNP Going for Consumption, Investment, and Government in 1984*

Investment 17%

Consumption 63%

Government 20%

Source: *Economic Report of the President, 1985*

numbers of workers are losing their jobs, there will be a substantial reduction in consumption spending. As consumption spending declines, GNP will decline even further and still more workers will become unemployed. In other words, a decline in the GNP will cause a reduction in income and in consumption spending, and the drop in consumption spending will cause an even bigger decline in the GNP. Economists use the term **recession** to describe periods when the GNP is declining and unemployment is rising. If the GNP falls to a very low level and remains there for a prolonged period of time while large numbers of people are unemployed, the term **depression** is used to describe the situation.

In addition to current income, individuals sometimes use past and future income for consumption expenditures. Past income takes the form of savings that have accumulated from previous income that was not spent. Future income takes the form of borrowed money that will have to be repaid with future earnings. Individuals who are unemployed for extended periods of time often have to use part or all of their savings and may have to borrow additional money for living expenses.

Expectations The expectations consumers have about the future also play an important role in determining consumption spending. If individuals become fearful that they will be laid off in the near future, they may cut back on their current consumption expenditures in an effort to save money. Although this is rational behavior for an individual, such behavior on the part of large numbers of people may very well cause them to lose their jobs. Cutbacks in spending because of a fear of unemployment will be matched by a reduction in production, which will result in the increased unemployment that the people fear.

Expectations of future inflation also can affect consumer spending. As we mentioned earlier, for purposes of our current analysis inflation can be defined as a general rise in prices. Put another way, inflation is a general reduction in the value, or purchasing power, of money.

As you will learn in the following chapter, the economy usually experiences increased inflation as it approaches the full-employment level of GNP. At such times, the economy is producing as much as it can, and any increase in spending usually causes prices to rise. Yet, the very fear of inflation often causes consumers to behave in such a way that they actually bring it about. If people fear substantial price increases in the near future, they may go on a spending spree in an effort to buy as many consumer goods and services as possible before these goods and services become so expensive that they no longer can afford them. This increased demand on their part, however, causes prices to rise even further.

In summary, if consumers expect increased unemployment in the near future, their attempt to prepare for it by reducing their consumption expenditures actually may cause the increased unemployment that they fear. If consumers fear increased inflation, their increased consumption expenditures actually may help to bring it about. In both cases, consumer expectations bring about the very occurrence that the consumers are trying to avoid.

Taxes Taxes are a third important determinant of consumption expenditures because they determine the amount of disposable personal income available to individuals. Any increase in taxes will result in a reduction in both disposable personal income and consumption expenditures. Any decrease in taxes will result in increased disposable personal income and, usually, increased consumption expenditures. This relationship between taxes and consumption provides the government with a very useful device for regulating the level of the GNP. If the government wants to increase the level of the GNP, it can reduce taxes, thereby giving consumers more money to spend. If the government wishes to reduce the growth of the GNP, it can raise taxes, which in effect reduces the spending power of consumers.

Investment

The term "investment" can be used two ways. We commonly think of investment as putting money into stocks and bonds. Thus, if you buy 100 shares of stock in a company, you will have invested in that corporation. This type of investment is personal investment. When economists talk about investment in the economy, however, they are referring to the spending for capital goods (factories, tools, and machines) to increase production in our economy. It is investment in the economy that we are concerned with here.

The amount of investment that will take place in the economy during any given time period depends primarily on two factors: (1) the availability of potentially profitable investment opportunities and (2) the cost and availability of investment funds. Let us examine each of these.

Availability of investment opportunities The availability of profitable investment opportunities depends on a number of factors. First and foremost among these is consumer demand. If an automobile company is unable to sell the cars that it is currently producing, there is no incentive for it to build new factories or buy new machines.

Government tax policies are also a factor that helps to determine the amount of investment that will take place. If business tax rates are high, businesses will have less after-tax profits and less incentive to invest. On the other hand, if businesses are offered tax incentives to invest, they are more likely to increase their investment.

The cost of new capital goods is a third factor that helps to determine investment. If the cost of new capital goods is too high, businesses may delay investment hoping that new technology will cause the price of these goods to drop. A decline in prices will spur increased investment.

New inventions and new technology are still other determinants of investment opportunities. Historically, periods of high investment in our economy usually have coincided with the development of new products and new technology. The invention of the automobile led to massive amounts of investment in factories, tools, and machines for the mass production of automobiles. The expansion in the automobile industry continued for many years. More recently, the electronics industry, including computers, has provided good opportunities for new investment.

Because the invention of new products and the development of new industries is somewhat sporadic, good investment opportunities are more plentiful in some time periods than in others. Since investment is one of the three basic determinants of the GNP, fluctuations in investment spending can cause fluctuations in the GNP.

Cost and availability of investment funds Much of the investment that takes place in the

An important measure of the economy's performance is investment in new construction.

United States is paid for with borrowed money. Therefore, the availability of loans and the interest rates that must be paid are important factors in determining the amount of investment that will take place in any given time period. In making investment decisions, businesses calculate the expected rate of return on the investment they are considering and compare it to the interest rate. The **rate of return** is the percentage of the total investment that the business gets back each year from the investment. For example, suppose a business makes its profits by renting out garden equipment. If the business pays $1,000 for a new heavy-duty rotary tiller and is able to earn $100 per year by renting out the tiller to customers, the rate of return on the investment is 10 percent.

Would the purchase of the tiller be a profitable investment? It depends on the interest rate. Suppose the business borrowed the $1,000 from a bank and had to pay 10 percent interest on the loan. In this case, the interest cost would be $100 per year, which is exactly the amount it receives from renting out the machine. Thus, with a 10 percent rate of return and a 10 percent interest rate, the business would not earn any profit at all, so this would not be a profitable investment.

What if the business could earn $200 per year in rent from the tiller and the interest rate was only 8 percent? In this case, since the rate of return (20 percent) is substantially above the 8 percent interest rate, the investment would be profitable.

As you will learn in later chapters when we examine the American banking system, interest rates vary a great deal from one time period to another. Also, the government has the power to raise or lower interest rates and to increase or decrease the amount of loanable funds available. Generally, the availability of loanable funds at low interest rates will tend to encourage businesses to increase their investment spending. A decreased availability of loanable funds accompanied by high interest rates usually will result in a decrease in investment.

Government Spending

Government spending, the sums the government spends on goods and services, is a major determinant of the gross national product, accounting for approximately 20 percent of the GNP each year. This includes all levels of government—from the federal government all the way down to village and township governments.

Changes in government spending can have a substantial effect on the GNP and on unemployment and inflation. If the economy is operating below the full-employment level, the government can increase spending in an effort to cause the GNP to rise and unemployment to decline. On the other hand, if the economy is operating at the full-employment level with GNP growing so fast that increased inflation is imminent, the government can attempt to reduce the danger of inflation by reducing government spending and slowing the growth of the GNP.

Check Your Understanding

1. What determines the level of GNP?

2. What are the three major components of total spending in the American economy?

3. What are the major determinants of consumption spending? How do changes in each affect the spending power of consumers?

4. What two factors determine the level of investment spending? How does each operate?

5. How important is government spending in determining the level of GNP?

BIOGRAPHY   Paul Samuelson

(1915—   )

Paul Samuelson, who in 1970 became the first American to receive a Nobel Prize in economics, is one of the world's most widely known economists, and some would argue that he is the greatest contemporary economist. Millions of college students both in the United States and abroad have used his introductory textbook, which first appeared nearly 40 years ago. In addition, millions of readers of American and foreign newspapers and magazines have been influenced by his articles on economic policies.

Samuelson received a bachelor's degree from the University of Chicago in 1935 and a doctorate in economics from Harvard University in 1941. At the age of 32, he became a full professor at Massachusetts Institute of Technology. Professional economists throughout the world have studied and been led toward further research by the extraordinary range of Samuelson's scientific work, which includes hundreds of papers and several books. Samuelson pioneered the use of mathematics in economics. His first book *Foundations of Economic Analysis* (1947), gave precise mathematical meaning to much of economic reasoning, thus breaking new ground by making economics a more precise and scientific discipline.

Samuelson has been a leading spokesman for Keynesian economics, a school of economic thought named after the British economist John Maynard Keynes. He also has been a leading critic of another school of economic thought known as monetarism. Samuelson believes that the government can and should use its spending and taxing powers to influence the level of total spending in the economy to control unemployment and inflation.

Equilibrium GNP

As you have just learned, the level of the GNP will depend on the total spending for consumption, investment, and government. Any time there is a change in the level of spending, the GNP will begin to move toward the new level of spending. When the GNP is exactly equal to the level of total spending, the economy is in equilibrium.

As you will remember from our analysis of supply and demand in Chapter 3, equilibrium is a point of rest. Once the GNP has reached the equilibrium level, there will be no tendency for it to change until total spending changes.

GNP is the *total supply* of goods and services. Consumption plus investment plus government spending is the *total demand* for goods and services. **Equilibrium GNP** is that level of GNP at which the *total demand* (consumption plus investment plus government spending) is equal to the *total supply* (GNP).

Don't make the mistake of assuming that equilibrium GNP is always desirable. Equilibrium simply means a point of rest, and equilibrium GNP simply means that the GNP is remaining at its current level and that there is no tendency for it to change in either direction. Equilibrium GNP is good only if the current level of GNP is the most desirable level.

When your car comes to a halt, it is in equilibrium. Is that good? Not necessarily. If the car runs out of gas and comes to a halt ten miles from your home, it is not at a good equilibrium point. You wanted it to take you home before it came to a stop. Your car also could go too far before reaching equilibrium. Suppose the brakes fail as you drive into your garage and the car goes crashing through the garage before coming to a halt in your backyard. This time the car went too far before reaching equilibrium. You are not content to have the car simply come to a halt. You want it to stop when, and only when, it has reached the desired destination.

The same is true of the economy. We are not content to simply have the GNP in equilibrium. Certainly, if large numbers of people are unemployed we don't want the GNP to be in equilibrium. When there is high unemployment, we want the GNP to be growing. Moreover, we want it to continue to grow until we reach full employment without excessive inflation. This is our overriding goal. Then, and only then, do we want the GNP to be in equilibrium.

Check Your Understanding

1. What are the necessary conditions for equilibrium GNP?

2. Why is equilibrium GNP not always the desirable position for the economy?

3. Under what conditions is equilibrium GNP desirable?

Economic Growth

As you have just learned, one of the goals of economic policy is to operate the economy at the full-employment level of GNP without inflation. That will enable our economy to produce as many goods and services as possible with our limited productive resources. Another goal is economic growth. **Economic growth** can be defined as an increase in full-employment real GNP (adjusted for inflation) over time. In other words, economic growth means that the economy's capacity to produce goods and services is increasing.

Economic growth is very important because it makes possible improvements in the standard of living. The **standard of living** can be defined as the quality of life of a society based on the amount of goods and services, leisure time, and so forth that its people have. Countries with more goods and services, leisure time, and so forth have a higher standard of living than countries with fewer of these things. The United States has one of the highest standards of living in the world.

If there is no growth in the productive capacity of the economy and no growth in the population, the overall standard of living for a nation as a whole would remain constant. This means that an improvement in the standard of living for any individual or group of individuals could come only at the expense of a reduced standard of living for another individual or group of individuals in the society. If there is growth in the population at a time when there is no growth in real GNP, there will be a reduction in the overall standard of living. This is true because the fixed quantity of goods and services will have to be divided among more people. Thus, it is important not only that there be some economic growth but that the economic growth be greater than the growth in the population.

The Determinants of Economic Growth

The rate of economic growth depends primarily on the quantity and quality of the basic factors of production—natural resources, capital goods, and labor—and on the efficiency with which these factors of production are used. Let us first examine the role that each of the factors of production plays in economic growth, and then we will examine the problem of *productivity*, which deals with resource efficiency.

Natural resources The quantity and quality of natural resources—land, water, forests, mineral deposits, and so forth—are a crucial determinant of potential economic growth. They are the starting point of all production, and thus they represent the most basic limitation on the productive capacity of an economy. If an economy has a shortage of natural resources, it will have very limited growth potential even if it is well-endowed with capital goods and labor. Fortunately, the United States has substantial natural resources compared to many other nations. However, we do not have an inexhaustible supply, and some critics fear that we are using them up so rapidly that future generations will suffer. Certainly, we need to find ways to employ our scarce natural resources as efficiently as possible.

Capital goods As you already know, capital goods are human-made resources that are used for the production of other goods and services. Capital goods include such things as factories, machines, tools, railroads, trucks, and business buildings. Without capital goods, natural resources are not very useful. We need more than fertile soil to produce an adequate food supply for the nation and surplus food for sale to foreign countries. We also need tractors, plows, mechanical planters, harvesting machines, and so forth. The United States has concentrated much effort on the production of capital goods.

When an economy is operating at the maximum, full-employment capacity, the only way to increase the production of capital goods is to reduce the production of consumer goods. The increased production of capital goods will, in turn, increase the total productive capacity of the economy. In other words, the newly produced capital goods will enable the economy to produce both more capital goods and more consumer goods in the future. The production of capital goods is important in order to maintain a strong rate of economic growth.

Labor Both the quantity and the quality of labor play important roles in determining potential economic growth. The quantity of labor depends on the size of the population, the age structure of the population, and the labor force participation rate. The quality of labor depends on the health as well as the educational and skill levels of the labor force.

In the United States, the population has grown from year to year, and more people have become part of the labor force. In addition, medical care has improved as a result of advances in science. Moreover, educational levels have been rising as more and more people choose to get a college degree. Along with education has come an increase in the skill levels of the population. The United States has benefited from a sizable healthy, well-educated, and highly skilled labor force. To promote continued economic growth, we must make sure that educational and skill levels keep pace with the changing needs of the economy.

The Productivity Problem

The efficiency with which labor is combined with the other factors of production determines labor productivity, which is an important determinant of economic growth. Specifically, **labor productivity** can be defined as the amount of output produced by a given quantity of labor. The more output a nation can get from its labor force, the greater will be its economic growth.

The quantity and quality of capital goods available to the labor force are important determinants of labor productivity. For example, the amount of snow that can be removed by one person in one hour depends on the equipment used. Someone equipped with only a snow

Both the horse drawn plow, above, and the mechanized harvester, below, are capital goods. However, the harvester greatly increases the productivity of the natural resource—the soil.

shovel cannot remove much snow from city streets in an hour. However, the same person equipped with a mechanical snow blower or a giant snow plow can remove a great deal of snow in that same period of time.

Increased research and increased investment in new technology are crucial to growth in labor productivity. American agriculture provides an excellent example of what can be accomplished with improved technology. In 1820, the average American farmer produced enough food to support only four people. How-

ever, by 1980, this figure rose to more than 60 people. This remarkable growth in agricultural productivity resulted primarily from the fact that extensive research yielded new and more efficient methods of food production. Because of these productivity gains, food prices in the United States are much lower than they otherwise would be. (See Figure 8-3.)

Unfortunately, many areas of production, including the heavy industries such as the steel industry, have not experienced the same kinds of growth in productivity as agriculture. As a

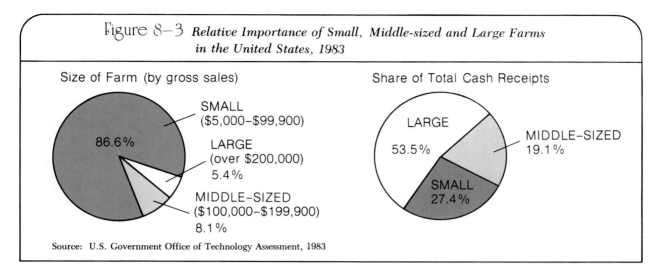

Figure 8–3 *Relative Importance of Small, Middle-sized and Large Farms in the United States, 1983*

Size of Farm (by gross sales)

SMALL ($5,000–$99,900)
86.6%

LARGE (over $200,000) 5.4%

MIDDLE-SIZED ($100,000–$199,900) 8.1%

Share of Total Cash Receipts

LARGE 53.5%

MIDDLE-SIZED 19.1%

SMALL 27.4%

Source: U.S. Government Office of Technology Assessment, 1983

result, production costs in these industries are higher in the United States than in some other countries, making it difficult for the United States to compete effectively in world markets. The cost of producing everything from automobiles to TV sets to shoes has been so high in the United States that equivalent imported items are often less expensive, despite the high transportation costs required to get them to American markets.

Some economists believe that inefficient management and labor practices have been major contributors to low growth in labor productivity in recent years. For example, they suggest that management and unions have often put too much emphasis on making gains at one another's expense and too little emphasis on working together to increase output so that both could benefit. Regardless of the causes of low labor productivity, there is general agreement that ways must be found to increase it if we want to have sustained economic growth in the future. Obviously, there is no single solution. However, efforts to increase productivity should include increased research and investment in new technology, upgrading the skill and educational levels of the labor force to match the new technology, and incentives to encourage increased efforts by workers.

Environmental Considerations

Unfortunately, there is often a conflict between the goal of economic growth and the goal of a clean environment. Americans have become increasingly aware that increased economic growth can lead to increased pollution. In recent years, problems of water, air, and land pollution have led to laws for the protection of the environment being passed at both the state and federal levels. In Chapter 14, we will examine the problems of pollution and the environment in some detail.

Check Your Understanding

1. What is economic growth?

2. Is economic growth alone sufficient for an economy? Explain.

3. What are the determinants of economic growth? What role does each one play?

4. What is labor productivity? What is the "productivity problem"?

CAREERS: Actuary

Have you ever wondered why young people pay more for automobile insurance than older people but older people pay more for life insurance than young people? Are you curious about how insurance companies decide what rate to charge different groups and individuals for insurance coverage? If you become an actuary, you will help to provide the answers to these questions.

Actuaries design insurance and pension plans and make sure that these plans are maintained on a sound financial basis. They collect and analyze data to calculate the probabilities of death, sickness, injury, disability, accident, unemployment, retirement, and property loss. For example, they might calculate what percentage of male drivers between the ages of 16 and 25 are likely to have an automobile accident in any given year. Or, they might calculate how many 25-year-olds are likely to die before they reach age 65. They use this information to determine the amount insurance companies must charge in order to be able to pay off all claims and still earn a profit.

Actuaries usually specialize in life and health insurance, property and liability insurance, or pension plans. Most work for private insurance companies, although some work for private consulting firms and for the government. Actuaries who work for the federal government deal with special programs, such as Social Security or life insurance for veterans or current members of the armed forces. Actuaries employed by state governments regulate insurance companies, supervise the operations of state retirement or pension systems, and deal with unemployment insurance and workers' compensation programs.

A strong background in mathematics is essential for anyone wishing to choose this career. A bachelor's degree with a major in mathematics, statistics, or actuarial science is usually required, although some companies hire applicants with a major in engineering, economics, or business administration, provided that they have a good working knowledge of advanced mathematics. In addition, you may need to pass one or more of the examinations offered by professional actuarial societies. Three societies—The Society of Actuaries, the Casualty Actuarial Society, and the American Society of Pension Actuaries—sponsor programs leading to full professional status in their specialty.

Chapter Highlights

1   The most basic and comprehensive measure of the nation's economic performance is the gross national product (GNP). GNP is the total dollar value of all goods and services produced in a year's time measured in terms of their market prices.

2   In measuring the GNP, the Commerce Department excludes certain items, avoids double counting, and adjusts the GNP for inflation.

3   Four useful related measures that can be derived from GNP are net national product, national income, personal income, and disposable personal income.

4   The GNP is used to make comparisons of an economy's performance over time to help policy makers formulate sound economic policies for a nation. It also is used to compare countries with similar lifestyles to get an idea of their economic well-being.

5   The rate of growth of the GNP is very important. If the GNP grows too slowly or declines, there will be an increase in the number of people unemployed. If the GNP grows too rapidly, it can cause inflation.

6   The level of GNP is determined by the level of total spending in the consumption, investment, and government sectors of the economy.

7   Consumption spending is dependent on consumer incomes and taxes and on consumer expectations about the future.

8   Investment spending is dependent on the availability of potentially profitable investment opportunities and on the cost and availability of investment funds.

9   Since government spending is a large component of GNP, changes in government spending can have a substantial effect on GNP and on unemployment and/or inflation.

10 Equilibrium GNP exists when the total demand (consumption plus investment plus government spending) is equal to the total supply (GNP).

11 The desired goal is for the GNP to be in equilibrium at the full-employment level without excessive inflation.

12 Economic growth is very important because it makes possible improvements in the standard of living. Determinants of economic growth include the quantity and quality of natural resources, capital goods, and labor. Labor productivity also is an important determinant of economic growth.

Important Terms

Match each of the following terms with the correct definition:

disposable personal income
consumption spending
gross national product
net national product
standard of living

national income
personal income
GNP deflator
depreciation
economic growth

government spending
investment spending
transfer payments
equilibrium GNP
labor productivity

1. All sources of income to individuals that do not represent current income earned for the production of goods and services.

2. The amount of output produced by a given quantity of labor.

3. The wear and tear of the nation's factories, tools, and machines that results from producing the GNP.

4. NNP minus indirect business taxes.

5. The quality of life of a society is based on the amount of the goods and services, leisure time, and so forth that its people have.

6. That level of GNP at which the total supply of goods and services is exactly equal to total spending.

7. The total income received by all persons before personal taxes are paid.

8. The increase in full-employment real GNP over time.

9. A special price index used to compensate for distortions in the GNP caused by inflation.

10. The purchase of consumer goods and services by consumers for their own personal use.

11. GNP minus depreciation.

12. The total spending by all levels of government.

13. The amount of income remaining after all taxes have been paid.

14. Business spending for factories, tools, and machines.

15. The total dollar value of all goods and services produced in a year's time measured in terms of their market prices.

Extending Your Understanding

1. Based on what you have learned in this chapter, what recommendations would you make for correcting a problem of inadequate growth in GNP? What should be done if GNP is growing too rapidly?
2. Why is economic growth so important? What can be done to increase economic growth?

Activities

1. Look through recent issues of news magazines and business magazines for statistics on the gross national product for the past quarter. Is the GNP growing or declining? What do economists say about the rate of growth? What sorts of predictions are they making?
2. Make a chart showing the pros and cons of economic growth. Consider such benefits as the resulting increase in the standard of living, as well as drawbacks such as an increase in pollution.

Building Skills in Economics: Reading a Bar Graph

Like pie graphs, bar graphs often are used for making comparisons. Unlike pie graphs, they usually do not show percentages of a whole. Rather, they show how each bar compares with the others.

The bars on a bar graph can be either horizontal or vertical. In a horizontal bar graph, the scale usually will be on the bottom. In a vertical bar graph, it usually will be on the lefthand side. The scale consists of the range of numerical values covered by the bars.

The bar graph that follows shows the GNPs of selected Western European countries in a recent year. The questions will help you interpret the graph.

Applying Economics Skills

1. Is this a horizontal or a vertical bar graph? Where is the scale located?
2. Which country shown here has the highest GNP? Approximately how large is its GNP?
3. Which country has the lowest GNP? What would you estimate its GNP to be?
4. Which two countries have similar GNPs?
5. Given what you have read in the chapter, what kinds of conclusions can you draw?

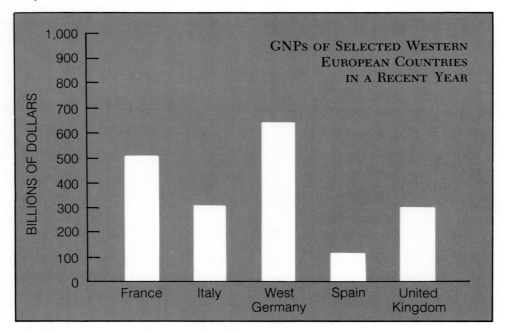

GNPs OF SELECTED WESTERN EUROPEAN COUNTRIES IN A RECENT YEAR

CHAPTER 9

BUSINESS CYCLES, UNEMPLOYMENT, AND INFLATION

In Chapter 8, you learned a great deal about the gross national product, the most basic and comprehensive measure of the nation's economic performance. You learned that the level of the GNP is determined primarily by the level of total spending for consumption, investment, and government, and that the rate of growth of the GNP is very important. If the GNP grows too slowly or actually declines, there will be an increase in the number of people unemployed. On the other hand, if the GNP grows too rapidly, increased inflation will result. You also learned that the desired goal is for the GNP to be in equilibrium at the full-employment level with minimal inflation.

Unfortunately, the desired objective of full employment combined with little or no inflation is seldom, if ever, achieved. Fluctuations in the rate of growth of the GNP have been a major problem throughout our nation's history. Much of the time the GNP has grown either too rapidly, or too slowly, and at times it has actually declined. These fluctuations in economic activity—or business cycles, as they are often called—are very costly in terms of unemployment and inflation.

In this chapter, we want to examine carefully the problems of unemployment and inflation. We will examine the various types and causes of unemployment and inflation, as well as the effects each has on individuals and on the economy. We also will discuss ways of alleviating these problems. Since business cycles are the most important cause of unemployment and inflation, let us begin the chapter with a look at the phases and causes of business cycles.

Business Cycles

Business cycles are simply recurrent but irregular fluctuations in economic activity. These fluctuations may last for a few months or they may go on for several years. Some economists dislike the use of the word "cycle" to describe such fluctuations because cycle implies a certain degree of regularity. For example, the four seasons of the year might be thought of as a cycle. Business fluctuations, however, are not regular or predictable. Although real GNP (GNP adjusted for inflation) has grown at an average annual rate of approximately 3.5 percent during the past 50 years, this growth often has been very uneven. Real GNP has grown by as much as 8 percent during some short periods and has actually declined during other periods. Nevertheless, the term "business cycle" has become the most common name for fluctuations in economic activity.

Phases of the Business Cycle

Although business cycles are not regular, it is often helpful to use a hypothetical cycle to explain them. Such a hypothetical business cycle is presented in Figure 9–1. As you can see, there are four phases to a business cycle: the peak, the recession, the trough (pronounced "trof"), and the recovery. The cycle can begin anywhere and then will continue through the four phases. From the high point, the **peak,** the GNP begins to decline. Business activity begins to slow down, factories start laying off workers, and people have less money to spend. (Remember, total spending determines the GNP.) This downward phase is called the **recession,** or contraction. Economists usually define a recession as a period of at least six months of continued decline in real GNP. The recession ends when GNP stops falling and levels off into the phase known as the **trough.** The trough will last until the cycle shows signs of **recovery.** During the recovery phase, there is economic expansion, laid-off workers are called

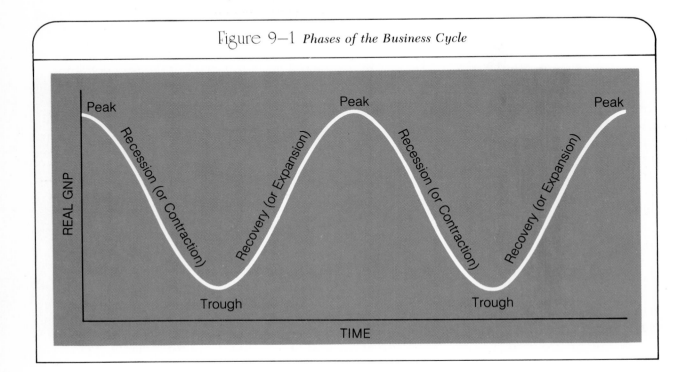

Figure 9–1 *Phases of the Business Cycle*

In the 1930s, the nation tumbled into the Great Depression. As business activity slowed, tens of thousands of businesses had to close.

back to their jobs, and overall unemployment declines. This economic upturn will last only so long, however. Once the GNP reaches a new peak, it will be just a matter of time until a new recession and a new business cycle begin.

Remember that Figure 9–1 represents only a hypothetical version of the business cycle. In actual practice, the phases of a business cycle are not of equal length. A recovery or a recession may last for a few months or it may last for a few years. A severe recession, which results in a prolonged period of little or no growth in the GNP, accompanied by high unemployment, is usually referred to as a **depression.** The Great Depression of the 1930s is the most well-known example in our nation's history.

Causes of Business Cycles

What causes business cycles? There is no easy answer to this question. The cause (or causes) of business cycles has long been the source of disagreement among economists. Perhaps the best answer is that anything that results in a major change in any of the components of total spend-ing—consumption spending, investment spending, and government spending—can contribute to a business cycle. For example, as you learned in Chapter 8, new inventions and new technology help to determine the availability of good investment opportunities. Many economists believe that the expansion phase of many past business cycles resulted from the heavy investment spending that was triggered by new inventions, new technology, the discovery of new mineral deposits, or the opening of new frontiers.

Political events and social upheavals also have been cited as major factors in some past business cycles. For example, some economists believe that World War II led to recovery from the Great Depression of the 1930s. The massive government spending on American war efforts helped to get factories running again, giving people jobs and money to spend on goods and services. Similarly, the Arab oil embargo in 1973–74 has been cited by many economists as a major factor contributing to the severe recession of 1974–75. After the oil-producing nations raised their prices and restricted oil shipments, prices of crude oil and oil-related products rose

The Arab oil embargo resulted in long lines at gas stations and restrictions on when motorists could buy gas. The fuel shortage and accompanying price rise also contributed to the recession of the mid-1970s.

dramatically. Because people had to spend more money on energy, they had less money to spend on other things.

Regardless of their causes, the beginning, the intensity, and the duration of the phases of business cycles are unpredictable. As a result, it is difficult to know what measures should be taken to prevent those consequences that can severely damage the economy—the high unemployment that can take place during the recession (or contraction) phase, and increased inflation that often occurs during the recovery (or expansion) phase. We will examine these two consequences of business cycles in the next section.

Check Your Understanding

1. What are business cycles?

2. What are the four phases of the business cycle?

3. What are some of the causes of business cycles?

Unemployment

Perhaps the most tragic of all economic problems is the problem of unemployment. During periods of high unemployment, millions of Americans find themselves without work, often through no fault of their own. They are without sufficient income to maintain their normal lifestyles; and some lose their savings, their automobiles, and their homes. In addition to the financial hardship, the unemployed experience a great deal of emotional and psychological pain. The inability to provide for their families causes the unemployed to lose self-esteem, and in some cases can lead to mental illness or even to suicide.

Are periods of high unemployment an inevitable part of American life? The answer to this question is a qualified no. As you will learn in this and the following chapter, some unemployment is unavoidable. However, we can attempt to avoid high unemployment for extended periods of time by following sound economic policies. As a first step toward understanding unemployment, let us see how unemployment is measured.

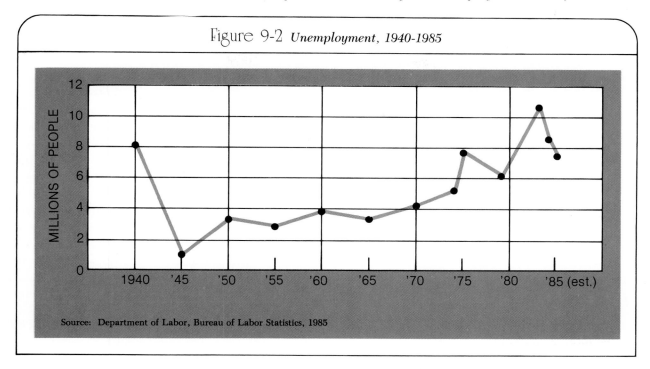

Figure 9-2 *Unemployment, 1940-1985*

Source: Department of Labor, Bureau of Labor Statistics, 1985

Measuring Unemployment

If the government announces that during a specific month 10 million Americans were unemployed, does this mean that the government actually counted each and every one of the 10 million unemployed people? If your mother or father was unemployed during that month, can you be sure that he or she was actually counted? The answer to both questions is no. It would be extremely difficult and very expensive for the government to count each and every unemployed worker every month. Instead, the government estimates the number of unemployed workers on the basis of a large sample survey.

Every month the Bureau of the Census conducts a sample survey of about 60,000 American households to determine the employment status of the members of these households. The sample includes households in every part of the country, and it is chosen very carefully so that it will be as representative of the total population as possible. The United States Department of Labor then uses the results of

this survey to estimate the employment status of the American population as a whole. Since the sample is large and very carefully selected, the estimate of the employment status for the nation as a whole is probably pretty accurate. (See Figure 9-2.)

In measuring unemployment, the Department of Labor places each person 16 years of age or older into one of the three catagories: (1) employed, (2) unemployed, or (3) not in the labor force. The Department of Labor then divides the number of unemployed persons by the total number of persons in the labor force to determine the unemployment rate. Let us examine each of these three categories to see who would be classified as unemployed.

Employed This category includes all those people who are actively working plus those who have a job but are temporarily absent from work because of vacations, illness, labor disputes, or bad weather.

Unemployed This category includes only those people who do not have a job and who *are actively seeking work*. Many people who do not have a job are excluded from the unemployed category. The fact that a person does not have a job does not mean that he or she is unemployed in the sense that the government uses the word. To be officially counted as unemployed, a person must be without a job and *must be actively looking for one*. Specifically, a person must have engaged in some sort of job-seeking activity (such as filling out a job application) within the past four weeks or be waiting to be called back to a job from which he or she has been laid off or be waiting to report to a new job within 30 days.

Not in the labor force Persons without jobs who are not actively seeking work are considered neither employed nor unemployed. They are classified as *not in the labor force*. Many people in this category are not interested in employment. Examples of such people are full-time students, mothers with young children, and retired persons. However, many of those classified as not in the labor force do want and need jobs. They are not actively seeking work because they think no jobs are available in their geographic area or line of work. Such people, too, are classified—as *discouraged workers*.

Shortcomings of the Unemployment Statistics

Although the unemployment statistics are very useful, they do have some serious shortcomings. As noted above, persons who want and need work but who are not actively seeking work are not counted as unemployed. Also, persons under 16 years of age who are actively seeking work are excluded from the unemployment statistics. In addition, the unemployment statistics exclude those individuals who are working only part time but who would like to work full time. If a person who has lost a regular full-time job finds a part-time job working only one afternoon per week, he or she is then classified as employed. Even a person who works as little as one hour per week is counted as employed rather than unemployed. Furthermore, an unemployed individual who wants to work only ten hours a week is counted the same as one who wants to work full time.

The Department of Labor releases monthly figures on unemployment. Here, hundreds of job seekers line up to fill out applications to become city sanitation workers.

Types of Unemployment

In the eyes of the unemployed, there is only one kind of unemployment. However, not all unemployment is the same in terms of causation. There are different causes of unemployment, and thus there are different solutions to the unemployment problem. Economists generally recognize four types of unemployment: frictional, cyclical, structural, and seasonal. Let us examine each type of unemployment.

Frictional unemployment Full employment does not mean zero unemployment. It would be both impossible and undesirable to attain zero unemployment in the American economy. Any attempt to do so would have to include the provisions that workers could not quit their jobs and employers could not dismiss employees.

During any given month, a certain number of people will quit their jobs, others will be fired, and still others will leave school and seek employment for the first time. By the following month, many of these people will have found new jobs but a new group of people will have just left their jobs. This type of unemployment —called *frictional unemployment*—involves people who are temporarily between jobs.

A certain amount of frictional unemployment is necessary to provide freedom and mobility to workers. However, there is some disagreement as to how much frictional unemployment is necessary. In the past, economists considered full employment to be approximately 4 percent unemployment, but in recent years some economists have argued that 6 percent unemployment is a more appropriate figure. With a labor force of over 100 million people, a 1 percent reduction in the unemployment rate means more than 1 million additional jobs. Thus, it makes a great deal of difference to a lot of people whether our government decides to accept 6 percent unemployment as the full-employment goal instead of 4 percent.

Some economists believe that frictional unemployment could be substantially reduced if there were a more efficient, systematic procedure for bringing together job seekers and job openings. At present, there is no central clearing house where all the job vacancies in a specific geographic area or a particular line of work are listed, although some job openings are listed with public or private employment agencies. Instead, most unemployed workers find new jobs simply by going out into the community and contacting as many potential employers as possible. If a way could be found to use computers, job-placement offices, and media advertising to shorten the time between the loss of a job and the finding of a new job, frictional unemployment could be reduced.

Cyclical unemployment Cyclical unemployment, which gets its name from the business cycle, is caused by insufficient total spending— or **aggregate demand,** as it is usually called by economists. Aggregate demand consists of consumption spending plus investment spending plus government spending. The level of aggregate demand determines the level of total production, which determines employment. If the level of aggregate demand is insufficient to purchase all of the goods and services that the economy can produce at the full-employment level, workers will be laid off and total production (GNP) will decline. As workers lose their jobs, they will be forced to reduce their spending, and this will lead to still more layoffs. This process can continue indefinitely, and the lower the level of aggregate demand, the higher the level of unemployment.

Since insufficient aggregate demand is the cause of cyclical unemployment, the solution is to find a way to increase aggregate demand. An increase in any or all of the three components of aggregate demand—consumption, investment, and government spending—can help to reduce cyclical unemployment. For example, the government might decide to increase its own spending directly by instituting new programs, or it might try to increase consumer spending by lowering taxes so consumers will have more money to spend. Still another option is to attempt to increase investment spending by

In coal mining areas of Appalachia, unemployed workers are often reluctant to leave their homes in the valleys although they have few other job opportunities there.

lowering interest rates on loans and making loans more readily available or by providing businesses with tax incentives.

Structural unemployment Structural unemployment involves a mismatch between job seekers and job openings. It can occur at a time when, even though the economy is operating near the full-employment level, a substantial number of unfilled job openings still exist. During such times there are usually labor shortages in some geographic areas and job fields and labor surpluses in others. Structural unemployment results from the fact that the unemployed workers are unable to fill the job openings, usually because of either a geographic or a skill mismatch.

A *geographic mismatch* occurs when there are job vacancies in some parts of the country while workers in other parts of the country remain unemployed. Usually the jobs will not move to the unemployed workers, and many of the unemployed workers are unable or unwilling to move to the areas where the job openings exist.

The employment situation in the coal mining regions of Appalachia provides an excellent example of structural unemployment caused by geographic mismatch. For generations, coal mining was the primary source of employment in this area. However, because coal deposits are exhausted in some areas and because there has been extensive use of technology in the mining process, there has been a substantial reduction in the number of jobs available. Thus, workers find themselves without jobs in an area where there are few alternative job opportunities. At the same time, job vacancies in other parts of the country remain unfilled.

There are two possible solutions to the unemployment problems of areas like Appalachia. One is to try to attract new potential employers into these areas. The other is to get the unemployed workers to move to other regions where employment prospects are better. Both of these potential solutions work better in theory than in practice, however. Many of the areas of high unemployment are located in remote areas that often lack good roads, airports, water resources, and other facilities that potential employers look for when they are selecting a site for a new manufacturing plant or other facility. With communities throughout the nation competing with one another for new potential employers, a region like Appalachia is at a great disadvantage.

It is also difficult to get unemployed workers to leave an area such as Appalachia. Many of the people have deep roots in their home communities, and they are hesitant or unable to move their families or to leave behind close friends and relatives. The result is that they must suffer the consequences of unemployment and poverty at home because they are unable or unwilling to move to a new and unfamiliar area in hopes of improving their economic status.

Some unemployed workers lack the skills needed to obtain jobs in industries that require high levels of education or technical training.

A **skill mismatch** occurs when both job vacancies and unemployed workers exist in the same geographic area but the unemployed workers lack the skills required to fill the job openings. In the past, it was generally believed that structural unemployment of this type was primarily the result of insufficient education. However, as the American population has become better educated, it has become clear that education alone is insufficient to solve the skill-mismatch problem. Job openings requiring a college degree can go unfilled at the same time that large numbers of college graduates find themselves unemployed. In addition to having a college degree, job applicants may need training in the specific areas required by the job openings. Four years of college training may be sufficient to train either a computer programmer or an elementary school teacher. However, training as an elementary school teacher is of little value if the only job openings are for computer programmers.

In recent years, the extensive use of new technology in many industries, such as mechanical robots in the automobile industry, has led to what some call **technological unemployment.** Actually, technological unemployment is just another form of structural unemployment. Workers' skills become obsolete because machines do the work that formerly was done by human hands. As the old jobs vanish, new jobs related to the new technology appear, but the workers who are displaced by the new technology seldom have the skills required by the new job openings. Thus, they are structurally unemployed.

There are two possible solutions to structural unemployment caused by skill mismatches. The first involves providing improved career guidance designed to help young people choose career fields in which job opportunities are likely to be available. This solution may help to prevent skill mismatches from occurring in the first place. The second solution involves retraining workers whose skills are obsolete or in such low demand that their chances of getting a job in their chosen field are very slim. Because there always will be some workers whose skills become obsolete as a result of changing technology, retraining programs are an important way of curbing this type of structural unemployment.

Seasonal unemployment involves workers who have jobs for at least part of the year but who find themselves without work at other times because of seasonal factors. For example, construction workers may be without work during part of the winter when weather conditions are not favorable for starting new projects. Also, migrant farm workers, who have plenty of employment during the harvest seasons, often find themselves unemployed between harvests. Even some manufacturing plants need more employees at certain times of the year than at others. For example, a firm that manufactures fireworks may be operating at maximum capacity during the months of April, May, and June. However, after July fourth it may temporarily lay off some of its employees. A certain amount of seasonal unemployment is unavoidable. However, some economists believe that seasonal unemployment in manufacturing could be reduced if manufacturers would spread the production of expected yearly output more evenly throughout the year instead of accelerating and decelerating production in response to seasonal changes in demand.

Costs of Unemployment

The costs of long periods of high unemployment are enormous, and they involve both the direct costs to those who are unemployed and the costs to the economy in terms of lost production. Let us briefly examine each of these types of costs.

Costs to the unemployed and their families As you have already learned, each time the unemployment rate rises by one percentage point, more than one million additional Americans lose their jobs. Thus, during even a mild recession millions of Americans suffer from unemployment.

During periods of prolonged unemployment, the suffering of the unemployed and their families is immense. In addition to the financial hardship, the emotional suffering can be extremely severe. As we mentioned earlier,

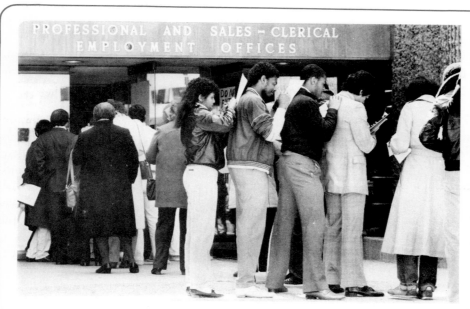

During the summer months, the number of people looking for jobs increases when high school and college students as well as new graduates enter the job market.

During the Great Depression, many of the jobless sold apples on the street. Some of these apple sellers once held high paying jobs.

the loss of self-esteem and the feelings of inadequacy that afflict many of the unemployed can lead to depression, increased domestic violence, and even to suicide in extreme cases. Even many of those who do not lose their jobs suffer from the fear of losing them. As they see more and more of their co-workers being laid off, the fear that they will be next puts them under a great deal of stress.

Costs to the economy Another tragedy of unemployment is the lost production that results from unused resources. During periods of prolonged high unemployment, resources lay idle while millions of Americans do without the things that these resources could have provided. During the Great Depression of the 1930s, enormous amounts of food rotted for lack of a profitable market while millions of Americans went hungry. Sheep farmers in the western states slaughtered sheep by the thousands and

destroyed their carcasses because the market price had fallen below the shipping costs and they would lose money on every shipment they made. Wheat was left in the fields uncut because the price was too low to cover the harvesting costs while millions were without bread.

In addition to the wasted food, many of the nation's factories sat partially or totally idle during the Great Depression. The factories did not operate because they could not sell their products. People could not buy these products because they didn't have jobs. It was a vicious cycle. The factories would have hired the unemployed workers if they could have sold their products, and the unemployed workers would have bought the factories' products if they had had jobs. The American economic system was simply allowed to break down. Without the proper policies to restore it to health, it remained broken down for a decade.

ISSUE: Should Government Serve as the Employer of Last Resort?

Ever since the Great Depression of the 1930s, some people have argued that during periods of high unemployment the government should provide jobs for the unemployed. They contend that instead of giving the unemployed handouts through such programs as unemployment compensation, welfare payments, and food stamps, it is far better to give them employment that will benefit both them and society. Others, however, oppose government employment projects on the basis that they are often wasteful and represent inappropriate government intervention in the economy.

The Case for Government Employment Projects

Proponents of government employment projects believe that there is nothing more wasteful than allowing individuals who are able and willing to work to remain idle. They point out that prolonged periods of high unemployment result in the financial hardship and emotional suffering of millions of Americans and cost the economy billions of dollars in lost production. They argue that the government should not allow such human suffering and such a waste of resources. Instead, they contend, the government should put the unemployed workers to work on projects that will benefit society.

In support of their argument, proponents of government employment projects point to the fact that many public facilities—including post offices, libraries, and city halls—were built during the Depression by workers who would otherwise have been unemployed, and that these facilities are still in use today nearly half a century after their construction. They argue that there is the potential for many similar projects today. For example, it is generally agreed that there is an urgent need for slum clearance, urban rehabilitation, and improvement of highways and mass transit systems in the United States. Many proponents of government employment projects contend that such projects could create jobs for many unemployed workers and at the same time provide benefits that would last for generations. Projects such as slum clearance and urban rehabilitation are especially attractive, say supporters, because such projects would create jobs in inner cities where unemployment among the young is highest.

The Case Against Government Employment Projects

Opponents of government employment programs contend that such programs are far too often just make-work projects that are hastily contrived, poorly planned, inefficient, and a waste of taxpayers' money. They argue that

although some of the public works projects of the 1930s had lasting benefits, many of them simply created jobs and little else. For example, some workers were employed simply to rake leaves, and others worked on inefficient road-building projects that used as little machinery as possible in order to prolong the work.

According to opponents, it takes too long to plan and develop sound public works projects for such projects to be used effectively during most recessions. Getting started on a new post office or putting into effect a road-building or slum-clearance project might take years. As a result, by the time such projects are implemented, the economy may have recovered from the recession and the additional government spending may just fuel inflation. Moreover, some of the work accomplished by such projects might have been undertaken by private enterprise if the government had not intervened.

Furthermore, according to some opponents, such programs represent inappropriate government intervention in the economy. The government's role in creating jobs, they argue, should be restricted to pursuing policies that would create an environment in which sufficient jobs would be provided by private employers. They believe that because private employers must earn a profit to remain in business, projects undertaken by private enterprise are likely to be far more efficient than those undertaken by government.

How do you feel about government employment programs? Do you think the government should serve as the employer of last resort? Why or why not? In investigating information to support your position, you might try to find out whether or not there were government employment projects that were carried out in your community during the Great Depression of the 1930s and decide whether or not you think they were beneficial.

The cost of the Great Depression was astronomical. Economic historians have estimated that if the economy had fully used all of its resources during the 1930s, the dollar value of the additional production would have been higher than the cost of World War II. Such a sum would have been large enough to have covered the cost of a new house and several new cars for every American family during the decade.

Although we have not had anything comparable to the Great Depression since that time, we have had a number of serious recessions that have been very costly in terms of both human suffering and lost production. The recession of 1981–82, which was the most severe economic decline since the Great Depression, resulted in a peak unemployment rate of 10.7 percent. During that recession, long lines of people waited for free food handouts in many cities across the country. At the depth of the recession, nearly one third of the nation's industrial capacity lay idle at a time when poverty was on the rise.

Check Your Understanding

1. How is unemployment measured?

2. Describe the three categories the government uses to measure unemployment. What are some shortcomings of unemployment statistics?

3. Describe the four types of unemployment. What are the causes of each? What are some possible solutions?

4. What are the costs of unemployment to the economy and to the unemployed workers and their families?

Inflation

Inflation is usually defined as a general rise in the price level or, to put it another way, a decline in the purchasing power of the dollar. Inflation became a serious problem in the United States in the late 1960s, and it has continued to be a problem ever since. As a first step in understanding this problem, let us see how inflation is measured.

Measuring Inflation

The most commonly used measure of the general inflation rate is the consumer price index. This measure, which is sometimes referred to as the "cost-of-living index," is used to determine the average increase in the prices of goods and services commonly purchased by American consumers. (See Figure 9-3.) Each month in every major part of the nation, the U.S. Department of Labor checks the prices of about 400 frequently used items in what it considers a "typical market basket" of consumer goods and services. If the total cost of all of the items in the typical market basket remains constant, there is no inflation even if the prices of several specific items rise but these price increases are offset by corresponding price decreases. However, if the total cost of all of the items is higher than it was during the previous month, according to this measure, inflation has taken place. The percentage increase in the total cost of all items in the typical market basket from one year to the next is the annual inflation rate.

Inflation has been a serious and persistent problem in the United States since the mid-1960s. From 1967 to 1984, prices more than tripled. This means that an item that cost $100 in 1967 would have cost more than $300 in 1984. In 1980 alone (the year with the highest inflation rate for that period), prices rose an average of 13.5 percent, meaning that an article that cost $100 in 1979 would have cost $113.50 the following year.

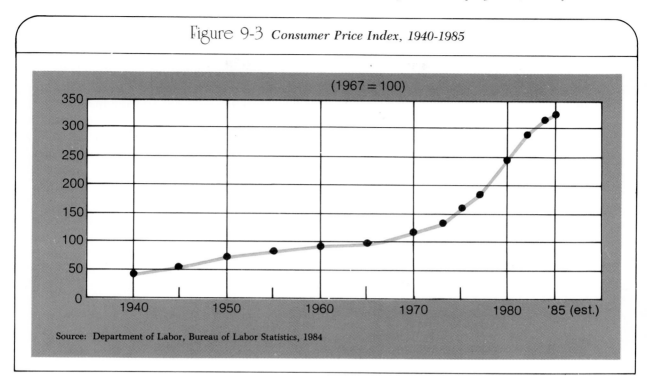

Figure 9-3 *Consumer Price Index, 1940-1985*

Source: Department of Labor, Bureau of Labor Statistics, 1984

As serious a problem as inflation has been in the United States in recent years, it has not reached the proportions some countries have experienced. Between 1967 and 1980, average prices in the United States rose by 146.8 percent. During the same period, average prices in Italy rose by 298 percent and average prices in Great Britain rose by 323.6 percent. Furthermore, in late 1980, at the same time that the United States had an inflation rate of 13.5 percent, Israel had an inflation rate of 200 percent. By 1984, Israel's annual inflation rate had risen to 400 percent. In early 1984, Argentina was running an annual inflation rate of about 450 percent.

Types of Inflation

All inflation involves a general rise in prices. However, there is more than one type of inflation. Economists generally recognize two types of inflation—demand–pull and cost-push. Let us examine each of these types of inflation.

Demand-Pull inflation Demand-pull inflation is caused when aggregate demand—the total spending for consumption, investment, and government—is too high. **Demand-pull inflation** occurs when aggregate demand exceeds the total dollar value of all the goods and services (GNP) that the economy is capable of producing at the full-employment level of production. In a sense, demand-pull inflation is just the opposite of cyclical unemployment. Too much aggregate demand results in demand-pull inflation, and too little causes cyclical unemployment.

If the economy is operating at the full-employment level of GNP, there can be no increase in the total supply of goods and services. In other words, the economy is producing as much as it is capable of turning out. Thus, any increase in aggregate demand must result in higher prices. Just as an increase in the demand for a single item relative to the supply will cause the price of that item to rise, an increase in the total demand for all goods and services at a time when the economy is operating at its maximum capacity (full-employment GNP) will cause average prices for the whole economy to rise.

Since demand-pull inflation is caused by too much aggregate demand, the solution must involve reductions in any or all of the components of aggregate demand: consumption, investment, and government spending. We will examine specific government policies for reducing demand-pull inflation when we cover fiscal policy in Chapter 10 and when we cover monetary policy in Chapter 12.

Cost-Push inflation Cost-push inflation occurs when production costs rise and sellers increase their prices in an effort to maintain their profit level. This type of inflation is often called "sellers' inflation" because it results from price increases initiated by sellers rather than from too much aggregate demand. Cost-push inflation can occur at times when the economy is operating below the full-employment level of GNP as well as when the economy is operating at maximum capacity.

Many factors can lead to increased production costs and, thus, to cost-push inflation. For example, the rapidly rising energy prices during the 1970s played a major role in the inflation of that period. Increased costs for raw materials have also contributed to cost-push inflation. One of the major causes of this kind of inflation has been increased labor costs brought about by wage increases demanded by workers who were trying to offset the loss in the purchasing power of their wages that was resulting from high inflation. For example, if a worker received a 7 percent wage increase at a time when the inflation rate was 9 percent, that worker's purchasing power actually declined. As a result, many labor unions negotiated cost-of-living provisions in their contracts that would give workers pay increases to keep pace with inflation. This caused labor costs to keep rising, which in turn fueled inflation. The term **wage-push inflation** is sometimes used to refer to cost-push inflation that is caused by rising wages.

The Effects of Inflation

Although inflation affects everyone to some degree, some people are affected far more severely than others. Let us examine the effects of inflation on different groups and aspects of the economy.

Effects on people with fixed incomes People living on fixed incomes probably are hurt more by inflation than any other group. As prices rise year after year, people with fixed incomes are able to buy fewer and fewer goods and services. As mentioned earlier, during the period 1967 to 1984, average prices in the United States more than tripled. This means that a person who retired in 1967 on a fixed income of $10,000 per year needed more than $30,000 in 1984 in order to buy the same amount of goods and services that he or she was able to buy with $10,000 in 1967. If the person's income remains fixed at $10,000 per year, he or she was able to buy less than one third as much in 1984 as was bought in 1967.

Although Social Security payments have been adjusted upward to keep pace with inflation in recent years, the major source of retirement income for many senior citizens is money

---

TABLE 9–1: CAUSES OF INFLATION

Type of Inflation	Cause
Demand-pull inflation	Too much aggregate demand; results when the total demand for goods and services exceeds the total supply.
Cost-push inflation	Results from price increases initiated by sellers who are responding to increases in production costs.

"It says here the full impact won't be felt till next month."

Modell
THE NEW YORKER

The immediate effects of inflation can be felt by shoppers when they look at prices in the stores, as this cartoon humorously shows.

that they saved during their working years. Because of inflation, this money is now worth considerably less than when it was earned. In a sense, they have been cheated out of a financially secure retirement by inflation.

Effects on long-term lending The high inflation of the 1970s and early 1980s had a disastrous effect on many lending institutions, and it resulted in major changes in long-term lending policies that will have an adverse effect on your generation. Until recent years, lending institutions were willing to make long-term home mortgage loans at fixed rates of interest. That is, if a person took out a 20-year loan at 6 percent interest, the person would pay 6 percent interest on the unpaid balance of the loan over the entire 20 years. Lending institutions were willing to do this because they were confident that there would not be high inflation over any prolonged period of time. As a result, during the prolonged high inflation of the 1970s and early 1980s many lending institutions lost a great deal

of money on long-term loans that had been made in previous years at fixed interest rates. For example, suppose a lending institution issued a loan at an interest rate of 10 percent. During 1980 when the interest rate was 13.5 percent, such a loan would have resulted in a net loss of 3.5 percent for the lender.

In the past, it was common practice for loan companies to make home mortgage loans at fixed interest rates for periods of up to 25 or 30 years. Today, it is almost impossible to obtain such loans. Most home mortgage loans now are issued over shorter periods of time and have provisions that allow interest rates to keep pace with inflation. With loans of this type, home buyers must live with the constant fear that their monthly payments might go up sharply as a result of higher inflation. In addition, many people may decide not to buy a home out of fear that they will be unable to meet the mortgage payments. Thus, the high inflation that hurt lenders in the past will hurt prospective home buyers today and in the future.

Effects on savings Inflation hurts individual savers the same way that it hurts lenders. When you deposit money in your savings account at the bank, you are in effect lending the money to the bank. If the bank does not pay you an interest rate at least as high as the inflation rate, you will suffer a net loss. For example, if you deposit $1,000 in an account that pays 8 percent interest, at the end of a year you will have $1,080. However if the inflation rate is 10 percent, you will need $1,100 to buy the same amount you could have purchased the previous year. In other words, although your original investment will have grown, you will now be able to buy less with this new amount than with the original amount.

Effects on international trade High inflation has a negative effect on a nation's trade with other countries. We will examine international trade in some detail in Chapter 15. However, at this point it is sufficient to say that when prices in the United States rise more rapidly than those of other countries, Americans buy more foreign-made products and foreigners buy fewer American-made products.

Beneficiaries of Inflation Some people benefit from inflation. As you have already learned, lenders are hurt when prices rise faster than interest rates. However, the lender's loss is the borrower's gain. People with low fixed-rate mortgages and other low-interest loans benefit from inflation. So, too, do people with investments in real estate and other commodities that rise in value during inflationary periods.

Wage and Price Controls as a Means of Combating Inflation

During periods of high inflation, many people advocate the use of government wage and price controls as a means of fighting inflation. To some, mandatory wage and price controls seem to be a logical answer to the problem. They urge the government to halt inflation by making it illegal for prices to rise; in other words, to help solve one of the most basic of all economic problems by passing a law against it.

Many economists oppose wage and price controls because they attack the symptoms of inflation instead of the causes and because they often do more harm than good. As you learned in Chapter 3, if the government establishes a legal price ceiling for a product at a level below the price that would be established if supply and demand were allowed to operate freely, there will be a shortage of the product. In fact, during periods of wage and price controls, there are usually shortages of many crucial items.

This is not to say that wage and price controls should never be used. During periods of war or other national emergencies, such controls may serve a useful purpose. During World War II, wage and price controls were used extensively, and the government rationed those items that were in short supply because the economy needed to concentrate on producing wartime goods. However, during peacetime most economists believe that wage and price controls do more harm than good.

Check Your Understanding

1. What is inflation? How is it measured?

2. Describe the two basic types of inflation. What are the causes of each?

3. How does inflation affect people on fixed incomes? How does it affect lenders and savers? Why does inflation have a negative effect on international trade?

4. Why do most economists oppose mandatory wage and price controls as a means of combating inflation?

CAREERS: Vocational Counselor

Vocational, or employment, counselors help people select, prepare for, and find employment in the careers for which they are best suited. Their clients usually include people of all ages and educational backgrounds, including school dropouts, high school and college graduates, and experienced professionals.

Vocational counselors have many responsibilities in the various settings in which they work—state employment service offices, college placement offices, and private employment agencies. They must be able to develop a friendly and trusting relationship with their clients so that they can help these people understand themselves and their abilities. In this capacity, counselors try to discover the kinds of work their clients are capable of doing and the kinds of jobs their clients will find most satisfying. To do this, counselors often administer and interpret aptitude and achievement tests, and study the educational backgrounds, work experience and skills, physi-

cal capacities, and personality traits of their clients. Counselors must be familiar with the training requirements, current job openings, and the future prospects for various career fields. In addition, they must be able to gain the confidence of employers, who will be interviewing and hiring the job applicants the counselors recommend.

Vocational counselors must have at least a bachelor's degree with a major in a field such as sociology, psychology, or educational guidance and counseling. They usually also must have successfully completed courses in standardized testing, occupational information, and counseling. For employment in a government tax-supported employment service, applicants usually must have a master's degree in a field such as guidance and counseling, psychology, social work, personnel work, or public administration. In addition, those counselors seeking employment with state employment service offices may have to pass a written examination.

Chapter Highlights

1   Business cycles are recurrent but irregular fluctuations in economic activity. They are very costly in terms of unemployment and inflation.

2   There are four phases to a business cycle: the peak, the recession (or contraction), the trough, and the recovery (or expansion).

3   Many economists believe that the expansion phase of many past business cycles was caused by heavy investment spending that resulted from new inventions, new technology, the discovery of new mineral deposits, or the opening of new frontiers. Political events and social upheavals also have been cited as major factors in some past business cycles.

4   Employment and unemployment statistics are based on a sample survey of about 60,000 households. In determining the unemployment rate, the Department of Labor categorizes each person 16 years of age and older as employed, unemployed, or not in the labor force. To be officially classified as unemployed, a worker who is without a job must be actively seeking work.

5   Economists generally recognize four types of unemployment: frictional, cyclical, structural, and seasonal. Frictional unemployment involves people who are temporarily between jobs. Cyclical unemployment results from insufficient aggregate demand. Structural unemployment occurs when there is a mismatch between job openings and job seekers. Seasonal unemployment involves workers who have jobs for part of the year but who are without work at times because of seasonal factors.

6   The costs of unemployment involve both direct costs to those who are unemployed and costs to the economy in terms of lost production.

7   Inflation is defined as a general rise in the price level or a decline in the purchasing power of the dollar. The consumer price index is the measure most often used to determine the general inflation rate.

8   Economists generally recognize two basic types of inflation: demand-pull and cost-push. Demand-pull inflation is a rise in prices that is caused by too much aggregate demand. Cost-push inflation occurs when sellers increase their prices in an effort to pass higher production costs on to their customers.

9   Although inflation affects everyone to some degree, some people are affected more severely than others. People on fixed incomes, long-term lenders, and savers are all hurt by inflation. Inflation also has a negative effect on international trade. Beneficiaries of inflation include borrowers and people with investments in commodities that rise during periods of inflation.

Important Terms

Match each of the following terms with the correct definition:

demand-pull inflation	aggregate demand	frictional unemployment
consumer price index	business cycles	cost-push inflation
cyclical unemployment	recession	structural unemployment
inflation	depression	trough
seasonal unemployment	recovery	peak

1. Unemployment that involves people who are temporarily between jobs.

2. Unemployment caused by a mismatch between job seekers and job openings.

3. The lowest phase of the business cycle.

4. The highest phase of the business cycle.

5. Temporary unemployment caused by seasonal factors.

6. A prolonged period of little or no economic growth accompanied by high unemployment.

7. A general rise in prices or a decline in the purchasing power of the dollar.

8. Recurrent but irregular fluctuations in economic activity.

9. Inflation caused by rising production costs.

10. The total of consumption spending plus investment spending plus government spending.

11. The downward phase of the business cycle.

12. Unemployment caused by insufficient aggregate demand.

13. The upward phase of the business cycle.

14. The measure most often used to determine the general inflation rate.

15. Inflation caused by too much aggregate demand.

Extending Your Understanding

[handwritten left margin: One start providing ways to decrease inflation so the Demand for product will increase and w which will cause Industries to Rev... demand for labour therefore less unemployment and also by allowing for more government jobs to fund (Army/Navy) air force (war)]

1. In what ways does unemployment hurt people who do not lose their jobs? Based on what you have learned in the chapter, what actions do you think government should take during periods of high unemployment? *[handwritten: Because it put a strain of the employed to buy more goods and services to maintain an increasing GNP to allow for more government]*

2. Which kind of unemployment do you think is easiest to reduce? Explain your answer. *[handwritten: p.177]*

3. Who is hurt most by inflation? Who is hurt least? If you had to choose between high unemployment and high inflation, which would you choose? Why?

[handwritten: Most people who are unemployed not people on fixed income. The rich - people who don't have to worry about money.]

[handwritten right: high unemployment because there are more ways to correct it by lowering inflation. Industries becoming increased with demand for labour]

Activities

1. Go to the library and look through copies of newspapers that are at least a year old. Pay particular attention to the advertisements. Jot down the prices of several items and then look through some recent newspapers for similar items. How do the prices of these items compare? Has there been any inflation in the economy over the past year?

2. Suppose you have just been appointed as an economic advisor to your governor. What policies would you propose for curbing unemployment in your state? Summarize your advice in a short report.

Building Skills in Economics: Understanding the Consumer Price Index

As you learned in this chapter, the consumer price index (CPI) is the most commonly used measure of the general inflation rate. To compute the consumer price index, economists choose a base year for comparison and set it equal to 100. The base year most often used in recent years is 1967. Economists then state any changes in prices in terms of the base year. For example, if prices in 1980 were 146.8 percent higher than in 1967, the consumer price index for 1980 would be 246.8.

The consumer price index also can be used to compare prices from year to year. To do this, you first determine the increase that took place between the two years you wish to compare. For example, suppose the CPI went from 217.4 in 1979 to 246.8 in 1980. The increase would be 29.4 points. You would then compute what percent that increase is from the earlier figure (29.4 ÷ 217.4 = .135). Prices rose 13.5 percent from 1979 to 1980.

The table that follows shows the consumer price index from 1970 through 1980 for selected items. The questions will help you interpret the table.

Applying Economics Skills

1. What was the consumer price index for all items in 1970? How much did prices increase since 1967? Which item showed the greatest increase?
2. What was the consumer price index for all items in 1980? How much did prices increase since 1967? Which item showed the greatest increase?
3. What was the consumer price index for medical care in 1979? In 1980? How much did the cost of medical care rise between 1979 and 1980?

CONSUMER PRICE INDEX FOR SELECTED ITEMS (1967 = 100)

Year	Food	Housing	Rent	Clothing	Medical Care	All Items
1970	114.7	118.2	110.1	116.1	120.6	116.3
1971	118.3	123.4	115.2	119.8	128.4	121.3
1972	123.2	128.1	119.2	122.3	132.5	125.3
1973	139.5	133.7	124.3	126.8	137.7	133.1
1974	158.7	148.8	130.6	136.2	150.5	147.1
1975	172.1	164.5	137.3	142.3	168.6	161.2
1976	177.4	174.6	144.7	147.6	184.7	170.5
1977	188.0	186.5	153.5	154.2	202.4	181.5
1978	206.3	202.8	164.0	159.6	219.4	195.4
1979	228.5	227.6	176.0	166.6	239.7	217.4
1980	248.0	263.3	191.1	178.4	265.9	246.8

Source: Bureau of Labor Statistics, 1984

CHAPTER 10

FISCAL POLICY, BUDGET DEFICITS, AND THE NATIONAL DEBT

What would most people do if they got an unexpected tax refund of $300 from the government? Would they spend it or save it? They would probably spend at least part of it. The money might go into the family clothing budget, or it could be used to buy new tires for the car. Perhaps it might even be used for a family vacation.

Now suppose that instead of receiving a tax refund, a family discovered that they were going to have to pay $300 more in taxes than they had counted on. Where would they get the extra money? Would they have to cut back on other spending in order to pay the extra taxes? Again, if they are like most people, the tax increase probably will cause at least some reduction in their consumption spending budget.

As you will learn in this chapter, increasing or decreasing taxes is one of the ways in which the government sometimes attempts to influence aggregate demand (total spending) in the economy. Another way is for the government to increase or decrease its own spending. The deliberate use of the government's spending and taxing powers to influence economic acitivity is known as **fiscal policy.** In this chapter, we want to examine fiscal policy both in theory and in practice. As a first step, let us look at the origin of fiscal policy.

The Origin of Fiscal Policy

As you learned in Chapter 2, economics as a discipline began with the publication of *The Wealth of Nations* by Adam Smith in 1776. The ideas that were formulated by Smith and refined by his followers became known as **classical economics.** This collection of ideas made up the predominant body of economic theory in the Western world from the late eighteenth century until the late 1930s.

A fundamental part of classical economics was the belief that a capitalistic economic system would tend toward full employment automatically through the free operation of the price system. Classical economists argued that a recession simply represented temporary surpluses of goods and workers and that through the forces of supply and demand, the economy would correct itself and soon reach a new equilibrium at full employment. According to classical economics, a prolonged deep depression could not occur.

The Great Depression of the 1930s caused many economists to question classical economics. The unemployment rate climbed to approximately 25 percent in 1933, and it never dropped below 14 percent for the remainder of the decade. Obviously, classical economics was inadequate to explain the Great Depression.

One of the harshest critics of classical economics was John Maynard Keynes, a British scholar. In 1936, Keynes published a monumental book, *The General Theory of Employment, Interest and Money*. In this book, Keynes strongly criticized classical economic theory and set forth a new theory that became known as **Keynesian economics.**

Keynesian economics soon replaced classical economics as the predominant body of economic theory in the Western world. Although his theories have undergone substantial refinement and revision, much of modern Keynesian economics is still rooted on the ideas set forth by him. Fiscal policy is a central part of Keynesian economics. Keynes argued that the government should play an active role in maintaining the proper level of aggregate demand in order to minimize both unemployment and inflation. He also believed that with the proper use of the government's spending and taxing powers, the extremes of the business cycle could be avoided.

As you soon will learn, fiscal policy doesn't work as well in practice as the theory suggests. However, before discussing the shortcomings of fiscal policy, let us see how it would work under ideal conditions.

The Objectives of Fiscal Policy

As you already have learned, fluctuations in economic activity can be very costly in terms of unemployment and inflation. During a severe recession, millions of workers become unemployed and billions of dollars worth of potential production are permanently lost. Likewise, prolonged periods of high inflation can have a devastating effect on both the economy and the American people.

The objectives of fiscal policy are to reduce business cycles, thereby minimizing unemployment and inflation. To accomplish this task, the government attempts to offset changes in consumption spending and investment spending—two components of aggregate demand—by regulating its own spending or by using its taxing powers.

For example, if consumption spending is falling, the government might increase its own spending or reduce taxes in an effort to encourage increased consumption spending. If investment spending is too low, the government might reduce business taxes to encourage increased investment spending. Because changes in consumption spending are inevitable, the government turns to fiscal policy to regulate aggregate demand, which in effect controls business cycles and minimizes unemployment and inflation.

BIOGRAPHY: John Maynard Keynes

(1883–1946) John Maynard Keynes has often been described as a genius with diverse talents. In addition to his teaching and writing, Keynes was a successful businessman who earned millions of dollars by speculating in the stock market.

With the publication of his monumental work, *The General Theory of Employment, Interest and Money*, in 1936, Keynes took his place alongside Adam Smith as one of the most influential economists of all time. In this book, Keynes challenged the generally accepted theory that capitalist economies always tended automatically toward full employment, and he set forth a new theory that soon became known as Keynesian economics. He argued that insufficient total spending can cause an economy to remain in recession or depression indefinitely. Pointing out that businesses will not produce products that they cannot sell, Keynes argued that government should use its taxing and spending powers to influence a nation's level of total spending.

Keynes's new ideas came at the time of the Great Depression of the 1930s, and they were soon accepted by many other economists. By the 1950s, Keynesian economics represented the dominant view among academic economists in the Western world, and by the 1960s Keynes's ideas formed the foundation of economic policy in the United States and most other Western nations.

The high inflation of the 1970s and early 1980s caused economists to reevaluate their thinking, and many now hold the view that the Keynesian approach is far more effective in stimulating demand and reducing unemployment than it is in controlling inflation. As a result, new theories and modifications of existing theories have been put forth, and further modifications will undoubtedly be made in the future. Nevertheless, many economists believe that although time may alter the specifics of Keynesian economics, the Keynesian approach will continue to form the core of economic theory and policy for the foreseeable future.

Ideally, fiscal policy would be used to fine-tune the economy. Any time aggregate demand fell short of the full-employment level of GNP, the government could increase its spending and/or reduce taxes in order to raise aggregate demand to the appropriate level. Any time aggregate demand exceeded the full-employment level of GNP, the government could reduce its spending and/or increase taxes in order to lower aggregate demand to the appropriate level. Let us use some hypothetical examples to show how fiscal policy would be used to influence the level of aggregate demand.

Figure 10–1 represents an ideal level of operation for the economy based on hypothetical data. It assumes that the economy is capable of producing $3,500 billion worth of goods and services at the full-employment level without inflation. If this were the case, we would want aggregate demand—consumption plus investment plus government spending—to be exactly $3,500 billion. Remember that the level of actual GNP (also called aggregate supply) is determined by the level of aggregate demand. Thus, if aggregate demand is less than $3,500 billion, GNP will fall short of the full-employment level and cyclical unemployment will occur. On the other hand, if aggregate demand is greater than $3,500 billion, GNP will exceed the full-employment level and demand-pull inflation will take place. Therefore, the objective of fiscal policy will be to assure an aggregate demand of $3,500 billion.

Figure 10–2 illustrates what will happen if aggregate demand falls short of $3,500 billion. In Figure 10–2, the combined demand for consumption, investment, and government spending totals only $3,200 billion, which is $300 billion less than the full-employment level of GNP. As you can see by comparing Figures 10–2 and 10–1, the reduction in aggregate demand was the result of a decrease in investment spending from $500 billion to $400 billion and a decrease in consumption spending from $2,200 billion to $2,000 billion. The net effect of the declines in investment and consumption spending will be a reduction in GNP as well as in employment. Just as an individual business firm will not produce more than it can sell, the economy will not produce more goods and services than can be sold. If aggregate demand remains at $3,200 billion for very long, the economy will go into a recession and the GNP will tend to adjust downward toward that level. This, of course, will lead to cyclical unemployment.

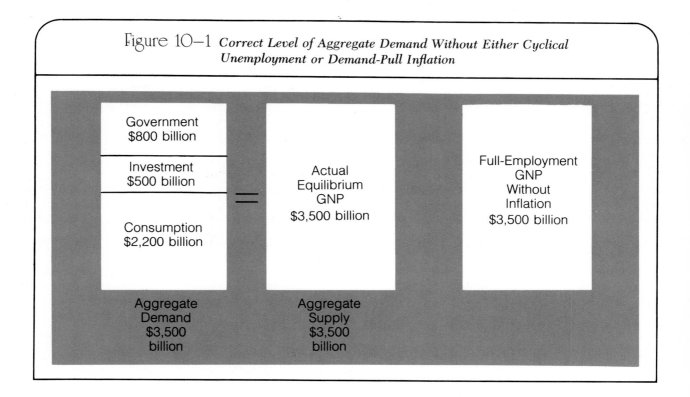

Figure 10–1 *Correct Level of Aggregate Demand Without Either Cyclical Unemployment or Demand-Pull Inflation*

Government $800 billion

Investment $500 billion

Consumption $2,200 billion

=

Actual Equilibrium GNP $3,500 billion

Full-Employment GNP Without Inflation $3,500 billion

Aggregate Demand $3,500 billion

Aggregate Supply $3,500 billion

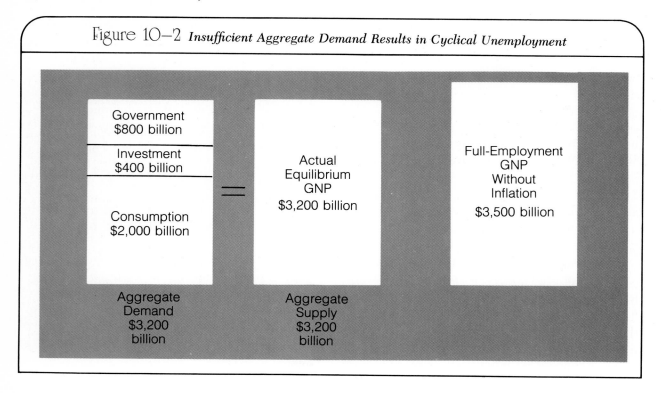

Figure 10–2 *Insufficient Aggregate Demand Results in Cyclical Unemployment*

What can the government do to head off the recession or at least minimize the severity of it? There are two fiscal-policy options available to government policy makers. The government could increase its own spending in an effort to offset some of the reduction in investment and consumption spending, or it could attempt to increase investment and/or consumption spending indirectly through reduced taxes. If a tax cut leaves consumers with more disposable income, there will be some increase in consumption spending. Also, a reduction in business taxes might lead to increased investment spending.

Figure 10–3 illustrates just the opposite problem of that in Figure 10–2. In Figure 10–3, aggregate demand is too high. The total combined spending for consumption, investment, and government is $3,800 billion, which is $300 billion above the full-employment level of GNP. Since the economy is capable of producing only $3,500 billion worth of goods and ser-

vices at current prices, any increase in aggregate demand above that amount can lead only to demand-pull inflation. If aggregate demand remains at $3,800 billion, there can be no increase in the actual physical volume of goods and services produced, but the dollar value of GNP will rise toward $3,800 billion. In other words, the rising prices will cause the previous $3,500 billion worth of goods and services to sell for approximately $3,800 billion. There is no increase in real GNP (GNP adjusted for inflation), but there is an increase in money GNP.

The goal of fiscal policy in this case would be to reduce aggregate demand by $300 billion in an effort to head off the inevitable demand-pull inflation that will occur if total demand exceeds the full-employment capacity of the economy for very long. The government might reduce its own spending in an effort to partially offset the increased investment and consumption spending. The other fiscal-policy option available to policy makers is to increase taxes.

Higher taxes on consumers would leave them with less disposable income and would lead to reduced consumer spending. Also, higher business taxes could help to reduce investment spending.

Of course, we are discussing here how fiscal policy operates in theory. The reality is somewhat different from what the theory suggests. We will soon focus on the shortcomings of fiscal policy.

Automatic Fiscal Stabilizers

Automatic fiscal stabilizers are built-in features of the economy that tend to change government spending and taxes in the desired direction automatically during the various phases of the business cycle. These automatic stabilizers tend to increase government spending and reduce the amount of taxes collected during times of recession. Conversely, they decrease government spending and increase taxes during periods of demand-pull inflation. Let us see how these changes in government spending and tax collections help to stabilize the economy.

Changes in government spending Most workers who lose their jobs through no fault of their own are eligible to collect government payments known as unemployment compensation. The funds for unemployment compensation come from a payroll tax imposed on employers. This program operates automatically without any deliberate action by government policy makers. As the economy slips into a recession and unemployment begins to rise, there is an "automatic" increase in government spending in the form of unemployment compensation checks. Conversely, as the economy recovers from the recession and heads toward inflation, there is an "automatic" reduction in government spending for unemployment compensation as the laid-off workers are recalled to their jobs.

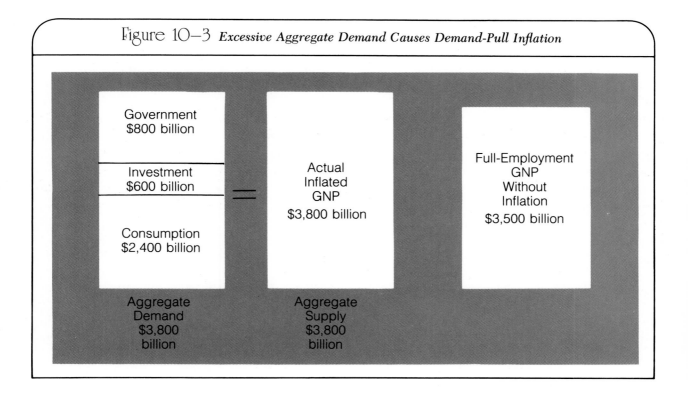

Figure 10–3 *Excessive Aggregate Demand Causes Demand-Pull Inflation*

Government $800 billion

Investment $600 billion

Consumption $2,400 billion

=

Actual Inflated GNP $3,800 billion

Full-Employment GNP Without Inflation $3,500 billion

Aggregate Demand $3,800 billion

Aggregate Supply $3,800 billion

The amount of income taxes collected will depend on the employment picture. High unemployment means fewer individuals will be earning wages on which to pay taxes.

In addition to unemployment compensation, other government programs—such as the welfare and the food stamp programs—also help to stabilize the economy. During periods of high unemployment, more people become eligible for food stamps and welfare and there is an increase in government spending for such programs. As the economy recovers from a recession, fewer people are eligible for these programs and spending for them declines.

Changes in tax collections As you learned in Chapter 7, the federal individual income tax, which is the major source of revenue for the federal government, is a progressive tax that takes an increasing percentage of income as income rises. When the economy is in a recession with rising unemployment, the government will collect fewer and fewer taxes as long as unemployment continues to rise. Those individuals who lose their jobs will have no wages on which to pay taxes, and those who are reduced to part-time work will pay a smaller percentage of their income in taxes as they drop into lower tax brackets. However, as the economy recovers from the recession and laid-off workers are called back to work in increasing numbers, the amount of taxes collected will rise. In addition, as more and more workers begin to work overtime, they will move into higher tax brackets and the government will collect an increasing percentage of income in taxes.

Discretionary Fiscal Policy

Automatic fiscal stabilizers work without any discretionary action on the part of government policy makers. They form what is called nondiscretionary fiscal policy. Although the automatic stabilizers help to cushion the extremes of the business cycle, they are not sufficient to prevent cyclical unemployment and demand-pull inflation. They must be supplemented with discretionary fiscal policies—deliberate actions taken by policy makers to change government spending and/or taxes.

During times of high unemployment, the government may take a number of deliberate actions to increase aggregate demand. For example, the government might increase spending for highways or other public works projects, thus directly providing a number of new jobs. The government took this kind of action during the Depression of the 1930s, although its efforts were not substantial enough to bring the economy out of the Depression. Or, the government might cut personal taxes in order to stimulate increased consumption spending. Still another approach might be to pass legislation giving businesses tax credit on investments. Such legislation would allow businesses to deduct from their taxes a part of the cost of new capital goods. This should encourage increased investment spending.

During times of demand-pull inflation, the government would want to take actions that are just the opposite from those just described. It would want to curtail its spending and/or increase taxes. For example, in 1968 a special one-year tax increase was enacted in an effort to reduce demand-pull inflation. In addition, some federal construction projects were temporarily halted in the early 1970s when the government withheld funds in an effort to reduce aggregate demand.

Fiscal Policy and the Federal Budget

Many economists believe that if fiscal policy were used properly, the government would have a balanced budget in some years, a surplus in the budget in other years, and a deficit in the budget in still other years. During periods when the economy is operating at or near the full-employment level, the government would spend just about the same amount of money that it collects in taxes. During periods of demand-pull inflation, the government would collect more dollars in taxes than it spends, thus resulting in a small surplus in the federal budget. Conversely, during times of recession and high cyclical unemployment, the government would pump more money into the economy than it takes out in taxes, resulting in a budget deficit. Unfortunately, as we have already mentioned, fiscal policy doesn't work nearly as well

Philadelphia Inquirer, 1933

In practice, fiscal policy does not operate as well as economic theory, as long periods with unbalanced budgets demonstrate. The public response, as this cartoon shows, is often insufficient to move Congress to act.

in actual practice as it does in theory. In the next section, we will examine fiscal policy in practice and explore in more detail various ways that might be used to balance the budget.

Check Your Understanding

1. What are the objectives of fiscal policy?

2. What are the mechanics of fiscal policy? How can fiscal policy be used to reduce unemployment and inflation?

3. Identify two automatic fiscal stabilizers. How do they work?

4. What is discretionary fiscal policy? Give some examples.

Fiscal Policy in Practice

As you know by now, both cyclical unemployment and demand-pull inflation have been serious problems in recent years. Why has fiscal policy failed to solve these problems? Not all economists agree on the answer to this question. Some economists, known as monetarists, disagree with the theory of fiscal policy. They believe that fiscal policy is completely ineffective in determining the level of total production except in the very short run. They base their argument on the fact that when the government tries to stimulate the economy by spending more than it collects in taxes, it must borrow the money to finance the extra spending. This borrowing, according to the monetarists, crowds out private spending that otherwise would have occurred. In other words, when the government borrows more money for public spending, there will be less money available for private borrowing and spending. We will examine the

Congress affects fiscal policy when it votes to increase or decrease federal expenditures.

views of the monetarist economists in more detail when we study monetary policy in Chapter 12.

Keynesian economists disagree with the monetarists. Many Keynesians believe fiscal policy could be effective if it were implemented properly. They argue that too often political considerations prevent the implementation of proper fiscal policies at the proper times. For example, in times of demand-pull inflation proper fiscal policy would call for higher taxes and/or reduced government spending. However, there is usually strong opposition to increased taxes, and it may not be politically feasible to raise them. Similarly, cuts in government spending usually mean cuts in government services, which also can lead to strong opposition. In summary, many Keynesian economists believe that the failure of fiscal policy to solve the problems of cyclical unemployment and demand-pull inflation is due to improper implementation of the theory rather than to a weakness of the theory itself.

The best example of successful use of discretionary fiscal policy is the long period of expansion in the economy during the 1960s. When President John F. Kennedy took office in 1961, the economy was still suffering from a recession that had begun in 1958. During the election campaign, Kennedy promised to get the economy moving if elected, and he brought into his administration economic advisors who were determined to use discretionary fiscal policy to bring the economy out of the recession. The first fiscal-policy steps included increased federal spending on highways, and legislation that allowed businesses to subtract from their taxes a part of the cost of new investment in capital goods.

When these early measures did not prove sufficient, the President proposed a major tax cut. President Kennedy was assassinated before the tax cut was enacted, but his successor, Lyndon Johnson, signed an $11 billion tax cut into law in February 1964. This large tax cut along with substantial increases in government

spending for the Vietnam War during the mid- and late 1960s fueled the longest economic expansion in the American economy in more than 100 years. The expansion lasted from February 1961 to December 1969. The unemployment rate dropped to 4.5 percent in 1965 and then fell below 4 percent and stayed there for four consecutive years.

Many economists believe the experience of the 1960s clearly demonstrates the potential effectiveness of fiscal policy in fueling an economic expansion. However, the experiences of the late 1960s and early 1970s also demonstrate the basic weakness of fiscal policy in controlling inflation. In 1966, after seven consecutive years with the inflation rate never as high as 2 percent, inflation began to rise. Many economists believe that proper fiscal policy at that time should have included higher taxes and reduced government spending in order to reduce aggregate demand. As mentioned earlier, however, it is difficult to get public support for tax increases and/or government spending cuts. There is often a basic conflict between economic goals and political goals, and it is not always possible for government leaders to carry out the recommendations of economic advisors. Such appeared to be the case in the late 1960s and early 1970s. Although a small temporary tax increase was enacted in 1968, it was not sufficient to stop the accelerating inflation that was fueled by the now rapidly rising government spending for both the Vietnam War and new social programs.

As you will learn in Chapter 12, the government also can use monetary policy—changes in the cost and availability of credit—as a means of trying to even out a business cycle. While both fiscal and monetary policy have their weaknesses, with the proper coordination they can both make some contribution toward economic stability.

Supply-Side Economics

The failure of fiscal policy based on Keynesian

TABLE 10–1: DEMAND- AND SUPPLY-SIDE ECONOMICS

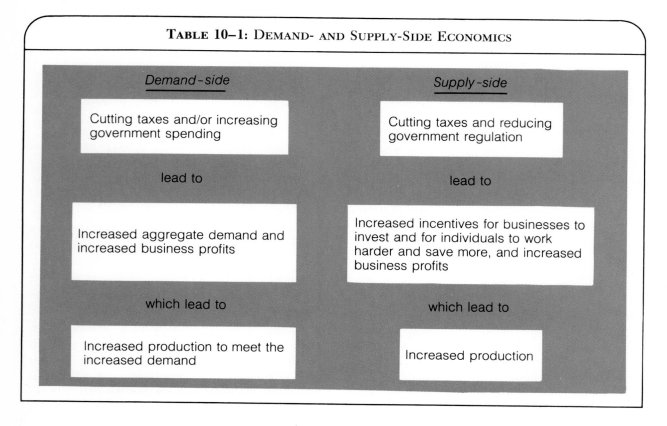

Demand-side

Cutting taxes and/or increasing government spending

lead to

Increased aggregate demand and increased business profits

which lead to

Increased production to meet the increased demand

Supply-side

Cutting taxes and reducing government regulation

lead to

Increased incentives for businesses to invest and for individuals to work harder and save more, and increased business profits

which lead to

Increased production

economics to control successfully the problems of unemployment and inflation led some economists during the late 1970s to advocate a new approach to economic policy called **supply-side economics.** The proponents of supply-side economics argued that the gradual rise in taxes over the years had led to a situation where taxes served to discourage work and investment. These economists contended that a sharp reduction in tax rates would provide strong incentives for workers to work harder and longer and for businesses to produce more goods and services. They argued that there would be so much additional work and production as a result of the tax cut that the government would actually collect more tax dollars then before, even with the lower tax rates.

In one sense, supply-side economics is just the opposite of Keynesian economics, which can be thought of as demand-side economics. Keynesian economists emphasize aggregate de-mand, whereas supply-side economists emphasize aggregate supply. In another sense, however, supply-side and demand-side economics are not so far apart because the goal of both is to increase production and reduce unemployment.

Table 10–1 presents the paths by which demand-side and supply-side economists propose to get to the increased production. Demand-side (Keynesian) economists believe that the government should actively intervene in the economy in order to maintain the proper level of aggregate demand. They believe that an increase in aggregate demand leads to increased business profits, which lead businesses to increase production to meet the increased demand. Supply-side economists, on the other hand, believe that cutting taxes and reducing government regulation will lead to increased business profits and increased incentives to invest. They argue that these increased profits and the resulting increase in investment will lead to increased production.

During the 1980 presidential election, candidate Ronald Reagan endorsed supply-side economics and proposed a 30 percent cut in tax rates over a three-year period. Reagan argued that if his policies were enacted into law, both unemployment and inflation would come down simultaneously and the increased production would generate enough revenue, even with the lower tax rates, to balance the federal budget by 1984.

In 1981, Congress enacted President Reagan's tax-cut proposal (which had been reduced from a 30 percent cut to a 25 percent cut in personal income tax rates over a three-year period), along with substantial cuts in federal spending for domestic programs. Inflation did come down but the unemployment rate climbed to 10.7 percent in December 1982, the highest since the Great Depression of the 1930s. Instead of the promised balanced budget by 1984, the federal government ran a budget deficit of $195.4 billion in fiscal year 1983, nearly three times the previous record of $66.4 billion set in 1976.

Some economists argued that the large budget deficits and high unemployment were proof that the theory of supply-side economics was unsound. However, other economists disagreed. They argued that the supply-side approach would succeed in the long run. They contended that the tax cuts and reduced government regulation would create a favorable environment for increased investment, which would eventually lead to increased economic growth.

By early 1985, the economy had recovered from the recession and the unemployment rate had dropped to 7.4 percent. Investment spending was up, and the annual inflation rate was holding steady at about 4 percent. Some supply-side economists argued that the improvement in the economy was evidence that supply-side economics was working. However, other economists pointed to the continuing large def-

icits and high interest rates as evidence that the economy is not in a good state of health. They argue that with the government continuing to borrow large amounts of money to finance the huge deficits, interest rates will remain high. They see high interest rates as an obstacle to reaching full employment, and some predict that the economy will enter a new recession long before full employment is attained.

Only time will tell whether supply-side economics can achieve in the long run what it did not achieve in the short run. In the meantime, there will be much debate over the ideas of the demand-side (Keynesian) and supply-side economists, as well as those of the monetarists.

Check Your Understanding

1. What are some of the reasons for the failure of fiscal policy to solve the problems of unemployment and inflation?

2. What are the main ideas behind supply-side economics? How does it differ from Keynesian economics?

3. How successful was supply-side economics in accomplishing the objectives promised by its advocates? Explain.

Balancing the Federal Budget

If the federal government uses its taxing and spending powers to influence the level of aggregate demand, it will seldom have a balanced budget in which tax revenue is exactly equal to government expenditures. This raises the important question of budget policy. Should the government attempt to balance its budget? If so, should it attempt to have a balanced budget each and every year or only in certain years? These questions have been the source of heated debate, both in and out of government, and have led some people to advocate a constitutional amendment requiring the federal government to balance its budget.

Most economists believe that the federal government should have a balanced budget under certain circumstances during some years. However, there is more than one way to balance the budget. Let us look at three alternative budget policies.

Annually Balanced Budget

Some people believe that the government should have a balanced budget each and every year. Such a policy may seem attractive in theory but few economists would support such a policy. Since most of the federal government's revenue comes from the individual and corporate income taxes, the government's revenue is very much influenced by the business cycle. During periods of recession, when many workers have lost their jobs and many corporations are losing money instead of making profits, government revenue falls off sharply. At the same time, government expenditures for unemployment compensation and other social programs will rise in response to the increased unemployment. The combined effects of reduced tax revenue and increased government spending will lead to larger budget deficits. Economists estimate that for every 1 percent increase in the unemployment rate, there will be a rise in the federal deficit of approximately $25 billion. Thus, if the unemployment rate rose by 2 percent during a recession, there could be a $50 billion increase in the federal deficit.

If the government attempted to balance such a budget by increasing taxes and/or reducing government spending, the resulting decline in aggregate demand would lead to still more unemployment and an even larger deficit. Thus, during periods of recession attempts to balance the budget through higher taxes and/or decreased government spending are likely to do more harm than good.

Cyclically Balanced Budget

A cyclically balanced budget would be one that was balanced over the course of the business cycle. During periods of recession, the government would run deficits in order to stimulate the economy. In other words, the government would increase spending and/or reduce taxes in order to increase aggregate demand. Businesses would then respond to the increased demand by recalling laid-off workers and increasing production. Conversely, during periods of high aggregate demand, the government would spend less than it collected in taxes and create budget surpluses. By pulling more tax dollars out of the economy than it spends, the government could reduce aggregate demand and help to prevent demand-pull inflation. If the surpluses offset the deficits, over a period of years total government spending would be approximately equal to total revenue.

In theory, such a policy would help to even out the high and low points of the business cycle and, at the same time, lead to a balanced budget over the long run. However, in actual practice the results would be different. Since business cycles are not uniform or predictable, it would be highly unlikely that the surpluses and deficits would exactly cancel one another out in any given time period.

Full-Employment Balanced Budget

A full-employment balanced budget policy is one in which the budget would be balanced when, and only when, the economy is operating at the full-employment level. Under this policy, the government would estimate the total revenue that it would receive if the economy were operating at the full-employment level and then attempt to restrict spending to this level. If the economy operates at the full-employment level, the budget will be balanced. If the economy operates below the full-employment level, tax collections will be less than what is needed and there will be a budget deficit. During periods when aggregate demand is insufficient for the economy to reach full employment, the government will be forced to spend more money than it collects in taxes.

This budget policy rejects the use of discretionary fiscal policy (deliberate changes in government spending and/or taxes) to change aggregate demand. Instead, it relies on the automatic fiscal stabilizers to keep the economy at a high level of employment. Supporters of this budget policy argue that it avoids the difficult problems connected with properly implementing discretionary fiscal policy and that it provides for a balanced budget during times of full employment. Furthermore, they contend that if tax rates are set high enough to generate a small surplus during years of full employment, the surpluses might offset the deficits of other years so that an approximately balanced budget could be attained over a period of many years. Critics of this policy charge that reliance on automatic stabilizers may not be sufficient to keep the economy operating at or near the full-employment level.

TABLE 10–2: BALANCING THE FEDERAL BUDGET

Type of Budget	Requirement	Problems
Annually balanced budget	Budget balanced every year	An increase in taxes or a reduction in government spending during a recession could lead to increased unemployment and an even larger deficit
Cyclically balanced budget	Budget balanced over the business cycle; deficits during recession and surpluses during inflation	Because business cycles are not uniform or predictable, surpluses and deficits would probably not cancel each other out during any given time period.
Full-employment balanced budget	Budget balanced only during periods of full employment	Automatic fiscal stabilizers, on which this type of budget depends, may not be sufficient to keep the economy operating at or near the full-employment level

TABLE 10–3: FEDERAL GOVERNMENT BUDGET RECEIPTS AND OUTLAYS
FOR FISCAL YEARS 1964–1984 IN BILLIONS OF DOLLARS

Fiscal Year	Receipts	Outlays	Surplus (+) or Deficit (−)
1964	112.7	118.6	−5.9
1965	116.8	118.4	−1.6
1966	130.9	134.7	−3.8
1967	148.9	157.6	−8.7
1968	153.0	178.1	−25.2
1969	186.9	183.6	+3.2
1970	192.8	195.7	−2.8
1971	187.1	210.2	−23.0
1972	207.3	230.7	−24.4
1973	230.8	245.6	−14.8
1974	263.2	267.9	−4.7
1975	279.1	324.2	−45.2
1976	298.1	364.5	−66.4
1977	355.6	400.5	−44.9
1978	399.6	448.4	−48.8
1979	463.3	491.0	−27.7
1980	517.1	576.7	−59.6
1981	599.3	657.2	−57.9
1982	617.8	728.4	−110.6
1983	600.6	796.0	−195.4
1984	666.5	841.8	−175.4

Source: *Economic Report of the President*, 1985

Deficits and the National Debt

Each of the above budget policies calls for balancing the federal budget in at least some years. However, in actual practice the federal government seldom has a balanced budget or a budget surplus. As you can see from Table 10–3, during the period 1964 to 1984, there was a surplus in the federal budget in only one year—$3.2 billion in 1969—despite the fact that the economy experienced full employment and demand-pull inflation during several of those years. The government ran a budget deficit in every other year for a total deficit of $943.6 billion during the period.

When the government spends more than it receives in revenue, it must borrow the extra money to finance the deficit. The government borrows money by selling bonds to banks, individuals, and other investors. Government bonds are simply IOUs that obligate the government to repay the borrowed money plus interest. Some government bonds have a very short maturity and must be repaid in a year or less. Others have a maturity of several years.

Government bonds are usually an attractive investment. Interest earned on United States bonds is not subject to state and local income taxes. Also, government bonds generally are considered the safest of all possible investments because the government can raise the necessary funds to repay the borrowed money when bonds come due. It can raise the money by selling new bonds, and if it can't sell enough bonds, it has the power to collect the needed money by raising taxes.

Over the years, the federal government has accumulated a large national debt as a result of borrowing money to finance deficits, and the debt becomes larger each time the government borrows more money. Figure 10–4 shows the growth in the national debt during the period 1945 to 1985. As you can see, the national debt rose from approximately $260 billion in 1945 to approximately $1.8 trillion in 1985.

The size and rate of growth of the national debt have been the source of much controversy. Some people fear that if the debt continues to grow at its present rate, it might eventually lead the nation into bankruptcy. This fear is based on a misunderstanding of the national debt. Unlike individuals and business firms, the United States government cannot go bankrupt because it has special revenue-raising powers. The gov-

ernment can raise money by selling additional bonds or by raising taxes. Although raising taxes to pay interest on the national debt may not be popular or desirable, the government does have the power to do so. Also, unlike private debts the national debt does not have to be paid off. When bonds come due, the government can and does sell new bonds to refinance the debt. Thus, the national debt probably will never be paid off.

Some people argue that we will be passing the burden of our current deficit spending on to future generations in the form of a larger national debt. It is true that the national debt is passed from one generation to the next, but so is the ownership of the debt. In other words, if some future generation should decide to pay off part or all of the national debt, the payment would be made to bondholders of that generation. The same is true of interest payments on the debt.

Many economists believe that growth in the debt must be looked at in relation to growth in the gross national product. Just as an individual can safely carry a larger debt as his or her income rises, many economists believe that the nation can safely carry a larger debt as the GNP rises. Figure 10–5 shows the national debt as a percentage of the GNP. As you can see, the national debt as a percentage of the GNP declined from 1946 until the early 1980s when it began to rise again because of unusually large budget deficits. Unless the large deficits continue indefinitely and the long-term decline in the national debt as a percentage of the GNP is reversed, some economists believe that the size of the national debt by itself is not a major problem.

Deficits and Interest Rates

Many economists believe that the most serious threat of large budget deficits is the effect that they have on interest rates. As you already know, an increase in the demand for any item will cause the price of that item to rise. The price of borrowing money is the interest rate,

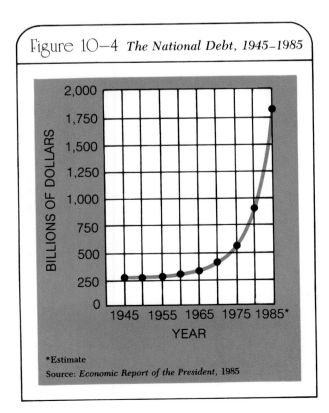

Figure 10–4 *The National Debt, 1945–1985*

*Estimate

Source: *Economic Report of the President*, 1985

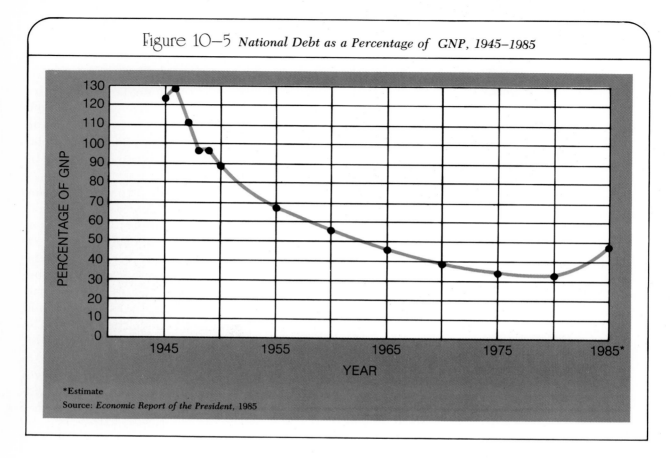

Figure 10–5 *National Debt as a Percentage of GNP, 1945–1985*

*Estimate

Source: *Economic Report of the President, 1985*

and any time the demand for loans increases relative to the supply, interest rates will rise. In 1983, the federal government had to borrow $195.4 billion to cover the federal deficit for that year and in 1984 it borrowed $175.4 billion. This means the government was competing for loans with individuals who wanted to borrow money to purchase homes, cars, and other things, and with businesses who wanted to borrow money to expand their business operations. The net result was higher interest rates. Everybody who borrowed money in 1983 and 1984 had to pay a higher interest rate than they would have if the federal government had not run such large budget deficits. By early 1985, many economists were voicing concern that if the government did not take action to reduce the federal deficit, the high interest rates would tend to limit both consumption and investment spending, and to prevent the economy from reaching full employment before heading into a new recession.

Check Your Understanding

1. Identify three budget policies. How do they differ from one another?

2. How do budget deficits affect the national debt?

3. How do budget deficits affect interest rates?

CAREERS: Buyer

If you like to travel and believe you can learn to spend large sums of money responsibly, you might be interested in becoming a professional buyer. Buyers purchase merchandise from manufacturers and wholesalers that is later sold to the general public in retail stores. Many buyers also supervise salespeople and take direct responsibility for successful sales of the products they choose. Others play only an indirect role in the resale of goods and rely on the store's sales staff to promote maximum sales.

Buyers must be familiar with the many manufacturers and wholesale distributors in their industry, and they must be able to assess the resale value of goods after a brief inspection. They must stay informed about changes in existing products as well as the development of new ones, and they must try to anticipate trends in consumer tastes. Buyers study economic conditions and examine industry and trade publications in an effort to purchase the best products at the lowest possible cost.

Resourcefulness, stamina, good judgment, and confidence in one's ability to make decisions and take risks are all requirements of the job. Buyers often have to work long hours and usually travel several days each month. Buying trips to such cities as New York, Chicago, San Francisco, and Philadelphia are an important part of the jobs of many buyers, and buyers of some specialized products may make yearly trips to major European or Asian cities.

Although a high school graduate might gain an entry-level position in a store that would eventually lead to a job as a buyer, an increasing number of employers prefer college graduates for buyer-trainee programs. These programs combine classroom instruction with short rotations to various jobs in the store. The trainees begin as assistant buyers and gradually assume buying responsibilities.

Chapter Highlights

1   Classical economics—the ideas formulated by Adam Smith and refined by his followers—proved inadequate to explain or solve the problems of the Great Depression of the 1930s. As a result, classical economics was soon replaced by Keynesian economics, based on the ideas of John Maynard Keynes.

2   Keynesian economists believe that the government should play an active role in regulating the level of aggregate demand in order to minimize both unemployment and inflation. They also believe that through proper use of its spending and taxing powers, the government can control fluctuations in the business cycle.

3   The deliberate use of the government's spending and taxing powers to influence economic activity is called fiscal policy. The objectives of fiscal policy are to reduce the size of business fluctuations and to minimize both unemployment and inflation.

4   Automatic fiscal stabilizers are built-in features of the economy that tend to change government spending and taxes in the desired direction automatically during the various phases of the business cycle. Two examples of automatic stabilizers are unemployment compensation and the progressive income tax.

5   Since automatic fiscal stabilizers are not sufficient to prevent cyclical unemployment and demand-pull inflation, most Keynesian economists advocate the use of discretionary fiscal policies—deliberate actions taken by policy makers to change government spending and/or taxes.

6   Fiscal policy does not work as well in actual practice as it does in theory. Political obstacles make it difficult for policy makers to change government spending and/or taxes by the proper amounts at the proper times.

7   Advocates of supply-side economics believe that large cuts in tax rates and reduced government regulation of business will provide strong incentives for workers to work harder and longer, and for businesses to produce more goods and services. They believe that the additional work and production that result from tax cuts will result in increased tax revenue even with the lower tax rates.

8   Three budget policies that might balance the federal budget under different circumstances are an annually balanced budget, a cyclically balanced budget, and a full-employment balanced budget.

9   The large federal budget deficits of recent years have caused the national debt to grow very rapidly. The large deficits also have tended to force interest rates up. High interest rates generally limit both consumption and investment spending and may affect our ability to reach a full-employment level.

Important Terms

Match each of the following terms with the correct definition:

supply-side economics	full-employment balanced budget
classical economics	annually balanced budget
fiscal policy	cyclically balanced budget
Keynesian economics	automatic fiscal stabilizers

1. The deliberate use of the government's spending and taxing powers to influence economic activity in order to accomplish desired economic objectives.

2. A body of economic theory that emphasizes aggregate supply as a means of increasing production and reducing unemployment.

3. A budget policy under which the federal budget would be balanced when, and only when, the economy is operating at the full-employment level.

4. A body of economic theory based on the belief that the government should play an active role in maintaining the proper level of aggregate demand.

5. A budget policy under which the government would attempt to balance its budget over the course of the business cycle.

6. The ideas that were formulated by Adam Smith in *The Wealth of Nations*, and refined by his followers.

7. Built-in features of the economy that tend to change government spending and taxes in the desired direction automatically during the various phases of the business cycle.

8. A budget policy under which the government would attempt to have a balanced budget each and every year.

Extending Your Understanding

1. Why is it often difficult for the government to follow consistent and sound fiscal policies?

2. Do you believe the federal government should have a balanced budget? If so, which budget policy do you believe is best? Give reasons for your answer.

3. Review the reasons why the government has run such large budget deficits in recent years. Do you think the large federal deficit is a serious problem? Why or why not?

Activities

1. Hold a panel discussion on the merits and shortcomings of Keynesian economics and supply-side economics. Compare how successful each has been, taking into account the problems that have been encountered by each. All participants should do the research they need ahead of time to be able to support their opinions.

2. Fiscal policy is carried out by all levels of government. To find out about your state's fiscal policy, write to your state government for a copy of the most recent state budget. Is it a balanced budget? Does it show a surplus or a deficit? Summarize your findings in a short report.

Building Skills in Economics: Interpreting a News Article

Economics is always in the news. If you pick up any newspaper, you are almost certain to find a story on economic issues. In order to understand what is being discussed, though, you need to know how to interpret a news article.

News articles usually begin with a dateline, which shows where and when the story was written. In addition, news articles focus on six important questions: who, what, where, when, why, and how. The opening paragraph usually answers the first four questions, and the rest of the article details the why and the how.

The article that follows discusses fiscal policy. The questions will help you interpret the article.

Applying Economics Skills

1. What does the dateline of the article tell you?
2. Which of the six questions are answered in the first paragraph? State the answers to these questions.
3. Where are the why and the how questions answered? Give the answers to these questions.
4. Write a brief summary of the article.

PRESIDENT PROPOSES BUDGET CUTS TO REDUCE DEFICIT

Washington, Dec. 5—The President announced at the White House today that he intended to recommend cuts of $34 billion in the coming year's federal budget. These reductions will be made up primarily of cuts in domestic programs such as Social Security benefits and student loans, and federal aid to transportation systems, farm support programs, and programs for the poor.

In addition, the President stated that recommendations will be made for cuts in the defense budget, as well as in programs affecting military pensions and aid to veterans.

Announcing his proposals at a Cabinet meeting, he stated, "We must make every effort to begin reducing government spending now. The record federal budget deficit and the cost of the national debt could lead to serious inflation or to a recession if the deficit is not reduced substantially over the next two years."

The President will submit his proposed budget to Congress early next month. He indicated that he also will be announcing proposals for major tax reforms in February.

Initial reactions to the President's proposed cuts are mixed. Those agreeing with the President's proposal argue that major reductions must be made in the record federal deficit. Those disagreeing with the President fear that those needing federal assistance the most—the poor and middle class citizens—will be severely hurt by his cuts. They generally would prefer across-the-board freezes in all spending programs rather than major reductions in selected budget areas. These reactions, for the most part, cut across party lines.

UNIT 4

Money, Banking, and Monetary Policy

CHAPTER 11

MONEY AND BANKING

Money is one of the most crucial and fascinating things in modern society. To a small child money is magic—pieces of green paper and metal coins that can be exchanged for all sorts of wonderful things. To adults, money is an important item that is needed to buy a home, food, clothes, a car, and many other things. Money is also one of the most misunderstood things in modern society. Some people believe that if only they could accumulate enough money, their problems would be solved. They see money as a means of obtaining happiness, prestige, power.

In this chapter, we will learn about the functions of money, the characteristics of money, and the kinds of money used in this country. In the latter part of the chapter, we will study the characteristics and functions of commercial banks and other financial institutions.

What Is Money?

Suppose you are asked to define "money." You might say money consists of coins and bills of various denominations—pennies, nickels, dollar bills, five-dollar bills, and so on. Suppose, however, you are told that at some time and place in history, stones, whale teeth, boar tusks, diamonds, fish hooks, seashells, grain, gold, silver, copper, and paper all have served as money. Would your definition of money change? Given this additional information, you might expand your definition of money somewhat. We will define **money** here as anything that is generally accepted and generally used as a medium of payments. In other words, people will accept it for whatever they have to sell because they know that other people will accept it, too. It doesn't matter whether money is made from gold, seashells, or just simple pieces of paper. As long as people are willing to accept it as payment for whatever they have to sell, it is money.

This definition tells us about one of the functions of money—its use as a medium of exchange. There are two other important functions of money.

Functions of Money

Money has three important functions: It serves as a medium of exchange, a measure of value, and a store of value. Any item that acts in these capacities can in fact serve as money.

A medium is anything that serves as a go-between and makes it easier for something to happen. Therefore, when we say that money is a medium of exchange, we mean that money makes it easier to exchange or trade things. Without money people would have to resort to **barter**—a form of trade in which people directly trade goods and services for other types of goods and services without using money.

Barter is a very cumbersome form of trade that is not practical in a modern, complex society. For barter to work, there must be a **double coincidence of wants.** This means that you must want what someone else has and the other person must want what you have. For example, suppose that in a barter society, John wants to buy a bicycle from his friend Linda. In exchange, Linda wants a tennis racquet, a book, and a cassette recorder—none of which John has. How is John going to get these items so he can buy the bicycle from Linda? The only way John has of earning anything of value is by mowing Mrs. Johnson's lawn. Mrs. Johnson raises chickens, and she will pay John five dozen eggs per week for 20 weeks to keep her lawn mowed all summer. That means John will earn a total of 100 dozen eggs for his summer's work. Because Linda will not accept eggs for the bicycle, however, John still has a problem. In order to be able to buy the bicycle, he must first find someone who is willing to trade a tennis racquet, a book, and a cassette recorder for 100 dozen eggs.

Just think how much simpler life would have been for John and Linda if money existed. Instead of paying John 100 dozen eggs for his summer's work, Mrs. Johnson could have paid him $100. John could have then paid Linda $100 for the bicycle, and Linda could have used the money to buy the things she wanted.

As you can see from this example, money is very important as a medium of exchange. Without money, it would be very difficult for people to obtain the things they need, even when they have other things of value. In fact, without money, life as we know it today could not exist.

Money also serves as a measure of value. This means that money is used to compare the worth of various things. For example, if the bicycle is worth $100 and the eggs are worth $1 per dozen, this means that the 100 dozen eggs have the same value as the bicycle. Without money, it would be necessary to state the price of each item in terms of all of the products for which it might be exchanged. In such a case, we might say that the bicycle is worth 100 dozen eggs, 4 footballs, 2 cassette recorders, 50 gallons of milk, 40 bushels of corn, and so forth. With money, the value of any item needs to be stated only in dollar terms.

In addition to serving as a medium of exchange and a measure of value, money also serves as a store of value. This means that people can use money as a means to store their wealth. For example, John wants to store his earnings from mowing Mrs. Johnson's lawn until he has enough to buy Linda's bicycle. If Mrs. Johnson pays him in eggs, he will have a difficult time storing his wealth. Eggs are not a good store of value because they spoil easily. If John tries to store his wealth in eggs, many of them will spoil before the end of summer. However, if Mrs. Johnson pays him $5 a week instead of 5 dozen eggs a week, John easily can store his earnings in the form of money because money is durable and will hold up well over time.

Characteristics of Money

There are five important characteristics that any item must have if it is to be used as money. It must be durable, accepted, portable, divisible, and stable in value.

As we just pointed out, eggs would be a poor choice when looking for something to serve as money. In order for an item to be useful as money, it must be able to endure the wear and tear of being passed from person to person over a long period of time. It is no wonder that gold and silver were often used as coins. Many ancient coins are still in existence today, thousands of years after they were first created. It is only recently that paper money has come to be used. Paper money is considered durable today because old bills can be replaced easily when they wear out.

Acceptability means that both parties to a transaction will accept the money in exchange for the goods or services being purchased. Acceptability is a very important characteristic. Just because something is called money doesn't

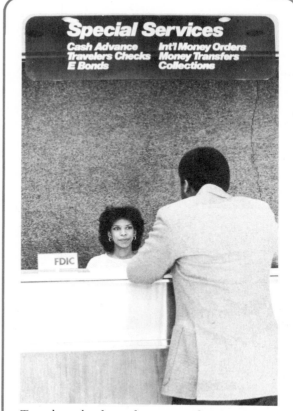

Travelers checks and money orders are considered money since they are widely accepted and generally used for payment.

necessarily mean that it will be accepted in that capacity. For example, suppose a Japanese family arriving in this country has only yen (Japanese money). How successful do you think the family will be if they try to use it to pay for a purchase in a small East Coast store? Chances are, the family will have to forgo its purchase because the merchant won't accept their money. Although we take dollars for granted, in many places outside of the United States they might not be accepted.

In order to serve as a medium of exchange, objects used as money must be able to be carried easily from place to place. Paper money easily can fit in a wallet. If you look at a list of items that have been used as money, you will see that they were portable. Items that were not portable could not be taken with people wherever and whenever they wanted to make a purchase. Imagine trying to take five beds with you if you wanted to make a major purchase.

In our society, the dollar is divisible into coins of different denominations—pennies, nickels, dimes, and so forth. These coins can be combined in varying amounts to make change for any purchase. For example, suppose a bag of flour costs 79 cents. A grocer might give you one penny and two dimes if you pay for your purchase with a dollar bill. All money must be easily divisible in this manner so that purchases of any size or price can be made.

Money must also be stable in value. If John decides to put aside the $100 he earns for mowing Mrs. Johnson's lawn, he is confident that a few months later he will still be able to buy the bicycle he wanted. This is because money is relatively stable in value. Of course, with inflation the purchasing power of money will go down. Money, however, is still relatively stable when all things are taken into account.

Check Your Understanding

1. What is money? Give some examples of items that have served as money.

2. What are the three functions of money?

3. Why is barter not practical in a modern, complex economy?

4. Describe five characteristics of money. How does the money we use fit each of these five characteristics?

Types of Money

All societies have created money that to a large extent meets the five criteria we just discussed. These five characteristics have made it possible for various items to serve as a medium of exchange, a measure of value, and a store of value in different societies. In the United States, there are basically three types of money: coins, paper money, and checkbook money. We will examine each of these kinds of money plus a related concept called near-money.

Coins

Coins—pennies, nickels, dimes, quarters, 50-cent pieces, and dollar coins—make up the smallest part of the nation's **money supply,** or the total amount of money in circulation. Only about 2 or 3 percent of the nation's total money supply is in the form of coins. Coins are convenient for buying inexpensive items and for use in automatic vending machines. However, coins are too heavy and inconvenient to use for large purchases.

Coins are made by the Bureau of the Mint—a part of the Treasury Department. At one time, all denominations of coins from dimes up contained 90 percent silver and 10 percent copper. The value of the silver in these coins was at least equal to the purchasing power of the coins. In other words, the silver in a quarter was worth at least 25 cents. Today, however, no coins produced for circulation contain silver. Pennies are made of copper and zinc, and all other coins are made of a combination of copper and nickel. The metal used to make a quarter today has a total value of approximately two cents.

Coins have value today not because of their metal content but because they are generally acceptable in payment and because the government says that they are money. Money that is declared money by government decree, or "fiat," is called **fiat money.** It has value because

The Treasury Department controls the issuing of paper money and coins, two of the three basic types of money in the United States.

the government has officially established it as **legal tender.** This means that it must be accepted for all debts, public and private.

Paper Money

Today, paper money in the United States makes up about 25 percent of the nation's money supply. Such money consists almost exclusively of Federal Reserve notes issued by the Federal Reserve Banks. (We will cover the Federal Reserve System and Federal Reserve Banks in Chapter 12.) Federal Reserve notes, which are issued in denominations of $1, $2, $5, $10, $20, $50, and $100, are printed by the Bureau of Engraving and Printing in Washington, D.C., and then shipped to the Federal Reserve Banks. (At one time denominations of $500, $1,000, $10,000, and $100,000 were also issued. However, these bills have since been recalled from circulation by the Federal Reserve.) Like

coins, Federal Reserve notes are fiat money. Printed on the front of each Federal Reserve note is the statement, "This note is legal tender for all debts, public and private." This means that Federal Reserve notes must, by law, be accepted as payment for any and all debts.

Some people have the mistaken notion that paper money is backed by gold or silver. This is not true today, although at one time it was. In fact, paper money evolved out of the custom of using paper receipts as proof of ownership of gold and silver. In the early seventeenth century, it was a common practice in England for people to keep their gold and silver in the vaults of local goldsmiths for safekeeping. When a person took gold or silver to a goldsmith, the goldsmith would issue a paper receipt to the owner as proof of ownership. When the person wanted to spend the gold or silver, he or she would take the receipt to the goldsmith and pick up the precious metal.

This was a cumbersome practice, and eventually people discovered that they could transfer ownership of their gold or silver by simply giving merchants the paper receipts. Merchants accepted the paper receipts because the paper represented actual gold or silver in the goldsmith's vault. It became a common practice to pay bills by simply endorsing, or signing over, the paper receipts. Eventually, goldsmiths began to write "payable to the bearer" on receipts instead of putting the owner's name on them. This eliminated the need to endorse the receipts when using them to make a purchase. Whoever possessed a receipt was the owner of the gold or silver. People willingly accepted the pieces of paper as money because they were "as good as gold."

Until 1933, paper money in the United States was convertible into gold and silver. The Treasury Department kept a substantial amount of gold and silver available so that people could exchange their paper money for the precious metals. In that year, however, the United States government abandoned the gold standard, and citizens no longer could convert paper money into gold. (Up until 1968, the government did require that a certain amount of gold be held as partial backing for Federal Reserve notes, but that requirement has been suspended as well.) Today, all paper money in the United States is fiat money. There is no gold or silver backing it up. It is money because the United States government has decreed that it is legal tender for all debts, public and private.

Checkbook Money

Checkbook money makes up more than 70 percent of the money supply in the United States, and approximately 90 percent of the dollar value of all transactions are carried out by the writing of checks. For example, we tend to pay our biggest bills by check rather than with other forms of money. To be able to write checks, a person deposits money in a checking account. The amount in the account is the amount for which the person can write checks. If the person wants to withdraw money from the account, either to pay a bill or to obtain cash, the person simply writes a check for that amount.

Because checkbook money is payable on demand to the depositor or to anyone else to whom the check is written, checking accounts are called **demand deposits.** Demand deposits are considered money because they are used as a medium of exchange, a measure of value, and a store of value. For example, if a person wants to pay for a purchase with a check, the person usually just has to show proper identification before being allowed to do so.

In the past, only commercial banks—often called full-service banks—could issue checking accounts, and no interest was paid on such accounts. However, changes in the banking laws in 1980 authorized other financial institutions, such as savings banks and savings and loan associations, to issue new types of checking accounts. The most popular of these new accounts is the Negotiable Order of Withdrawal, or NOW account. NOW accounts pay interest, as do some other types of checking accounts, and today they are offered by most commercial banks as well as other financial institutions.

Many people prefer to pay for large purchases with checkbook money rather than with paper money or coins.

Near-Money

Two kinds of bank balances that are similar to money, but which are not usually considered a part of the nation's money supply, are time deposits and savings accounts. Both kinds of accounts pay interest to the depositor. The major difference between the two is that depositors usually must give prior notice to a financial institution before withdrawing money from a time deposit, whereas money can usually be withdrawn from a savings account at any time.

Unlike demand deposits, money cannot be withdrawn from savings accounts or time deposits by writing checks. You cannot use your savings account passbook to pay a bill. Instead, you must go to the bank and withdraw cash or have money transferred from your savings account to your checking account. Because you cannot use savings accounts and time deposits to make purchases or pay bills, they usually are not considered a part of the nation's money supply. However, since funds in savings accounts and time deposits easily can be converted into cash or checking account balances, such deposits usually are considered **near-money.**

Taken together, coins, paper money, and demand deposits comprise the nation's money supply. (Sometimes economists also include near-money to get a broader measure of the potential money supply.)

Check Your Understanding

1. Describe the three basic types of money used in the United States today. How did paper money originate?

2. What is meant by the terms "fiat money" and "legal tender"? Why does paper money have value?

3. What are demand deposits? Why are they considered money?

4. Describe what is meant by "near-money."

Near-money includes interest-bearing savings accounts such as Christmas Club accounts, where depositors add to their accounts at intervals throughout the year.

The Development of Banks and Banking

As we already have mentioned, during the seventeenth century in England it was a common practice for people to keep their gold and silver in the vaults of local goldsmiths for safekeeping. Goldsmiths issued paper receipts, or notes, to people who deposited gold and silver with them, and over time people began to use these paper notes as money. These early goldsmiths gradually developed into goldsmith-bankers and were the forerunners of modern bankers.

As the paper notes became more and more acceptable as money, the goldsmith-bankers discovered that much of the gold and silver never left their vaults. Given this situation, they began to lend out part of the money in the form of additional paper notes. As long as the goldsmith-bankers were careful not to make too many loans and as long as borrowers repaid their loans on time, the system worked to the benefit of all parties. Borrowers were able to obtain funds to finance purchases without having to wait until they had saved enough cash. The goldsmith-bankers earned interest on the loans. In some cases, the depositors may even have been paid a small fee for leaving their money in the goldsmith's vaults.

During the late 1700s and early 1800s, many banks in the United States operated on the same principle as the early goldsmith-bankers in England. Some banks, however, did not follow sound banking practices. In an effort to earn as much interest as possible, they issued far too many loans. Holders of bank notes started becoming concerned, and increasing numbers of them went to the banks to exchange their notes for gold and silver. Since the gold and silver reserves of many banks were low, the banks were forced to suspend redemption of these notes. By 1814, most of the banks in the nation, except for those in New England, stopped exchanging gold and silver for bank notes.

Commercial Banks

People sometimes use the term "bank" to refer to different kinds of financial institutions. The term "bank," however, should be used to refer only to **commercial banks,** which are financial institutions that have been chartered by the federal government or a state government to receive deposits and make loans. In the past, commercial banks easily could be distinguished from other financial institutions by the fact that only they could offer checking accounts (demand deposits). Changes in the banking laws in 1980, however, authorized other financial institutions to issue new types of checking accounts, such as NOW accounts. Today, the most important distinguishing feature of commercial banks is that they make short-term commercial loans to businesses and short-term personal loans to the general public. In contrast, savings and loan associations make mostly long-term home-mortgage loans.

In order to start a new bank, the group wishing to do so must obtain a *charter* from either the federal government or a state government. Banks chartered by the federal government are called **national banks.** Banks chartered by state governments are called **state banks.** This dual system of banking evolved over 100 years ago as a number of state banks maintained their independence despite the development of a national banking system. Today, many newly organized banks choose to become state banks rather than national banks because the requirements for doing so are less rigid. For example, national banks must become members of the Federal Reserve System. State banks have the option of joining this organization but they are not required to do so.

All banks that are members of the Federal Reserve System also must belong to the Federal Deposit Insurance Corporation (FDIC). Non-member state banks can become members of

The letters FDIC are prominently displayed in most American banks to inform customers that their accounts are insured to a maximum of $100,000.

the FDIC, and most state banks have chosen this option. The FDIC was established by Congress in 1933 to insure bank depositors against bank failures. During the Great Depression, prior to the establishment of the FDIC, many people became concerned about the safety of their deposits and rushed to the banks to withdraw their money. Since banks lend most of the money that is deposited with them, they couldn't possibly repay all their depositors within a short time period. These "runs on the bank," as they were called at the time, caused many banks to fail and many people to lose their life savings.

Today, the FDIC guarantees bank deposits up to a maximum of $100,000 and the majority of American banks do carry FDIC insurance. Thus, depositors do not have to worry about the safety of their deposits up to that amount. FDIC insurance adds stability to the American banks that have it by making future runs on those banks unlikely.

Primary Functions of Commercial Banks

Modern commercial banks serve three primary functions: (1) they provide safekeeping services; (2) they make loans; and (3) as a group, they create money. The safekeeping function of banks originated with the early goldsmiths in seventeenth-century England. As you already have learned, it was a common practice at that time for people to keep their gold and silver in the strong vaults of local goldsmiths. Today, modern banks provide a similar service in the form of safe-deposit boxes, which can be rented for an annual fee. However, the most important safekeeping service provided by banks today is that depositors can place their savings in FDIC-insured bank accounts.

The second function of banks is to make loans. Most of the money that is deposited with commercial banks is loaned out. These banks channel the savings of depositors into credit-worthy loans—business loans, real estate loans, home-improvement loans, automobile loans, personal loans, and so forth. Of course, commercial banks earn substantial profits by charging borrowers a higher interest rate on loans than these banks pay to depositors on savings.

Creating money is the third function of commercial banks. These banks create money in the form of demand deposits (checking accounts) when they make loans and add them to the demand deposit balances of their borrowers. As you will learn in the next chapter, banks are required by law to keep only a certain percentage of money that is deposited with them as **required reserves** to back up deposits. Any money in excess of the required reserves is called **excess reserves** and can be loaned out. Let us look at how this process works.

Suppose Sam Lucas deposits $10,000 in a checking account. The bank might be required to keep only 10 percent on reserve and therefore loans out the remaining $9,000. Let us assume Jane Grady needs $9,000 to make improvements on her home. She borrows and spends the money. The contractor she hired and paid deposits the $9,000 in another bank. Because the bank that receives the new deposit is required to keep only $900 on hand, it loans out the remaining $8,100. As you can see, several transactions may take place because of Sam Lucas's original $10,000. The net result of this process leads to an expansion in the nation's money supply. In Chapter 12, you will learn about actions that the Federal Reserve can take

that affect the capacity of banks to create new loans and promote such expansion.

Objectives of Commercial Banks

Commercial banks have three primary objectives: liquidity, profitability, and safety. These objectives conflict with one another, and most banks continually struggle to achieve and maintain proper balance among the three.

Liquidity can be defined as the ease with which an asset can be converted into cash quickly without loss of value in terms of money.

Security guards and bank vaults symbolize one of the services provided by banks—the safekeeping of valuables.

Liquidity is a matter of degree. Cash is perfectly liquid because it can be used as a medium of exchange and it always retains the same value in terms of itself. At the other extreme, a bank building is not very liquid. It cannot always be sold quickly and easily, and it might have to be sold at a loss. In between these two extremes are the **income-earning assets** of banks. A bank's income-earning assets fall into two categories: loans and government securities.

Loans represent IOUs from businesses and individuals who have borrowed money from the banks. The liquidity of loans depends on their length. A bank's loans will range from 30-day or 60-day notes to 4-year auto loans to long-term real estate loans. Short-term loans are usually more liquid than long-term loans because they are more likely to be repaid quickly.

Government securities include securities (IOUs) issued by the United States Treasury, various agencies of the federal government, and state and local governments. Government securities earn interest for the banks, and they are relatively liquid since they can be sold at any time. Short-term government securities are the most liquid since they can be readily sold for cash with little or no loss of value. Longer term securities can be sold at any time but there is a greater potential for some loss of value because they may decrease in value over time.

Profitability is most affected by the loans a bank makes. The goal of profitability is in direct conflict with the goal of liquidity. A bank's most liquid assets are its cash in the vault and its deposits with the Federal Reserve Bank, but neither of these assets earns any interest at all. In contrast, the loans a bank makes are its most profitable assets because of the interest they earn. Loans, however, are among the least liquid of a bank's assets since they cannot be readily converted to cash. Government securities fall between these two extremes. They usually earn less interest than loans but they are considerably more liquid.

Safety refers to the probability that loans and other investments will be repaid on time with interest. Safety is a matter of degree. The safest of all investments for banks are government securities. The least safe are certain high-risk loans that some banks occasionally make. However, there is a conflict between safety and profitability because the high-risk loans usually earn substantially more interest than the low-risk government securities.

Bank officials must constantly weigh the goals of liquidity and safety against the goal of profitability. A bank must at all times be able to pay cash upon demand to its depositors. The moment a bank is unable to meet the cash demands of its demand deposits, it must close its doors. Thus, banks must make a compromise between their desire for maximum profitability and the need for safety and liquidity. This means holding a certain portion of their assets in nonearning vault cash and reserves at Federal Reserve Banks and an additional portion in very liquid short-term government securities.

Check Your Understanding

1. How did banks come into being?

2. What is a commercial bank? How are commercial banks distinguished from other financial institutions?

3. What are the three primary functions of commercial banks?

4. What are the three primary objectives of commercial banks? How do these objectives conflict with one another?

Nonbank Financial Institutions

In addition to commercial banks, there are other types of financial institutions that accept deposits from savers and make loans to investors and consumers. Three of the most important types of nonbank financial institutions are savings and loan associations, mutual savings banks, and credit unions.

Savings and loan associations are owned and operated by savers who as shareholders elect a board of directors to manage the organization. Technically, savers buy shares of ownership in the associations when they make deposits, but actually their savings are much like deposits in commercial banks. Most of the loans made by savings and loan associations historically were long-term loans—usually 20 years or longer—made for the purpose of buying or building homes. Today, however, savings and loan associations are also offering other types of loans that are usually shorter term.

In the past, savings and loan associations could not offer checking accounts, but today they can offer NOW accounts. In addition, deposits at most savings and loan associations are insured up to a maximum of $100,000 per account by the Federal Savings and Loan Insurance Corporation (FSLIC), a federal government agency very similar to the FDIC.

Mutual savings banks originated in the United States in the early 1800s at a time when commercial banks were not interested in the small savings deposits of wage-earners. Their purpose was to pool the savings of many small depositors so that this money could be invested profitably. Mutual savings banks are totally owned by their depositors and are operated for the benefit of these individuals. The depositors also receive any profits earned by mutual savings banks, as well as interest on deposits.

Mutual savings banks can offer NOW

Nonbank financial institutions are offering more services today than in the past.

accounts or regular checking accounts. They can make both consumer and business loans, but business loans are limited to a small fraction of their total assets. They are chartered by the state in which they are located, or by the federal government, and deposits are usually insured up to $100,000 by the FDIC or, in some cases, by the FSLIC.

Credit unions, as you learned in Chapter 4, are nonprofit cooperative associations owned and operated by their members for the purpose of offering high-interest savings accounts and low-interest loans. They are often organized by the employees of large companies or the members of large labor unions for the benefit of their membership, some of whom would have difficulty getting loans from commercial banks or other financial institutions.

Check Your Understanding

1. What are savings and loan associations?

2. What are mutual savings banks?

3. What are credit unions?

CAREERS: Bank Teller

If you enjoy working with people and feel you can handle large amounts of money responsibly, you might consider becoming a bank teller. Bank tellers deal directly with bank customers, cashing checks, accepting deposits, and paying out withdrawals. In some cases, they also may sell savings bonds and travelers checks and perform other clerical duties.

In cashing checks, tellers are responsible for identifying the person cashing the check, verifying signatures, and making sure that the account has sufficient funds to cover the check. They also must avoid making errors when counting out money or when recording deposits or withdrawals in passbooks.

Tellers' duties begin before the bank opens and continue past the time when the bank closes. Tellers begin the day by receiving and counting an amount of working cash for their drawer. They use this cash for transactions during the day and are respon-

sible for its safe and accurate handling. At the end of the day, tellers must count their cash and balance the day's account on a settlement sheet. They also may be responsible for sorting deposit slips and checks and for other duties assigned by their supervisor.

Although a high school education usually is required for employment as a bank teller, increasing numbers of tellers are college educated. College graduates who want careers in banking often begin as bank tellers and then work their way up to higher level positions. Tellers also can prepare for better jobs by taking courses accredited by the American Institute of Banking (AIB) or the Bank Administration Institute (BAI). Both institutes assist banks in conducting cooperative training programs. Some banks have their own training programs that result in teller certification. In addition to formal education, maturity, neatness, and a pleasant personality also are important requirements for the job.

Chapter Highlights

1 Money is anything that is generally accepted and generally used as a medium of payments.

2 Money has three important functions: It serves as a medium of exchange, a measure of value, and a store of value.

3 Five characteristics of money are durability, acceptability, portability, divisibility, and stability.

4 In the United States, there are basically three types of money: coins, paper money, and checkbook money. Coins, which are made by the Bureau of the Mint, make up the smallest part of the money supply. Paper money consists of Federal Reserve notes, which are printed by the Bureau of Engraving and Printing and issued by the Federal Reserve Banks. Checkbook money consists of demand deposits in banks and other financial institutions.

5 Coins and Federal Reserve notes are called fiat money because they are declared money by government decree. They have value because the government has officially established them as legal tender, which means that they must be accepted for all debts, public and private.

6 Near-money consists of time deposits and savings accounts that can easily be converted into cash or checking account balances.

7 A commercial bank is a financial institution that has been chartered by the federal government or a state government to receive deposits and make loans. All national commercial banks must become members of the Federal Reserve System, but state commercial banks may choose whether or not to join.

8 Almost all banks are members of the Federal Deposit Insurance Corporation (FDIC), which insures bank deposits up to a maximum of $100,000.

9 Modern commercial banks serve three primary functions: (1) they provide safekeeping services; (2) they make loans; and (3) as a group, they create money. Commercial banks operate on the basis of liquidity, profitability, and safety.

10 In addition to commercial banks, there are other types of financial institutions that accept deposits from savers and make loans to investors and consumers. Three of the most important types of nonbank financial institutions are savings and loan associations, mutual savings banks, and credit unions.

Important Terms

Match each of the following terms with the correct definition:

liquidity	commercial banks	credit unions
FDIC	demand deposits	state banks
barter	savings and loan associations	national banks
money	mutual savings banks	near-money
fiat money		

1. Money that is declared legal tender by government decree.

2. Financial institutions that have been chartered by the federal government or a state government to receive deposits and make loans.

3. Checkbook money.

4. A form of trade in which people directly trade goods and services for other types of goods and services without using money.

5. Savings accounts and time deposits that are not payable on demand but that can easily be converted into currency.

6. Anything that is generally accepted and generally used as a medium of payments.

7. The ease with which an asset can be converted into cash quickly without loss of value in terms of money.

8. Financial institutions, totally owned by their depositors, whose purpose is to pool the savings of many small depositors so that these savings can be profitably invested.

9. Banks chartered by the federal government.

10. Banks chartered by state governments.

11. Financial institutions, owned and operated by savers, that historically made mostly long-term loans for the purpose of buying or building homes.

12. A government agency established by Congress in 1933 to insure bank depositors against bank failures.

13. Cooperative associations often organized among the employees of large companies or the members of large labor unions for the purpose of offering high-interest savings accounts and low-interest loans.

Extending Your Understanding

Suppose you lived in a society without money. How would that society differ from the one you live in? What kinds of special problems would exist in such a society?

Which of the three primary objectives of commercial banks—liquidity, profitability, and safety—do you think is the most important? Explain your answer.

Activities

1. Try to locate someone in your area who lived through the Great Depression. If they are willing to be interviewed, ask that person to talk about the period and particularly to describe the "runs on the bank" that occurred during that time. With the person's permission, you may wish to tape the interview and present it to the class. Otherwise, present your findings in a brief oral report. If you cannot interview someone in your community, visit your local library and ask the librarian to help you locate books that contain firsthand accounts of the Depression era. Use these personal accounts as the basis for your report.

2. Some banks have electronic banking, a system that allows consumers to make deposits or withdraw money from an automatic-teller machine and pay bills by phone. If possible, visit a bank that offers this service. Ask a bank officer to explain how this system works.

Building Skills in Economics: Understanding a Bank's Balance Sheet

A bank's *balance sheet* is a statement showing a bank's financial condition on any given day. On the left side, it presents the bank's **assets,** or properties, possessions, and anything else of value that the bank owns. On the right side, it presents the bank's **liabilities,** or debts and obligations and net worth. Both sides of a balance sheet must always be equal.

Any checking accounts, or demand deposits, appear as part of a bank's liabilities. This is because the bank is holding money that really belongs to its customers. If these customers write a check for the amount they are owed, the bank would have to turn over this money. All savings account balances and time deposit balances also are listed in the liability column.

The balance sheet that follows presents a bank's assets and liabilities. The questions will help you interpret the balance sheet.

Applying Economics Skills

1. What items form the bank's assets? its liabilities?
2. How much do each of the items in question 1 amount to?
3. If Mary Walker withdraws $10,000 from her time deposit account, how will this be reflected in the bank's balance sheet?
4. If the bank lends Jason Rinaldo $10,000 by setting up a checking account for him in that amount, what would happen to the bank's balance sheet?

BALANCE SHEET

Assets		Liabilities	
Total cash	$300,000	Demand deposits	$350,000
Loans	$ 50,000	Time deposits	$200,000
Bonds	$ 10,000	Net worth	$ 50,000
Property	$240,000		
Total	$600,000	Total	$600,000

CHAPTER 12

BUILT BY... **SOLD**
WEST RIVER
BUILDERS, INC.
BEULAH, N. DAK.
Call
● 873-4642
● 873-5633
● 873-5726

THE FEDERAL RESERVE SYSTEM AND MONETARY POLICY

Have you ever thought about the possibility of owning your own house or apartment someday? Home ownership is a major goal of many adults. When you are finally ready to buy a home, you probably will have to borrow at least part of the money because few people have enough cash to pay for such a large purchase. How easy will it be for you to get a home loan? How much interest will you have to pay? The answers to these questions will depend at least partly on the policies of the Federal Reserve.

In this chapter, you will learn about the organization and functions of the **Federal Reserve System,** which serves as the nation's central monetary authority or "central bank." We will examine also the actions it can take to affect the money supply and thus the economy. Let us begin with a look at the organization.

Organization of the Federal Reserve System

The Federal Reserve System—or the Fed, as it is commonly called—was established by Congress in 1913. Prior to that time, there were several severe financial panics during which many businesses failed and many banks were forced to close. The national banking system that existed at that time was ill-equipped to deal with such crises, and it was decided that major reforms were needed. The result of these reform efforts was the Federal Reserve System.

As you can see from Figure 12–1, the Fed consists of three levels of organization. At the very top of the organizational structure are the Board of Governors, the Federal Open Market Committee, and the Federal Advisory Council. The second level consists of 12 Federal Reserve Banks scattered throughout the United States. The third level is made up of approximately

5,800 member banks. Together, these components make decisions that have far-reaching effects on our economy and our lives.

Board of Governors

The Board of Governors, which is the central policy-making body of the Federal Reserve System, is responsible for supervising the overall operation of the Fed and for formulating and carrying out monetary policy. It consists of seven members—prominent bankers, economists, and business executives—appointed by the President of the United States and confirmed by the Senate. Each member is appointed for a 14-year term and is ineligible for reappointment. The terms of the seven members are staggered so that a new member is appointed by the President every two years. The President also appoints one of the seven members as chairperson of the Board for a term of four years.

In actuality, many of the Board's members do not complete their entire 14-year terms. Many resign because of their age or to pursue other interests. Although Board members can

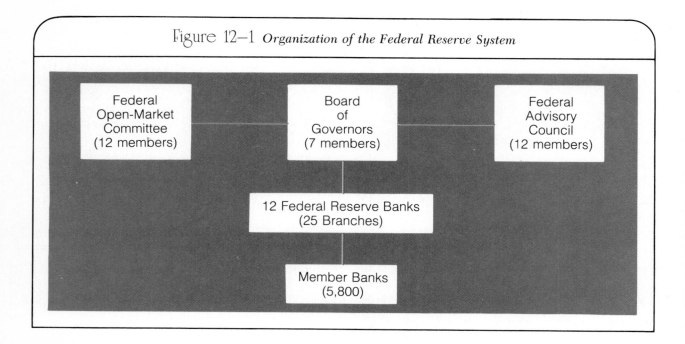

Figure 12–1 *Organization of the Federal Reserve System*

Federal Open-Market Committee (12 members)

Board of Governors (7 members)

Federal Advisory Council (12 members)

12 Federal Reserve Banks (25 Branches)

Member Banks (5,800)

be removed for not doing their job satisfactorily, none have ever met this fate. The average term completed by Board members is between five and six years.

The members of the Board of Governors are seven of the most powerful people in the nation in terms of the effect their decisions have on the economy. It is extremely important that their decisions not be influenced by partisan politics. The creators of the Federal Reserve were aware of this danger and took precautions to prevent this from happening. For one thing, Board decisions do not have to be approved by the President or Congress. In addition, because Board members serve long terms and are ineligible for reappointment, they do not have to fear losing their jobs because a new President has been elected. As a result, the Board of Governors remains relatively independent of politics.

Federal Open Market Committee

The Federal Open Market Committee is made up of 12 members—the seven members of the Board of Governors and five presidents of Federal Reserve Banks. This committee is responsible for directing the buying and selling of government securities in the open market in order to influence interest rates and the availability of credit. We will discuss the activities of the Open Market Committee in more detail later in the chapter.

Federal Advisory Council

The Federal Advisory Council consists of 12 commercial bankers, with one member selected by each of the 12 Federal Reserve Banks. As the name implies, the duties of this council are strictly advisory. It meets periodically with the Board of Governors to report on general business conditions throughout the nation and to give the Board advice about future banking policy. Although this council performs an important service by providing a link between bankers and the Board, in reality it has virtually no power and little impact on the way the Fed carries out its day-to-day activities.

The Federal Reserve Banks

The 1913 Federal Reserve Act divided the United States into 12 districts and established a separate Federal Reserve Bank for each district. One reason for this move was that the framers of the Act feared a centralized banking authority. Although other nations already had centralized their banking operations (the Bank of England, for example, was founded in 1694), Americans did not wish to place all their banks under one central power.

The map in Figure 12–2 shows the boundaries of each of the 12 districts. The Federal Reserve Banks are located in Boston, New York, Philadelphia, Cleveland, Richmond, Atlanta, Chicago, St. Louis, Minneapolis, Kansas City, Dallas, and San Francisco. Some of the 12 Federal Reserve Banks have branch offices so that transactions between the Federal Reserve Banks and member banks can be carried out more speedily. The activities of the 12 Federal Reserve Banks are coordinated by the Board of Governors, although the Board may allow individual Federal Reserve Banks to adopt policies designed to deal with special economic conditions existing within their districts.

The Federal Reserve Banks do not deal directly with the public. You cannot open an account or cash a check at a Federal Reserve Bank. They are "bankers' banks" that deal only with financial institutions and the government. Each Federal Reserve Bank is owned by the member commercial banks in its district, which are required to buy shares of stock in their Federal Reserve Bank when they become members of the Fed. Although they are privately owned, the primary objective of the Federal Reserve Banks is to carry out the monetary policies established by the Board of Governors. In fact, most of the earnings of the Federal Reserve Banks are returned to the U.S. Treasury each year.

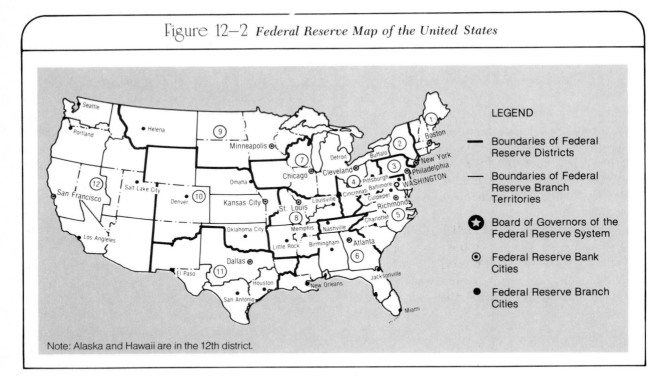

Figure 12–2 *Federal Reserve Map of the United States*

LEGEND

— Boundaries of Federal Reserve Districts

— Boundaries of Federal Reserve Branch Territories

★ Board of Governors of the Federal Reserve System

⊙ Federal Reserve Bank Cities

● Federal Reserve Branch Cities

Note: Alaska and Hawaii are in the 12th district.

Member Banks

As you learned in the previous chapter, all national banks are required to become members of the Fed but state banks can choose to join or not to join. Currently, there are approximately 5,800 member banks. This figure includes all of the approximately 4,750 national banks plus about 1,050 state banks. The remaining 8,600 or so state banks are not members.

Prior to 1980, nonmember state banks were not subject to controls by the Fed. This is one of the major reasons they chose not to join. Instead, they were subject to less strict controls by state agencies. However, the 1980 changes in the banking laws eliminated much of the distinction between member and nonmember banks. Today, even state banks that are not members of the Fed must keep reserves equal to those required of member banks. In addition, nonmember banks as well as member banks have access to Fed services, such as the Fed's check-clearing facilities and computerized funds transfer system. Thus, there is little reason today for state banks to join the Fed.

Check Your Understanding

1. How is the Federal Reserve System organized?

2. What functions are performed by the Board of Governors? The Federal Open Market Committee? The Federal Advisory Council?

3. How are Federal Reserve Banks distributed? What functions do they serve?

Functions of the Federal Reserve System

The Fed performs a number of important functions in the American economy, the most important of which is controlling the nation's money supply. Let us briefly examine some of the other functions of the Fed before we study in detail how it affects the amount of money in circulation.

One of the major functions of the Fed is clearing checks. Each year billions of checks are written by individuals, businesses, and the various agencies of government. Each of these checks represents an order to transfer funds from the account of the check writer to the recipient of the check. Sometimes the check clearance procedure can be very simple. For example, suppose you write a check for $20 to a local store in payment for merchandise. If the store owner banks at the same bank as you, when he or she deposits the check at the local bank, the bank can simply subtract $20 from your account and add $20 to the account of the store owner. However, the check clearance procedure for many checks is far more complicated, and the Federal Reserve Banks play an important role in the process. In order to better understand how the check clearance system works, let us look at a specific example.

Suppose Pamela Rissler of Albany, New York, mails an order for art supplies along with a check to an art supply store in Sacramento, California. Figure 12–3 shows the various steps involved in clearing this particular check. As you can see from the chart, the art supply store will deposit Pamela's check in its account at a Sacramento bank. The Sacramento bank in turn will deposit the check in its account at the Federal Reserve Bank of San Francisco. The Federal Reserve Bank of San Francisco will send the check to the Federal Reserve Bank of New York, which will deduct the amount of the check from the account of Pamela's bank in Albany and then forward the check to Pamela's bank. Finally, Pamela's bank will deduct the amount of the check from her account and mail the canceled check to Pamela along with her other checks that have been processed that month.

The Fed also serves as a fiscal agent for the federal government. The U.S. Treasury collects huge sums of money through taxation and then

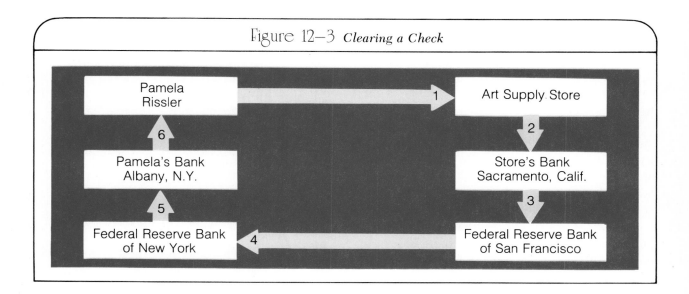

Figure 12–3 *Clearing a Check*

deposits much of this money in Federal Reserve Banks. The Treasury then keeps checking accounts for such things as tax refunds and Social Security payments. Moreover, the Fed helps the Treasury in its efforts to borrow money by selling government securities, such as U.S. Treasury bonds.

In addition, the Fed performs various supervisory functions intended to ensure that the member banks are in compliance with the banking laws and that they are engaging in sound banking practices. Among these functions are making sure that member banks have adequate funds, overseeing bank mergers, and setting limits for loans by member banks. Because national banks are supervised by the Comptroller of the Currency, a federal agency, the Fed's primary supervisory responsibility is overseeing the operations of member state banks. The Fed also works closely with another federal agency, the Federal Deposit Insurance Corporation, in making sure that all bank deposits are insured.

Another responsibility of the Fed is to hold **required reserves.** Banks and other financial institutions are required by law to keep a certain percentage of money that is deposited with them as required reserves to back up the deposits. One of the important functions of each Federal Reserve Bank is to hold the required reserves of the depository institutions within its district. As you soon will learn, changing the percentage of deposits that must be kept as required reserves is one of the ways the Fed can increase or decrease the money supply of the nation.

The Fed also is responsible for supplying paper currency. As you learned in Chapter 11, paper currency in the United States consists almost exclusively of Federal Reserve notes issued by the Federal Reserve Banks. The actual printing of the notes is done by the Bureau of Engraving and Printing in Washington, D.C. However, each Federal Reserve note has a seal on the left side of the front indicating which of the 12 Federal Reserve Banks issued it. For

example, Federal Reserve notes issued by the Chicago Federal Reserve Bank have a capital letter *G* printed on them with the name of the bank indicated in the circle that surrounds the *G*.

Many of the new Federal Reserve notes are issued simply to replace old ones that are taken out of circulation because they are worn out or torn. However, more paper currency is demanded by the public at certain times of the year than at others. For example, each year during the Christmas shopping season Americans withdraw large amounts of cash from banks. To meet the increased demand for paper money, commercial banks withdraw additional Federal Reserve notes from their accounts with the Federal Reserve Banks. After Christmas, much of the currency is returned to commercial banks, and they find themselves with a surplus of currency on hand. They in turn redeposit that currency with the Federal Reserve Banks.

The most important function of the Fed is regulating the amount of money in circulation, which affects the cost and availability of credit and, thus, the level of business activity in the economy. Much of the remainder of this chapter will be devoted to an examination of how and why the Fed changes the money supply. As a first step toward understanding monetary policy, let us see how banks create money.

Check Your Understanding

1. What are the primary functions of the Federal Reserve System? Which is the most important?

2. Describe the check-clearing process.

3. Why does the demand for paper currency change? How does the Fed meet this changing demand?

How Banks Create Money

In this section, we want to see how banks as a group are able to create money and how the Fed regulates the capacity of banks to create money. Let us begin with a look at the relationship between demand deposits and the money supply.

Demand Deposits and Money Creation

As you learned in Chapter 11, demand deposits (checking accounts) are the largest component of the money supply, accounting for approximately 90 percent of the dollar value of all transactions. There are two ways that demand deposits can originate or change in size. The first involves the deposit of cash or checks in demand deposits. The second involves borrow-

ing money and having it deposited in demand deposits. Only the second, however, involves an increase in the money supply.

In the first kind of transaction, money is simply changing hands. An example of this kind of transaction might occur if your neighbor gave you a $10 check for washing his car. You would take the check and either cash it or deposit it in your checking account. In either case, your neighbor would be $10 poorer and you would be $10 richer. No new money has been created. A fixed amount—$10—has simply gone from one person to another.

In the second kind of transaction, however, the money supply is increased. For example, suppose Debbie Light goes to her bank and borrows $500 with which she opens a checking account. Debbie was carrying no money when she entered the bank but she walks out of the bank with $500 of "checkbook money." At the

A bank customer can borrow money to open a checking account. This kind of transaction involves an increase in the money supply.

same time, nobody else's account was decreased by $500 to enable Debbie to get the money. Debbie's bank just created $500, and the money supply of the nation increased by that amount. Is this some kind of magic? Can banks create as much money as they wish by simply making loans?

The answer to both questions is no. There is no magic involved, and banks cannot create an unlimited amount of money by making loans. The amount of money that banks can lend out is restricted by reserve requirements imposed on them by the Fed.

Reserve Requirements

A **reserve requirement** is a rule that stipulates the percentage of deposits that must be kept as reserves to back up those deposits. For example, if a bank has $100 million of deposits and a reserve requirement of 10 percent, then $10 million must be kept as required reserves. If the reserve requirement is 12 percent, then $12 million must be kept as required reserves. The reserves must be kept in the form of cash in the banks' vaults or as deposits with Federal Reserve Banks. Because banks are required to keep only a fraction of their deposits as reserves, the rest of the money either can be invested or loaned out. Because of the reserve requirements, our banking system operates under what economists call **fractional reserve banking.**

Usually a bank's deposits with its Federal Reserve Bank plus its vault cash, which together are called actual reserves, exceed the amount that must be kept as required reserves. This difference between actual reserves and required reserves is known as **excess reserves.** A bank cannot lend out any more than it has in excess reserves. If, for example, a bank has $12 million of actual reserves of which $10 million is required reserves, it would have excess reserves of $2 million with which to make loans. By making such loans it creates money and expands the money supply.

Deposit Expansion by the Banking System

Although a single bank can make loans and thus increase the money supply by the amount of its excess reserves, the banking system as a whole can make enough loans to increase the money supply by a multiple of its excess reserves. Let us use a hypothetical example to explain how the banking system as a whole can create money.

Suppose Don and Paula Nguyen receive a $1,000 tax-refund check from the Internal Revenue Service that they deposit in their checking account at Bank A, as shown in Table 12–1. How does this affect the lending capacity of Bank A? If the reserve requirement is 10 percent, Bank A must set aside $100 (10 percent of the $1,000 demand deposit) as required reserves. The remaining $900 is excess reserves, which Bank A can use to make new loans and thus expand the money supply.

Now assume that Bank A indeed loans out this $900, and the person who borrows it spends it. The person who receives the $900 of new spending deposits it in his or her checking account at Bank B. Bank B now has $900 of new reserves. It must set aside 10 percent ($90) as required reserves but the remaining $810 is excess reserves that it can use to make new loans. The $810 of new loans made by Bank B is spent and ends up as new demand deposits at Bank C. Bank C then sets aside $81 as required reserves and uses the remaining $729 to make new loans. As you can see from Table 12–1, this process of multiple deposit expansion can continue until a maximum potential of $9,000 of new money is created. Note that although each individual bank can lend only the amount of its excess reserves, the banking system (all the banks as a group) can make enough loans to expand the money supply by ten times the initial excess reserves of $900. This example is based on a 10 percent reserve requirement. If the reserve requirement had been 20 percent, Bank A would have had to set aside $200 (20 percent of the $1,000 demand deposit) as required reserves, leaving it with $800 of excess

TABLE 12–1: EXPANSION OF THE MONEY SUPPLY BY THE BANKING SYSTEM WITH A 10 PERCENT RESERVE REQUIREMENT

Bank	Demand Deposits	Required Reserves	Excess Reserves	New Loans
A	$1,000.00	$100.00	$900.00	$900.00
B	900.00	90.00	810.00	810.00
C	810.00	81.00	729.00	729.00
D	729.00	72.90	656.10	656.10
E	656.10	65.61	590.49	590.49
F	590.49	59.05	531.44	531.44
G	531.44	53.14	478.30	478.30
H	478.30	47.83	430.47	430.47
I	430.47	43.05	387.42	387.42
J	387.42	38.74	348.68	348.68
K	348.68	34.87	313.81	313.81
Other Banks	3,138.10	313.81	2,824.29	2,824.29

Total amount of money created $9,000.00

reserves. In this case, the banking system could make enough loans to expand the money supply by five times the initial excess reserves of $800 for a total expansion of $4,000.

Thus, the potential money supply is determined by the amount of reserves that banks hold and by the reserve requirement. Any action that results in a change in the reserves held by banks or a change in the reserve requirement will affect the potential money supply. As you will soon learn, the Fed has the power to change both the amount of reserves held by banks and the reserve requirement. These powers enable the Fed to regulate the nation's money supply. In the next section, we will examine how the Fed accomplishes this task.

Check Your Understanding

1. In what two ways do demand deposits originate or change in size? Which of these ways changes the money supply? Why?

2. What are excess reserves? How are they calculated?

3. How does the banking system as a whole increase the money supply?

"WELL, YOU LOOK GOOD! HOW WOULD YOU LIKE THE SAME OPERATION OVER AGAIN?"

The Federal Reserve System attempts to achieve economic goals through policies such as reducing or increasing interest rates.

Monetary Policy

Monetary policy is made up of actions taken by the Federal Reserve System to control the nation's money supply as well as interest rates, in order to achieve desired economic objectives. The desired economic objectives that the Fed attempts to achieve through monetary policy are the same as those the President and Congress attempt to achieve through fiscal policy—low unemployment combined with relatively stable prices.

At a time of low unemployment and high inflation, the Fed would want to restrict the growth in the money supply. A decline in the growth of the money supply would make money more scarce and the cost of borrowing money more expensive. This cost would be reflected in higher interest rates. Higher interest rates would in turn cause businesses to cut back on investment spending and consumers to cut back on consumption spending—two components of aggregate demand. In this manner, by making credit more difficult to obtain and more costly the Fed can reduce the level of aggregate demand and thus reduce inflationary pressures. During times when the Fed is restricting the availability of credit and forcing interest rates up, economists say that it is pursuing a **tight-money policy** (see Table 12–2).

At the other extreme, during a severe recession the Fed would want to increase the availability of credit, leading to a decline in interest rates. Lower interest rates would tend to encourage more credit spending and thus increase aggregate demand. When the Fed is expanding the money supply and reducing interest rates, economists say that it is pursuing an **easy-money policy** (see Table 12–2).

TABLE 12–2: MONETARY POLICY

Conditions	Desired Goal	Monetary Policy
Low unemployment High inflation	Restrict growth in money supply	Tight-money policy
High unemployment Low inflation	Expand money supply	Easy-money policy

Instruments of Monetary Policy

The Fed has three major instruments that it can use in its attempt to control the money supply and interest rates. They are (1) changing reserve requirements; (2) changing the discount rate; and (3) open-market operations. Let us examine each of these instruments.

Changing Reserve Requirements

The Fed has the power to change the reserve requirements within stipulated limits established by law. By using this power, the Fed can increase or decrease banks' excess reserves and thus their lending capacity. For example, suppose a bank has $100 million in demand deposits at a time when the reserve requirement is 10 percent. In this case, the bank must keep $10 million in required reserves. Now suppose the Fed reduces the reserve requirement from 10 percent to 8 percent. The effect of this change on the bank will be to reduce its required reserves from $10 million to $8 million. This will give it $2 million of additional excess reserves that it can use to make loans.

Of course, the change in the reserve requirement described above would not affect just one bank. If the Fed reduced the reserve requirement from 10 percent to 8 percent, all banks would have increased excess reserves and thus increased lending capacity. This would result in a substantial increase in the money supply, as well as a reduction in interest rates. These two changes in combination could help to bring the economy out of a recession.

If the Fed wants to restrict loans instead of making them more readily available, it can raise the reserve requirement. An increase in the reserve requirement will reduce excess reserves and the lending capacity of banks. Such a policy could help to reduce demand-pull inflation by decreasing the amount of money that people have to spend.

Changing the Discount Rate

Although banks obtain most of their funds from depositors, they do occasionally borrow funds from their Federal Reserve Banks. If a bank experiences large unexpected withdrawals, for example, it may have to borrow funds from its Federal Reserve Bank just to meet its reserve requirement. The rate of interest that Federal Reserve Banks charge banks and other financial institutions for such loans is called the **discount rate.**

By changing the discount rate, the Fed can encourage or discourage borrowing by member banks. In theory, a low discount rate might cause member banks to borrow more than they need. They could then build up their reserves and lend out the excess reserves. In practice, though, most banks don't borrow any more than they have to, so a decline in the discount rate does not prompt the amount of borrowing you might expect. A change in the discount rate, however, sends a signal to the banking and business communities about the kind of monetary policy the Fed plans to pursue. If the discount rate is lowered by the Fed, it probably indicates that the Fed is pursuing an easy-money policy. In contrast, an increase in the discount rate usually indicates a tight-money policy.

When the discount rate goes up, commercial banks usually increase the rate of interest that they charge their customers. The **prime rate**—the rate of interest that large banks charge their best business customers—usually moves in the same direction as the discount rate. Thus, any increase in the discount rate usually signals a rise in the prime rate and other interest rates charged to the general public.

Open-Market Operations

Open-market operations involve the buying and selling of United States government securities by the Fed in the open market. The term "open market" refers to the fact that the buying and selling is done in the same securities markets as those open to ordinary citizens and businesses.

Open-market operations, the monetary policy instrument most often used by the Fed, are directed by the Federal Open Market Committee, which was described earlier in this chapter. The purpose of open-market operations is to increase or decrease the reserves, and thus the lending capacity, of banks and other financial institutions. Let us see how open-market operations work.

When the Fed buys securities in the open market, the reserves of banks and other financial institutions are increased. If the Fed buys securities directly from banks, it increases their reserve balances with the Federal Reserve Banks by the amount of the purchase. For example, suppose the Fed buys $1,000 in government securities from a bank and adds the $1,000 to that bank's account in its district Federal Reserve Bank. The bank then can increase loans by the amount of the new reserves. More importantly, this $1,000 of new reserves can enable the banking system (all banks as a group) to increase loans by a multiple of this amount through the process we described earlier.

The same holds true if the Fed buys securities from private individuals and businesses. It pays them with checks that they will deposit in their banks, which will bring about an increase in bank reserves. It doesn't matter who the Fed buys securities from, because in either case the net result is increased reserves and lending capacity for the banks and thus an increase in the money supply. In short, when the Fed buys securities in the open market, it pumps additional money into the economy. This will bring about lower interest rates, increased availability of credit, and thus an increase in aggregate demand.

When the Fed sells securities in the open market, the reserves of banks and other financial institutions are decreased. If the Fed sells securities directly to banks, their reserves with the Federal Reserve Banks are reduced by the amount of the purchase. If the Fed sells securities to private individuals and businesses, they will pay for the securities by writing checks against the balances in their banks, thus reducing the reserves of the banks. For example, if the Fed sells $1,000 worth of government securities to either a bank or an individual or a business, bank reserves are decreased by $1,000, and thus the lending capacity of the banking system is reduced by a multiple of this amount. In summary, when the Fed sells securities in the open market, it reduces banks' reserves and lending capacity and thus reduces the nation's money supply. The net effect of this action will be higher interest rates, a reduction in the availability of credit, and a reduction in aggregate demand.

Check Your Understanding

1. Define monetary policy. What is meant by a tight-money policy? An easy-money policy?

2. How do changes in the reserve requirement affect the lending capacity of banks?

3. What is the discount rate? Why does the Fed change it from time to time?

4. What are open-market operations? What is their purpose?

Monetarism

Most economists agree that the money supply plays an important role in the American economy. However, some economists place much more emphasis on the relationship between the money supply and economic activity than others. One school of economic thought called **monetarism** takes the position that the money supply is the key factor determining the economic health of the nation. The monetarists—economists who believe in the doctrine of monetarism—argue that erratic changes in the money supply are the dominant cause of business cycles. They believe that the economy would be relatively stable if it were not for the large fluctuations in the rate of growth of the money supply that are caused by the Fed's monetary policies.

Monetarists generally oppose the use of fiscal policy to regulate aggregate demand. Because they believe that changes in the money supply are the chief determinant of economic activity, they argue that fiscal policy is of little or no value as a stabilizing device. Monetarists also oppose the use of monetary policy as a means of attempting to increase or decrease aggregate demand. They believe that deliberate efforts to change aggregate demand by the use of either fiscal or monetary policies do more harm than good. Instead, the monetarists believe that the money supply should grow at a fixed rate of about 3 to 4 percent per year, which is compatible with what economists believe is the economy's long-term potential rate of growth in GNP. According to the monetarists, such a policy would permit the economy to stabilize itself and avoid both high inflation and high unemployment.

Keynesian economists believe that the view of the monetarists is too narrow and too simplistic. They argue that both monetary and fiscal policy should be used to smooth out the extremes of the business cycle. They believe that the failure to use fiscal policy to stimulate the economy during periods of severe recession or depression will result in unnecessary prolonged high unemployment that imposes a heavy cost on society in individual suffering as well as lost production.

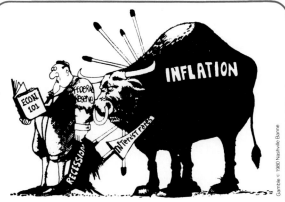

'According to the book...he should be giving ground any minute!'

Monetarists oppose the Fed's control of the money supply and interest rates.

Monetary Policy and the Economy

As you already know, the Federal Reserve System has the power to influence both interest rates and the availability of loans. Changes in the cost and availability of loans affect the entire economy. However, we will concentrate our attention on how monetary policy affects three important areas of the economy: investment in factories and equipment, the housing market, and consumer spending.

Investment in Factories and Equipment

As you learned in Chapter 8, the amount of investment that will take place in any given time period depends on the availability of prof-

BIOGRAPHY: Milton Friedman

(1912–   )

Like Paul Samuelson, Milton Friedman is one of the best-known contemporary American economists and a recipient of a Nobel Prize in economics (1976). Friedman's economic views are very different from those of Samuelson, however. Whereas Samuelson has been a proponent of Keynesian economics, Friedman has been a harsh critic of Keynesian economics and a leading spokesperson for monetarism.

Friedman, who holds a bachelor's degree from Rutgers University and a Ph.D. degree from Columbia University, taught economics at the University of Chicago from 1946 to 1977. Best known for his monetarist views, Friedman believes that neither monetary nor fiscal policy will eliminate minor business fluctuations. As a result, he generally opposes the use of either for purposes of influencing aggregate demand. Instead, he favors an automatic policy designed to increase the money supply by a given amount each year.

Friedman is also well known for his outspoken criticism of government intervention in the economy. He argues that government intervention often does more harm than good. For example, he believes that minimum wage laws designed to help the disadvantaged actually hurt them by reducing their employment opportunities. Friedman holds similar views about many other government programs designed to help the disadvantaged or to protect consumers. Friedman's strong support for free markets is reflected in the titles of two of his books: *Capitalism and Freedom* and *Free to Choose*.

Milton Friedman is highly respected for his scholarly contributions to the economics profession, and he was awarded the Nobel Prize for his scholarly research on consumption. Many economists believe that his most significant work may well be *A Monetary History of the United States, 1867–1960*. This book (co-authored with Anna Schwartz) is considered by many economists to be a gold mine of monetary and aggregate economic data.

itable investment opportunities and on the cost and availability of investment funds. Monetary policy can have a big impact on investment spending. For example, during periods when loans are scarce and interest rates are high, businesses will reduce their investment in new factories and equipment. This can result in increased unemployment and a slower rate of economic growth.

In contrast, an easy-money policy under which loans are more readily available at lower interest rates may lead to increased spending for new factories and equipment and thus to a reduction in unemployment and an increase in economic growth. Of course, if during such a period businesses are unable to sell what they can produce with their current factories and equipment, they may not increase investment even at the existing low interest rates. However, businesses generally will invest more when interest rates are low and loans are readily available than they would otherwise. Keep in mind, however, that increased investment spending is not always desirable. If aggregate demand is already too high, the increased investment spending resulting from an easy-money policy can lead to increased inflation.

The Housing Market

Monetary policy plays a major role in determining how many new houses will be built and how many existing houses will be sold. High interest

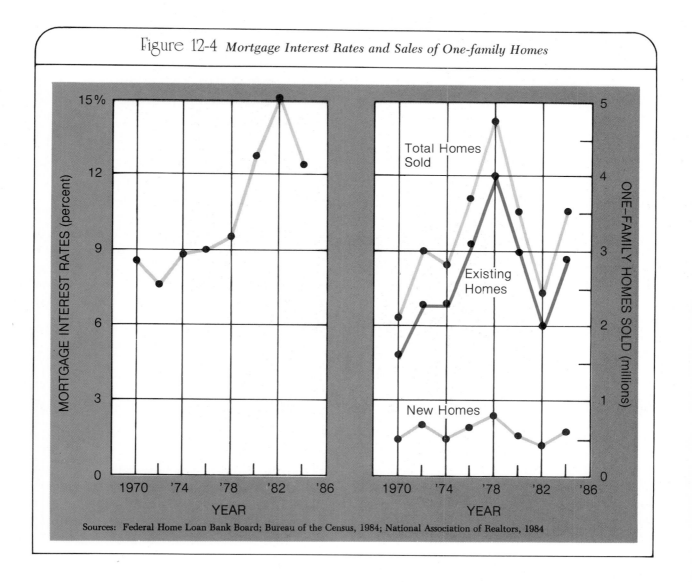

Figure 12-4 *Mortgage Interest Rates and Sales of One-family Homes*

Sources: Federal Home Loan Bank Board; Bureau of the Census, 1984; National Association of Realtors, 1984

Monetary policy can affect whether or not consumers make major purchases such as buying homes or appliances as well as whether they buy those extra clothes for the family.

rates and a shortage of loans can lead to a sharp reduction in the construction of new houses and in the sale of existing homes. (See Figure 12–4.) During periods of very restrictive monetary policy, it is often difficult for many potential home buyers to obtain mortgage loans at any interest rate. Moreover, the high interest rates on those loans that are available push the monthly payments to levels that are beyond the reach of many families.

A decline in housing construction can lead to substantial unemployment. In addition to the carpenters, plumbers, electricians, and others who will have difficulty finding work, there will be far-reaching effects in many related industries. For example, fewer new homes will mean fewer sales of appliances, furniture, carpeting, and other household items. This in turn will lead to reduced employment in these industries as well.

In contrast, when the policies of the Fed lead to a situation where loans are more readily available at lower interest rates, there will be an increase in the construction and sale of homes. This in turn will lead to increased employment opportunities.

Consumer Spending

Since a great deal of consumer spending is done with borrowed money, changes in monetary policy can have a substantial impact on consumer spending. This is especially true in the case of major purchases, such as automobiles, home appliances, and furniture. When interest rates are high and loans are difficult to obtain, sales of such items usually decline and unemployment in the corresponding industries rises. In contrast, lower interest rates and increased availability of loans usually lead to increased sales of automobiles, appliances, furniture, and so forth. Thus, monetary policy helps to determine the production and sale of consumer goods, as well as the level of employment in industries that produce such goods.

In summary, monetary policy has important effects on the economy and you. Whether or not you will be able to get a good job in the future and whether or not there will be high inflation depend at least partly on the policies of the Fed. Similarly, whether or not you will be able to get an automobile or home-mortgage loan in the future, and the interest rates you will have to pay on such loans, will be determined in part by monetary policy.

Check Your Understanding

1. What is monetarism? Describe the main ideas of the monetarists.

2. How does monetary policy affect investment in factories and equipment? How does it affect the housing market? Consumer spending?

CAREERS: Bookkeeper

In many small businesses, a general bookkeeper does all the bookkeeping. If you were employed as a general bookkeeper in such a business, your duties might include recording and analyzing all financial transactions, checking money taken in against money paid out to be sure that all accounts balance, calculating the firm's payroll and making up employees' paychecks, and mailing bills to customers.

Every business needs accurate, up-to-date records of accounts and business transactions. These records, which show the financial condition of the business, are necessary for making business decisions and for preparing income tax reports. Bookkeepers maintain these records in journals, ledgers, and—in many cases—the memories of computers. They also prepare periodic financial statements showing total receipts and expenditures. Bookkeepers are employed in all types of businesses, including small retail businesses, banks, insurance agencies, and manufacturing firms of all sizes.

In large businesses, several bookkeepers usually work under the direction of a head bookkeeper or accountant. In these cases, individual bookkeepers often specialize in one or a few bookkeeping duties. For example, some might prepare statements of a company's income from sales or its daily operating expenses, others might deal only with payroll matters, and still others might be responsible for keeping track of freight charges or making sure that bills are paid when they are due. Virtually all bookkeep-

ers use calculating machines, and many work with computers.

A high school graduate who has taken business arithmetic, bookkeeping, and principles of accounting would meet the minimum educational requirements for some bookkeeping jobs. However, many employers prefer applicants who have completed accounting programs at community or junior colleges or who have attended business school. In addition to the educational requirements, bookkeepers need to be good at working with numbers and concentrating on details.

Chapter Highlights

1   The Federal Reserve System, which was established by Congress in 1913, consists of three levels of organization. The first level consists of the Board of Governors, the Federal Open Market Committee, and the Federal Advisory Council. The second level consists of 12 Federal Reserve Banks, and the third level is made up of approximately 5,800 member banks.

2   The Board of Governors is responsible for supervising the overall operation of the Fed and for formulating and carrying out monetary policy. It consists of seven members who are appointed by the President and confirmed by the Senate for 14-year terms.

3   The Federal Open Market Committee is made up of the seven members of the Board of Governors plus five presidents of Federal Reserve Banks. It is responsible for conducting open-market operations in order to influence interest rates and the availability of credit. The Federal Advisory Council consists of 12 commercial bankers who advise the Board of Governors about banking policy.

4   The 1913 Federal Reserve Act divided the United States into 12 districts and established a separate Federal Reserve Bank for each district. The Federal Reserve Banks are "bankers' banks" that deal only with financial institutions and the government. They are owned by the member banks in their districts but their primary objective is to carry out the monetary policies established by the Board of Governors.

5   Important functions of the Federal Reserve System include clearing checks; serving as the fiscal agent for the federal government; supervising member banks; holding required reserves of banks and other financial institutions; supplying the nation's paper currency; and regulating the money supply.

6   Banks as a group can create money in the form of demand deposits by making loans. The capacity of banks to create money depends on the amount of excess reserves—actual reserves minus required reserves—they hold and the Fed's reserve requirements.

7   Monetary policy can be defined as actions taken by the Fed to control the nation's money supply and interest rates in order to achieve low unemployment and relatively stable prices. The three major instruments of monetary policy are changing reserve requirements, changing the discount rate, and open-market operations.

8   One school of economic thought called monetarism takes the position that the money supply is the key factor determining the economic health of the nation. The monetarists argue that erratic changes in the money supply are the dominant cause of business cycles. They generally oppose the use of either fiscal or monetary policy to influence aggregate demand. Keynesian economists believe that the view of the monetarists is too narrow and too simplistic. They believe both monetary and fiscal policy should be used to smooth out business cycles in order to avoid extremes in those cycles.

9   Monetary policy affects the entire economy, but in particular it affects investment in factories and equipment, the housing market, and consumer spending.

Important Terms

Match each of the following terms with the correct definition:

Federal Advisory Council
Federal Open Market Committee
member banks
Federal Reserve System
Board of Governors
required reserves
excess reserves

Federal Reserve Banks
open-market operations
monetarism
tight-money policy
easy-money policy
monetary policy
prime rate
discount rate

1. Commercial banks that are members of the Federal Reserve System.

2. The nation's central monetary authority or "central bank."

3. A school of economic thought that takes the position that the money supply is the key factor determining the economic health of the nation.

4. The amount of reserves that a bank is required to hold as backing for money that has been deposited with it.

5. The buying and selling by the Fed of government securities in the open market.

6. The rate of interest that Federal Reserve Banks charge banks for loans.

7. The central policy-making body of the Federal Reserve System.

8. The Board of Governors plus five presidents of Federal Reserve Banks.

9. Actual reserves minus required reserves.

10. Twelve commercial bankers who advise the Board of Governors on banking policy.

11. Twelve banks established by the Federal Reserve Act of 1913.

12. The rate of interest that large banks charge their best business customers.

13. A policy of expanding the money supply and reducing interest rates.

14. Actions taken by the Fed to control the nation's money supply and interest rates.

15. A policy of restricting the availability of credit and forcing interest rates up.

Extending Your Understanding

1. Do you think the decisions of the Board of Governors should be regulated by the President or Congress? Why or why not?

2. Which instrument of monetary policy—changing reserve requirements, changing the discount rate, or engaging in open-market operations—do you think is most effective in regulating the money supply? Explain your answer.

Activities

1. Draw two cartoons or charts, one showing the effects of an easy-money policy and the other showing the effects of a tight-money policy.

2. Read the business section of your local newspaper for one week, keeping an eye out for articles on monetary policy. Clip these articles and bring them to class. Discuss the kind of policy the Fed is pursuing.

Building Skills in Economics: Writing a Check

As you learned in this chapter, billions of checks are cleared annually by the Federal Reserve System. This also means that billions of checks are written each year.

The process of writing a check is relatively simple. In the upper right-hand corner, you insert the date. Then, on the line beginning with the words "Pay to the Order of," you insert the name of the person or the company to whom you are writing the check. At the end of the line, print the amount of the check in numbers. Make sure to print this amount as close to the dollar sign as possible to prevent anyone from inserting additional numbers and thereby increasing the amount of the check. Then, on the next line, write the dollar amount in words and the cents amount as a fraction. Once again, to avoid possible tampering begin writing this information as far to the left as possible and follow your entry with a squiggly line. Finally, sign your check in the lower right-hand corner. If you wish, you can write the reason for writing the check in the space marked "Memo."

The check shown below is a typical example of the billions of checks written each year. Use it to answer the questions and do the activity that follow.

Applying Economic skills

1. Who is writing this check? Who will be receiving the money?
2. When was this check written? What is the amount of the check?
3. On a separate sheet of paper, create a blank check using the completed check as a model. Then write a check to Main Street Fashions for $32.95 for the purchase of a new jacket.

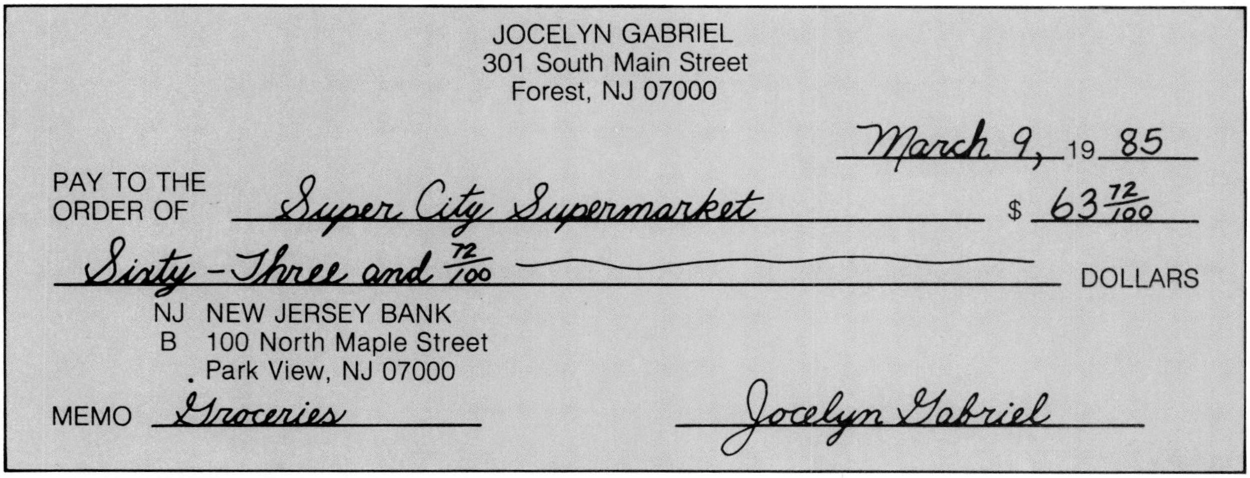

JOCELYN GABRIEL
301 South Main Street
Forest, NJ 07000

March 9, 19 *85*

PAY TO THE ORDER OF *Super City Supermarket* $ *63 $\frac{72}{100}$*

Sixty – Three and $\frac{72}{100}$ ———————————————— DOLLARS

NJ NEW JERSEY BANK
B 100 North Maple Street
. Park View, NJ 07000

MEMO *Groceries* *Jocelyn Gabriel*

UNIT 5

Problems on the Home Front

CHAPTER 13

INCOME DISTRIBUTION, POVERTY, AND URBAN PROBLEMS

The United States is one of the most affluent nations in the world. Eight out of every ten families own a car, and many people consume far more food than they need. At the same time, poverty is widespread in the United States. Millions of Americans do not have adequate food or shelter, and many lack the money to buy even the basic essentials.

What causes poverty? Who are the poor? What can be done to reduce poverty in the United States? These are some of the questions that we will explore in this chapter. We will look at the distribution of income and the reasons for income inequality. We also will examine the extent of poverty, the characteristics of the poor, and proposed solutions to the poverty problem. In addition, we will examine the special problems of the nation's cities, in which many of the poor reside. Because the unequal distribution of income is a major cause of poverty, we will begin with an examination of income distribution.

Income Distribution

In virtually all nations of the world, income distribution is unequal, with some people receiving more income than others. The United States is no exception to this statement. Let us see how income is distributed and why such inequality exists.

Analyzing Income Distribution

The method most often used by economists to analyze income distribution is to break the population down into quintiles, or fifths, based on income rank and then observe the percentage share of total income received by each fifth of the population. Table 13–1 shows the percentage share of total income received by each quintile of all families in the United States in 1983. As you can see, those in the lowest fifth received only 4.7 percent of the nation's income, while those in the highest fifth received 42.7 percent. In other words, the 20 percent of American families with the highest income received more than nine times as much income as the 20 percent with the lowest income.

It is true that the above figures represent income received before taxes. Therefore, since families with high incomes pay more taxes than those with low incomes, the degree of income inequality after taxes is less than that shown in Table 13–1. However, even after taxes there is still a wide disparity between the incomes received by those in the highest and those in the lowest brackets.

Reasons for Income Inequality

There are many reasons for differences in income. Among the most important are differences in ability, education, opportunity, occupations, wealth, and luck.

People in the middle income quintiles have enough education, ability, opportunity, and luck to live comfortably and provide opportunities for their children.

TABLE 13–1: PERCENTAGE SHARE OF TOTAL INCOME RECEIVED BY EACH ONE FIFTH OF ALL FAMILIES IN 1983

Income Rank	Percentage of Total Income Received
Lowest Fifth	4.7
Second Fifth	11.1
Third Fifth	17.1
Fourth Fifth	24.4
Highest Fifth	42.7

Source: *Current Population Report of Consumer Income: Money Income and Poverty Status of Families and Persons in the United States,* issued August 1984

Differences in ability Not all people are born with equal ability—either physical or mental. Some people are born with healthy bodies and good mental abilities, while others are born with physical and/or mental handicaps. Moreover, some people have developed their above-average intelligence or their unique talents to become superstars in their field. Because the demand for such superstars is high relative to the supply, these superstars earn much higher incomes than most people. This is not to say that mental and physical abilities are the only factors determining career success. Motivation and determination are also crucial factors. Many handicapped individuals defy the odds and experience phenomenal success, while other highly talented individuals fail to develop their potential. In the overall picture, however, differences in ability are an important reason for differences in income.

Differences in education Many Americans with low incomes are poorly educated and possess few marketable skills. Compared to supply, the demand for these people is low and they find it almost impossible to get high-paying jobs. In fact, many of those without a high school education may find it difficult to find employment of any kind. In contrast, although there are exceptions, those with high education levels generally earn more money than those with less schooling. Individuals in some of the higher paying career fields, such as medical doctors and lawyers, have many years of formal education beyond high school.

Differences in opportunity Many experts believe that a substantial portion of the inequality in income distribution today is the result of differences in the opportunity to receive a good education and to enter the high-income career fields. In the past, discrimination on the basis of race, sex, religion, ethnic background, and age prevented many individuals from entering certain career fields and served as a barrier to promotion to the higher paying jobs in these fields.

Many of the effects of past discrimination are still with us today. Moreover, although such discrimination is now against the law, there is little doubt that it still occurs to some degree and will continue to affect income distribution for many years.

Occupational Differences Not all jobs are equally attractive to workers. Some jobs are especially unattractive because they may involve danger, low prestige, or other negative working conditions. For example, most people would consider jobs such as working with explosives, working on high-rise construction projects, collecting garbage, and mining coal very unattractive. Therefore, in order to get people to work at these jobs it is often necessary to pay them above-average wages. Of course, because of supply and demand conditions or the degree of skill involved, some unattractive jobs pay substantially more than others.

Wealth There is an important difference between the terms "income" and "wealth." A person's income is the money he or she receives from various sources during any given time period. A person's wealth is the value of the goods and property that the person owns. People hold wealth in many forms, including ownership of stocks, bonds, bank accounts, and real estate. Wealth is an important source of income for some people. Persons who own wealth receive income in the form of dividends, interest, and rents in addition to any income they may receive from work. In fact, many of the people with the highest income in the United States receive most of their income from wealth rather than from work. Moreover, wealth often is passed from one generation to another in the form of inheritance. Some experts argue that a widely distorted distribution of wealth in the United States is the most important cause of income inequality. They base this argument partially on the fact that the richest one fifth of American families owns more than 70 percent of the nation's wealth, while the poorest one fifth of American families owns less than 1 percent of the nation's wealth.

Luck In addition to all of the above factors, luck also plays a role in income inequality. Luck can include everything from circumstances of birth to occurrences throughout the life of an individual. For example, a child born to an unemployed wage earner is generally more likely to have a lower lifetime income than a child born to a wealthy oil magnate. An actor or actress fortunate enough to be at the right audition for the right movie might become a star overnight. At the same time, accidents and poor health can destroy the earning power of any worker, and choosing a profession in which there is an unexpected decline in demand can lead to reduced earnings.

Check Your Understanding

1. How do economists determine how income is distributed in the United States?

2. How does the percentage share of income of the lowest income group in the population compare with that of the highest income group?

3. Identify six reasons for differences in income.

Those with minimal education and few marketable skills may find employment in fields having a large supply and a low demand for workers.

Poverty

Poverty is a problem in almost all nations of the world, and the United States is no exception. Millions of Americans suffer considerable hardship because of their poverty. As a first step in examining poverty in the United States, let us see how it is defined.

Defining Poverty

Poverty is a relative term, and different individuals have different ideas about what constitutes poverty. What some would consider poverty might be considered by others to be a comfortable lifestyle. Moreover, what is considered poverty in one time period may not be considered so in another. At a time when nobody had indoor plumbing or electricity, we could not say that everybody lived in poverty. Yet, given our present standard of living, we might say that people forced to live under these conditions today might be considered poverty stricken.

In an effort to provide an objective and consistent measure of poverty in the United States, the federal government has established an official definition for poverty known as the **poverty level.** This is the income level that the government believes is needed to meet the costs of the basic essentials—food, clothing, and shelter. Any family or individual with an income below the poverty level is officially classified as poor. In 1983, the official national poverty level for a family of four was $10,178. The poverty level rises each year by the same percentage as the annual consumer price index, which you learned about in Chapter 9.

The Extent of Poverty

Table 13–2 shows the number and percentage of Americans living below the poverty level during the years 1972–83. As you can see, 35.3 million Americans—15.2 percent of the population—were living below the poverty level in 1983. The sharp rise in the poverty rate between 1979 and 1982 was primarily the result of the rising unemployment that accompanied the severe recession of 1981–82. The unemployment rate peaked out at 10.7 percent in late 1982, the highest level in more than 40 years. In addition to the recession, another factor contributing to the rise in poverty during this period may have been the tightening of eligibility standards for certain government aid programs.

Characteristics of the Poor

Table 13–3 shows selected characteristics of the poor. As you can see, minorities have a much higher poverty rate than whites. In 1983, 12.1 percent of whites lived below the poverty level, while 35.7 percent of all blacks and 28.4 percent of all persons of Spanish origin were officially classified as poor. In actual numbers, however,

---

TABLE 13–2: NUMBER AND PERCENTAGE OF AMERICANS LIVING BELOW THE POVERTY LEVEL 1972–83

Year	Number Below Poverty Level in Millions	Percentage Below Poverty Level
1972	24.5	11.9
1973	23.0	11.1
1974	23.4	11.2
1975	25.9	12.3
1976	25.0	11.8
1977	24.7	11.6
1978	24.5	11.4
1979	26.0	11.7
1980	29.3	13.0
1981	31.8	14.0
1982	34.4	15.0
1983	35.3	15.2

Source: *Current Population Report of Consumer Income: Money Income and Poverty Status of Families and Persons in the United States,* issued August 1984

more whites lived below the poverty level than any other group because whites make up the bulk of the population. There were 24 million whites, 9.9 million blacks, and 4.2 million persons of Spanish origin living below the poverty level in 1983.

The average poverty rate for metropolitan areas is lower than that for nonmetropolitan areas because metropolitan areas include suburbs, which usually have a low poverty rate. However, the central cities within metropolitan areas have a very high poverty rate. In 1983, the average poverty rate for all central cities was 19.8 percent, with a total of 12.9 million of the nation's poor living in such areas.

Individuals living alone have a higher poverty rate than families, and women have a higher rate of poverty than men. In 1983, the poverty rate for individual women was 26.2 percent, compared to a poverty rate of 19.9 percent for individual men. In that same year, families headed by a woman with no husband present had the highest poverty rate of all categories, with 36 percent of all such families living below the poverty level. Many of these families were headed by mothers of preschool children.

Other characteristics of the poor, not listed in Table 13–3, involve age, geographic location,

TABLE 13–3: CHARACTERISTICS OF PERSONS LIVING BELOW THE POVERTY LEVEL IN 1983

Characteristic	Percentage Below Poverty Level
All Persons	15.2
White	12.1
Black	35.7
Spanish Origin	28.4
In Metropolitan Areas	13.8
In Central Cities	19.8
Outside Central Cities	9.6
Outside Metropolitan Areas	18.3
All Families	12.3
Married Couple Families	7.6
Male Householder, No Wife Present	13.0
Female Householder, No Husband Present	36.0
All Unrelated Individuals	23.4
Male	19.9
Female	26.2

Source: *Current Population Report of Consumer Income: Money Income and Poverty Status of Families and Persons in the United States*, issued August 1984

Poverty is greatest in central cities, especially during periods of high unemployment.

When land is available, a family can often supplement its income by growing food for themselves.

and work status. The young and the old have the highest rate of poverty. In 1983, there were 13.7 million children under the age of 18 and 3.7 million persons 65 years of age and over living below the poverty level. These two groups combined made up approximately half of the nation's poor.

In terms of geography, the South had both the largest number of poor and the highest poverty rate. In 1983, nearly 13.5 million of the nation's 35.3 million poor lived in that region, where the average poverty rate was 17.2 percent as compared to an overall national rate of 15.2 percent.

Solutions: Dealing with the Causes

There are no easy, simple solutions to the poverty problem. However, over the years a number of government programs aimed at helping the poor have been established, and still others have been proposed. Many of the existing and proposed programs deal with the causes of poverty, one of the most important of which is the inability of the poor to find stable employment at jobs that will enable them to rise above the poverty level. Any program designed to get at the causes of poverty must attempt to increase the employability of the poor. A comprehensive program aimed at increasing the employability of the poor would include three parts: (1) increasing educational opportunities; (2) reducing discrimination; and (3) increasing overall employment.

Increasing educational opportunities Many of the poor lack the educational and skill levels required by most jobs today. Many are high school dropouts, but even those who have graduated from high school often find that they do not have the technical skills necessary for many jobs in today's changing economy. The nation's high schools are currently offering more training in specific occupational skills than they have in the past, and future graduates will be better qualified for jobs than were past graduates. For those no longer in high school, programs have been and are being developed to provide the unemployed and the underemployed with job skills. Community colleges offer technical training classes, and government and private businesses have offered cooperative training programs.

Many people believe that greater educational opportunities today will decrease the amount of poverty in the future. (See Figure 13–1.) Unfortunately, the quality of education in general is still uneven. School districts in areas that have a large tax base often can offer far more to students than school districts with a small tax base can offer.

Reducing discrimination Many experts believe that many of today's poor are victims of past and present discrimination. In the past, educational opportunity was far from equal in the United States, and many individuals were denied good employment opportunities on the basis of race and sex, among other things. Although such discrimination is illegal today, some critics argue that it still exists to a substantial degree.

Even if all discrimination could be eliminated, the effects of past discrimination would continue to contribute to poverty for many years to come. The poor are concentrated in inner cities and rural regions where educational expenditures per pupil are often substantially less than in the suburbs and other more affluent areas. In addition, faced with a lack of opportunities, many of the poor have simply given up hope that they will ever escape their poverty. They, in turn, present to their children a bleak picture of the future. Any program that aims to combat poverty must deal with the effects of both past and present discrimination.

Increasing overall employment During recessions the poverty rate usually increases dramatically. For example, as a result of the severe recession of 1981–82, the number of persons living below the poverty level rose from 29.3

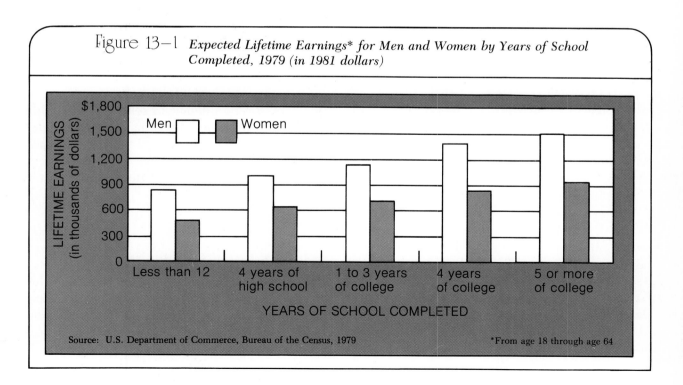

Figure 13–1 *Expected Lifetime Earnings* for Men and Women by Years of School Completed, 1979 (in 1981 dollars)*

Source: U.S. Department of Commerce, Bureau of the Census, 1979

*From age 18 through age 64

Structural unemployment in some regions has forced many who lost their jobs to seek employment in new fields.

million in 1980 to 34.4 million in 1982. This two-year increase of 5.1 million people caused enormous suffering and put a severe strain on the nation's capacity to provide relief for the poor. Any actions that could have prevented or even reduced the magnitude of the recession would have resulted in much less poverty during the period. Thus, pursuing sound fiscal and monetary policies in an effort to avoid the extremes of the business cycle is perhaps the strongest contribution the government can make toward reducing poverty.

Since recessions cannot be completely avoided, some economists advocate government employment programs during periods of high unemployment. They believe that it is better to provide employment opportunities in the form of useful public works programs, such as road construction and maintenance projects, than to provide the poor with cash assistance.

In addition to the cyclical unemployment caused by recessions, there is the problem of structural unemployment caused by skill mismatches and geographic mismatches. Increased educational opportunities can help to reduce unemployment caused by skill mismatches. However, as you learned in Chapter 9, unemployment resulting from geographic mismatches can be difficult to solve. Because this type of unemployment is a major cause of poverty in some regions, some people advocate special government programs designed to increase employment opportunities in affected regions as a way to reduce poverty in these areas.

Solutions: Dealing with the Symptoms

Long-term programs aimed at reducing the causes of poverty do little to reduce the suffering of those currently living in poverty. In addition, because many of the poor are too old, too young, or too disabled to work, there always will be the need for programs aimed at alleviating the hardship resulting from poverty. These programs deal with the symptoms of poverty and attempt to provide direct economic assistance to the poor. Such programs usually are referred to as **welfare programs,** and they fall into two categories: direct cash payments and noncash assistance.

Direct cash payments The most important program that provides direct cash payments to the poor is the **Aid to Families with Dependent Children (AFDC)** program. Under this program a family in need because of the death, absence from home, disability, or (in some states) unemployment of a parent can receive cash payments based on income. Although the federal government helps pay for AFDC programs, each state runs its own program, and benefits vary widely from state to state. Another program that provides direct cash payments to the poor is **Supplemental Security Income for the Aged, Blind, and Disabled (SSI).** This program, which is administered by the federal government, guarantees a minimum income for persons who are at least 65 years old, blind, or disabled. Eligibility is based on need and is not tied to Social Security coverage.

In addition to the above programs, unemployed workers usually receive cash payments in the form of unemployment insurance benefits for several months after being laid off from their jobs. This program is funded by a payroll tax on employers, and benefits vary from state to state.

Noncash assistance There are a number of government programs that provide assistance to the poor in a form other than through direct cash payments. The two most important such programs are the food stamp program and Medicaid. The food stamp program was designed to improve the diets of low-income individuals and families. **Food stamps** are government-issued coupons that can be exchanged for food. Food stamps are given or sold for a fraction of their value to eligible low-income persons, and they can be used only to purchase approved food

Food stamps are a form of noncash assistance to allow low-income families to sustain minimum dietary needs by increasing their ability to purchase food.

items. For example, a low-income family might be able to buy $100 worth of food stamps for $50. The family then can use the food stamps to purchase $100 worth of food.

Medicaid Medicaid is a joint federal–state medical insurance program that provides health care for the poor. Under this program, states and the federal government pay physicians, dentists, and hospitals for medical services to individuals who are too poor to provide for their own medical needs.

A Proposed Alternative to Current Welfare

Programs

Without a doubt, many of the nation's poor have been helped by current welfare programs. Many poor people have been able to obtain goods and services that would have been impossible for them to obtain otherwise. However, there are many critics of the American welfare system. Some say it does not meet the needs of the poor, and others say it costs the taxpayers too much money. Still others cite the fraud and abuse within the system. They cite as examples instances in which doctors are overcharging the government and instances where people are receiving benefits that they are not entitled to receive.

All three criticisms may be valid to a certain extent. The major problem lies in the fact that the current program is very costly to administer. A large staff of workers is needed to make sure that the needs and resources of welfare applicants are documented. This is very expensive and at the same time allows matters to become entangled in the bureaucratic web of operating the system. People who want to cheat the system sometimes are able to sneak through the cracks, and others who are eligible for benefits sometimes get caught up in the bureaucracy.

Because of these problems, there have been many proposals for welfare reform—both by economists and by public officials. The proposal receiving the most support from economists is the **negative income tax,** which is a program in which people who earn less than a certain income would receive cash payments from the government. Proponents of the negative income tax advocate transferring the responsibility for administering welfare payments from the current welfare bureaucracy to the Internal Revenue Service—the agency that already administers the federal income tax system.

Employees of state and federal governments help citizens fill out their tax forms. Some people have suggested a negative income tax as an alternative to the current welfare programs.

The negative income tax proposal calls for a modification of the current federal income tax. Under the current system, the lower an individual's income, the less he or she pays in federal income taxes. When income falls below a certain minimum level, the individual pays no federal income tax at all. With a negative income tax, if income should fall below a certain level the individual would not only be exempt from paying a tax but he or she would also receive a cash payment from the Internal Revenue Service. For example, a family earning only $6,000 in income might receive $1,500 in negative income tax payments from the government for a total income of $7,500. If the family earned $7,000, it would receive $1,000 in negative income taxes for a total income of $8,000; and if the family earned $8,000, it would receive $500 in negative income taxes for a total income of $8,500. If the family earned $9,000, it would neither receive any negative income tax payments nor owe any taxes to the government. However, all income above $9,000 would be taxed at a progressive rate.

The idea behind the negative income tax is simple. Since the government is currently receiving tax payments from individuals with incomes above a certain minimum and making payment in the form of welfare checks to poor individuals, why not eliminate the welfare bureaucracy and allow one agency of government—the Internal Revenue Service—to perform both fuctions? Proponents of the negative income tax argue that the reduction in administrative costs resulting from such a change would enable the government to provide larger benefits to the poor at less cost to the taxpayers.

Not all proponents of the negative income tax agree on the specifics of such a program. However, most agree that any workable plan must provide incentives for the poor to work. Some propose that benefits under such a plan be reduced by only 50 percent of any additional earnings that recipients might receive from working. For example, suppose a family of four with a total income of $8,000 (in earnings plus negative income tax payments) had the opportunity to earn $2,000 of additional income. If the negative income tax payments were reduced by $2,000, because of the $2,000 of earnings there would be no incentive to work. However, if the payments were reduced by only 50 percent of the family's earnings, the family would end up with a total income of $9,000, for a net gain of $1,000.

Opponents of the negative income tax argue that such a program would require a large increase in the staff of the Internal Revenue Service so that they might mail out checks monthly or weekly and prevent abuse of the program. They also contend that workers with incomes only slightly above those required to qualify for benefits would resent having to subsidize families with incomes perhaps only a few hundred dollars less than theirs.

Check Your Understanding

1. What is meant by the term "poverty level"? What percentage of the population was living below the poverty level in 1983?

2. Describe the segments of the population that have the highest poverty rate.

3. Describe three actions that could be taken to reduce the causes of poverty.

4. Describe two programs that provide direct cash payments to the poor. Which two programs provide noncash assistance to the poor?

5. What is a negative income tax? How would such a program work?

ISSUE: Should There Be a Guaranteed Minimum Income?

Widespread dissatisfaction with the current welfare system as a means of dealing with poverty has led to many proposals for reform. Some propose the establishment of a family allowance system, under which every family would receive a certain amount of money based on the number and age of its children. Those families with incomes above a designated level would return part or all of the money to the government when they pay their income taxes. Those below the established level would keep the money. Others propose a negative income tax, under which people below a certain income level would receive cash payments from the Internal Revenue Service. Still others propose various combinations of these two proposals. Although the specifics differ, all of these proposals have a common objective—the establishment of a guaranteed minimum income for all families. Aside from the debate over which proposal is best, there is much disagreement over the basic question of whether or not there should be a guaranteed minimum income.

The Case for a Guaranteed Minimum Income

Proponents of a guaranteed minimum income argue that the current welfare system is inadequate and inefficient. They contend that poverty is far too widespread in this country and that the extensive red tape connected with the current system often prevents needy persons from obtaining benefits while others cheat the system and obtain benefits for which they are not qualified.

Moreover, they see the wide range of benefits and qualification standards among the various states under the current system as unfair both to welfare recipients and to taxpayers. They contend that because some states are either unable or unwilling to provide adequate benefits for their welfare recipients, there is a great deal of inequity in the benefits available to the poor in the various regions of the country. Furthermore, they argue that there is an incentive for welfare recipients in those states with the lowest benefits to move to other states where benefits are higher, putting an added burden on the taxpayers in those states.

In a nation as affluent as the United States, proponents say, no individual or family should be without enough income to provide for at least the most basic essentials such as adequate nutrition and shelter. With a guaranteed minimum income, they argue, everyone would be assured of at least a subsistence level of living. Furthermore, such a program would be a more efficient way of dealing with the problem of poverty than the current welfare system.

The Case Against a Guaranteed Minimum Income

Opponents of a guaranteed minimum income object to such a program on a number of grounds. Many oppose the whole idea of having the federal government take money from one group to give to another group for the purpose of ensuring a minimum income for everyone. They argue that some low-income working Americans would be taxed to provide benefits for others whose incomes were only slightly lower. Furthermore, they contend that such a program would not solve the problem of poverty. They argue that there is a basic conflict between the goal of guaranteeing a minimum income and the goal of providing incentives to work. They believe that if the government guaranteed everyone a minimum income regardless of whether or not they were able to work, some low-income workers actually might be encouraged to quit their jobs.

They also believe that recipients of government payments must be accountable to someone, such as a local welfare caseworker. They point to the fact that if the head of a household is addicted to drugs, drinking, or gambling, or is simply irresponsible with money, the other members of the family might receive little or no benefits from government income payments.

Finally, opponents of a guaranteed minimum income are very concerned about the cost of such a program. They believe that because such a program would reduce incentives to work, the cost would be far greater than proponents believe. Furthermore, once such a program was established, they fear that there would be a tendency for benefits to be increased gradually over the years, leading to even greater costs.

How do you feel about a guaranteed minimum income? Do you favor such a program? Why or why not? Do you believe such a program would substantially reduce incentives to work? Give reasons for your answer.

Urban Problems: Housing

In 1800, only 5 percent of all Americans lived in urban areas. By 1920, this figure had grown to approximately 50 percent. Today, more than 70 percent of the population is urban and lives on only about 1 percent of the land. This urbanization of the population has created many serious social and economic problems, one of the most important of which is housing.

Housing

One of the most critical of all urban problems is the shortage of adequate housing for the poor. The problem has existed for decades, and although there have been serious efforts by both government and private enterprise to solve it, these efforts have met with very limited success. Let us examine some of the causes of the urban housing shortage.

Urban poverty As you learned earlier in this chapter, the poverty rate is very high in central cities. In 1983, central cities had an average poverty rate of 19.8 percent, with 12.9 million of the nation's poor living in such areas. One of the reasons for the high urban poverty rate is the fact that many former employers have left the inner cities and relocated to the suburbs or to other geographic areas of the country, such as the South. With no means of commuting or relocating to new jobs, the poor have been forced to remain in the cities—unemployed, and with few marketable skills.

Because of their poverty, many urban dwellers cannot afford to pay sufficient rent to cover the cost of adequate housing even if such housing were available. This gap between the cost of housing and what low-income families can afford to pay is the most fundamental part of the urban housing problem. Government estimates have indicated that even if a sufficient number of apartments to meet the needs of urban dwellers could somehow be constructed, more than two thirds of inner-city families could not afford to pay even half the estimated rents that would be required to recover construction costs.

Zoning laws and building codes Most units of local government have zoning laws that stipulate the types of structures that can be built in various areas of the community and building codes that specify construction standards. For example, some areas are zoned for industrial and/or commercial buildings, some are zoned for multiple-family apartment buildings, and others are zoned exclusively for single-family dwellings. Anyone wishing to build a house or apartment building must comply with both the zoning laws and the building codes.

Although zoning laws and building codes serve a useful purpose, some critics argue that they are often far too restrictive and that they serve as a barrier to solving urban housing problems. These critics believe too much land is allocated to single-family dwellings and too little is made available for the type of multiple-family apartment buildings that can provide affordable housing for urban dwellers. They also argue that building codes often specify construction standards that result in much higher building costs than necessary and, thus, push the cost of housing beyond the reach of many who might otherwise be able to afford it.

Government rent controls Some cities have resorted to government-imposed rent controls, or rent ceilings, in an effort to keep rents from rising beyond the reach of many urban dwellers. Although rent controls may provide some short-term relief to renters, many economists believe that over the long run they do more harm than good. Since rent controls limit the returns to landlords as compared to other investments, landlords are more likely to allow their rental properties to deteriorate or in some cases even to abandon them for tax purposes. Because rent ceilings can discourage the construction of new housing as well as the renovation of existing units, a decline in the supply of housing over the long run can result.

Government Housing Policies

Over the years, the government has engaged in a number of activities aimed at reducing the housing shortage. These include promoting the construction of private housing, providing public housing, and sponsoring urban renewal projects.

Promotion of private housing For many years, the government has sought to encourage the construction of private housing through a number of agencies, including the Federal Housing Administration and the Veterans Administration. The government has sought to promote home ownership by making home-mortgage loans available at very reasonable interest rates. However, while this program has helped many middle-class families to purchase a single-family dwelling, it has done little to aid poor urban families in obtaining adequate housing.

Public housing Since the late 1930s, the government has been involved in public housing. There have been a number of government programs over the years, most of which involve federal aid to state and local governments for the purpose of providing low-rent housing for the poor. The housing units are privately built but they are owned and operated by public-housing authorities.

An increase in multiple-family dwellings is needed to provide affordable housing for people in cities.

Urban renewal generally increases available housing for middle- and upper-income families, but often reduces the number of low-income units.

Although these government-funded public housing projects have helped reduce the housing shortage, many critics argue that they have been far from adequate. In addition to the fact that most programs have been insufficiently funded, critics charge that some programs have been poorly conceived and have overlapped and conflicted with earlier programs.

Urban renewal   During the past 30 years, more emphasis has been placed on rehabilitating cities than on constructing new housing for the poor. Most of the **urban renewal** projects have been sponsored jointly by federal and municipal governments, and their purpose has been to rebuild old neighborhoods in an effort to attract new industry and to encourage affluent suburbanites to return to the central cities.

Although many of the urban renewal programs have been impressive, many critics charge that they have hurt the poor and made the urban housing problem worse instead of better. They base their criticism on the fact that most local units of government have used the urban renewal projects, which are funded primarily by the federal government, to broaden their local tax base. In other words, most of the emphasis has been placed on constructing new commercial buildings and housing for middle- and upper-income families instead of on building low-income housing. Since many low-income units are demolished as a part of the urban renewal projects, the result is less low-cost housing instead of more.

Solutions to the Housing Problem

There is general agreement that ways must be found to make urban housing more affordable for the poor. Among the various proposed solutions are development of a uniform national building code, rent supplements, and interest subsidies.

A uniform national building code   There is a wide variation in the standards of local building codes throughout the United States. Critics argue that the codes go far beyond the requirements of safety and durability and often specify the kinds of materials that must be used and the methods of construction. They charge that many of the codes are designed to protect special-interest groups, such as manufacturers of building materials or trade unions, rather than to provide safe and durable housing at the least possible cost.

Proponents of a uniform national building code argue that the establishment of a code specifying safety and durability standards instead of construction methods would enable the housing industry to develop more efficient, lower cost ways of constructing housing. This would, of course, help to close the gap between building costs and what low-income families can afford to pay for housing.

Rent supplements Some people argue that since there is insufficient public housing to

Would government rent supplements for low-income families increase the range of housing choice for poor people? There are good arguments on both sides of this question.

meet the needs of the poor, the government should supplement a portion of the rental payments of qualified low-income families living in private housing. They argue that this would give the poor a wider range of housing choices and would eliminate the stigma of "poorness" that many people associate with public housing. However, others argue that such a program would be difficult and costly to administer because both tenants and landlords would have to be audited periodically to make sure the government was not being overcharged.

Interest subsidies Proponents of interest subsidies argue that by contributing a portion of the monthly interest that a family must pay on its home mortgage loan, the government could enable more low-income families to become homeowners. The amount of subsidy would depend on family income, and as a family's income rose the subsidy payments would decline. However, critics of this approach fear that such a program would enable some people who otherwise would have found a way to pay the full cost of their interest to receive subsidies. They argue also that it would not make a major contribution toward solving urban housing problems.

Check Your Understanding

1. What are the basic causes of the urban housing problem?

2. How effective have public housing programs been in solving the urban housing problem?

3. What is meant by urban renewal? What effect have urban renewal projects had on the housing problem?

4. What are some of the proposed solutions to the urban housing problem?

Urban Problems: Transportation and Financing Local Government

Two other important urban problems are transportation and financing local government. We will focus on both of these problems in this section.

Transportation

One of the most essential ingredients of a strong urban economy is a good transportation system. Such a system must be capable of transporting hundreds of thousands—and in some cases millions—of people to and from work in the central business districts, or downtown areas, with maximum safety and minimum congestion and discomfort. Unfortunately, many of today's cities are experiencing serious problems with their transportation systems.

The most serious problems facing the transportation systems of most cities are congestion during rush hours and insufficient revenues from fares to finance mass-transit systems adequately. Massive traffic jams during morning and evening rush periods are an everyday occurrence in many cities. They are a constant source of frustration to commuters, and they often prevent people from getting to work on time. Most experts believe that the excessive traffic congestion is the result of an imbalance between the use of automobiles and mass-transit systems such as buses and trains. Urban freeways, bridges, and tunnels simply cannot handle adequately the large volume of commuters who elect to drive their own cars rather than use mass-transit alternatives.

Although most experts believe that more commuters should be using mass-transit systems, these systems, too, are often overcrowded during rush hours. This is because many mass-transit systems do not generate enough revenue from fares to cover even operating costs. Safety problems and a general dissatisfaction with the quality of service are producing a further decline in the total ridership in many cities, causing revenues to drop even further. As a result, expansion and modernization of the systems are financially impossible. Many economists believe that both problems stem

Traffic jams are a regular problem during rush hours in most cities.

Mass-transit systems help relieve some traffic problems, but some systems cannot attract enough riders to cover operating costs.

from the fact that the government subsidizes automobile travel to a much higher degree than mass transit. The Federal Highway Act allows 90 percent federal funding for freeways, and thus most cities have been more interested in expanding highways than mass-transit systems.

Some economists believe that many of the problems of urban transportation could be solved by the proper use of economic incentives. They advocate the use of variable tolls on freeways—both to encourage commuters to switch from automobile to mass-transit travel and to even out the flow of traffic throughout the day. They argue that if higher tolls were charged on the major freeways during rush hours, some motorists would use alternative routes, others would delay travel until after the rush periods, and still others would switch to mass-transit travel.

Because automobile travel is more heavily subsidized than mass transit, many economists believe that funds generated by the higher tolls on the freeways should be used to expand and improve mass-transit systems. However, most do not believe that such funds would be adequate, and they advocate channeling additional funds into mass transit. These economists do not necessarily support fare increases. Too often when fares are raised to increase the revenues of mass-transit systems, they tend to encourage more commuters to switch to auto travel. This, of course, is just the opposite of what is needed. Many economists believe that by upgrading the capacity and quality of mass-transit systems and by implementing policies that would make the cost of traveling by automobile approximately equal to the cost of using mass transit, cities could take a big step toward solving their transportation problems.

Financing Local Government

One of the most difficult of all urban problems is the financing of local government. Over the years, the costs of providing public services in American cities has grown almost continuously at the same time that the cities' ability to pay for such services has been declining. For decades, the groups that pay the largest share of taxes—businesses and middle-income families—have been leaving the cities and moving to the suburbs. They, in turn, have been replaced by a growing population of poor individuals and families who have a greater need for the public services that the cities provide but less ability to pay taxes to support such services. The problem is compounded by the fact that many of the people who have moved outside the city limits still work in the city. Thus, they still benefit from city streets, mass-transit systems, police protection, ambulance service, and so forth, although they contribute little toward financing such services.

There are no easy solutions to the problem of financing city governments. However, ways must be found to generate more revenue. One proposal is to collect more revenue from non-city residents who work in the city or regularly visit the city. Many city services—such as public libraries, museums, and parks—are now financed primarily by local taxes on city residents, although these services are regularly used by people who live outside the city as well. One solution to this problem is to finance such services primarily with user fees charged to people regardless of their place of residence.

Some economists advocate restructuring the property tax as a partial solution to the problem of local finance. They argue that the present property tax is too heavily weighted toward buildings relative to land. They believe that a heavy tax on the increased value of land that results from community development and population growth would be more equitable and yield more revenue than the present property tax. Such a tax also would tend to encourage the building of structures on land and dis-courage land speculators from withholding land from productive use in the hope of earning large future profits after adjacent properties have been developed.

Another proposed solution to the problem of financing city governments is the establishment of metropolitan governments. Economists and others who advocate this approach argue that local government authority in most metropolitan areas is too fragmented to provide balanced public services to all the people in the metropolitan area efficiently. They argue that some form of government consolidation is needed in order to provide more efficient government administration. However, there is often strong public opposition to government consolidation, and this approach may not be politically feasible in many areas.

Many economists believe that the problems of the cities are too big for the cities to solve by themselves. They point to the fact that many of the poor who currently live in inner cities migrated to urban areas in search of work when they were displaced by the mechanization of the industries in which they worked. They see the problems of the cities as national problems and argue that the federal government must provide more financial assistance toward solving them.

Check Your Understanding

1. What are the two most serious problems facing urban transportation systems today?
2. Describe two possible solutions to the problems of urban transportation.
3. What are the basic underlying causes of the problems of financing city government?
4. Describe the proposed solutions to the problems of financing city government.

CAREERS: City Planner

City planners play a vital role in determining the future of our cities. They develop programs to provide for future growth and revitalization of cities, and they help local government officials make decisions on social, economic, and environmental problems. One of the responsibilities of city planners is to make sure that community facilities—such as water supplies, health clinics, and schools—are able to meet the demands placed on them. Planners must also prepare for the likely results of population growth or for other social and economic changes. In this capacity, they estimate the long-range needs for housing, transportation, and business and industrial sites, and propose alternate ways to achieve more efficient and attractive urban areas.

City planners prepare detailed studies showing the current use of land for residential, business, and community purposes, as well as the current locations of streets, highways, water and sewer lines, schools, libraries, and recreational sites. These studies also provide information about the types of industries in the community, the characteristics of the population, and employment and economic trends. Such information is important when planning zoning regulations—which stipulate the specific use of land and buildings in any area—on how undeveloped land can and should be used.

A bachelor's degree with a major in city planning, architecture, or engineering may qualify candidates for some entry-level jobs in city planning. However, most entry-level positions with federal, state, and local government agencies require at least two years of graduate study in urban or regional planning, or the equivalent in work experience. Many colleges and universities offer a two-year graduate program leading to a master's degree in urban planning, which includes both classroom study and on-the-job training. This is the preferred course of study for people wanting to enter this field.

Chapter Highlights

1   Income distribution is unequal in the United States. In 1983, the 20 percent of the population with the highest income received more than nine times as much income as the 20 percent with the lowest income.

2   Among the most important reasons for differences in income are differences in ability, education, opportunity, occupations, wealth, and luck.

3   The United States government has established an official definition of poverty known as the poverty level. In 1983, the official poverty level for a family of four was $10,178.

4   In 1983, there were 35.3 million Americans—15.2 percent of the population—living below the poverty level. There was a sharp rise in the poverty rate between 1979 and 1982, primarily because of the severe recession of 1981–82.

5   Groups with high poverty rates include minorities, central city residents, families headed by a woman with no husband present, the young, and the old.

6   Programs aimed at eliminating the causes of poverty should attempt to increase educational opportunities, reduce discrimination, and increase overall employment.

7   Programs dealing with the symptoms of poverty fall into two categories: direct cash payments and noncash assistance. Two programs that provide direct cash payments to the poor are the Aid to Families with Dependent Children (AFDC) program and the Supplemental Security Income for the Aged, Blind, and Disabled (SSI).

8   Two important programs that provide noncash assistance to the poor are the food stamp program and Medicaid. Food stamps are government-issued coupons that can be exchanged for food. Medicaid is a joint federal–state medical insurance program under which states pay physicians, dentists, and hospitals for medical services to individuals who are too poor to provide for their own medical needs.

9   A proposed alternative to current welfare programs is the negative income tax. Proponents of the negative income tax believe that this program would enable the government to provide larger benefits to the poor at less cost to the taxpayer.

10 Housing is one of the most serious urban problems. It is caused by a shortage of adequate housing; a gap between what many urban dwellers can afford to pay for housing and the cost of supplying such housing; current zoning laws and building codes; rent controls; and urban renewal programs. Proposed solutions to the housing problem include a uniform national building code, rent supplements, and interest subsidies.

11 The most serious problems facing the transportation systems of most cities today are traffic congestion during rush periods and insufficient revenues from fares to adequately finance mass-transit systems. To solve these problems, some economists advocate both the use of variable tolls on major freeways to encourage commuters to switch from automobile to mass-transit travel and the use of additional public funds to subsidize mass-transit systems.

12 Over the years, cities have found it increasingly difficult to finance public services. Proposed solutions have included instituting user fees for certain services, restructuring the property tax, and establishing metropolitan governments.

Important Terms

Match each of the following terms with the correct definition:

food stamps   SSI   poverty level
Medicaid   urban renewal
AFDC   negative income tax

1. A federal government program that guarantees a minimum income for persons who are at least 65 years old, blind, or disabled.

2. A joint federal–state medical insurance program designed to provide health care for the poor.

3. That level of income at or below which the government officially classifies individuals and families as poor.

4. Programs designed to rehabilitate cities.

5. A government program under which a family in need because of the death, absence from home, disability, or unemployment of a parent can receive cash payments.

6. Government-issued coupons that are given or sold for a fraction of their value to eligible low-income persons in an effort to improve their diets.

7. A proposed alternative to current welfare programs that would transfer the responsibility for administering welfare payments to the Internal Revenue Service.

Extending Your Understanding

1. Do you think income distribution in the United States is too unequal? Why or why not?

2. What are some of the ways in which the United States government has tried to deal with the poverty issue? Do you think the government is doing enough to solve the problem of poverty? Why or why not?

3. Which proposed solution to the housing problem do you think is the most workable? Explain your answer.

Activities

1. Suppose you have been given the job of drawing up a plan to solve the problems of cities. Prepare a brief outline that reflects what you think the most important first steps should be. Then state the reasons why you have chosen the approach you have outlined.

2. Hold a debate on whether or not a negative income tax should be established as an alternative to the current welfare program. Both sides should do research ahead of time so that all arguments are backed by specific information.

Building Skills in Economics: Computing Averages

Very often when reading statistics about poverty and about income levels, you hear such terms as "median" and "mean." These are types of averages that are used for comparison purposes. The **median** is the income level or data entry that falls in the middle of a series when the entries are arranged from the lowest to the highest. For example, in the series $10,000, $10,000, $13,200, $14,135, and $17,190, the median is $13,200. Two figures fall above this income level, and two fall below it.

The **mean** is what we usually think of when we think of average. It is computed by adding all pieces of data together and dividing by the number of pieces. In the above example, the mean is $12,905 ($10,000 + $10,000 + $13,200 + $14,135 + $17,190 = $64,525; $64,525 ÷ 5 = $12,905).

A third kind of average is the **mode.** The mode is the term that appears most often in any given list. In the above example, the mode is $10,000 because that figure appears twice.

Each kind of average is used at different times. The median doesn't take into account extremes, whereas the mean does. For example, if the last entry in the above list was $35,000, the mean would be much higher than $12,905 but the median would remain the same. The mode is used least frequently because an entry would have to appear several times before it would be useful to researchers.

The list that follows shows the incomes of the workers in a particular factory. The questions will help you compute the various types of averages.

Applying Economics Skills

1. What would you have to do first before being able to find the median? After doing this, determine the median.
2. Compute the mean income for these factory workers.
3. Which figure appears most frequently? What is this figure called?
4. Which average do you think presents the most realistic picture of incomes in this factory? Explain your answer.

Incomes of Factory Workers

$ 7,000
$12,000
$65,000
$ 7,000
$ 9,200
$12,500
$10,400

CHAPTER 14

ENERGY, POLLUTION, AND THE ENVIRONMENT

Energy is one of the most crucial of all resources. Without it life could not exist. Energy in the form of food powers our bodies. In other forms—such as gasoline, fuel oil, natural gas, and electricity—energy is used to power our automobiles, locomotives, airplanes, and factories. Energy also is used as a source of heat and light, providing us with warmth and brightness even on the coldest and darkest days. Most of the energy on earth comes from the sun and is stored in such forms as wood, coal, gas, and oil.

For many years, Americans took energy for granted. It was relatively inexpensive and seemed to be available in unlimited quantities. That all changed, however, in late 1973 when a group of Arab nations—members of the Organization of Petroleum Exporting Countries (OPEC)—halted oil shipments to the United States and some other Western nations.

The oil embargo shattered the belief of many Americans that supplies of cheap energy would last forever. It also played a major role in the high inflation of the 1970s and helped to trigger the 1974–75 recession. As a result, more Americans both inside and outside of government began to take the energy problem seriously. It became increasingly apparent that the future of the American economy was closely linked to the availability and cost of energy.

In this chapter, we will examine the energy problem, look at the various sources of energy, and consider the need for energy conservation. We also will examine a closely related problem—pollution. Let us begin with a look at the energy problem.

The Energy Problem

In 1973, the world market price of crude oil—the raw material from which gasoline, fuel oil, kerosene, and many other products are manufactured—was about $3 per barrel. When the OPEC nations instituted their embargo, however, the price of crude oil rose dramatically. Moreover, prices continued to rise even after the actual embargo ended the following year, as OPEC continued to restrict oil production. By 1980, the price of crude oil had risen to about $33 per barrel.

This eleven fold increase in the world price of crude oil had an enormous impact on prices in the United States. The price of almost everything—not just gasoline and other fuels—rose because part of the manufacturing cost and much of the transportation cost, of all manufactured items is energy cost. The same is true of farm products. Planting farm crops, harvesting them, and transporting them to consumers all require considerable energy expenditures.

This sudden and unexpected change in the world energy situation put the United States in a difficult predicament because it had become highly dependent on oil, including imported oil, as a major source of its energy supply. The nation's heavy reliance on oil stemmed from two basic factors. The first is that of all common fuels, oil is the most versatile and the most convenient for transportation. The second is that until the early 1970s, oil had seemed endlessly abundant and relatively inexpensive. In the words of some critics, the nation had become addicted to oil. (See Figure 14–1.)

As long as foreign oil remained abundantly available and the price remained relatively low, this dependency did not pose a serious problem. However, the 1973–74 embargo and the skyrocketing prices that accompanied and followed it changed the whole picture. In 1970,

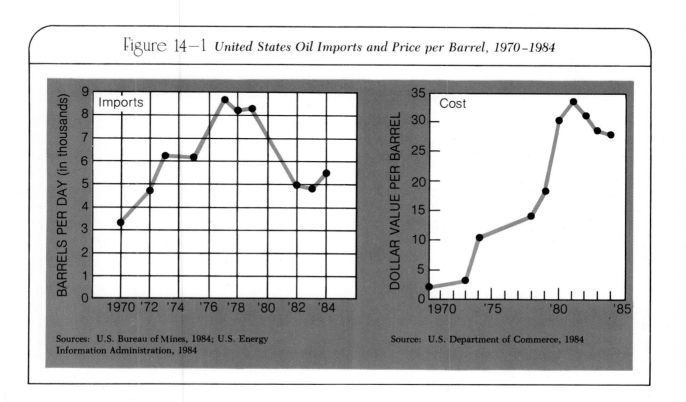

Figure 14–1 *United States Oil Imports and Price per Barrel, 1970–1984*

Sources: U.S. Bureau of Mines, 1984; U.S. Energy Information Administration, 1984

Source: U.S. Department of Commerce, 1984

To decrease their dependence on imported oil, many countries encouraged more offshore oil drilling, a process that had been too expensive when imported oil was cheap and readily available.

our national bill for imported oil was only $3 billion; in 1978, it had swelled to $42 billion. By 1980, it had reached a staggering $80 billion. As a result of these developments, the United States faced what many called an "energy crisis." It became abundantly clear that we needed to reduce our dependence on imported oil. It also was becoming clear that we had to seek alternative sources of energy because our own oil reserves were being depleted.

There are a number of potential sources of energy. However, most experts do not believe that any other single source of energy will ever replace oil. Instead, they believe we must seek additional energy from several possible sources.

Check Your Understanding

1. Why did Americans take energy for granted for so many years?

2. How did the OPEC oil embargo of 1973–74 change people's attitude toward energy?

3. Why did the United States face an energy crisis after the OPEC oil embargo was lifted?

Energy Sources

Among the major sources of energy are fossil fuels, synthetic fuels, nuclear energy, and solar energy. Each of these energy sources probably will play some role in meeting our future energy needs, although some will be more important than others.

Fossil Fuels

Fossil fuels include petroleum, natural gas, and coal. These valuable fuels were formed millions of years ago from plants and animals that became buried, decayed, and were subjected to centuries of pressure from the earth. The quantity of these fuels is limited. Although there are probably additional reserves not yet discovered, there is still a limited quantity in the sense that they are not being replaced. Once a barrel of oil is used, it is gone forever. Let us examine each of the fossil fuels.

Petroleum Petroleum comes from the earth as a dark liquid, usually called crude oil. Gasoline, fuel oil, kerosene, jet fuels, and LP gas all are manufactured from petroleum. In addition, petroleum is used to make many nonfuel products, such as asphalt, paint, synthetic rubber, plastics, drugs, fertilizers, and nylon.

The American oil industry was born in 1859 when Edwin L. Drake punched a hole 70 feet deep just outside Titusville, Pennsylvania, and struck oil. Oil from this first well sold for as much as $20 a barrel. Many other wells soon were drilled nearby, however, and the price of oil dropped to ten cents a barrel in less than three years.

Once the American oil industry started, workers and investors flocked to Pennsylvania to share in the opportunities. The population in this Pennsylvania town jumped from 100 to 14,000 in six months.

Petroleum became a major source of energy for the nation as oil consumption continued to increase over the years. Whenever it appeared that we soon might run out of oil, new strikes were made and the needed oil became available. However, by 1948 the United States was unable to produce enough petroleum to meet all of its needs and began to supplement its domestic oil supply with imported oil. The amount of oil consumed and imported continued to climb year after year. In 1980, the United States consumed more than 25 percent of the worldwide production of 60 million barrels of oil per day. Nearly nine million barrels a day came from American oil wells. The remainder was imported.

At 1984 production levels, the known oil reserves in the United States were projected to last less than ten years. While some new reserves will likely be discovered, experts fear that few large reserves remain to be found. Their pessimism is based at least partly on the fact that 2.5 million oil wells already have been drilled in the United States. That's four times as many as in the rest of the world combined. Given these statistics, many experts believe that the odds of finding large new reserves are not good.

Natural gas Natural gas is found in the holes of limestone, sandstone, and other porous rocks. It also is often found on the top of oil deposits because the same natural forces formed both fuels. Natural gas has long been a major source of heat in the United States. Like petroleum, however, there is a limited quantity remaining. Not all experts agree about future supplies of gas. Some experts consider gas a slowly dwindling resource, while others are optimistic that substantial reserves remain to be discovered.

Coal Coal is the most plentiful fossil fuel in the world. At present rates of consumption, the known reserves of coal would last the world more than 200 years, according to conservative estimates. Some geologists believe that actual

coal reserves—known reserves plus undiscovered reserves—may be as much as 15 times this amount.

More than one quarter of the world's known coal reserves are in the United States. Coal mining in this country began in the 1700s, and in the 1880s coal overtook wood as the major fuel source. As recently as 1925, the nation relied on coal for 70 percent of its energy. In the late 1940s, however, oil and gas surpassed coal as the major energy sources

Natural gas, another fossil fuel, is often found near oil deposits. Experts disagree on just how much remains of this limited source of energy.

Although the United States has vast reserves of coal, it is expensive to mine and transport and raises more pollution concerns than do other fossil fuels.

because they were cheaper, cleaner, and easier to transport. Today, coal provides only about one fifth of the energy we use each year, and most of it is used to generate electricity.

Coal might seem to be the logical replacement for oil, but unfortunately there are some serious problems connected with increased coal use. First of all, mining and transporting coal are very costly—so, too, is the process for converting electrical generating plants and other facilities from oil and gas to coal. Furthermore, much of the nation's coal has a high sulfur con-

tent and other impurities, and many people fear that increased use of such coal could pose serious threats to our environment and to our health.

Synthetic Fuels

Synthetic fuels, which are potential substitutes for petroleum, can be made from oil shale, coal, and various forms of plant life. The United States possesses vast resources for making synthetic fuels—more than any other nation in the world.

Large deposits of oil shale, a type of rock from which oil can be obtained, are found in Colorado, Utah, and Wyoming. Some energy experts have estimated that as much as 600 billion to a trillion barrels of recoverable oil exist in these deposits. The major problem, however, is the cost. Most experts believe that with our present level of technology, oil obtained in this way would be more expensive than imported crude oil.

Scientists have known for a long time that they could make synthetic fuels from coal. During World War II, German war planes burned gasoline made from coal, and today a giant refining plant in South Africa converts coal into 55,000 barrels of transport fuel and other products each day. Since the United States possesses more than one quarter of the world's known coal reserves, some argue that synthetic fuels made from coal offer one of the best prospects for solving our long-term energy problem. However, as we mentioned earlier, there are a number of health and safety hazards connected with coal, and some experts counsel against moving too far and too quickly in that direction.

Alcohol, which can be manufactured from corn, sweet sorghum, sugar beets, and many other types of vegetation, can be used as fuel. Some alcohol has been marketed for fuel in the United States in the form of gasohol, which is 10 percent alcohol and 90 percent gasoline. Other countries are taking the process even further. Brazil is currently converting sugar cane into alcohol in large quantities, and some auto plants in that country are turning out models designed to run on straight alcohol. Critics of the use of alcohol as an energy source in the United States argue that increased use of crops for fuel could lead to food shortages and rising food prices.

Nuclear Energy

Nuclear energy comes from fission—the splitting of the atoms of uranium. Nuclear power plants generate approximately 10 percent of the electricity in the United States as a whole, and

Nuclear energy appealed to many people as a good solution to demands for increasing production of electricity until news of an accident at a nuclear plant raised questions about the safety of nuclear power.

they are the major source of electrical power in some states. For example, 80 percent of the electricity in Vermont, 60 percent in Maine, and 50 percent in both Connecticut and Nebraska is generated by nuclear power. During the early 1970s, the future of nuclear energy in the country seemed very bright, with some optimists envisioning as many as 1,500 nuclear power plants by the year 2000. However, a highly publicized accident at a nuclear power plant at Three Mile Island, Pennsylvania, in 1979 raised serious doubts in the minds of many Americans about the safety of nuclear energy. As a result, there has been little growth in the use of nuclear energy since that time.

Solar Energy

Every year the sun drenches the United States with 500 times more energy than we use. Some experts estimate that by tapping just 10 percent of the energy from the rays that strike only 2 percent of the nation's surface, the entire energy needs of the country could be met. Of course, we do not now have and may never have the technology to accomplish this objective. Still, solar energy is one of the most attractive of all future energy sources.

Solar energy is apparently a safe unlimited energy resource, but it is still awaiting the technology to permit fuller use.

Solar energy comes in many forms. In the broadest sense of the term, almost all energy comes from the sun. The energy in food, wood, oil, gas, and coal is all stored solar energy. Even if we restrict our discussion to nonstored solar energy, it still comes in many forms. In addition to the direct solar rays that can be used to provide heat for buildings and to generate electricity, both wind energy and water power are forms of solar energy. It is the unequal heating of the earth by the sun that causes the wind to blow. When the sun causes water to evaporate, it is carried to higher elevations where it then can flow to lower levels and, in the process, create water power.

Solar energy supplies only a very small percentage of our total energy today. However, as more and more buildings are constructed to use solar energy as heat and as new technology is developed for using solar energy in other ways, this percentage is likely to increase. Some experts believe that by the year 2000 the nation will be able to obtain approximately 20 percent of its energy needs directly from the sun.

Check Your Understanding

1. Identify three kinds of fossil fuels. Why is there concern about the future of these fuels?

2. What are synthetic fuels? Describe some of the problems associated with creating and using them.

3. Why has there been less growth in the use of nuclear energy than expect ed?

4. In what forms is solar energy found? Why is it one of the most attractive of all future energy sources?

Energy Conservation

Most energy experts believe that, in addition to seeking new sources of energy, we must improve how we use existing energy through energy conservation—that we must learn to reduce our energy demands and to use our scarce resources more efficiently.

In fact, the nation already has made substantial gains in energy efficiency through conservation measures. In 1983, the nation used 20 percent less energy to produce each dollar of GNP than ten years earlier. Much of the progress in energy conservation has come from better-insulated buildings and more energy-efficient automobiles.

There is much progress that still can be made, however. Experts estimate that about two thirds of all American homes could use more insulation, and many homes still have no insulation at all. Many nonresidential buildings built in the past also have no insulation, and it would be difficult and costly to insulate many of them because of the way they are constructed. Of course, homes and nonresidential buildings constructed in the future will be more energy efficient.

Private automobiles use over half of all transportation energy and approximately 30 percent of all oil used in the United States. Thus, increased efficiency of automobiles has been one of the major goals of national energy policy. Lowering the speed limit from 70 mph to 55 mph has made a major contribution toward reducing fuel consumption. Experts estimate that the average automobile uses about 20 percent less fuel at 55 mph than at 70 mph. Even more important in terms of energy saved are the minimum mileage standards established for new cars. In 1983, new cars were required to average 26 mpg—double the 1973 average. In 1985, they were required to average 27.5 mpg.

The Role of Government in Energy Policies

How big a role should government play in solving the nation's energy problems? There is no easy answer to this question. Some critics argue that the government helped to create the problems by imposing price controls on domestically produced oil and natural gas. They base their argument on the fact that government price ceilings on oil and natural gas during the 1970s kept prices artificially low, thus creating shortages. The intent of the price ceilings was to protect consumers by keeping prices at what some termed reasonable levels. However, many critics argue that the price controls actually hurt consumers by restricting production.

Most energy price controls were removed in the early 1980s, and prices have been allowed to seek their free-market levels. Many economists believe the long-term effect of price

Automobile designs such as this one increase the energy efficiency of cars by reducing wind drag. Although this futuristic design has not been mass-produced, some of its ideas have been used.

Increasing energy costs have made it profitable to install insulation, thereby reducing the amount of energy needed for heating.

deregulation will help to solve our energy problems. Higher prices will encourage oil and gas companies to increase exploration and production. At the same time, higher energy prices will provide stronger incentives for energy users to install insulation and switch to alternative energy sources such as solar heat.

Some economists believe that the government should leave the solution of our energy problems primarily to private enterprise. They argue that the higher market prices will provide the necessary incentives for private enterprise to develop adequate supplies of energy. Others, however, believe that adequate energy supplies at affordable prices are so crucial to the future of our economy that the government should play an active role in assuring their development. For example, they argue that the production of synthetic fuels is too costly and too risky for private enterprise to handle alone, and in the event of another oil embargo such fuels may be essential. Thus, they believe the government should help to finance development of these alternative energy sources.

Check Your Understanding

1. What conservation practices have contributed to increased energy efficiency in recent years?

2. Why did the government impose price ceilings on domestically produced oil and natural gas? How did the price ceilings affect the supply of oil and gas?

3. Why do some economists believe that the solution to our energy problems should be left primarily to private enterprise? Why do others believe the government should play an active role in helping to develop new energy supplies?

Environmental Pollution

An **environment** is made up of the resources, forces, and conditions that surround and influence living things. Our natural environment includes three major types of resources—air, water, and soil—which are essential to the survival of all forms of life. The contamination of these resources is called **pollution,** and it is potentially one of the most serious problems facing the world today. Too much pollution in the air can lead to serious illness and even death. Water pollution kills fish and other marine life, and soil pollution reduces the quantity and quality of land available for growing crops and other uses.

Most Americans are very concerned about environmental pollution. Survey after survey has shown that people think protection of the environment should be a high priority and that pollution should be reduced. Why, then, is pollution still such a serious problem? The answer is because the problem of pollution is a very complicated one. The most serious pollution is caused by things that benefit people. Exhaust emissions from automobiles cause a large percentage of air pollution, but automobiles are an important part of the American way of life. Factories are responsible for a substantial amount of both air and water pollution, but factories provide jobs and produce products that the American people want. Thus, reducing pollution is not nearly as simple as many people would like to believe. We'll examine the costs associated with reducing pollution later in this chapter. First, we will examine the various kinds of pollution.

There are many kinds of pollution, but most pollution falls under one or more of three categories: air pollution, water pollution, and soil pollution. Each has serious consequences that can affect us all.

Air Pollution

Air pollution is caused by the release into the atmosphere of artificially created wastes in the form of gases or **particulates,** which are tiny particles of dust, ash, or liquids. Every year, the human race pours hundreds of millions of tons of these gases and particulates into the earth's atmosphere. As a result, clear, odorless air is transformed into hazy, foul-smelling air that can kill plants, damage property, and in some cases pose serious threats to human health.

Most air pollution results from the burning of fuels. As part of the combustion process, pollutants are released into the air. These pollutants range from small amounts of colorless poison gas to clouds of thick, black smoke. The

'THERE GOES THE <u>ENTIRE</u> NEIGHBORHOOD'

One aspect of pollution may be apparent while other aspects of pollution remain unnoticed, as this cartoon suggests.

burning of coal and oil to heat buildings, manufacture products, and generate electricity is a major source of air pollution—so, too, is the burning of gasoline to power automobiles and other vehicles.

People have been polluting the air to some degree since the beginning of civilization. However, so long as the concentration of pollutants remained relatively low, nature could deal with the problem. Wind scattered pollutants, and rain and snow washed them into the ground. As the population grew and became more and more urbanized, however, pollutants were put into the air faster than weather conditions could dispose of them. In today's large crowded cities, the thousands of automobiles, factories, and furnaces can add tons of pollutants to a small area of the atmosphere in a single day.

Certain weather conditions can increase the danger from air pollution. For example, when a layer of warm air settles over a layer of cooler air that lies near the ground, the warm air holds down the cool air and prevents pollutants from rising and scattering. Such a condition—called a **thermal inversion**—can cause serious health hazards in a city where tons of pollutants are being released into the air. The pollutants burn people's eyes and irritate their lungs. They can worsen such respiratory diseases as asthma and bronchitis, and some experts believe they even may help cause such illnesses as emphysema and pneumonia.

In addition to posing direct threats to human health, air pollutants in sufficient concentrations can restrict growth and eventually kill almost any type of vegetation. Certain pollutants that pose a particular danger are those that return to the earth in the form of **acid rain.** This is rainfall that contains a high concentration of harmful acids produced by sulfur and nitrogen oxides emitted during the combustion of fossil fuels. Acid rain—which may fall to the ground hundreds of miles from where the pollutants were released into the air—can poison lakes, killing off fish and plant life, and damage agricultural crops and forests.

Air pollution even can affect the weather. By scattering the sun's rays and reducing the amount of sunlight that reaches the ground, pollutants in the form of particulates may cause average temperatures in an area to drop. On the other hand, gases may allow sunlight to reach the ground but prevent the sun's heat from rising again. This would cause average temperatures in an area to increase.

Water Pollution

Water pollution is caused by dumping of wastes into rivers, lakes, oceans, and other bodies of water. These wastes include human and animal wastes, chemicals, metals, oil, and many other substances. The three chief sources of water

Fuel combustion, which has aided industrial growth, has also led to enormous increases in air pollution.

Some water pollution is readily visible. Industrial waste in this harbor led one person to remark, "It looks like suds in a washing machine."

pollution are industrial wastes, sewage, and agricultural chemicals and wastes. Large areas of some rivers and lakes as well as some coastal waters in the United States have become dangerously polluted, according to many experts. Cities with large populations and many factories have the most water pollution. However, water pollution resulting from farming and mining exists even in rural areas.

Pollution makes water unfit for drinking, bathing, swimming, and so forth. It also can kill fish and other living organisms and interfere with the natural processes by which water uses oxygen to make small amounts of wastes harmless. Water contaminated with human and animal wastes can help to spread various diseases, and polluted water can give off unpleasant odors. Although community water supplies are disinfected to kill disease-causing germs, the disinfection process does not remove chemicals and metals, many of which in large quantities can be harmful to human beings.

Toxic waste dumps have polluted both soil and water in many regions, leading to high spillover costs.

Soil Pollution

One form of soil pollution can result from excessive applications of chemical fertilizers and pesticides which can harm bacteria and other helpful organisms in the soil, reducing their ability to decay plant vegetation and produce nutrients naturally. However, the type of soil pollution that has received the most publicity in recent years involves the disposal of toxic wastes by burying them under soil. Toxic waste dumps (sites where toxic wastes have been buried) have been the source of much controversy, and some experts believe that many of these dumps may pose serious health hazards to nearby residents. Abnormally high rates of certain illnesses have been found in areas of some toxic waste dumps, and in a few cases the government has considered the threat to human health so serious that it has purchased the homes of nearby residents and evacuated the areas.

Check Your Understanding

1. Why is environmental pollution such a serious problem? Why is the problem of pollution so complicated?

2. What is the source of most air pollution? How can weather conditions increase the danger from air pollution?

3. What causes acid rain? Why is it a serious problem?

4. Identify the chief sources of water pollution.

5. Identify two types of soil pollution. Why has soil pollution received increasing publicity in recent years?

The Economics of Pollution Control

Although there is general agreement that pollution is undesirable, a certain amount of pollution is inevitable because pollution is a by-product of production. Generally speaking, the level of pollution is directly related to the level of production; and in the past, increased production usually meant increased pollution. This relationship has led some people to question the wisdom of continued economic growth. They argue that the quality of our environment is more important than the production of more goods and services. However, many experts believe that pollution can be reduced without curtailing economic growth. They contend that much of our past pollution occurred because it was economical to pollute, and they believe that pollution can be reduced by making it economically unattractive. In order to better understand the economics of pollution, let us examine two important concepts: costs of pollution and methods of pollution control.

Costs of Pollution

In order to understand why polluters often have found it economical to pollute, we must make a distinction between two types of costs: private costs and spillover costs. **Private costs** are the costs borne by an individual or a business firm as a result of a particular act such as producing a product. **Spillover costs** are the costs borne by other members of society as a result of an act by an individual or business firm. Because of spillover costs, the costs of producing a product often are much higher than the private costs. Let us look at an example.

Suppose that a manufacturing plant disposes of its wastes by dumping them into a river. The private costs of this act are very small.

All the firm has to do is dig a ditch or install a pipe from the factory to the river. Once this is done, the wastes will flow directly into the river and be carried downstream by the current. What about the spillover costs, however? Suppose that communities downstream have to spend a great deal of money to remove the pollutants from the water before they can use it. This expenditure to remove the pollutants that were discharged into the river by the manufacturing plant upstream is the spillover cost. Thus, the cost of disposing of wastes by dumping them directly into a river includes both private and spillover costs.

If the manufacturing plant had to pay both the private costs and the spillover costs of disposing of wastes in the river, it might find that it no longer could afford to dispose of its wastes in that way. Instead, it might find an alternative method of waste disposal that would be less expensive. As you learned in earlier chapters, when a business firm has alternative methods of producing a product, it usually will choose the method that is least costly. Indeed, if the firm faces stiff competition from other firms, it may be forced to use such a method or else go out of business. Generally, when a firm chooses the least costly method of production, society benefits. However, if there are substantial spillover costs, the least costly method will not be in the best interests of society.

Like water pollution, air pollution also can involve substantial spillover costs. For example, some coal-burning electrical generating plants discharge large quantities of sulfur dioxide into the air. Winds may blow this sulfur dioxide hundreds of miles before it returns to earth in the form of acid rain. As you learned earlier, acid rain in sufficient quantities can poison lakes and damage agricultural crops and forests. Thus, the spillover costs of discharging sulfur dioxide directly into the air may be enormous.

There is an alternative. It is possible to reduce the amount of sulfur dioxide discharged into the air by installing devices known as

Chemicals stored in drums and then abandoned left a community with the problem of identifying the contents and disposing of the hazardous wastes within.

Methods of Pollution Control

The problem of pollution is a complicated one and there are no simple answers. However, a number of alternative methods of pollution control have been proposed. They include (1) levying emission fees on polluters; (2) subsidizing pollution-reduction efforts; and (3) imposing direct regulations. Let us examine each of these approaches.

Levying emission fees on polluters Proponents of this approach believe that the costs of pollution should be built into the price—profit system as an incentive. They advocate the use of metering devices to measure the amount of pollution each firm discharges into the environment and the imposition of fees based on that amount. The fees could be based on how much pollution could be safely emitted at various times and in various locations. For example, the fee could be lower at those times of the day when the least total amount of pollution normally is emitted. This would tend to spread the pollution more evenly throughout the day. Furthermore, lower fees could be charged in sparsely populated areas than in densely populated regions. This would serve as an incentive for factories to locate away from cities where the pollution would be less of a problem.

Proponents of emission fees argue that in addition to spreading pollution more evenly, such an approach would encourage firms to find ways of reducing the amount of wastes discharged into the environment. For example, firms might explore the possibility of recycling certain kinds of wastes. Also, since these fees would add to the costs of production, firms would take pollution into consideration when making production and pricing decisions. Critics of this approach point out that not all types of pollution can be measured with metering devices. Moreover, it often is not possible for factories to locate in sparsely populated areas because they must be near raw materials, an adequate labor supply, and good transportation facilities.

scrubbers on smokestacks. These devices, however, are very expensive. If power plants installed such devices, who would pay for them? Should the entire costs be passed on to public utility customers in the form of higher utility bills? Or, since the public will benefit from the cleaner air, should the government pay a portion of the costs? Such questions are difficult to answer. There is general agreement that reduced pollution is desirable, but there is much disagreement over who should pay the costs.

Subsidizing pollution-reduction efforts Advocates of this approach argue that since the public as a whole would benefit from reducing pollution, at least a part of the cost of such efforts should be borne by the taxpayers. However, there is much opposition to this approach. First of all, there is the question of who should pay the taxes to finance government-subsidized pollution-reduction efforts. Because pollution is not an equally serious problem in all parts of the nation, reduced pollution would benefit some people more than others. Thus, would it be fair to ask all taxpayers to pay an equal share of the cost of pollution reductions? Some would say no. They would argue that those people who benefit most from pollution reduction should pay most of the costs. The problem with this approach is that it would be impossible to determine the net benefits of pollution reduction to any individual or group of people.

ISSUE: Should Federal Antipollution Laws Be Loosened?

In the early 1970s, after decades of increasing pollution, the United States government established the Environmental Protection Agency and enacted some very strong antipollution laws. These laws set strict standards and timetables for cleaning up the environment. Although substantial progress has been made, these laws have come under increasing criticism in recent years by people both in and out of government who suggest that the environmental standards are too strict. These critics believe that the provisions of the federal laws should be loosened and more freedom should be given to the individual states to set and enforce environmental standards. However, many people are strongly opposed to any loosening of federal antipollution laws.

The Case for Loosening Federal Antipollution Laws

Advocates of weaker federal antipollution laws argue that current laws set unrealistically high standards that can be attained only at extremely high costs. They contend that many industrial plants cannot afford to comply with the laws, and if the laws are enforced, at least some of these plants will have to shut down, which will cost many people their jobs. They argue that because United States firms must compete in world markets against firms from nations that have much weaker environmental laws, the increased cost of pollution control often pushes prices of American-made products too high for successful competition. In addition, they point out that because manufacturers must recover the costs of antipollution devices, American consumers are the ones who ultimately pay the cost of reduced pollution in the form of higher prices.

Many of the critics of current antipollution standards believe that sufficient progress already has been made in cleaning up the environment to

302 UNIT 5 / Problems on the Home Front

warrant some relaxation in environmental standards. They argue that we now must weigh the benefits of further improvements in environmental quality against the costs in terms of plant closings, lost jobs, and higher product prices. Moreover, many critics believe that because pollution is a more serious problem in some regions of the country than others, more power should be given to the states to set and enforce environmental standards. Such a policy, they argue, would allow tough standards in areas with serious pollution problems and weaker standards in those states where pollution is not so serious.

The Case Against Loosening Federal Antipollution Laws

Those who oppose any relaxation of federal environmental standards argue that although progress has been made in reducing pollution, environmental quality is still unacceptably low. For example, they point to the fact that more than 100 counties and parishes in the United States failed to meet the minimum standards of the 1970 Clean Air Act by the law's deadline in 1982. Furthermore, they argue that there has been even less progress in reducing water pollution. They fear that any relaxation in environmental standards now would result also in the loss of the gains already made.

Many of these people argue that instead of weaker environmental standards, the nation needs stronger standards. They contend that instead of asking whether we can afford to clean up the environment, we should be asking whether we can afford not to clean it up. They argue that we cannot continue to pollute the resources upon which our health and welfare depend without serious long-term consequences. They point out that in addition to the known health hazards connected with many pollutants, there may be many other hazards not yet recognized.

Opponents of weaker federal pollution standards argue that allowing each state to establish and enforce its own environmental standards would be a serious mistake. They fear that some states would establish weak standards in order to attract new industry and that state pollution laws would become a major factor in determining the location of new manufacturing facilities. If this happened, they contend, there would be a tendency for most states to reduce environmental standards in order to avoid losing jobs to other states. Furthermore, they point out that because air pollutants travel hundreds of miles across state lines, states with strong environmental standards might suffer substantial pollution from firms located in neighboring states with weaker standards.

How do you feel about loosening federal antipollution laws? Do you favor such action? Why or why not? Do you believe that states should be given more freedom to establish and enforce their own pollution standards? Give reasons for your answer.

Imposing direct regulations This approach involves establishing specific rules and regulations with regard to pollution. Under the "general welfare" and "police power" clauses of the Constitution both the federal and state governments have the power to impose such direct regulations. The government does use these powers in an effort to protect the environment.

Protecting the Environment

In 1899, the United States government passed a pollution control law that made it a crime to dump any liquid wastes into navigable waters except those from sewers. But the law was almost never enforced, and for the next 60 years the government did very little to deal with the problems of pollution. During the 1960s, however, Americans became increasingly aware of the need to protect our environment. Groups of citizens throughout the nation formed organizations to fight pollution. They attempted to alert the public to the dangers of pollution and pressured government and industry officials to take appropriate actions. One of the highlights of the antipollution movement took place on April 22, 1970, which was called Earth Day. On that day, more than 20 million persons throughout the United States took part in antipollution demonstrations and other activities.

Government responded to public concern about pollution by passing a number of laws. In 1970, 15 federal pollution programs were combined to form the **Environmental Protection Agency (EPA),** an independent federal agency directly responsible to the President. This agency has the power to set and enforce pollution standards, conduct research on the effects of pollution, and provide grants and technical assistance to states, cities, and other government units that seek to prevent pollution.

In addition to the federal EPA, most local and state governments have developed pollution control programs. These programs vary widely from one area to another, depending on the nature and seriousness of local pollution problems. However, common provisions of local pollution laws include prohibiting such practices as burning trash in the open air and dumping untreated sewage in water.

Substantial progress in reducing pollution has been made since 1970. Both air and water are cleaner today, and some toxic waste dumps have been cleaned up. However, the progress has not been as fast as anticipated. Many communities still are unable to meet basic pollution standards established by the government, and pollution experts believe it will take many more years of effort to undo the environmental damage of the past.

Check Your Understanding

1. Differentiate between private costs and spillover costs. Why is it important to distinguish between these two types of costs when studying the problems of pollution?

2. Describe three proposed methods of pollution control.

3. What was the antipollution movement? Identify one of the highlights of this movement.

CAREERS: Petroleum Engineer

The energy shortages of recent years have emphasized the importance of energy to our economy and the need to find new energy sources and supplies. Petroleum engineers play a key role in the search for additional energy. They explore and drill for oil and gas and work to recover the maximum profitable amount of oil and gas from reservoirs.

Because only a small proportion of the oil or gas in a reservoir will flow out naturally, petroleum engineers develop and use various methods—such as flooding an oil field with water to force the oil to the surface—to increase the proportion of petroleum that can be recovered. However, even with the best methods in use today, only about 50 percent of the oil in a reservoir can be recovered. Thus, much of the future research of petroleum engineers will be directed toward finding new methods that will enable them to recover a larger proportion of these resources. In addition, with oil and gas becoming harder to find, engineers

will need to develop new technologies in order to tap new sources.

Petroleum engineers are employed by major oil and gas companies as well as by the hundreds of smaller independent companies involved in oil and gas exploration, production, and services in both the United States and foreign countries. Many engineers also work for government agencies, equipment suppliers, and engineering consulting firms.

A bachelor's degree in engineering is the minimum educational requirement for an entry-level job in a company or agency, but a master's degree with specialization in petroleum engineering is the preferred training. Students planning to become engineers should take as many courses in advanced mathematics and physical sciences as possible while still in high school and college. Engineers should have an analytical mind and a capacity for detail, be able to communicate their ideas well, and be able to work as part of a team.

Chapter Highlights

1   Although energy is one of the most crucial of all resources, for many years Americans seemed to take it for granted. The 1973 Arab oil embargo made Americans realize that the United States had a serious energy problem.

2   Among the major sources of energy are fossil fuels, synthetic fuels, nuclear energy, and solar energy. The fossil fuels—which include petroleum, natural gas, and coal—are limited in supply. Coal is the most plentiful of the fossil fuels, but the serious problems connected with increased use of coal make it a doubtful replacement for oil.

3   Synthetic fuels, which are potential substitutes for petroleum, can be made from oil shale, coal, and various forms of plant life. Large quantities of recoverable oil exist in oil shale located in Colorado, Utah, and Wyoming. Gasoline and other fuels can be manufactured from coal. Alcohol, which can also be used as a fuel, can be made from crops such as corn and sugar beets and from many other types of vegetation.

4   Nuclear power had been considered a major potential source of energy until a highly publicized accident at a nuclear power plant in Pennsylvania in 1979 raised doubts about the safety of nuclear energy. As a result, there has been little growth in the use of nuclear power in recent years.

5   Solar energy, which includes wind power and water power as well as energy obtained directly from the sun's rays, currently supplies a very small fraction of our total energy needs. However, some experts believe that this figure will increase to approximately 20 percent by the year 2000.

6   The nation already has made substantial gains in energy efficiency through conservation measures such as insulating homes and other buildings and making automobiles more fuel efficient. However, many experts believe additional progress remains to be made.

7   There is substantial disagreement over how big a role the government should play in solving the nation's energy problems. Some economists believe the government should leave the solution primarily to private enterprise. Others argue that adequate energy supplies at affordable prices are so crucial to the future of our economy that the government should play an active role in future energy development.

8   Environmental pollution—contamination of the air, water, and soil—is potentially one of the most serious problems facing the world today. Air pollution is caused by the release into the atmosphere of artificially created wastes in the form of gases or particulates. Most air pollution results from the burning of fuels such as wood, coal, oil, and gasoline. Acid rain, a particularly dangerous kind of pollution, can poison lakes and damage agricultural crops and forests.

9   Water pollution is caused by the dumping of wastes into rivers, lakes, oceans, and other bodies of water. The three chief sources of water pollution are industrial wastes, sewage, and agricultural chemicals and wastes. Soil pollution can be caused by excessive applications of chemical fertilizers and pesticides and by burying toxic wastes under the soil. Toxic waste dumps have been the source of much controversy in recent years.

10   Many economists believe that much pollution in the past resulted from the fact that the private costs of polluting were small relative to the spillover costs. Private costs are those borne by an individual or a business firm as a result of a particular act. Spillover costs are costs borne by other members of society as a result of an act by an individual or a business firm. Many economists believe that if polluters had to pay both private and spillover costs, many would find alternative ways of disposing of wastes.

11   Proposed methods of pollution control include levying emission fees on polluters, subsidizing pollution-reduction efforts, and imposing direct regulations. Levying emission fees on polluters would involve the use of metering devices and fees based on the quantity of pollution emitted by each firm. Subsidizing pollution-reduction efforts would involve some government assistance in paying for pollution reduction. Imposing direct regulations involves establishing specific rules and regulations to protect the environment.

12   During the 1960s, Americans concerned about the dangers of pollution pressured government and industry officials to take actions designed to protect the environment. In 1970, the Environmental Protection Agency, an independent federal agency, was established to deal with the problems of pollution. In addition to the federal EPA, most local and state governments have developed pollution control programs.

Important Terms

Match each of the following terms with the correct definition:

fossil fuels	pollution	environment
thermal inversion	private costs	spillover costs
synthetic fuels	acid rain	EPA
nuclear energy	solar energy	particulates

1. Fuels which are potential substitutes for petroleum that can be made from oil shale, coal, and various forms of plant life.

2. The resources, forces, and conditions that surround and influence living things.

3. Rainfall that contains sulfur and nitrogen oxides—pollutants that can cause serious damage.

4. Fuels—including petroleum, natural gas, and coal—that were formed millions of years ago from the remains of plants and animals.

5. Costs borne by an individual or a business firm as a result of a particular act.

6. Energy created by splitting the atoms of uranium.

7. An independent federal agency created in 1970 for the purpose of dealing with the problem of pollution.

8. A condition under which a layer of warm air settles over a layer of cooler air and holds it near the ground.

9. The contamination of air, water, and soil.

10. Energy coming from the sun.

11. Costs borne by other members of society as a result of an act by an individual or business firm.

12. Tiny particles of dust, ash, or liquids emitted into the air.

Extending Your Understanding

1. Why is an adequate supply of affordable energy so crucial to the future of the American economy? If you had to draw up a master plan for meeting the nation's future energy needs, what would your plan include? Which sources of energy do you think should be used to replace petroleum when and if our supplies run out?

2. Why is environmental pollution such a serious problem? Which kinds of pollution do you think pose the greatest threat to our future? Who do you think should pay the cost of reducing pollution? Why? Do you think the government should move faster in its efforts to clean up the environment? Explain your answer.

Activities

1. It has been said that many of the most harmful pollutants are found at home or at work. For example, benzene, a suspected cause of leukemia, is found in many cleaners. Write to the Environmental Protection Agency to learn about these indoor pollutants. Summarize the information you receive in a short report.

2. Prepare a class chart entitled "Ways Americans Can Conserve Energy." Each student should contribute at least one suggestion.

Building Skills in Economics: Understanding Trends

A **trend** is the general movement or course of an event over a substantial period of time. Economists and other policy makers try to discover trends in order to make predictions and decisions about the future. For example, if a government official finds that there is a trend toward smaller families across the nation, the official might recommend that the size of proposed government housing units be decreased and that the number of proposed new elementary schools be reduced.

Trends are often easier to identify when information is illustrated by a graph. The graph that follows shows the world production of crude oil for the years 1973–83. The questions will help you understand the trends revealed in the graph.

Applying Economics Skills

1. What does the graph tell you about the production of crude oil during the years 1973–1979?
2. What kind of trend in crude oil production was taking place during the years 1979–1983?
3. Given the trend you identified in question 2, do you think more people turned to other energy sources such as solar energy and synthetic fuels during this period? Why or why not?
4. Given what you know about the quantity of fossil fuels, do you think this trend is likely to continue? Why or why not?

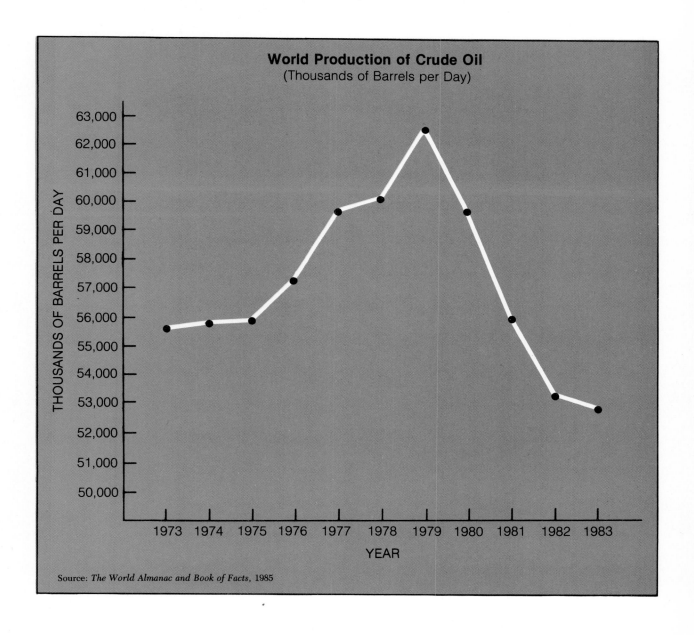

World Production of Crude Oil
(Thousands of Barrels per Day)

Source: *The World Almanac and Book of Facts*, 1985

UNIT 6

The International Picture

CHAPTER 15

INTERNATIONAL TRADE AND FINANCE

Picture for a moment a world in which all international trade suddenly comes to a halt. No nation would be able to **import,** or buy anything from other nations. Similarly, no nation would be able to **export,** or sell anything to other nations. Each nation would have to get by with what it alone produces. How would such a world compare with the world we live in today? First of all, there would be a big increase in world hunger and starvation because many nations cannot produce enough food to feed their people. In addition, there would be worldwide shortages of crude oil because relatively few nations produce vast quantities of this commodity. This also would mean critical shortages of gasoline and manufactured goods, both of which depend on crude oil for their production. Moreover, there would be mass unemployment in many industrial nations that depend on foreign markets for much of what they produce.

Many nations would be affected much more severely than the United States by such a halt in international trade because the value of goods and services that the United States imports is less than 10 percent of our GNP. In some nations, this figure might run as high as 40 percent. Yet, this does not mean that the United States would not be seriously affected by a complete halt in foreign trade. The dollar amount of goods and services imported from other nations comes to more than $260 billion a year. Moreover, any halt in foreign trade would result in substantial inconvenience or severe hardship for most people. There would be no bananas or coffee, because we buy virtually 100 percent of these items from foreign nations. In addition, more than half of all radios, television sets, and motorcycles sold in this country are foreign made. We also depend on foreign nations for much of our oil and for many other raw materials. Furthermore, many jobs in the United States hinge on sales to foreign countries. Thus, international trade is very important to the United States as well as to most other nations. Let us see why.

Why Countries Trade

Countries engage in international trade for the same reasons that individuals specialize in specific careers—the recognition that specialization increases total output. In order to better understand this concept, imagine yourself trying to become totally self-sufficient. You would have to grow your own food, build your own shelter, make your own clothes, build your own source of transportation, take care of your own medical problems, and so forth. You would have so many chores to do that you probably would not be very good at any of them, and perhaps there would be some that you would not be able to do at all. As a result, your standard of living would not be very high.

For this reason, most people specialize in a specific career. For example, if you choose to become a physician, you eventually would become very good at treating people's illnesses. This would enable you to earn enough money to buy all the other things you need from other "specialists"—skilled carpenters, plumbers, and electricians to construct your house and farmers to produce the food you consume. As a result, you would have more than you could possibly have if you had to produce everything yourself. With everybody specializing in what he or she does best, more goods and services are produced and everyone is better off.

Differences in Resources of Nations

Just like individuals, different regions of the country and different nations of the world specialize. The net result is increased total produc-

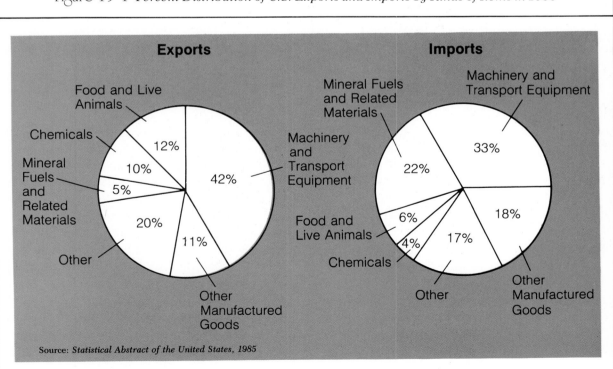

Figure 15-1 *Percent Distribution of U.S. Exports and Imports by Kinds of Items in 1983*

Exports

Food and Live Animals — 12%
Chemicals — 10%
Mineral Fuels and Related Materials — 5%
Other — 20%
Other Manufactured Goods — 11%
Machinery and Transport Equipment — 42%

Imports

Mineral Fuels and Related Materials — 22%
Machinery and Transport Equipment — 33%
Food and Live Animals — 6%
Chemicals — 4%
Other — 17%
Other Manufactured Goods — 18%

Source: *Statistical Abstract of the United States, 1985*

Oranges, like most crops, are grown in the regions where the soil, temperature, and moisture are best suited to their production.

tion. Before looking at other nations, let us first see how the United States benefits from specialization within the various regions of the country.

Apples and oranges are two crops that are grown in different parts of the country. New York, Washington, and several other states are known for apple production, while Florida and California are known for the production of oranges. Although apples and oranges could be grown in any region of the United States, the soil, temperature, and moisture requirements for each make some regions far more suited for apple production and others far more suited for orange production. For example, in order for

orange trees to be grown in the northern states, expensive heated greenhouses would be required. This would make the price of oranges so high that very few people could afford to buy them. As a result, it makes better sense for the regions best suited for orange production to produce the nation's oranges while other regions focus on the crops for which they are best suited. In fact, this does occur, and about 95 percent of the oranges produced in the United States are produced in Florida and California, with the remainder grown in small regions of Texas, Arizona, and Louisiana.

There are substantial differences in the resources of various nations of the world as well.

For example, Canada has huge forests that enable it to produce lumber and paper products for sale to foreign nations. Ecuador has an ideal climate for banana production, and thus it exports more bananas than any other nation. Both Brazil and Colombia have ideal growing conditions for coffee, and they are the world's leading producers of that crop. Many countries in the Middle East have large reserves of oil, and many coastal nations have rich fishing grounds off their coasts. The United States has a highly skilled labor force, considerable technological knowledge, and large quantities of capital goods: factories, tools, machines, and so forth. Thus, the United States is well suited for the production of many complex manufactured products, such as farm machinery and computers and other electronic equipment. The United States also has some of the best soil and growing conditions found anywhere in the world. As a result, our nation is able to produce much more food than the American people can eat, making us a major food exporter.

The Concept of Absolute Advantage

Because of the differences in resources of nations, some countries are able to produce certain products more efficiently than other countries. A country that can produce a product more efficiently than another country is said to have an **absolute advantage** in the production of the product. This means that given a set amount of resources, the country can produce more of the product than the other nation can. Put another way, one nation has an absolute advantage over another nation in producing a product when it can use fewer resources than the other nation to produce the same quantity of the product.

Ecuador certainly has an absolute advantage over the United States in the production of bananas. Ecuador has the ideal climate for growing bananas naturally, whereas the United States could produce bananas only by building expensive heated greenhouses with controlled

environments. Thus, it would take substantially more resources in the United States to produce a given quantity of bananas than would be required to produce an equal quantity in Ecuador. The United States, however, has an absolute advantage over Ecuador in the production of corn, wheat, beef, steel, and most other items. In fact, the United States has an absolute advantage over most nations in the production of most commodities. Does this mean that the United States should not trade with other nations? No. A country can benefit from international trade even when it has an absolute advantage in the production of most products. Let us see why this is true.

The Concept of Comparative Advantage

Individuals and nations can benefit from specialization and trade even when one of the parties can produce most products more efficiently than the other. Suppose, for example, that a lawyer is a better typist than his or her secretary. This means that the lawyer has an absolute advantage over the secretary in both typing and the practice of law. Should the lawyer, then, do the typing in addition to practicing law? No. The time spent practicing law is far more profitable than the time spent typing. If the lawyer can earn $50 per hour practicing law and pays a secretary only $5 per hour to type, the lawyer can earn ten times as much per hour practicing law as he or she can earn typing. Therefore, the lawyer should retain the services of a secretary.

In economic terms, we would say that the lawyer has a **comparative advantage** in the practice of law. This means that the absolute advantage of practicing law is greater than that of typing. Any time an individual or a nation has an absolute advantage in the production of two goods or services, the individual or nation has a comparative advantage in the production of that good or service where the absolute advantage is greater.

TABLE 15–1: SOYBEAN AND PEANUT PRODUCTION CAPABILITIES OF BEANADELPHIA AND PEANUTORPHIA

	Soybean Production Capability with All Resources Devoted to Soybean Production (million bu. per year)	Peanut Production Capability with All Resources Devoted to Peanut Production (million lbs. per year)
Beanadelphia	15	100
Peanutorphia	5	50

Let us look at an example of comparative advantage involving two nations. Suppose that two countries, Beanadelphia and Peanutorphia, have approximately the same area and population and that both nations grow only two crops: soybeans and peanuts. Table 15–1 shows each country's production capabilities for both crops. If Beanadelphia devotes all its resources to the production of soybeans, it can produce 15 million bushels per year. If it devotes all its resources to peanut production, it can produce 100 million pounds of peanuts each year. Peanutorphia, on the other hand, can produce annual yields of either 5 million bushels of soybeans or 50 million pounds of peanuts.

Note that Beanadelphia has an absolute advantage over Peanutorphia in the production of both crops. However, it has a greater absolute advantage in the production of soybeans than in the production of peanuts. Beanadelphia can produce three times as many soybeans as Peanutorphia but only twice as many peanuts. Put another way, although Beanadelphia outranks Peanutorphia in the production of both soybeans and peanuts, it is more efficient in the production of soybeans. Thus, Beanadelphia has a comparative advantage in the production of soybeans.

What can we say about Peanutorphia? If we look at Table 15–1, we can see that it ranks below Beanadelphia in the production of both crops. Yet its "absolute disadvantage" in the production of peanuts is smaller than in the production of soybeans. Peanutorphia can produce half as many peanuts as Beanadelphia but only one third as many soybeans. In other words, Peanutorphia is less efficient than Beanadelphia in the production of both soybeans and peanuts, but of the two crops, it is more efficient in the production of peanuts. We can say, then, that Peanutorphia has a comparative advantage in the production of peanuts. Even though a nation has an absolute disadvantage in the production of two products, it still has a comparative advantage in the production of the product in which the absolute disadvantage is less.

In this case, Beanadelphia would find it advantageous to specialize in the production of soybeans, where it has a comparative advantage, and buy its peanuts from Peanutorphia and/or other nations. Similarly, Peanutorphia could benefit from specializing in the production of peanuts and buying its soybeans from Beanadelphia or other soybean producers. Of course, if Beanadelphia and Peanutorphia were the only two countries producing soybeans and peanuts, Peanutorphia might not be able to produce enough peanuts to meet both its own needs and the needs of Beanadelphia. If this occurred, Beanadelphia might be forced to produce some of its own peanuts even though it has a comparative advantage in the production of soybeans. However, in a world of many nations, Beanadelphia could find other nations from which to buy peanuts if Peanutorphia was unable to produce an adequate supply.

In summary, a nation has a comparative advantage in the production of those products where its absolute advantage is greatest or where its absolute disadvantage is least. In other words, given two products, a nation has a comparative advantage in the production of whichever product it can produce more efficiently even though it may be less efficient than other nations in the production of both products.

Gains from Trade

When nations specialize in the production of those things that they can produce most efficiently, total world production is much greater than it would be if all nations tried to be totally self-sufficient. Moreover, when a nation trades those products that it can produce most efficiently for products that other nations can produce most efficiently, both nations benefit. The actual gains that a particular nation will experience from trade depend on exchange rates, which you will learn about later. However, trade between two nations usually will not occur unless both nations experience some gains, although both may not benefit equally.

Check Your Understanding

1. How would a sudden halt in international trade affect the United States and other countries?

2. Why do countries engage in international trade?

3. Explain the concept of absolute advantage.

4. Explain the concept of comparative advantage.

5. Who gains from international trade? Explain.

Barriers to Trade

Despite the benefits of specialization and international trade, most nations put some restrictions on trade in order to protect home industries from foreign competition. They fear that unrestricted free trade would cause some workers to lose their jobs and some industries to lose their standing. Let us examine the most important barriers to trade.

Tariffs

A **tariff** is a tax imposed by the government on imported products. A tariff may be a specific fixed amount charged per unit of imported

When a country specializes in growing those crops it produces most efficiently, both the exporting and importing countries benefit.

Increased sales of Japanese automobiles in the United States at a time when sales of U.S. cars were decreasing led many Americans to call for import quotas on cars from Japan.

goods, such as a tax of $2 per pair on imported shoes; or it may be a percentage of the value of the imported product, such as a 5 percent tax on the value of imported automobiles. A tariff imposed on an imported product raises the price of that product and gives domestic producers of the product a competitive advantage. For example, suppose that a pair of jeans manufactured in the United States sells for $25 and comparable imported jeans sell for $18 per pair. With such a wide price difference, American consumers might prefer the imported jeans. However, a tariff of $5 per pair on the imported jeans would raise their price to $23 per pair, thus making them almost as expensive as the American-made jeans.

A tariff also raises a small amount of revenue for the government, but that is a secondary consideration. Most tariffs are imposed for purposes of protecting domestic producers, not for purposes of raising revenue.

Import Quotas

An **import quota** places a precise legal limit on the number of units of a particular product that can be imported into the country during a specified time period. For example, the United States government might establish an import quota on the number of television sets that could be imported from Japan per year. Once the quota had been reached, no more sets could be imported during that year no matter how willing American consumers were to buy them.

Like tariffs, import quotas give American industries a competitive edge. When imports of popular products are restricted, the potential supply is reduced, making it possible for American producers to charge a higher price.

Unlike tariffs, import quotas do not produce any revenue for the government. Their only purpose is to limit the quantity of imported products.

Other Barriers

In addition to tariffs and import quotas, there are a number of other actions that governments sometimes take to restrict trade. By requiring licensing of importers, the government can gain some control over the number of importing firms and thus the volume of imports. High license fees may drive away some competitors, and delays in processing application forms may cause other competitors to become discouraged. The government also may establish rigorous health standards for imported foods that in effect limit the quantity imported. Still another approach is to put pressure on foreign nations to restrict exports "voluntarily." Sometimes the government orders a total ban, an **embargo,** on the import or export of a particular product. Embargoes usually are politically motivated. As you learned in Chapter 14, in 1973 the OPEC nations placed an embargo on oil shipments to several Western nations. This was OPEC's response to Western support of Israel. Similarly, in 1980 President Jimmy Carter ordered a halt to all grain sales to the Soviet Union in response to the Soviet military intervention in Afghanistan. This embargo was not lifted until 1981 by President Ronald Reagan.

Arguments For and Against Trade Barriers

Policies designed to restrict international trade are always controversial because such policies usually help some people and hurt others. Let us briefly examine the arguments most frequently used by supporters of trade barriers, as well as the responses given by their opponents.

National Security Argument

This argument is based on the assumption that a nation should be as self-sufficient as possible in the production of goods needed for war and national defense. For example, some argue that the United States should not become too dependent on foreign-made steel because steel is a crucial ingredient in the manufacture of military weapons. In the event of war, they argue, foreign supplies might be interrupted. The same argument is used for many other products, but some critics believe that some industries have overstated their case in seeking protection on these grounds.

The U.S. steel industry has suffered from competition with countries that produce steel more efficiently. Some Americans have urged that the United States protect its steel industry for reasons of national security.

Infant Industry Argument

This argument is based on the belief that certain new industries—infant industries—should be protected from foreign competition until they have developed sufficient technological efficiency and economies of scale to enable them to compete in world markets. For example, suppose one of the developing nations of the world wishes to develop a domestic automobile industry. During the first few years of such an industry, the costs of producing automobiles probably would exceed the cost of importing automobiles from other nations. Thus, in order to ensure the survival of the infant industry, the nation might impose high tariffs or import quotas on foreign-made automobiles to drive their price up and make them less attractive.

Critics of this argument believe that far too often the infant industries never grow out of the "infant" stage. In other words, once the industry has protection against foreign competition, it will attempt to persuade the government to continue that protection indefinitely. The infant industry argument might have merit in some of the less-developed countries of the world but it is difficult to make a case on these grounds for protection of American industries.

Diversified Economy Argument

This argument is used by those who believe that too much specialization can make a country highly vulnerable to changes in world demand for products. For example, the economies of those countries that were highly dependent on the exports of wool and cotton were severely damaged by the introduction of synthetic fibers. Thus, proponents of trade barriers on this basis argue that nations should be diversified even if this means producing some products in which they do not have a comparative advantage. However, many economists believe that this argument is of little significance for the American economy, which is already very diversified.

Employment Protection Argument

The employment protection argument is based on the notion that a reduction in imports would lead to more American jobs or at least provide protection for existing jobs. This is perhaps the most emotionally charged and frequently used of all arguments in favor of trade barriers. Those who argue for employment protection often attempt to appeal to people's sense of patriotism by urging Americans to buy American-made products. They often suggest that people who buy foreign-made products are contributing to the nation's unemployment problem. Economists, however, point out that many American jobs are dependent on sales to foreign countries and that in international trade, goods pay for goods. In other words, a nation that exports goods also must import goods. Any attempt to

Do restrictions on exports and imports slow down world trade? What does the cartoonist believe?

reduce imports probably will result in a similar reduction in exports. Thus, although trade barriers may help to protect the jobs of some workers, they tend to cost other workers—those who produce goods for export—their jobs.

In addition, although in the short run trade barriers do offer protection to some American workers, in the long run they may do more harm than good. By limiting imports that enter this country, trade barriers protect inefficient industries. In time, the high prices that result from the inefficiency will cause people to buy less of the products these industries produce. These industries may then lose money and be forced to lay off workers anyway.

Wage Protection Argument

Some people argue that because wages in the United States are higher than in most other industrialized nations, tariffs or import quotas are needed to protect the wages of American workers from the threat of "cheap labor" from abroad. Advocates of this argument contend that a high-wage nation cannot compete successfully with low-wage nations. Many economists disagree with this contention. They point out that many products produced in the United States do compete successfully with products made elsewhere because labor is only one component of the price of goods. In many American industries, labor is combined with highly efficient capital goods that are absent in some other countries. As a result, the prices of American products and similar foreign-made products are often comparable.

The Inevitability of Trade Barriers

Most economists agree that barriers to trade benefit some groups at the expense of the rest of society. According to one recent study, 97 percent of economists agree that tariffs and import quotas lower real income. Thus, if the only goal of society was to maximize world production of

Many American jobs depend on sales of U.S. products in foreign countries, such as these canned goods in Nigeria.

goods and services, all nations would produce those products in which they have a comparative advantage and there would be no trade barriers.

However, life is not that simple. Nations must worry about national security; and many prominent people, including some business executives, labor leaders, and politicians, continue to support restrictions on international trade. As a result, there probably always will be some trade barriers, although most economists will continue to argue that it is in society's best interests to keep such barriers to a minimum.

Check Your Understanding

1. Why do nations put restrictions on international trade?

2. What is a tariff? Explain how tariffs give domestic producers a competitive advantage.

3. What is an import quota? Explain how import quotas operate.

4. Give five arguments that are frequently used in support of trade barriers.

5. Do economists generally favor or oppose trade barriers? Explain.

International Finance

Since different countries have different units of money, international trade involves international financial transactions. Let us see how international trade is financed.

Financing World Trade

When Americans wish to buy goods from other nations, they usually must pay for the goods in the currency of the exporting country. For example, Japan probably will demand yen, France will demand francs, West Germany will want deutsche marks, Great Britain will insist on pounds, and Mexico will demand pesos in payment for the goods they sell. Foreign currencies are known as **foreign exchange,** and they are bought and sold in **foreign exchange markets.** These are markets that deal in the

Computerized systems have enabled people to learn quickly about changes in the prices of gold, silver, and foreign currencies.

buying and selling of foreign currencies. The major participants in foreign exchange markets are banks that specialize in financing international trade. If an American importer wishes to buy television sets from a Japanese manufacturer, he or she will go to a bank that specializes in financing international trade and exchange dollars for yen.

Exchange Rates

When an American importer exchanges dollars for a foreign currency, the quantity of foreign currency received for each dollar will depend on the foreign exchange rate. The **foreign exchange rate** is the price of one currency in terms of another. For example, the British pound might be worth $1.50 in United States money, the West German mark might be worth 40 cents, and the Canadian dollar might be worth 80 cents. Historically, there have been two major types of foreign exchange rates: fixed rates and flexible rates.

Fixed exchange rates Under this system, the price of one currency is fixed in terms of other currencies so that the rate does not change. For example, the exchange rate between the British pound and the United States dollar might be fixed at 1 pound equals $1.50. The advantage of such a system is that importers and exporters know exactly how much foreign currency they can purchase with a given quantity of their own nation's currency. From 1944 to the early 1970s, foreign exchange markets operated under a fixed-exchange-rate system. Prior to 1971, the value of the United States dollar was tied to gold at the rate of $1 equals 1/35 ounce of gold. Since the value of other currencies was also fixed in relation to gold, the dollar price of British pounds, French francs, Japanese yen, and so forth remained constant.

The disadvantage of such a system is that it does not make allowances for changing economic conditions in various countries. For example, if the United States is experiencing high inflation at a time when West Germany is experiencing little or no inflation, American-made goods will become increasingly expensive in relation to German-made goods. As a result, the West Germans will tend to decrease their purchases from the United States. At the same time, Americans will find it increasingly attractive to buy German-made goods. This would lead to a serious imbalance in imports and exports between the two countries.

During the period of fixed exchange rates, some countries tried to solve such trade imbalances by devaluing their currencies. A **devaluation** is the lowering of a currency's value in relation to other currencies by government order. In the above example, if the United States devalued its currency, less West German currency would be required to purchase a dollar; thus, American goods would become less expensive to German buyers. Similarly, since Americans would receive less German currency for each dollar exchanged, German goods would become more expensive to Americans.

For example, suppose that before any devaluation, $1 was equivalent to 3 German marks, or 1 mark was equal to about 33 cents. If the American dollar was devalued, the new exchange rate might be $1 equals 2 marks. Put another way, the mark would now be worth 50 cents. Before the devaluation, it took 30 marks to buy $10 worth of American goods; now it would take only 20. In contrast, before it took about $3.30 to buy something that cost 10 marks; now it would cost $5.00.

The motive for devaluation is usually to increase exports and decrease imports. However, it is usually only a temporary solution. If other nations retaliate by devaluing their currencies, the planned improvement in a nation's trade status will not occur.

Flexible exchange rates Under a system of flexible exchange rates, the forces of supply and demand determine the value of a country's currency in terms of the value of other currencies. Thus, under this system the price of a country's currency can fluctuate up and down daily in response to market conditions. For example, on Monday the dollar may be trading at 3.01 marks. On Tuesday this figure may rise to 3.07. The foreign exchange markets have operated under a flexible-exchange-rate system since the early 1970s.

The supply and demand for foreign exchange usually are determined largely by the supply and demand for goods and services. For example, if United States importers wish to import large quantities of goods from Japan, there will be a strong demand for the Japanese yen. This could lead to a substantial increase in the price of the yen. If at the same time, however, the Japanese want to increase imports of soybeans or other products from the United States, they may be willing to supply large quantities of yen in exchange for dollars. In this case, the increases in demand and supply may cancel one another out and the price of the yen may remain relatively stable.

Factors other than the demand for goods can cause an increase in the demand for a nation's currency. Political or economic instability in other countries may cause people in those countries to exchange their currency for a more stable currency, such as the United States dollar. Also, high interest rates in a particular country may encourage foreign investors to convert their currencies into the currency of that nation so that they can invest there. This is exactly what happened in the United States during the early 1980s. The high interest rates in the United States prompted many foreign investors to exchange their currency for dollars for investment purposes. This increased demand for dollars increased the value of the dollar in terms of other currencies and made American-made products more expensive in world markets. As a result, foreigners bought fewer American-made products and Americans bought more foreign-made products.

Balance of Trade

The difference between the dollar amount of exports and the dollar amount of imports is called the **balance of trade.** If the United States sells more goods to foreign countries than it buys from foreign countries (if exports exceed imports), the nation has a **trade surplus.** On the other hand, if the nation buys more foreign goods than it sells abroad (if imports exceed exports), the nation has a **trade deficit.** In 1971, the United States recorded its first trade deficit—$4.8 billion—in this century, and in recent years the deficit has been running larger and larger. The figure for 1984 set an all-time record of $123.3 billion. Figure 15–2 shows the United States' balance of trade for the years 1974–84.

Not all economists agree on how serious a problem the trade deficits are. Some say that in the long run market adjustments will correct the problem. Others are not so sure. Some economists believe that the high trade deficits of the early 1980s are directly linked to the large deficits in the federal government's budget. As you learned in Chapter 10, heavy government borrowing to finance high budget deficits has helped to keep interest rates high. Moreover, many foreign investors have been exchanging their foreign currencies for dollars so that they could benefit from the high interest rates. These actions have contributed to the high value of the dollar. Thus, some economists believe that the trade deficit will remain high as long as interest rates in the United States remain high relative to those of other nations. They also believe that interest rates will remain high as long as the government continues to run large budget deficits.

How do trade deficits affect the economy and the American people? The answer to this question is not as simple as it might seem. The high value of the dollar, which contributes to the large trade deficits, is beneficial to many Americans. It means that foreign-made products cost less in dollar terms. In addition, since Americans buy a large volume of foreign-made products, lower prices for these products means a lower inflation rate for the nation. However, many Americans have been severely hurt by

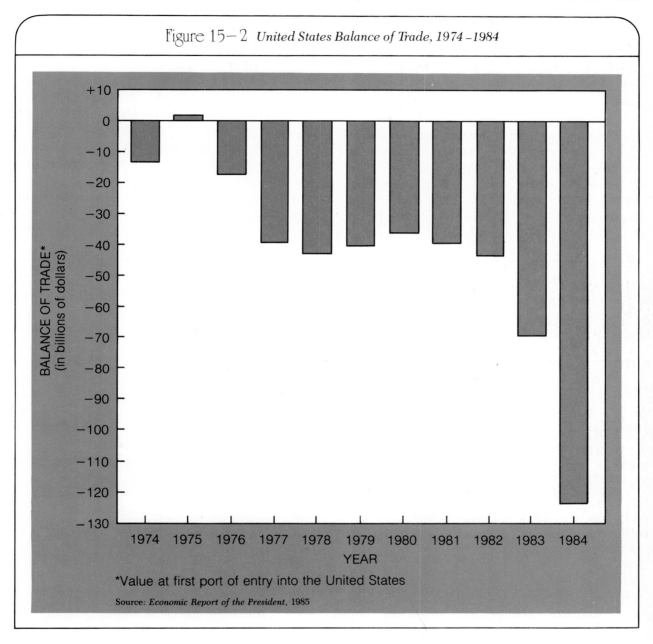

Figure 15–2 *United States Balance of Trade, 1974–1984*

*Value at first port of entry into the United States

Source: *Economic Report of the President*, 1985

the trade deficits. Farmers and other businesses that sell much of their output in world markets have been especially hard hit by the high value of the dollar. For example, suppose a bushel of wheat cost $3.91. In 1980, it would have cost 7 German marks to purchase this wheat, but in 1984 it would have cost 12 marks because of the rise in the value of the dollar. As a result, Amer-ican farmers have found it very difficult to com-pete in world markets. Many other industries that produce goods for export also have been severely hurt, and thousands of employees in these industries have been laid off. Thus, the trade deficits have both positive and negative effects on the economy and on the American people.

Balance of Payments

Economic relations between nations are not restricted to imports and exports alone. There are many other kinds of transactions that involve the exchange of money between nations. For example, the United States government spends money for foreign aid and to support military personnel stationed abroad. In addition, American businesses invest funds in foreign nations, and American banks make foreign loans. Furthermore, Americans spend money for goods and services when they travel abroad, and American citizens often send money to relatives living in other nations. Similarly, money flows into the United States from other nations when foreign citizens travel in this country, when foreign businesses make investments in the United States, when Americans receive dividends on foreign investments, and so forth.

Each nation keeps an accounting record of all its monetary transactions with other countries. This accounting record is called the **balance of payments.** A nation's balance of payments account includes all payments that it

Imported and exported goods comprise the major category in a country's balance of payments.

makes to other nations and all the payments it receives from other nations during a year. It includes imports and exports of goods (the balance of trade), flows of investment funds into and out of the country, loans between nations, and all other transactions that involve payments between countries. Because the total balance of payments account includes all financial transactions, including loans and debts, it always will be in balance. However, individual categories in the balance of payments account will not necessarily be in balance. The most important category of the balance of payments is the import and export of goods, and as you have just learned, this category is usually not in balance in any given year or group of years. Over the long run, however, there is a tendency for the deficits and surpluses to balance out.

Trade Agreements and the Future of World Trade

Despite the continuing support for trade barriers by many people, the future of world trade is bright. The benefits of free trade are so substantial that nations undoubtedly will engage in more—not less—trade in the future. In fact, over the past 50 years substantial progress has been made toward reducing trade barriers. The Reciprocal Trade Agreements Act of 1934 authorized the President to negotiate reciprocal agreements that promised to lower American trade barriers or tariffs in return for similar concessions abroad. In 1947, the General Agreement on Tariffs and Trade (GATT), which was signed by 23 countries, greatly enhanced the atmosphere for tariff reduction among nations. Since its creation, GATT has provided an ongoing forum for the negotiation of tariff reductions, and today more than 90 nations are members. The success of these efforts to reduce trade barriers is evident in the fact that the average tariff rate among nations has been reduced from about 59 percent in 1932 to less than 7 percent today.

In addition to GATT, several groups of nations have entered into their own agreements to reduce trade barriers among themselves. The most successful is the European Economic Community (EEC), popularly known as the European Common Market. Founded in 1957 by the Treaty of Rome, the EEC began operation in 1958. It originally consisted of six nations: Belgium, France, Italy, Luxembourg, the Netherlands, and West Germany. Today, Denmark, Ireland, Great Britain, Greece, Spain, and Portugal also are members. The objectives of the EEC are to eliminate tariffs among the member nations and to establish common tariffs against goods from outside countries. In a sense, the member nations of the EEC have united their economic resources into a single economy. They experience the same kinds of benefits from free trade among themselves as the United States does from free trade among the 50 states.

Check Your Understanding

1. What is foreign exchange? What are foreign exchange markets?

2. What is meant by the term "foreign exchange rate"? Describe two types of foreign exchange rates. Which type is used for world trade today?

3. What is the balance of trade? Do economists agree on the severity of recent trade deficits? Explain.

4. What is meant by the term "balance of payments"? What does it include?

5. What do the initials GATT and EEC stand for? What are the objectives of GATT and EEC?

ISSUE: Should the United States Restrict Imports?

One of the most controversial economic issues is the question of whether it is in the best interest of the nation and the American people to place restrictions on the import of foreign-made products. Many people advocate substantial restrictions in the form of tariffs and import quotas. Others argue that such restrictions do more harm than good. This controversy has existed throughout our history and will probably continue for the forseeable future.

The Case for Restricting Imports

Advocates of import restrictions argue that such restrictions are necessary to protect the jobs and wage levels of American workers. They contend that if fewer foreign-made goods were imported, more American-made goods would be sold and this, in turn, would provide additional jobs. For example, they point to the large number of foreign-made automobiles sold in the United States and to the fact that many auto workers in this country have lost their jobs in recent years. They argue that if greater restrictions had been placed on the import of foreign-made automobiles, many former American auto workers would still have their jobs.

In addition, they maintain that import restrictions are necessary to protect the wages of American workers. They point to the fact that many imported products are produced in countries where both wages and living costs are much lower than in the United States. Without restrictions, they contend, wages in this country would be reduced to the point where many workers would have difficulty making ends meet because the reduction in wages would not be met by a corresponding reduction in the cost of living.

Advocates of import restrictions argue also that without protection some American industries would be severely weakened. For example, they point to the large number of steel factories in the United States that have closed down and contend that these closings are directly related to the import of lower priced foreign-made steel. They argue that in time of war the nation might not be able to depend on foreign sources of steel and it is in the national interest to make sure that a strong steel industry continues to exist in the United States.

The Case Against Restricting Imports

Opponents of import restrictions argue that all nations benefit from international trade, and any restrictions on such trade would have a negative impact on the nation. They argue that many American jobs are dependent on exports to foreign countries, and that any reduction in imports would be offset by similar reductions in exports. Thus, they argue, trade restrictions designed to save the jobs of some American workers would result in the loss of jobs by other American workers who produce products for foreign markets.

In addition, those against import restrictions argue that importing products from nations with lower wages than those in the United States does not necessarily reduce wages in this country. This is true, they say, because by combining a great deal of technology and capital goods with labor, many firms in this country are able to compete successfully with firms in nations where labor costs are much lower. Furthermore, they contend that import restrictions tend to protect inefficient industries and result in higher prices for American consumers. They argue that if American industries were forced to compete in world markets without protection, most of them would find ways of increasing efficiency so that they could compete successfully. They do not believe it is fair to deny American consumers the opportunity to buy less expensive foreign-made products in order to protect inefficient industries.

Opponents of trade restrictions point to the gains that result when countries specialize in the production of those products in which they have a comparative advantage and trade with other nations for the things in which they have a comparative disadvantage. They believe that advocates of import restrictions take too narrow a view of the economy and fail to understand that such restrictions often do more harm than good to the nation and its people.

What view do you take on the issue of import restrictions? Do you believe there should be more or fewer restrictions? Why? Do you think import restrictions increase or decrease the number of jobs available to American workers? Explain your answer.

CAREERS: Computer Programmer

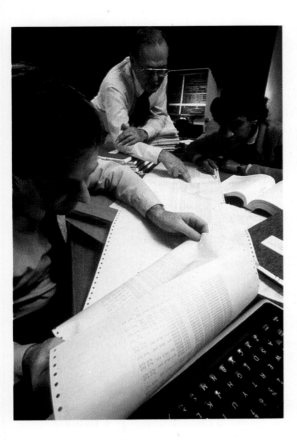

Computers can process vast quantities of information rapidly and accurately. They can retrieve data stored on tapes and disks, organize it, and perform complex calculations with it. However, in order to perform these functions, computers need to be given detailed, step-by-step instructions. Computer programmers are the people who write these specifications, which are called programs.

To prepare a program, programmers usually work from specifications prepared by other experts called systems analysts.

These analysts have carefully studied the tasks that the computer is going to be asked to perform and have prepared a detailed list of the steps the computer must follow. The programmer then writes the specific program for the task by breaking down each step into a series of coded instructions using a language—such as BASIC, PASCAL, COBOL, or FORTRAN—developed especially for computer applications.

Although simple programs can be written in a few hours, most require several months, and some complex programs may require more than a year of work. Sometimes several programmers work together on a program under the supervision of a senior systems programmer. A systems programmer—a person who is knowledgeable about the operation of the entire computer system—also helps programmers determine the source of problems, or "bugs," that may occur with their programs and how to eliminate such problems.

Training requirements for computer programmers vary. Although not all employers require a bachelor's degree, employers using computers for scientific or engineering applications seek college graduates with degrees in computer or information science, mathematics, engineering, or the physical sciences. Employers who use computers for business applications prefer applicants who have had college courses in programming and business. Computer programmers should be able to think logically, work with abstract concepts, and do technical analysis. In addition, the job requires patience, persistence, and the ability to work with extreme accuracy even under pressure.

Chapter Highlights

1   International trade is very important to most nations of the world. Without international trade, many countries would be unable to feed their people. Even in the United States, we are dependent on other countries for certain products.

2   There are substantial differences in the resources of the various nations of the world. However, the more each nation engaged in trade specializes in the production of those products that it can produce most efficiently, the more the total world production of products will increase.

3   One nation has an absolute advantage over another nation in producing a product when it can use fewer resources than the other nation to produce the same quantity of the product.

4   Any time a nation has an absolute advantage over another nation in the production of two products, it has a comparative advantage in the production of that product in which the absolute advantage is greater. Similarly, when a nation has an absolute disadvantage in the production of two products, it has a comparative advantage in the production of that product in which the absolute disadvantage is less.

5   Despite the benefits of specialization and international trade, most nations put some restrictions on trade in order to protect home industries from foreign competition. These restrictions usually take the form of tariffs or import quotas.

6   Arguments used in support of trade barriers include the national security argument, the infant industry argument, the diversified economy argument, the employment protection argument, and the wage protection argument. Although most economists believe it is in society's best interest to keep trade barriers to a minimum, there will probably always be some trade barriers.

7   When Americans wish to buy goods from other nations, they usually must pay for the goods in the currency of the exporting country. Foreign currencies are known as foreign exchange, and they are bought and sold in foreign exchange markets.

8   The foreign exchange rate is the price of one currency in terms of another. There are two major types of foreign exchange rates: fixed rates and flexible rates. The foreign exchange markets have operated under a flexible-exchange-rate system since the early 1970s.

9   The difference between the dollar amount of exports and the dollar amount of imports is called the balance of trade. If United States exports exceed imports, the nation has a trade surplus. If imports exceed exports, the nation has a trade deficit. In recent years, the United States has been running large trade deficits. Trade deficits have both positive and negative effects on the economy and on the American people.

10   In addition to imports and exports, there are many other kinds of transactions that involve the exchange of money between nations. The accounting record of all of a nation's monetary transactions with other countries is called the balance of payments.

Important Terms

Match each of the following terms with the correct definition:

foreign exchange	trade surplus	comparative advantage
balance of payments	embargo	flexible exchange rates
absolute advantage	devaluation	foreign exchange rate
import quota	tariff	foreign exchange market
balance of trade	trade deficit	fixed exchange rates
import	export	

1. The ability of one nation to produce a product with fewer resources than another nation.

2. A tax imposed by the government on imported products.

3. To buy a product from another nation.

4. Foreign currencies.

5. A situation in which a country has a greater absolute advantage or less of an absolute disadvantage in the production of one of two products.

6. A situation in which a country's imports exceed its exports.

7. To sell a product to another nation.

8. A government policy that places a precise legal limit on the number of units of a particular product that can be imported into a country during a specified time period.

9. An exchange rate system under which the forces of supply and demand determine the value of a nation's currency in terms of the value of the currencies of other nations.

10. A total ban by the government on the import or export of a particular product.

11. The price of one currency in terms of another.

12. The lowering of a currency's value in relation to other currencies by government order.

13. The difference in the dollar value of exports and imports.

14. An accounting record of all of a nation's monetary transactions with other countries.

15. A situation in which a country's exports exceed its imports.

16. An exchange rate system under which the price of one currency is fixed in terms of other currencies so that the rate does not change.

17. Market on which foreign currencies are bought and sold.

Extending Your Understanding

1. Suppose the United States were to suddenly halt all trade with other countries. How would such an act affect your life and that of other Americans?

2. How does the concept of comparative advantage relate to your life? In what areas do you have a comparative advantage over other people?

3. Do you think the United States should have more or fewer restrictions on international trade? Why? Who benefits from trade barriers? Who is hurt by them?

4. Which system do you think is better—a system of flexible exchange rates or a system of fixed exchange rates? Why?

5. Overall, do you think the nation has benefited from or been hurt by the recent trade deficits?

Activities

1. The next time you go shopping for items such as food, clothing, sporting equipment, stereo equipment, and so forth, make a list of some of the items in the store that are imported. Include the country they came from. Compare the quality and price of these foreign-made items to the quality and price of similar items made in this country. What conclusions can you draw?

2. Suppose you are shopping for a car. Prepare a chart showing arguments that can be made for buying an American-made car and for buying a foreign-made car.

Building Skills in Economics: Understanding Foreign Exchange

As you learned in this chapter, when the United States trades with another country, it usually must pay for its purchases in the currency of the exporting country. The same would hold true if you traveled abroad. Shopkeepers and hotel managers in many countries would be unwilling to accept your dollars.

The table below shows the rates of exchange for some major currencies. The first column shows the dollar value of the currency. For example, on the particular day represented in the table, the British pound was worth about $1.14. The second column shows how much of the currency you would get for each dollar you exchange. Using this same example, you would get .88 pound for each dollar. Use the table to answer the questions.

Applying Economic Skills

1. About how much was the French franc worth in American dollars? How many francs would you get for each dollar?
2. About how much was the West German mark worth in American dollars? About how many marks would you get for each dollar?
3. Which country's currency is worth less than a penny for each individual unit exchanged? How many would you get for each dollar?
4. Which country's currency has the highest dollar value?

FOREIGN EXCHANGE RATES		
	$ Value per Unit of Foreign Currency	*Unit of Currency per Dollar*
Austria (schilling)	.0451	22.17
Great Britain (pound)	1.1389	.8780
France (franc)	.1029	9.7115
Japan (yen)	.0039	254.67
Switzerland (franc)	.3772	2.6510
West Germany (mark)	.3154	3.1405

CHAPTER 16

COMPARATIVE ECONOMIC SYSTEMS AND PROBLEMS OF DEVELOPING NATIONS

Alice and Martin Kellar live in the United States. If the Kellars want new clothing, they might visit their nearest local clothing store. If that store doesn't have the style or the color of clothing they want, they probably can go to a number of other clothing or department stores in their area. Because they live in the United States, the Kellars have a varied selection of stores from which to choose.

If the Kellars lived in the Soviet Union, however, the process of shopping for clothing probably would be very different. First of all, they would not have a variety of stores from which to choose. In addition, they would have to go to a store owned and operated by the government, and at the government store they might have little or no choice of styles and colors. More likely than not, they each would have just one style of clothing on which to base their decisions.

The economy of the Soviet Union is very different from that of the United States. In the United States, a system of free markets helps to make decisions about what to produce, how to produce it, and for whom to produce it. In contrast, in the Soviet Union the government makes most of these decisions. Most of this book thus far has been devoted to a study of the American economy. In this chapter, we want to examine some of the other major economies of the world. We also want to study the problems faced by developing nations.

Capitalism, Democratic Socialism, and Authoritarian Socialism

As you learned in Chapter 1, economists often classify economies as traditional economies, command economies, and market economies on the basis of how economic decisions are made. Economies are categorized also on the basis of who owns the means of production, such as factories, natural resources, and machinery. Under pure **capitalism,** all businesses are privately owned and operated. In contrast, under pure **socialism,** all businesses are owned and operated by the government. Just as there have never been examples of pure market economies, there also have never been examples of pure capital-

ism or pure socialism. In every economy, some of the means of production are owned by individuals and others are owned by the government. We can say that the United States is predominantly a capitalist economy because most businesses are privately owned and operated. There are, however, two different types of socialism: democratic socialism and authoritarian socialism.

Under **democratic socialism,** the people take part in the decision-making process by electing government leaders. There is also a substantial amount of private enterprise, with the government owning and operating some major industries and individuals owning the rest. In addition, the government is responsible for providing such services as free education and medical care. Sweden often is considered an example of democratic socialism. Other democratic nations that now or formerly have

Under capitalism and democratic socialism, small businesses are privately owned and a system of free markets operates.

Figure 16–1 *Characteristics of Three Types of Economic Systems*

	Capitalism	Democratic Socialism	Authoritarian Socialism
Ownership of the Means of Production	Most factories, natural resources, machinery, and so forth are privately owned.	Government owns some of the major industries, such as steel factories and iron ore mines. The rest are privately owned.	Factories, natural resources, machinery, and so forth are owned by the government.
Method of Answering the Basic Economic Questions	Basic economic questions are answered primarily through a system of free markets.	Basic economic questions are answered partly by free markets and partly by the government.	Basic economic questions are answered by the government.
Amount of Government Economic Planning	Very limited government economic planning.	Moderate amount of government economic planning.	Extensive government economic planning in both the short run and the long run.
Source of Government Power	Government leaders are usually chosen by free democratic elections.	Government leaders are usually chosen by free democratic elections.	Government leaders are chosen by a political party.

had some socialism in their economies include Great Britain, France, West Germany, Denmark, and Norway.

Under **authoritarian socialism** (or Marxian socialism), however, the government controls most of the means of production and decides what goods and services will be produced. The people have little or no say in the decision-making process. Countries, such as the Soviet Union, that today are known as "communist" nations are examples of authoritarian socialism. Whereas the word "communist" refers to a classless society in which there is no government, countries currently thought of as "communist" are characterized by extensive government control by the Communist Party, the only political party permitted to exist. In addition to the Soviet Union, other examples of authoritarian

socialism include Bulgaria, Czechoslovakia, East Germany, Hungary, Poland, Romania, and China.

Figure 16–1 presents the characteristics of capitalism, democratic socialism, and authoritarian socialism. We will examine specific examples of each later in this chapter, but first let us look at the origins of socialism and the development of Marxian socialism.

The Origins of Socialism

The origins of modern socialism date back to the Industrial Revolution of the early 1800s. Prior to that time, people generally worked singly or in small groups to produce goods with simple tools. Many employers had a close relationship with their workers and felt some responsibility for them. With the onset of the Industrial Revolution, however, the relationship between employer and employee changed. The rapid growth in factories and in mass production during the period led to a social distance between employer and employee and to the development of many social problems. In addition, factory work was often dangerous, and most workers worked 12 to 14 hours a day for six days a week. Wages were very low for men, and women and children made only a small fraction of what men earned. Many children as young as 10 years of age worked 10 to 14 hours a day.

Moreover, as more and more people from rural areas moved into the cities in search of factory jobs, severe overcrowding resulted, which led to unsanitary conditions and outbreaks of disease.

Many critics at the time felt that factory owners were taking advantage of their workers, and some advocated socialism as a means of attaining economic and social equality. Some proposed the creation of communities in which the means of production would be owned collectively by all the people and where income would be shared equally. In fact, some commu-

During the Industrial Revolution, critics charged that mine and factory owners exploited their workers. They pointed to child labor, low wages, and dangerous working conditions as evidence of this exploitation.

BIOGRAPHY: Kark Marx

(1818–1883) Karl Marx was a German economic historian and social philosopher whose ideas formed the foundation of modern communism. The son of a successful lawyer, he was educated at the universities of Bonn, Berlin, and Jena. After receiving his doctorate in philosophy in 1841, Marx tried to get a teaching job but failed because of his radical views. During the 1840s, while he was still in his twenties, Marx spent short periods in Germany, France, and Great Britain, where the police sought to expel him because of his articles advocating revolution. In 1848, at the age of 30, Marx and his close friend Friedrich Engels published *The Communist Manifesto*, which included the statement: "Workers of the world unite! You have nothing to lose but your chains."

In 1849, after being expelled from both Germany and France, Marx moved to London where he spent the final 34 years of his life writing and struggling for survival. Engels, who was the son of a wealthy industrialist, has been credited with keeping Marx, his wife, and their five children from starving during this period. Marx worked almost continuously from early morning until late at night doing research and writing. In 1867, the first volume of his major work, *Das Kapital*, was published.

Marx viewed capitalism as a struggle between the "ruling class," the capitalists who owned the means of production, and the "oppressed class," the workers who were "exploited" by the capitalists. He argued that private ownership of the means of production under capitalism was the heart of class conflict, and he urged the workers to rise up and overthrow capitalism.

Marx's ideas have altered the course of history, shaping the policies of nations and affecting the lives of millions. Yet during his life he had few friends. When he died in 1883, his eulogy was delivered by Engels, and the funeral was attended by only eight people.

nities of this type were actually established, but almost all of them failed.

Although some of the early socialists worked peacefully to bring about changes within existing political and economic systems, others advocated the use of force to replace capitalism with socialism. The most influential of those who wanted to overthrow capitalism was a nine-teenth-century German economic historian and social philosopher named Karl Marx.

Marxian Socialism

Karl Marx was a harsh critic of capitalism. He saw capitalism as a struggle between the capitalists—the owners of land, factories, and machines—and the workers whom he called the **proletariat.** Marx believed that the capitalists were exploiting the workers by selling goods for more money than they had paid the workers to produce them. According to Marx, the value of any good was equal to the value of labor that went into it. Thus, Marx argued, profits represented exploitation of the workers.

Marx believed capitalism was doomed to fail. Since workers were not being paid the full value of the goods they produced, they would not have sufficient purchasing power to buy all the goods produced. This, Marx believed, would lead to severe recessions and depressions that would cause many people to be without work. The gap between the rich (the capitalists) and the poor (the workers) would grow wider and wider, Marx argued, until the workers eventually would unite and revolt to overthrow capitalism.

Marx urged workers to rise up and overthrow capitalism and replace it with a classless society in which the people as a whole owned everything. Marx viewed socialism as only a temporary step in the development of what he called communism. He believed a strong government under the control of the workers would be necessary at first. Once everyone became equal, however, there no longer would be a need for government. At this point communism would exist. It would be a system where there was no poverty or crime and where everyone would work hard for the good of society as a whole and consume only what was necessary for basic needs.

Marx's ideas had strong appeal for workers and sparked the development of what is called communism in many nations of the world. Modern communism, however, is very different from the communism that Marx described. Most Communist leaders today argue that they are still in the socialism stage of their evolution toward true communism. They say that during this stage it is necessary for the government to force people to work for little reward in order to enable the country to become wealthy enough

to satisfy everyone's economic wants. When that stage is reached, "pure communism" will exist and each person will work according to his or her abilities and consume according to his or her needs. At that point, there no longer would be a need for government actions. However, no nation has ever reached this stage, and few people outside the Communist world believe that any nation ever will.

Marx's predictions that capitalism was doomed to fail have not proved correct. This is partially true because modern capitalism is very different from the capitalism of nineteenth-century Europe about which Marx wrote. Moreover, Marx viewed capitalists and workers as two distinct groups and believed that there was nothing workers could do to change their status except to unite and overthrow capitalism. However, in the societies that developed in the United States and many other countries, workers are free to change their status, and even to become capitalists themselves.

Check Your Understanding

1. Define socialism. How does it differ from capitalism?

2. Identify two types of socialism. How do they differ?

3. When and why did modern socialism originate?

4. Briefly describe the main ideas of Karl Marx.

The Soviet Union

The Soviet Union is the largest country in the world in terms of area—larger than the United States and Canada combined. The population of the Soviet Union in 1980 was an estimated 262 million, compared to a population of 220 million in the United States. As a first step toward understanding the Soviet economy, let us briefly examine its history.

A Brief History of the Soviet Economy

Karl Marx predicted that it would be in industrial nations, such as Britain and Germany, that workers would revolt and set up socialism. Instead, the revolution came in Russia, an agricultural nation. At the time of the Russian Revolution in 1917, approximately 80 percent of the people were peasants who lived and worked on the farms of rich landowners.

After the 1917 revolution, one of its leaders, Vladimir Lenin, set up a new government controlled by members of the Communist Party. Lenin was a strong believer in the theories of Karl Marx, and he took land away from the rich landlords and gave it to the peasants. He also turned the few factories that existed over to the workers.

The workers, however, were unable to manage the factories properly, and production soon decreased dramatically. There were also critical food shortages in the cities, and when the government attempted to use military force to confiscate food from farms to feed the hungry city dwellers, the farmers retaliated by cutting back on their production. By 1921, the Russian economy had deteriorated to the point that Lenin decided to restore some capitalist methods. Under the new approach, which was called the **New Economic Policy** (**NEP**), small, privately owned businesses could operate. Also, farmers were permitted to sell a portion of what they produced directly to customers through private markets.

In 1924, Lenin died and Joseph Stalin came to power. Stalin wanted to convert the nation from a predominantly agricultural country to an industrial nation, and to do so he ordered the government to take over almost complete control of the economy, including ownership of property. Stalin's long-term goals were put forth in a series of Five-Year Plans—comprehensive programs of economic planning designed to achieve the maximum potential economic growth. Through these Five-Year Plans, Stalin hoped to industrialize the nation as rapidly as possible and to increase farm production by combining small farms into larger units. The first Five-Year Plan was introduced in 1928 and was followed by other long-term plans through which the Soviet Union attempted to reach maximum production levels without returning to capitalist methods. To a certain extent, the Soviet Union follows similar economic policies today.

The Soviet Economy Today

As we mentioned earlier, the Soviet Union is an example of authoritarian socialism. Economic activity is strictly controlled by the government, which is controlled by the Communist Party—the only political party permitted to exist. Although membership in the Communist Party is limited to less than ten percent of the total population, the Communists maintain firm control over every aspect of Soviet life including the economy. The government, which owns and operates most of the nation's businesses, engages in elaborate planning and gives each business firm detailed instructions about what and how much to produce.

Economic planning The government's central planning agency, **Gosplan,** is responsible for economic planning in the Soviet Union. Gosplan formulates both five-year plans, which focus on long-range objectives, and detailed annual plans. The detailed annual plan establishes production targets for each business firm. Each firm is told how many resources (raw

Under central government planning, Soviet agriculture is responsible for meeting certain annual production goals.

materials, labor, machines, and so forth) it will receive and how much it is supposed to produce with these resources.

There is much that can go wrong with the economic plans. Because the output of one firm (a steel mill, for example) is generally the input of another firm (a farm-machinery plant, for example), the failure of one firm to meet its production quota can set off a domino effect. In other words, a shortage of steel can lead to a shortage of farm machinery, which can lead to a shortage of farm products.

Providing incentives Soviet managers are under considerable pressure to meet the production quotas established by Gosplan. Those managers who meet or exceed their quotas are usually rewarded with bonuses, promotion, and medals. Those managers who fail to meet their quotas usually can expect demotion. The intense pressure on managers to meet their quotas often can lead to the production of low-

quality goods. For example, a firm that manufactures jam may not receive enough sugar to meet its monthly quota. In this case, the firm might put less sugar in the jam than the recipe calls for in order to maintain its required production level.

Soviet agriculture There are three types of agricultural production units in the Soviet Union: state farms, collective farms, and private plots. **State farms** are owned by the government and operated just like industrial firms. The government establishes annual quotas and determines the wages paid to workers. The output of state farms is sold to the government for processing and distribution through state stores and for export. State farms are usually quite large, averaging about 112,000 acres each, and they account for approximately 25 percent of total agricultural output.

Collective farms are made up of varying numbers of individual peasant families who combine their resources and talents to operate on a collective basis. This is the dominant form of agricultural organization in terms of number of farm units, share of land area cultivated, and number of workers employed. The average size of collective farms is about 16,000 acres, and more than 500 families live on each farm. In the past, members of collective farms were not paid wages. Instead, they shared in the income from the farm's products. However, in recent years there has been a shift toward regular cash wages similar to those paid on state farms.

Private plots consist of the tiny plots of land that collective farm households and state farm workers are allowed to farm. Products produced on these plots can be sold on the open market. Although the typical private plot is only two thirds of an acre and total private land holdings account for only 3 percent of all cultivated land, a substantial amount of production comes

Some Soviet farm workers have tiny private plots on which they raise produce or even flowers to sell on the open market.

from such plots. In 1980, the private sector in the Soviet Union produced 30 percent of the total meat supply, 35 percent of the eggs, 35 percent of the milk, 34 percent of the vegetables, and 44 percent of the fruit.

Distributing goods As in other countries, the amount of goods that an individual consumer gets depends on his or her income and on the prices of goods. Wages are the major source of income in the Soviet Union; and despite the distributional ethic of equality set forth by Marx, substantial wage differentials do exist. Skilled craftworkers generally earn two to four times as much as unskilled workers; and the earnings of scientists, engineers, and high-level government officials are several times greater than the national average.

Ordinary Soviet citizens shop at government-operated stores or regulated cooperatives. Consumers are free to spend their income as they desire. However, since the government determines what will be produced and the prices of goods, many products often are unavailable to ordinary consumers or they are priced so high that consumers cannot afford them. Shortages of goods are a way of life, and people often must wait in lines for hours to purchase needed goods. In contrast, government officials, upper-level Communist Party members, and members of favored groups—such as scientists, ballet stars, and economic managers—often are allowed to shop in special stores that offer lower prices and a more varied stock.

Personal freedom Personal freedom in the Soviet Union is strictly limited. Persons who outwardly criticize the Communist Party and the government may be expelled from their city or even sent to a prison labor camp. Even a move into a city or from one apartment to another requires government approval. There is some freedom of occupational choice, and the government uses wage differentials to encourage workers to enter career fields or work in geographic areas where there are labor short-

Soviet shoppers face frequent shortages of consumer goods and are accustomed to waiting in long lines to buy goods that become available.

ages. However, the government is the only employer, and it establishes wage rates. Although there are labor unions in the Soviet Union, they are very different from unions in the United States. They do not engage in collective bargaining or participate in wage determination. Instead, they are supposed to cooperate with management in achieving the objectives established by the Communist Party and the government.

The COMECON Countries of Eastern Europe

Six other countries in Eastern Europe have economic systems patterned after that of the Soviet Union. They are Bulgaria, Czechoslovakia, East Germany, Hungary, Poland, and Romania. These countries are members of the Council for Mutual Economic Assistance (COMECON), an economic organization that was founded in 1949 to promote trade within countries politically influenced by the Soviet Union. Over time, however, the economies of these countries have taken on some individual characteristics. Some have reduced the level of central planning and adapted some capitalist ideas to meet their needs.

These economies have experienced varying degrees of success. Czechoslovakia and East Germany have been the most successful, and they have higher per person incomes than the Soviet Union. Poland, on the other hand, has had serious economic and political problems. In 1980, in response to extensive government control and high food prices, workers formed a union called **Solidarity** and staged a series of strikes. Solidarity was allowed to function freely for a brief period. However, in December 1981, under pressure from the Soviet Union, the Polish government outlawed the union and arrested many of its leaders.

Check Your Understanding

1. Why was the New Economic Policy established in the Soviet Union? What changes took place under the NEP?

2. What changes did Stalin make when he came to power?

3. What agency is responsible for economic planning in the Soviet Union? What kinds of incentives are used to pressure managers of Soviet business firms to meet their quotas?

4. Describe the three types of agricultural production units found in the Soviet Union.

5. How are goods distributed in the Soviet Union?

6. Identify the six COMECON countries of Eastern Europe.

The People's Republic of China

China, with an estimated population of one billion, has more people than any other nation. Although it is the third largest nation in terms of area, however, less than 15 percent of its land is suitable for producing crops. Providing for the needs of so many people with such limited resources has always posed a difficult problem for the Chinese, and this problem has been complicated by a great deal of political instability. Let us begin our study of China with a brief look at its recent history.

Recent History

Like the Soviet Union, China is an example of authoritarian socialism. Since seizing power from the Nationalist Chinese government in 1949, the Communists have worked to transform China into a communist economic system with industrialization as the primary economic goal. The period from 1949 to 1952 was a period of consolidation during which the new govern-

After gaining power in China, the Communists introduced many far-reaching economic reforms. They set up communes, or huge farms, to increase agricultural output.

ment announced a series of nationwide reforms, the most important of which was land redistribution. In order to win the support of the masses of peasants, the Communists redistributed millions of acres of land and eliminated landlords as a class.

The second stage of economic development, covering the period from 1953 to 1957, was guided by the First Five-Year Plan. During this stage, the Chinese relied heavily on Soviet expertise and entered into agreements with the Soviet Union that called for extensive Soviet aid. The Soviets built power plants, modern iron and steel complexes, refineries, and many other manufacturing plants. They also trained Chinese technicians to operate them.

Although substantial progress was made during the First Five-Year Plan, in 1958 the Chinese decided to use a new approach to drive the economy forward at an even faster pace. This new approach, known as the **Great Leap Forward,** called for the development of production techniques that could make the greatest possible use of China's enormous population. In agriculture, the policy called for the formation of communes, which forced peasants to give up their land and their homes in exchange for communal housing.

In industry, the policy of the Great Leap Forward called for the creation of thousands of tiny industrial units throughout the country. Small industrial plants—including handicraft workshops, iron and steel foundries, fertilizer plants, machine shops, and many others—were created to make use of the abundant labor supply. Top priority was given to the iron and steel industry, which the Communists saw as the key to industrial success. Two million backyard furnaces designed to manufacture steel were built throughout China. Millions of Chinese worked day and night producing steel while millions of others mined iron ore and coal.

The policies of the Great Leap Forward did not succeed. The agricultural communes never lived up to their promise, and the iron and steel was of very poor quality because of a lack of

Today, the Chinese government encourages the production of traditional handcrafts, which can be sold abroad and earn the country foreign currency.

quality-control standards. The net result was that the gains made during the First Five-Year Plan were lost.

The period from 1961 to 1965 marked a return to the policies that preceded the Great Leap Forward. More rational economic policies toward industry and agriculture were adopted, and farmers were again permitted to have private plots of land for their own use. These gains were short-lived, however. During the period from 1966 to 1969 the **Cultural Revolution,** a political drive to free the Chinese from their traditional customs, was led by Communist leader Mao Tse-tung. This upheaval brought disruption to the economy and a sharp reduction in economic growth. Following the Cultural Revolution, systematic economic planning was reintroduced, but political instability continued to interfere with economic progress. Since the death of Mao Tse-tung in 1976, Chinese leaders have been attempting to restore orderly growth to the economy.

In China, as in the Soviet Union, some farm workers sell produce on the open market although the government often sets a limit on how much a seller can charge.

The Chinese Economy Today

Overall, the Chinese political and economic systems are similar to those of the Soviet Union. The government is controlled by the Communist Party, which establishes the economic objectives and policies. The government engages in long-term planning and determines what will be produced, how it will be produced, and for whom it will be produced. In addition, all major industrial firms are under government control. However, much of the country's industry is decentralized and under the control of authorities at the provincial, or local, levels. Moreover, there seems to be more flexibility of organization and administration in China than in the Soviet Union.

Until recently agricultural organization in China was similar to that of the Soviet Union. The key agricultural production unit was the **commune,** which was similar to the collective farm in the Soviet Union. In recent years, however, agricultural organization in China has become more decentralized. Although the commune is still the most comprehensive agricultural unit, there has been a shifting of control over production from communes to production brigades, which usually consist of several villages, and to production teams, which consist of single villages.

Today, the production team is the key economic unit in agriculture. Each team consists of an average of 30 households, and it owns and operates a production unit consisting of about 50 acres of land. Each household usually owns its own house, but not the land on which it sits. The team is given production quotas by the government, and it is permitted to sell anything it produces in excess of the quotas in free markets for any price it can get. These extra earnings are then divided among the members of the production team on the basis of the quantity and quality of work that each member has contributed to the team.

China also has some state farms, which are managed by government-appointed directors, and private plots from which peasants can sell their products in free markets. Production from private plots has become increasingly important in recent years, and most of the poultry, pork, and vegetables consumed in China is produced on these plots.

It appears that China may be about to depart from its Soviet-style planned economy and move toward a modified free-market system. In 1984, Chinese leaders announced that beginning in 1985 Chinese factories would operate under the same system that has allowed Chinese farmers to sell their homegrown produce in free markets. Under the new system, supply and demand would determine economic planning. Government business firms would function as independent companies responsible for making profits and determining production. Fixed quotas would be abolished, and unprofitable factories would be closed down. Although property still would be owned by the government, market forces would be used to help solve the problems of shortages and surpluses that have plagued the economy in the past. Not all Chinese government officials approved of the new reforms, however, and only time will tell whether or not they will become permanent changes.

Check Your Understanding

1. How did the Communist government of China come to power?

2. What was the purpose of the Great Leap Forward? Describe the economic policies of this period. Did these policies succeed?

3. What was the Cultural Revolution? How did it affect economic growth?

4. How do the current political and economic systems of China compare with those in the Soviet Union today?

Sweden

As we mentioned earlier, Sweden often is considered an example of democratic socialism. Although approximately 90 percent of Swedish industry is privately owned, the government owns some of the most basic industries, including the iron ore, steel, and shipbuilding industries. This substantial amount of socialism in the Swedish economy, however, has not meant restricted democracy. Sweden has one of the most participatory democracies in the world. Whereas in the United States approximately 50 percent of the eligible voters vote in presidential elections, as many as 90 percent vote in Sweden's national elections, which are held every three years.

Businesses are run very differently in Sweden than they are in the United States. Employees as well as stockholders must be represented on the boards of directors of large Swedish corporations, and both play important roles in corporate decision-making. For example, companies cannot establish foreign branches without the consent of their Swedish employees. Moreover, Swedish companies are required to share their profits with workers.

Sweden does engage in economic planning, but it is very different from the planning that takes place in the Soviet Union. The plans usually are for only one year at a time, and they require agreement by representatives of the various sectors of the economy, such as business, labor, and agriculture. One special feature of the Swedish economy is the special investment reserve. This consists of a portion of a corporation's profits that is exempt from taxes when used for investment under certain conditions stipulated by the government. These funds usually can be invested tax free only at times of rising unemployment and in those regions of the country where there is a surplus of labor. This helps to keep unemployment in Sweden relatively lower than in many other industrial nations.

Sweden often is referred to as a welfare state because of its extensive government social programs. The government provides free education from grade school through college, as well as subsidized medical care. It also pays generous pensions to retired persons, widows, and orphans, and it provides financial aid for housing. Because of these comprehensive social programs, taxes in Sweden are very high, and in recent years, the government has experienced increasing opposition to the high taxes. Growing discontent with government policies resulted in the removal from power of the Socialist Party in 1976 after 44 years of rule. However, rising unemployment led Swedish voters to return the Socialist Party to power in 1982.

Check Your Understanding

1. What kind of economic system does Sweden have?

2. How are businesses run in Sweden?

3. What kind of economic planning does Sweden engage in?

4. Why is Sweden often referred to as a welfare state?

Japan

The performance of the Japanese economy since 1950 has been so remarkable that it often is referred to as the "Japanese miracle." In 1950, Japan's GNP per person was only one eighth that of the United States. Today, the Japanese economy is the third largest in the world, ranking below only that of the United States and the Soviet Union. During the period from 1950 to 1980, Japan's GNP adjusted for inflation grew by approximately 9 percent per year. During the same period, the income of the typical Japanese family adjusted for inflation almost doubled every eight years.

This phenomenal performance is even more remarkable when we consider the economic base from which Japan operates. The

The Japanese have gained worldwide markets for products such as cameras, cars, and electronic equipment. Here, a Japanese child in traditional dress takes pictures at a national festival.

Many Japanese factories benefit from having the latest in equipment and technology. The Japanese were pioneers in the use of robots.

land area of Japan is smaller than the state of California but its population is approximately one half as large as that of the entire United States. Furthermore, Japan has limited natural resources and has to import most of its petroleum. Given these circumstances, how do we explain Japan's phenomenal success? There are a number of factors underlying the success of Japan's economy. Although it is basically a capitalist market economy, it differs from the economy of the United States in a number of important respects.

Labor–Management Relations

The relationship between employees and employers in Japan is very different from that in the United States and most other market economies. Most Japanese workers are intensely loyal to their employers, and they take great pride in the quality of their work. In many Japanese factories, workers and managers stand side by side at the beginning of each shift and sing a company song that reflects their pride in the company.

This close relationship between employees and employers is reflected by the fact that many Japanese firms and employees make a **lifetime employment commitment** to one another. After a brief probationary period (usually less than one year), employees are guaranteed continued employment until retirement age, and workers usually do not leave one company for another. Given this arrangement, employees know that their future depends on the future of their company, and they are motivated to work hard so that the company will prosper.

Government and Business Relations

The government plays an important role in coordinating economic activity in Japan. The Ministry of International Trade and Industry (MITI), a powerful government agency, regulates all Japanese business firms and decides in broad terms the direction in which each industry should proceed. For example, because building a steel industry was one of Japan's most important postwar priorities, MITI encouraged Japanese banks to supply the money to buy the equipment and technology needed to establish such an industry. Low interest rates, tax incentives, and other forms of financial privileges also were given to the steel industry.

Taxation, Savings, and Investment

In Japan, employers provide many of the services that government provides in most other market economies. For example, along with the lifetime employment commitment, many firms also provide employees with free medical care, low-cost housing, and subsidized meals. Because of this policy, Japan does not have a comprehensive Social Security system such as that of the United States. In addition, Japan engages in only limited military spending. As a result of these factors, taxes are much lower in Japan than in most other market economies. Furthermore, because of the high rate of economic growth, Japan has been able to reduce the rates of both personal and corporate income taxes in almost every year since 1950.

The savings rate in Japan is the highest in the world. This is partly the result of the tax system. Interest income from small savings deposits is exempt from the personal income tax, and an individual can set up several savings accounts in the names of family members so that each can get the maximum tax-free interest. In addition, income from stock dividends is taxed at a much lower rate than most other income.

Japan also has a very high investment rate, with the major share of corporate profits being reinvested in new capital goods. The government provides special tax incentives to encourage investment, especially in key industries. The share of Japan's GNP going for investment is much higher than that of other industrial market economies, and this high investment rate is a major factor in Japan's high rate of economic growth.

Productivity

Labor productivity (output per worker) growth has been much higher in Japan in recent years than in most other industrial countries. Since 1960, the annual rate of productivity growth in Japan has averaged approximately three times that of the United States. The high level of investment in capital goods is a major factor contributing to this productivity growth. As Japan has added more and more capital goods, such as industrial robots, the output per worker has continued to rise. Another major factor has

Some Japanese employers arrange vacation tours for their workers in addition to providing other work and health benefits.

been the high level of investment in the training and retraining of workers. Since most workers are hired with the idea that they will continue to work for a company until retirement, employers find it profitable to invest heavily and continuously in on-the-job training and retraining. Still another factor contributing to Japan's high productivity growth is the fact that in the past Japan was able to borrow technology and production methods from the more advanced countries, including the United States. However, because Japanese industry is now as modern as that of other industrial countries, it cannot continue to make large gains in this way. For this reason, many economists believe that Japan's rate of productivity growth will decline somewhat in the future.

Check Your Understanding

1. Why is the performance of the Japanese economy since 1950 often referred to as the "Japanese miracle"?

2. How does the relationship between employees and employers in Japan differ from that in the United States?

3. What role does the government play in the Japanese economy?

4. How do taxes in Japan compare with those of other market economies? How do the savings and investment rates compare with those of other countires?

5. Why has productivity growth in Japan been so high in the past? Why do some economists believe it will decline in the future?

The Developing Nations

In many nations of the world, people face a constant struggle with poverty, hunger, and sometimes starvation. These nations usually are referred to as the developing nations or, more commonly, the **less developed countries (LDCs).** Approximately three fourths of the world's people live in such countries today. The remainder of this chapter will be devoted to a look at the problems facing these countries. Let us begin by examining the characteristics of the less developed countries.

Characteristics of Less Developed Countries

Like the developed countries, the less developed countries are different from each other in many respects. For example, the political system, the economic system, and the quantity and quality of productive resources vary from country to country. Yet most of the less developed countries share a set of common characteristics.

Poverty levels of income The per capita (per person) income level of most less developed countries is so low that poverty and hunger are widespread. More than two billion people live in countries with an average GNP of less than $500 per person, compared to more than $14,000 per person in the United States. Many of these people live continuously on the margin of bare survival, and any interruption in the scarce food supply can lead to mass starvation. In 1984, Africa suffered the worst famine in its history as a result of a severe drought that spread across much of the continent. Nearly 30 countries were officially listed as "hungry," and experts warned that in some of these countries whole populations faced possible extinction. By late 1984, when the news media in the United States and other advanced countries began to devote extensive coverage to the mass hunger and starvation, an estimated 200,000 people

In less developed countries, herders and subsistence farmers are largely self-sufficient and require few goods from outside their local areas.

already had died of starvation in Mozambique. In Ethiopia, one of the hardest hit countries, the famine had killed an estimated 300,000 people, and some experts estimated that as many as one million more might perish before the disaster was over.

Predominantly agricultural economies Nearly two thirds of the work force of most less developed countries are employed in agriculture, as compared with less than 4 percent in the United States. In addition, most families in the less developed countries raise their own food, make most of their own clothing, and construct their own shelter. Thus, the specialization and exchange of goods that are so important in the advanced nations are either uncommon or nonexistent in many less developed countries.

Rapid population growth The population of most of the less developed countries is growing much faster than that of most developed countries. For example, the population of Kenya has been growing at an annual rate of 3.8 percent, compared to a rate of less than 1 percent in the United States. If this rate continues, Kenya will double its population in 19 years. Since the population is growing faster than the food supply in many less developed nations, survival will become more and more difficult.

Unequal income distribution In addition to having a low per capita income, many of the less developed countries have a very distorted income distribution pattern. In many countries, a relatively small group of people own much of the nation's wealth and receive a substantial portion of the income. They often control the government and oppose changes that would harm their economic interests. In contrast, the majority of the people often have little political power, own very little of the nation's wealth, and receive a relatively small share of the nation's income.

Poor health care and educational facilities In many parts of most less developed countries, physicians and hospitals are unavailable. In such areas, disease often runs rampant and many people die of diseases and illnesses that might have been prevented if medical services were available. Similarly, many citizens of these countries have no opportunity for formal schooling. In some nations, fewer than one third of the adults can read and write.

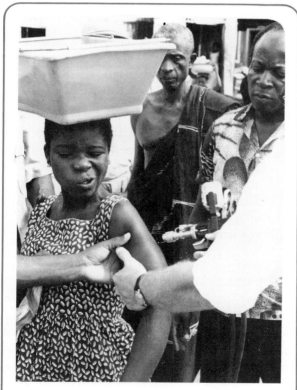

Mass vaccinations by both national and international organizations are an important method of trying to improve health conditions in less developed countries.

Special Problems of the Developing Countries

There is no single or easy way for a less developed country to progress toward the status of a developed country. However, there are a number of specific problems that must be overcome in order for economic development to take place.

The need for agricultural development Most economists believe that an important first step in the development of most less developed countries must be increased efficiency in agriculture. In addition, a surplus of agricultural products is needed to provide raw materials for manufacturing and to earn foreign exchange through exports. Increased efficiency in agriculture can lead to a surplus of output over and beyond what the agricultural sector consumes. This makes labor and raw materials available for manufacturing.

Many economists also believe that land reform is absolutely essential to agricultural development. In many of the less developed countries, the land is owned by a few rich families but farmed by many poor families. Advocates of land reform argue that land ownership by those who actually farm the land leads to increased incentives to maximize farm production. However, land reform alone will not solve the agricultural problems. In fact, studies have shown that if the land is fragmented into too many small units, it can cause a decrease in efficiency because the land units become too small to keep the farmer-owners fully employed. Thus, any land reform must be accompanied by new farming techniques, such as irrigation systems, fertilization programs, and improved plant strains.

The need to escape the "population trap" In order for a country to achieve an improved lifestyle for its people, the GNP must grow faster than the population; otherwise, any growth in the GNP is offset by the increasing population and the nation will not make any economic progress. A number of countries, including China and India, have instituted family-planning

Investment in capital goods such as this mining equipment is a basic need for economic development.

programs to help escape the "population trap." However, such programs often conflict with local social and religious traditions, and it is often difficult to implement them. For example, many people in developing countries believe that a large family will assure that someone will be available to care for them in old age. As a result, they try to have as many children as possible.

The need for investment in capital goods   One of the most urgent needs of the less developed countries is increased capital goods. The needs range from large irrigation dams and electrical generating plants to simple hand tools, such as shovels and hoes. Aside from such major projects as irrigation dams, electrical generating plants, and transportation systems, many of the most urgent needs are for small items that are relatively inexpensive by American standards. For example, such simple tools as steel plows that can be pulled by horses or oxen can make a

sizable difference to some nations. Since most of the less developed countries have an abundance of labor, investing in many simple farm tools that can be combined with that labor can yield larger returns than investing in a few large farm tractors and other complex machines that will replace some workers and be difficult for other workers to operate and maintain.

The need for investment in human resources   Most less developed countries have a surplus of unskilled workers and a critical shortage of skilled workers. Technical education and on-the-job training in such fields as agriculture, commerce, industry, and construction are absolutely essential to development.

Many less developed countries send their most gifted young people to developed nations for advanced education. Although this is a practical way to gain expertise in many essential fields, it does have one major drawback. Some of these talented young people decide to remain in the developed nations rather than return to their home countries where they are so desperately needed. Because of this problem, some experts believe that the less developed countries should have foreign experts train their young people at home instead of sending them abroad.

The quality of a nation's labor force depends on the health of the workers as well as the level of education. The poor health of workers can result in many lost workdays. Thus, in addition to education, less developed countries need to invest in health programs to reduce disease.

Foreign Aid

The poverty of most less developed nations makes it impossible for them to finance the needed investment in capital goods and human resources without foreign assistance. The cost of power facilities, transportation systems, factories, education, public health, and so forth are astronomical when compared to the meager savings that most less developed countries are able to accumulate. Thus, they must seek foreign funds in the form of either private foreign investment or aid from foreign nations.

Foreign aid can take the form of loans, outright grants of money, or direct technical assistance. One important source of foreign aid is the International Bank for Reconstruction and Development, or the **World Bank,** as it is popularly called. The World Bank, a specialized agency of the United Nations, was created in 1944 and began operations in 1946. Its purpose was to provide loans for postwar reconstruction and to promote development of poorer countries. The chief function of the World Bank today is to finance basic development projects such as dams, communication and transportation facilities, and health programs. It insures, or guarantees, private loans to the developing countries; and when private loans are not available, it makes direct loans.

The United States and several other nations also provide foreign aid to the less developed countries. Some of this aid, especially to the poorer nations, is in the form of outright grants and/or direct technical assistance. The remainder is in the form of long-term loans, usually at low interest rates. Foreign aid has long been a source of much controversy in this country. Some critics charge that too often the foreign aid is in the form of military assistance to nations friendly to the United States instead of in a form that will help the poor nations achieve economic development. Others charge that foreign aid dollars are not always spent wisely by recipient nations. Some feel that the United States should use the foreign aid dollars to reduce poverty in this country, while others argue that as an affluent nation the United States has a moral obligation to do more to reduce hunger in the poorer nations of the world. There probably will never be agreement over the proper role of the United States in helping the less developed countries of the world. However, there is general agreement among experts that many of the less developed countries will be unable to achieve much progress without some foreign assistance.

Check Your Understanding

1. List five characteristics of less developed countries.

2. What kinds of special problems must the less developed countries overcome in order for economic development to take place?

3. Why is foreign aid necessary for economic development to take place in most less developed countries? What are the sources of foreign aid?

CAREERS: Peace Corps Worker

Peace Corps workers help people in developing countries improve their living and working conditions. They serve only in countries that have asked for them; and at present there are about 5,000 men and women working in 60 countries, including countries in Africa, Asia, Latin America, and on various islands in the Pacific Ocean.

Peace Corps workers live with the people they help. They teach these people technical skills as well as provide them with nutrition and health care information. Some Peace Corps volunteers work in teacher training schools and technical institutes. Others work on community projects, such as those developed to build hospitals, schools, roads, and bridges, or to vaccinate communities against disease. Those who work on such projects teach as they work. For example, carpenters teach construction skills as they help build schools and other community facilities, and agricultural workers teach improved farming techniques that will increase food production as they work on farms.

To qualify for service in the Peace Corps, a person must be an American citizen and must be at least 18 years old. Potential Peace Corps workers must be dedicated individuals who can adapt to cultures and living conditions very different from those in the United States. Most of those selected are college graduates, but the Peace Corps does not require applicants to have college training. Once accepted into the Peace Corps, volunteers receive 8 to 14 weeks of training, which usually is conducted in the host country. The training program includes study of the culture, history, and language of the country in which the volunteers will serve, as well as technical training for their specific assignments. Volunteers usually serve for two years. During this period, they receive an allowance for living costs and at the end of the period they receive a small payment ($175) for each month of service completed.

Chapter Highlights

1   Economies are often classified as being examples of capitalism, democratic socialism, or authoritarian socialism. Capitalism is a form of economic organization in which the means of production are privately owned. Under democratic socialism, the government owns some major industries and individuals own the rest. Under authoritarian socialism, the government controls most of the means of production.

2   The origins of modern socialism date back to problems resulting from the Industrial Revolution during the early 1800s. During this period, some social critics advocated socialism as a means of attaining economic and social equality. The most influential of these critics was a German economic historian and social philosopher named Karl Marx.

3   Marx saw capitalism as a struggle between the capitalists and the workers. He urged the workers to rise up and overthrow capitalism and replace it with a classless society in which the people as a whole owned everything. Marx's ideas were the inspiration that led to the development of what is called communism.

4   After the 1917 Russian Revolution, one of its leaders, Vladimir Lenin, set up a new government controlled by the Communist Party. When Lenin died in 1924, Joseph Stalin came to power in the Soviet Union. He took over almost complete control of the economy, including ownership of property, and in 1928 he introduced the first of many Five-Year Plans, which were intended to stimulate economic growth and to industrialize the nation.

5   The Soviet economy today is strictly controlled by the government, which is controlled by the Communist Party. The government engages in elaborate planning and gives each business firm detailed instructions about what to produce and how much to produce. The three types of agricultural production units in the Soviet Union are state farms, collective farms, and private plots. Although private plots account for a very small portion of the total cultivated land, they account for a substantial portion of the production of certain farm products.

6   Bulgaria, Czechoslovakia, East Germany, Hungary, Poland, and Romania are members of the Council for Mutual Economic Assistance (COMECON) and are closely allied with the Soviet Union. Although the economies of these nations originally were patterned after that of the Soviet Union, over time they have taken on some individual characteristics.

7   The Communist government of The People's Republic of China was formed in 1949 after the Communists seized power from the Nationalist Chinese government. There has been a great deal of instability in China's economic policies, and the economy was damaged by both the Great Leap Forward and the Cultural Revolution. Overall, the Chinese political and economic systems are similar to those of the Soviet Union. However, in 1984 China announced that beginning in 1985 Chinese factories would operate under a new system where supply and demand would determine economic planning.

8   Sweden is often considered an example of democratic socialism. The government owns some major industries and the rest are privately owned. Sweden is often referred to as a welfare state because of its extensive government social programs.

9   Japan currently has the third largest economy in the world. Most Japanese workers are intensely loyal to their employers, and many Japanese firms make a lifetime employment commitment to their employees. The government plays an important role in coordinating economic activity in Japan. Taxes are much lower in Japan than in most other market economies, while savings and investment rates are high. In addition, in recent years labor productivity growth has been much higher in Japan than in most other industrial countries.

10 In many nations of the world, people face a constant struggle with poverty, hunger, and sometimes starvation. Approximately three fourths of the world's people live in less developed countries. Characteristics of less developed countries include poverty levels of income, predominantly agricultural economies, rapid population growth, unequal income distribution, and poor health care and educational facilities.

11 Special problems facing the less developed countries include the need for agricultural development, the need to escape the "population trap," the need for investment in capital goods, and the need for investment in human resources. Less developed countries receive foreign aid from the World Bank, the United States, and other countries.

Important Terms

Match each of the following terms with the correct definition:

socialism	less developed countries	World Bank
Gosplan	democratic socialism	Cultural Revolution
COMECON	collective farms	commune
proletariat	authoritarian socialism	communism
New Economic Policy	Great Leap Forward	state farms

1. A theoretical system characterized by a classless society.

2. A policy designed to drive China's economy forward at a very fast pace.

3. International Bank for Reconstruction and Development.

4. A political drive designed to free the Chinese from their traditional customs.

5. Large farms in the Soviet Union that are owned by the government and operated just like industrial firms.

6. The term Marx used to refer to the workers or the working class.

7. Those nations that share a common set of characteristics, including poverty levels of income, predominantly agricultural economies, rapid population growth, unequal income distribution, and poor health care and educational facilities.

8. The type of socialism in which the government controls most of the means of production.

9. A type of socialism under which the people take part in the decision-making process by electing government leaders.

10. The most comprehensive agricultural unit in China.

11. An organization of which Bulgaria, Czechoslovakia, East Germany, Hungary, Poland, Romania, and the Soviet Union are members.

12. Farms in the Soviet Union that are made up of large numbers of peasant families who combine their resources and talents to operate on a collective basis.

13. Lenin's economic policy.

14. The central planning agency of the Soviet Union.

15. A form of economic organization in which businesses are owned and operated by the government.

Extending Your Understanding

1. Why do you think that private farm plots in the Soviet Union account for such a large portion of the production of many farm products?

2. Why do you think the Chinese are planning to make greater use of market forces in future economic planning?

3. Do you think the United States should play any role in helping the less developed countries achieve economic development? Explain your answer.

Activities

1. Write to the embassies of some of the nations discussed in this chapter (your school or local librarian can help you find the addresses). Ask for information about each nation's economic activities. Based on the information you receive, prepare a short report. Include in your report a section on whether or not you would like to live in these nations and why.

2. Over a period of two weeks, clip newspaper articles on nations with economic systems different from that in the United States. Summarize these articles in a brief report. Present your report to the class.

Building Skills in Economics: Comparing Standards of Living

The standard of living differs from country to country. In some less developed countries of the world, the standard of living is low, with many people lacking the basic necessities. In many developed countries, much of the population has adequate food, clothing, and shelter; is educated; and has such luxury items as TVs, radios, and cars.

The table that follows presents selected statistics to help you compare the standard of living in various countries. Before studying the table, however, you should keep in mind that certain aspects of life cannot be translated into statistics. For example, in several of the authoritarian socialist countries, the people have very little control over certain aspects of their lives. In addition, numbers often reflect quantity and not quality. The fact that there are more physicians in the Soviet Union than there are in any of the other countries listed on the table does not necessarily mean that the quality of health care in the Soviet Union is better. Still, we can get a general idea of the standard of living by examining statistics. The questions will help you interpret the table.

Applying Economics Skills

1. Which country has the highest per capita income? What do the other statistics tell you about the standard of living in that country?
2. Which country has the lowest per capita income? What do the other statistics indicate about the quality of life there?
3. Which countries would you consider to be less developed? Why?

COMPARATIVE STANDARDS OF LIVING

Country	Population (in millions)	Per Capita Income	Percent of Labor Force in Agriculture	Life Expectancy at Birth	Physicians (per 100,000)	TVs in Use (in thousands)	Daily Newspaper Circulation (per 1,000)	Literacy Rate (%)
China	1,022	$ 566	74	68.0	87	15,000	74	75
Egypt	45.8	$ 560	50	55.9 m[a] 58.4 f	92	1,400	124	40
Ethiopia	31.2	$ 117	80	37.0 m 40.1 f	1	30	1	8
Great Britain	56	$ 7,216	1.5	70.2 m 76.2 f	153	22,600	419	99
India	730.5	$ 150	70	52.9 m 50.5 f	26	1,100	21	36
Japan	119.2	$ 8,460	11	73.2 m 78.4 f	131	62,900	569	99
Peru	18.6	$ 655	40	56.7 m 59.7 f	64	850	118	72
Poland	36.5	$ 4,670	27	66.0 m 74.4 f	178	8,100	287	98
Soviet Union	272.5	$ 2,600	20	64.0 m 74.0 f	346	80,000	312	99
Sweden	8.3	$14,821	5	73.1 m 79.1 f	178	3,200	578	99
Uganda	13.8	$ 240	90	48.3 m 51.7 f	20	72	2	25
United States	234.2	$11,675	4	70.8 m 78.2 f	176	80,000	312	99

[a] m = male; f = female

Source: *The World Almanac and Book of Facts*, 1985

UNIT 7

Personal
Economics

CHAPTER 17

GETTING THE MOST FOR YOUR MONEY

Some people always seem to have money problems. Although they may have good jobs, they never seem to have enough money to pay all the bills and buy all the things they want. Other people may earn the same or even less money but they seem to be able to make ends meet and to be financially secure.

How do some people live so well with their limited financial resources? The answer is that they manage their money more carefully than others do. For example, rather than owning and driving a full-sized car every day, they may rely on a compact car. Similarly, they may not replace their wardrobes every year or eat in restaurants several nights a week. By watching their money closely, they find that they can keep better control over where their money goes.

As you get older and your wants seem to increase, you too will find that you won't have enough money to buy everything you want. It's the same problem of scarcity that you learned about in the first chapter of this book. There's just not enough of everything to go around. As a result, you always will have to make difficult choices and do without some things in order to have other things.

There is, however, a great deal you can do to get the most satisfaction from your money. In this chapter we'll examine some of the strategies you should follow and the decisions you will have to make to manage your money well. We will discuss such topics as budgeting, renting or buying a home, buying a car, buying appliances and furniture, buying food and clothing, and buying insurance. Let us begin with a look at how you can develop your personal money-management plan.

Developing Your Personal Money–Management Plan

Using a spending plan based on expected income is called **budgeting.** The spending plan itself is called a **budget.** All businesses and units of government use budgets to guide them in their spending. Similarly, individuals and families who want to get the greatest possible satisfaction from their limited income should use a budget, too.

Reasons for Budgeting

Budgeting will not increase your income but it can help you get greater satisfaction from your spending. It helps you get what you want most, prevents you from spending beyond your income, often helps reduce conflicts, helps you keep track of expenditures, and puts you in control of your money.

Without a spending plan, many people buy things that will not give them much satisfaction over the long run. They often engage in **impulse buying,** which is unplanned buying that results from a sudden urge to have something. For example, they might walk into a store and buy an expensive coat, although they had planned to buy only an inexpensive pair of jeans. They then often find that they don't have enough money to buy the things they want most. Budgeting helps reduce impulse buying. If you don't have money budgeted for a specific item, you are not likely to buy it without at least considering whether the item would give you more satisfaction than other items included in your budget.

Budgeting also prevents you from spending beyond your income. Without a budget, it's very easy for a person to spend more money than he or she earns. Of course, this is possible only in the short run, but the long-term consequences of such actions—being unable to pay bills on time and not having enough money for

necessities—can be very painful. If you make a budget and follow it carefully, you can avoid spending beyond your means.

In addition, budgeting can help you keep track of expenditures and of how well you are progressing toward your goals. For example, if you are saving for a new car, your budget can help you calculate how long it will take to accumulate enough for the down payment. Budget records can be helpful also in calculating taxes and in determining when and from whom a particular item was purchased.

Finally, budgeting puts you in control of both your money and your life. Many people who do not plan their spending buy too many things on credit and get themselves deeply into debt. They then feel that they have lost control of their lives. Instead of working to earn money for future purchases, most of their income is going toward paying off their debts. Such a situation can greatly reduce the joy that one gets out of life, and in some cases the stress caused by unpaid debts can lead to severe depression. Budgeting enables you to stay in control of your purchases and to plan for the future.

Designing Your Budget

Designing a budget involves matching expenditures to income. The first step is to gather information on how you are currently spending your money. Once you have this information, you can design a plan that will enable you to adjust your spending to correspond to your income.

The monthly budget The best way to determine how you are currently spending your money is to keep a detailed record of all expenditures for an entire month. Table 17–1 presents a sample worksheet that could be used for this purpose. Column 1 shows a detailed list of budget items that would cover most of the expenditures of a typical family. Any expenditure not included in the list could be recorded in the miscellaneous category. Column 2 provides blanks for recording the actual monthly expenditure for each category.

TABLE 17–1: BUDGET WORKSHEET FOR USE IN DESIGNING A MONTHLY FAMILY BUDGET

Item	Actual Current Monthly Expenditure	Proposed Adjustments	Proposed Budget Allotment
FOOD			
Groceries	_____	_____	_____
Eating Out	_____	_____	_____
CLOTHING			
New Purchases	_____	_____	_____
Dry Cleaning/Laundry	_____	_____	_____
HOUSING			
Mortgage or Rent Payment	_____	_____	_____
Utilities	_____	_____	_____
Homeowner's Insurance	_____	_____	_____
Real Estate Taxes	_____	_____	_____
Maintenance	_____	_____	_____
TRANSPORTATION			
Auto Payments	_____	_____	_____
Auto Insurance	_____	_____	_____
Gas and Oil	_____	_____	_____
Maintenance	_____	_____	_____
MEDICAL CARE			
Health Insurance	_____	_____	_____
Medicine	_____	_____	_____
Doctor Bills	_____	_____	_____
Dental Care	_____	_____	_____
TAXES			
Federal Taxes	_____	_____	_____
State Taxes	_____	_____	_____
Local Taxes	_____	_____	_____
EDUCATION	_____	_____	_____
RECREATION	_____	_____	_____
MISCELLANEOUS	_____	_____	_____
TOTAL MONTHLY EXPENDITURE	_____		_____
PLUS MONTHLY SAVING	_____		_____
EQUALS MONTHLY INCOME	_____		_____

Once a family has a record of their total spending for an entire month, they can compare that total with their expected future income. If their total expenditures exceed their expected income, they will have to find ways of cutting their spending. Even if their total spending is equal to or slightly below their expected income, they still will have to reduce their spending in order to save at least enough money to provide for emergencies. Most experts believe that a family should have a minimum of two months' income saved for such emergencies as loss of job, unexpected illness, or major auto repairs. These savings are in addition to the money set aside for such specific goals as a down payment on a house or a car.

Column 3 of Table 17–1 can be used to record proposed adjustments to the amount a family is currently spending for each item. They may find it necessary to reduce spending for some items and increase spending for other items. For example, a family's average monthly utility bills may be higher in certain months than in others. Allowances need to be made also for any expenses that were not included in the month's expenses. For example, real estate taxes and homeowners' insurance may be paid in only one or two annual installments. If this is the case, a family will need to set aside money for these items each month so that they will be able to pay these bills when they come due. Once a family has given careful consideration to each item and made sufficient adjustments to cover all items, they are ready to record their proposed monthly budget allotment for each item in Column 4.

The annual budget and long-term planning A monthly budget can be used to construct an annual budget. If a family has provided for all of its expenditures in their monthly budget and if their estimated monthly expenses are the same each month, their annual budget will simply consist of the monthly budget multiplied by 12. However, if they have much higher expenses in some months than others, they may want to draw up a detailed annual budget reflecting these variations. For example, they may be planning a major vacation trip sometime during the coming year. They can budget for this expenditure by setting aside a specific amount each month or by planning to save the money during certain months when some of their other monthly expenditures are lower than normal.

In addition to planning their spending for an entire year at a time, a family should give some consideration to long-term goals. For example, they may want to save money toward a down payment on a house. What will they do with the extra money they will have when some of their loans are paid off? What will they do with any extra money they might have saved? By establishing long-term goals and planning spending so that these goals can be achieved, they should be able to get more satisfaction from their limited income.

Check Your Understanding

1. List five good reasons for budgeting your money.

2. What is impulse buying? How does it prevent people from getting what they want most?

3. List the steps involved in preparing a monthly budget. Why is it also important to prepare an annual budget and to do long-term planning?

Housing

Sooner or later you will have to make important decisions about housing. You will have to decide which type of housing you wish to live in, whether to buy or to rent, and whether you should buy or rent a house or an apartment. If you decide to *buy* a home, you also will have to decide how to finance it. First, let us look at the various types of housing available to people in this country.

Types of Housing

There are five basic types of housing. They are single-family homes, rental apartments, cooperatives, condominiums, and mobile homes. Each has its own unique features that make it suitable for different individuals and families.

Single-family homes have traditionally been the most popular choice of housing for Americans. Such homes are separated from other houses on either side and have at least a small front or back yard. These homes provide more privacy and more living space both inside and outside than apartments. However, single-family homes also require considerable maintenance, which could amount to substantial expenditures of time and money. In addition, in recent years, rising housing costs have made it increasingly difficult for many families to afford single-family homes. Because of these factors, increasing numbers of Americans have been turning to other housing options.

Rental apartments provide a broader selection of living arrangements than any other type of housing. Apartments can be small and relatively inexpensive, making them affordable for young single persons with limited incomes as well as for retired persons. On the other hand, many apartments are sufficiently large for families, and high-rise apartment buildings in large cities often enable residents to live close to their jobs and to shopping facilities and cultural events. Also, many large apartment buildings provide recreational facilities and other special benefits for residents.

Cooperatives are apartment buildings or groups of dwellings that are owned by a non-profit corporation and managed by a board of directors elected by the residents. The residents of the cooperative buy shares of stock in the building proportional to the share of living space they occupy. For example, if a resident's apartment consists of 5 percent of the total living space in the building, the resident will buy shares of stock equal to 5 percent of the value of the entire building. Because cooperatives are nonprofit, the cost of living in a cooperative apartment is usually less than in a comparable rental apartment.

Condominiums are apartment buildings or groups of dwellings in which each individual housing unit is privately owned. Ownership of all common areas such as grounds, corridors, lobbies, and recreational facilities is shared by the owners of the individual units who also pay a monthly fee to maintain these areas. This fee is in addition to the cost of owning the units. Yet even with these expenses, condominiums often are less expensive than single-family homes because they usually are smaller and share common elements.

Mobile homes have become increasingly popular in recent years, and they account for approximately one third of all new homes. A primary reason for their popularity is the fact that their cost per square foot of living space is less than half that of a conventional house. Buyers of mobile homes usually rent a space in a mobile-home park as a permanent parking space for their home. Their monthly rental fee generally covers grounds maintenance, recreational and laundry facilities, property tax, and sometimes some utilities. Despite their name, most mobile homes are not very mobile. Once installed, large mobile homes are difficult and expensive to relocate, and thus more than 90 percent of mobile homes are mobile only once—when they are transported from the factory to their permanent parking space.

Renting Versus Buying

You may not have the luxury of choosing between renting and buying for your first home. Unless you have sufficient funds for a down payment on a house, condominium, or mobile home, your only option is to rent. However, in a few years you may reach the point where you can choose between renting and buying. When you reach that point, which option should you choose? There is no easy answer to this question. Both options have their advantages and disadvantages.

Advantages and disadvantages of renting Perhaps the most important advantage of renting is that no major cash outlay is required. A tenant usually is required to pay the first month's rent in advance as well as a refundable deposit equal to one or two months' rent to cover possible property damage by the tenant. However, this is a small amount of money compared to what is usually required for a down payment on a home. A second important advantage of renting is the flexibility it allows the tenant. If tenants need to move because of a job transfer, the need

for larger living accommodations, or other reasons, they usually can move more easily than homeowners who first must sell their homes. In addition, many apartments are at least partly furnished. This is an important advantage for young people who cannot afford to buy all of their own furniture and appliances. Still another advantage of renting is the freedom from home-repair and maintenance chores.

On the negative side, tenants have no property rights. They usually cannot make any changes, such as painting the interior a different color, without the permission of the owner. Also, the owner may refuse to make prompt repairs, thus creating problems and inconveniences for tenants. In addition, owners may sometimes raise rents when leases on rentals are renewed. Furthermore, there are no financial breaks for tenants. Homeowners can deduct the cost of real estate taxes and interest on home loans from their income when paying federal income taxes; and over the years as they make their monthly payments, they build up equity (the value of the home minus what is still owed on it) in their homes. None of these advantages are available to renters.

Many mobile homes are bought complete with furniture, drapes, and carpeting. Once installed in a mobile-home park, a unit like this one will probably be left in place.

Advantages and disadvantages of buying As we have just mentioned, real estate taxes and interest on home loans are tax deductible for homeowners, and part of each month's home mortgage payment adds to the homeowner's equity in his or her house. In addition, owning a home is usually a good financial investment. During periods of high inflation, the value of real estate usually rises as fast or faster than prices in general. However, the most attractive advantage of home ownership may be the feeling of pride and independence it gives the homeowner. Homeowners can remodel and redecorate to suit themselves, and they don't have to worry about waiting for repairs or being told to move out.

One of the biggest disadvantages of home ownership is that it can be very expensive. In addition to the substantial down payment and sizable monthly payments that are usually required, the homeowner also must pay real estate taxes and homeowners' insurance. Upkeep on a home also can be quite expensive both in terms of money and time. Moreover, home ownership greatly restricts mobility. If homeowners want to move, they usually must sell their homes first. During certain times and in certain locations, it may take months to find a buyer.

Renting Housing

Now that we have examined the various types of housing and discussed the pros and cons of both renting and buying, let us briefly examine some of the things you should consider when selecting a specific housing unit to rent.

Families or individuals must weigh the advantages and disadvantages of renting or buying a home. Today, many Americans are buying or renting in cluster housing complexes such as this one.

Whether you decide to rent an apartment or a house, there are certain factors that you should consider before entering into a rental agreement: Is the unit the right size for your needs? Is the unit close to your job and to shopping facilities? Is the unit in good condition? Who takes care of repairs? Is there someone you can easily contact when problems arise? Who pays for utilities? Is the unit in a high crime area? What kind of security measures are available? Are there safe fire exits? Are children and pets allowed? Are there any rules and regulations that will cause a problem for you?

After you have considered each of these factors and feel that a particular housing unit meets your needs, you are ready to sign a rental agreement. There are two basic kinds of rental agreements: month-to-month agreements and leases. With a month-to-month agreement, the owner can change the rental fee and other terms of the agreement at the end of any month. However, such an agreement gives you more flexibility if you wish to move. You may have to give the owner some advance notice but you don't have to worry about breaking a lease, which can be costly. In contrast, a lease fixes the rent payment and other terms of the agreement for a specific time period, usually at least one year. Generally, a lease provides the tenant with more budgetary security than a month-to-month agreement, but most leases are written to protect the owner. Before signing any lease, you should read it carefully to see if there are any provisions with which you will have difficulty complying. For example, if the lease prohibits having pets, you could be forced to move for failing to comply with that provision.

Buying Housing

Buying a home is a much larger undertaking than renting. It usually involves a substantial financial commitment and, as we already have mentioned, often restricts mobility. Therefore, careful consideration should be given to selecting the right home and the right kind of financing.

Selecting your home Many of the considerations listed above for selecting a rental unit apply to selecting a home for purchase as well. Because as owner you'll have to pay for any repairs, you will want to make sure that the dwelling is structurally sound and that there are no major problems with the plumbing and electrical wiring. Location is even more important when purchasing a home than when renting because if you decide to move, location can play a major role in your home's resale value. Therefore, you will want to check the zoning regulations to make sure that a business or industrial unit that could reduce the value of your home cannot be constructed nearby.

In addition, before selecting a specific home, you will need to give careful consideration to the question of how much you can afford to spend for housing. A careful examination of your budget will help you answer this question. There are also some general rules that you can use as a guide. One rule is that total housing costs—loan payments, taxes, insurance, utilities, and maintenance—should not exceed 40 percent of your annual budget if other debts are low. (If you have other substantial debts, then your total housing expenditures should be considerably less.) Another rule is that the purchase price of a home should not be more than 2½ times as much as a household's annual income. For example, if the total income is $30,000, more than $75,000 should not be spent on a home.

Financing your home In order to buy a home, you usually will need a down payment of 10 to 20 percent of the purchase price, and you will have to obtain a mortgage loan to finance the balance. A **mortgage loan** is a long-term loan that will be repaid in many installments, and it gives the lender a claim (mortgage) against your home. This means that if you do not or cannot repay the loan, the lender can take your home in place of the money you owe. Most mortgage loans are obtained from savings and loan associations, savings banks, or commercial banks.

Most home buyers shop for mortgages much as they do when making other large purchases. They look for the home mortgage that best meets their needs.

There are several different types of home mortgage loans. Let us examine the four most common types.

A **standard fixed-rate mortgage** is one in which the monthly payment and the interest rate remain at one level for the lifetime of the loan, which is usually 25 or 30 years. Until recently, this was the only type of mortgage loan that lenders could make. However, changes in state and federal laws have allowed the creation of alternative types of loans, such as those described below.

An **adjustable-rate mortgage** is one in which the interest rate for the loan can rise or fall with interest rates in general throughout the period of the loan. Monthly payments also can change along with the interest rate. However, there are usually limits on how much and how often interest rates and payments can change.

A **graduated-payment mortgage** is one with a fixed interest rate and variable monthly payments. With such a loan, monthly payments start out low and gradually increase over a period of years. During the early years, the borrower is in effect borrowing the difference between what would be paid with a standard fixed-rate mortgage and what he or she actually is paying. However, over time this borrowed money is repaid with interest as the monthly payments increase. This type of loan is designed for people who expect their annual income to increase substantially over the long run.

A **flexible loan insurance program** is similar to a graduated-payment mortgage except that all or part of the down payment is deposited in an interest-earning account from which some money is withdrawn each month during the early years of the loan to supplement the borrower's low payment. Over the years, as the funds in the account are used up, the borrower's monthly payments gradually increase until the borrower is finally making full monthly payments.

The best type of mortgage loan for you will depend on both your individual circumstances and on the options available to you. In recent years, it has been increasingly difficult to obtain standard fixed-rate mortgage loans, and when they are available the interest rate is usually very high. When you are ready to obtain a mortgage loan, your best bet is to compare the loan options of all lending institutions in your area and then choose the one that best fits your individual needs.

Check Your Understanding

1. List and describe the five basic types of housing.

2. What are the advantages and disadvantages of renting housing? Of buying housing?

3. What are some of the factors you should consider when selecting a rental unit? Why is it important to read a rental lease carefully before signing it?

4. What factors should you consider when selecting a home to purchase?

5. Describe the four most common types of home mortgage loans.

Transportation

Transportation is an essential part of our mobile society, and the automobile plays a central role in the nation's transportation system. The United States, with only 5 percent of the world's population, has over half of the world's automobiles.

Owning and operating an automobile is a considerable expense. In addition to the cost of the car, there is the cost of insurance, taxes and licensing fees, parking fees, interest on auto loans, fuel, and maintenance. Moreover, unlike homes, a car usually depreciates, or loses value, during the time you own it. Table 17–2 gives the cost per mile of owning and operating five different-sized cars. It assumes that the cars were bought new, owned for 12 years, and driven 120,000 miles before being junked. The cost of a subcompact, for example, would be 18.9 cents per mile, which would come to $22,680 over the life of the car. These expenses make a car the second most expensive item that most consumers ever buy. Given these expenses, you should consider carefully whether you can afford to own a car. If you then decide to buy a car, you must decide whether it will be a new car or a used one.

Buying a New Car

Shopping for a new car can be even more costly than it should be if you are not careful. Some people pay hundreds of dollars more than they have to because they do not shop around. To avoid this pitfall, you should make a firm resolution not to buy a car, or even to decide on a particular make of car, until you have visited several dealers and looked at alternative makes, sizes, and styles. Tell the salespeople that you are thinking about buying a new car but are not yet ready to make a decision. Look at all the makes and styles, test drive the models that you are most interested in, ask each dealer to quote you a price, and then go home and give the

TABLE 17–2: ESTIMATED COST OF OWNING AND OPERATING AUTOMOBILES AND VANS IN 1982 WITH SUBURBAN BASE OF OPERATION (CENTS PER MILE)

Size	Depreciation	Maintenance	Gas and Oil	Garage, Parking, and Tolls	Insurance	Taxes	Total Cost
Subcompact (weighs less than 2,500 lbs. empty)	4.7	4.8	4.5	0.8	3.1	1.0	18.9
Compact (weighs less than 3,000 lbs. empty)	5.9	5.0	5.3	0.8	3.3	1.1	21.4
Midsize (weighs less than 3,500 lbs. empty)	6.2	5.6	6.6	0.8	3.3	1.3	23.8
Standard (weighs more than 3,500 lbs. empty)	7.7	6.0	7.3	0.8	3.3	1.5	26.6
Passenger Van (weighs less than 5,000 lbs. empty)	10.7	7.2	8.9	0.8	4.4	1.9	33.2

Source: *Cost of Owning Automobiles and Vans*, 1982

whole matter some careful thought. Don't be pressured into making a premature decision by some salesperson who tells you that the car you like most will soon be sold. If it is, you probably can find another one like it at another dealer. If not, you can have the dealer order one from the factory.

The most important thing is to get as much information as possible and then spend some time thinking about your needs and wants before making a final decision. Check consumer-oriented periodicals, such as *Consumer Reports*, which is published by Consumers Union of the United States, Inc., an independent, nonprofit organization that tests and rates vari-

ous products. *Consumer Reports* publishes an annual *Buying Guide* and usually reports on all new cars in its April issue. You also can ask friends and acquaintances who recently have bought new cars about how satisfied they are with their purchases. Determine the maximum amount you can afford to spend and don't allow a high-pressure salesperson to talk you into violating your budget guidelines. A general rule is that not more than 15 percent of your monthly income should be devoted to *total* transportation costs (car payments, auto insurance, fuel, maintenance, and so forth).

Once you have decided on the car you want, visit several dealers to see which will offer the best price. Don't ever pay the asking price without trying to negotiate a lower one. Most dealers allow themselves some bargaining room when they quote a price, and you usually can get a better deal than the initial offer. Also, many dealers tend to stock models with a lot of optional equipment. There is no point in paying extra for such things as power windows unless you really want those options. Shop for a car that has just the optional equipment that you need and want.

Buying a Used Car

The chances are good that your first car may be a used car—three out of every four cars sold for personal use in the United States are used. The biggest advantage of buying a used car is the cost. You can buy a used car for as little as a few hundred dollars, although you can spend several thousand dollars for a late-model car. As with anything else, you usually get what you pay for. There is always some risk when you buy a used car, and generally the older the car the greater the risk. If you buy an old, high-mileage car that turns out to have a bad engine, it could cost you more to repair it than the car is worth.

Usually, the best place to buy a used car is from a new-car dealer. New-car dealers usually offer for sale to the general public only the best of those cars that they take in on trades. They generally have these cars inspected by their service departments and often offer a limited warranty on them. These new-car dealers are concerned with their local reputations and usually will not knowingly sell a car that has major mechanical problems. The older trade-ins and those with suspected mechanical problems usually are sold in wholesale auto auctions and end up on the lots of used-car dealers, along with former taxis and police cars. Used-car dealers often offer cars at lower prices, but they often do not have their own service facilities and seldom offer a warranty. Of course, there are always exceptions. As with new cars, once you find a used car you want, don't hesitate to try to negotiate a lower price than what the dealer is asking.

Buyers of used cars take certain risks, but they are willing to do so because of the high cost of new cars.

Appliances and Furniture

Some of the most important and difficult choices that consumers have to make involve the purchase of appliances and furniture. These items fall into the category of **durable consumer goods** because they usually last for several years. Because these items are purchased less often than **nondurable consumer goods,** such as food and clothing, most consumers have little experience in shopping for them and often have difficulty recognizing quality. Yet, mistakes in the selection of durable goods can be very costly both in terms of money and in terms of consumer dissatisfaction.

The best way to avoid such mistakes is to comparison shop in a number of stores and give a lot of thought to your needs and wants before making a final decision. When buying a major appliance, you should consider whether your needs are likely to change in the future. For example, a refrigerator that might be large enough for you now might not be large enough in five years. It also is important to make sure you are buying the make and model you really want, or you may either regret your choice for many years or end up trading it in at a loss to buy the model you really wanted in the first place. Another important consideration is the availability of service for the appliance. It is sometimes better to purchase an appliance from a reputable local dealer who provides repair service, even if it means paying a little more than you would have to pay at a discount store that does not have a service department.

Shopping for furniture is usually more difficult than shopping for appliances. There are only a few major brands of appliances, and most of them have good performance records. Furniture is a different story. There is an enormous difference in the quality of furniture, and it is often difficult for the inexperienced shopper to recognize this difference. The types of wood and fabric used to manufacture furniture as well as the actual construction determine durability. Many young people with limited budgets are tempted to buy the cheapest furniture they can find. Often this "cheap" furniture turns out to be quite expensive in that it must be replaced years sooner than would have been the case with more expensive furniture. When shopping for furniture, it is wise to seek the advice of a trusted friend or an acquaintance who is a good judge of furniture quality.

Check Your Understanding

1. What are some of the costs involved in owning and operating a car?

2. What are some of the things you should keep in mind when shopping for a new car? When shopping for a used car?

3. What difficulties can you encounter when shopping for appliances and furniture?

4. What factors should you consider when selecting an appliance?

5. Why is shopping for furniture often more difficult than shopping for appliances?

Food and Clothing

Food and clothing are two of the most essential items purchased by consumers, and together they account for approximately 22 percent of the average consumer's total spending. Because they are so important in the budgets of most consumers, it is important for consumers to develop good shopping skills so that they get the most for their money. One of the best ways of getting the most for your money is to stick to your budget. Use a realistic figure when establishing your monthly budget allotment and then keep within the limit. It is very easy to engage in impulse buying, especially when you go shopping for food. Stores often create tempting displays and place cookies and candies near the cash register. However, if you make a list of the items you plan to buy before going to the store and buy only those items on your list, you can avoid spending more than you planned.

A second way of using your money wisely involves comparison shopping. Compare the prices of similar food and clothing items in different stores. Also, keep your eye out for advertised specials. Stores often run sales to attract shoppers and to clear out selected merchandise. However, always keep in mind that clothing sales often represent the efforts of retail stores to get rid of clothing that is going out of style or has already gone out of style. You also should recognize that there are limits to comparison shopping. If you go around to too many stores, your savings may be offset by the extra transportation costs and time required.

There are other specific factors to consider when shopping for food and clothing. Let us look at a few of them.

Shopping for Food

When shopping for food, you always should consider the type of food store you are shopping in, brand labels, and price comparisons. Each of these factors usually affects the price of your purchases.

In large supermarkets, consumers have many opportunities for comparison shopping among different brands.

Types of food stores There are basically three types of food stores: food supermarkets, discount food stores, and convenience stores. **Food supermarkets** carry a wide selection of most food items, including fresh produce, meat and dairy products, canned foods, and frozen foods. Because of the wide selection, most consumers are able to buy all of their needed food at such stores. There is, however, often a wide variation in the prices of various supermarkets in a community. By shopping regularly at several local supermarkets, a consumer can get a pretty good idea of which stores usually have the lowest prices.

Discount food stores, sometimes called warehouse food stores, usually sell food at lower prices than food supermarkets. However, they often do not carry a complete line of food items. Some sell only basic canned and packaged foods and carry only a few brands of these items. Also, some discount stores sell goods only by the case. Nevertheless, for consumers who can buy in large quantities, these stores can offer substantial savings on some items.

Convenience stores are plentiful in most large communities, and they are often open 24 hours a day. They carry only a limited selection of food items, and the prices of most items are much higher than in supermarkets. As the name implies, these stores offer convenience to consumers. They are open when most supermarkets are closed and often are in more convenient locations than supermarkets. However, consumers should avoid making major food purchases at such stores because of the higher prices.

In some areas there are **food co-ops.** These are nonprofit organizations created for the

Shoppers often use convenience stores near their homes to pick up a few last-minute items.

purpose of offering their members lower food prices. Co-ops often buy items in large quantities and pass along the savings to their members. However, they generally stock only certain items, and some of them are open only to those who belong to the co-op.

Brand labels Consumers often have a wide range of brands from which to choose. Most supermarkets offer both nationally advertised brands and less well-known regional brands. Many supermarkets also carry their own brands, which are produced exclusively for the supermarket chain. Nationally known brands are usually of high quality but they cost more than the regional and supermarket-chain brands. To save money, you might try some of the lower-priced brands. They often are produced by the same companies that make the nationally known products. If you don't like them, you always can switch back to the brands you had bought earlier.

In recent years, many supermarkets have begun to offer **generic brands** of some items. A generic brand has only the name of the product on the package. For example, generic sugar is simply labeled "sugar" with no company name. Generic foods often sell for as much as 10 to 40 percent less than national brands. Some generic products are of low quality. However, others may be comparable to more expensive brands. For example, generic sugar is often indistinguishable from the most expensive brands.

If you prefer to buy national brands, one way of getting the most for your money is to look for manufacturers' coupons in newspapers and magazines. These coupons can help to reduce your shopping bills, sometimes up to several dollars each week. To use coupons, all you have to do is buy the correct size of the product advertised and present the coupon to the store cashier. The cashier then will subtract the amount on the coupon from your bill.

Price comparisons Wise shoppers compare the price per unit of different brands and different-sized packages. Sometimes stores have unit pricing labels on the shelf that give the price of each item per serving, per ounce, per pint, per gram, and so forth. This is necessary because different brands are not always packaged in the same size containers, and it is often difficult to determine which size container of the same brand is the better buy without determing the unit price of the item. If your store doesn't offer unit pricing labels, a small pocket calculator can be very helpful in making such comparisons. Of course, the fact that a larger size package costs less per unit than a smaller container of the same item does not mean that the larger size is the better buy for you. If the item is perishable and it will spoil before you use it up, you are better off buying the smaller size package.

Shopping for Clothing

Shopping for clothing can be a very frustrating experience for people with a limited budget because they often cannot afford the kind of clothing they really want. Part of the problem is the fact that for most people clothing serves both a physical and a psychological need.

Clothing meets physical needs in that it is worn for protection against the weather. For example, warm sweaters and coats protect people's bodies from the cold, and boots help to keep feet dry. If meeting physical needs were the only objective in shopping for clothing, people would look for warm, durable clothes that would last for a long time. Moreover, once a person had purchased enough clothing to meet his or her physical needs, there would be no need to buy any more clothes until some of the clothing items became badly worn. However, meeting physical needs is not the only reason for buying clothes. For many people, meeting psychological needs is possibly more important when shopping for clothing.

Most people want variety in their clothing, and they want their clothes to help make them attractive. They also see clothing as a way to achieve status and self-esteem, and they feel insecure unless they are wearing clothing that is currently in style. Because clothing styles change so frequently, keeping up with current

Style, fit, and price are a few of the factors that shoppers take into account when they make decisions about buying new clothes.

fashions usually means buying new clothes each year. Since the psychological needs of people differ so much, it is difficult to establish general guidelines for shopping for clothing. If keeping up with current fashions is not extremely important to you, you will get more clothing for your money by buying more basic clothing designs that are attractive but do not change so frequently. However, if you feel you must always have up-to-date clothing styles, you will have to settle for fewer clothing items at any one time and/or cut back on spending for other things in order to have a larger clothing budget.

One factor you always should take into consideration is the manufacturer's recommendation for cleaning the item. The cost of dry cleaning can be very expensive, and a "bargain" might turn out not to be a bargain at all if the cost of cleaning the item will eventually amount to five times what you paid to purchase that item initially.

Check Your Understanding

1. What are two ways of getting the most for your money when shopping for food and clothing?

2. Describe the three basic types of food stores. What are food co-ops?

3. Why is it important to compare the prices of different brands? Why is it necessary to determine the unit price of food items when making price comparisons?

4. Clothing serves different kinds of needs. In what ways do these needs affect the way people shop for clothes?

Insurance

The chances are good that you will buy several different kinds of insurance during your lifetime. When you buy your first automobile, you'll have to buy automobile insurance. If you buy a home, the loan company will require you to buy homeowner's insurance. In addition, you'll probably buy life insurance and health insurance at some time in the future.

When you buy insurance, you are buying protection against certain risks. For a fee called a premium, insurance companies are willing to assume risks that you cannot afford to assume yourself. They can do this because not everyone who buys insurance will ever collect it. For example, although in many states all car owners must have insurance, only relatively few file a claim in any given year. In addition to providing a profit for the insurance companies, the money collected from all car owners is available to pay for any accident-related injuries or repairs that occurred in that year. In other words, the losses of a few are paid for by all of the other insured people who do not have losses. There are four basic types of insurance that you are most likely to buy.

Automobile Insurance

All states require that drivers of motor vehicles be financially responsible for any damage done by their vehicles. This means that if you are involved in an accident in which someone is injured or in which there is significant property damage, you must be able to pay for the damages. Because such damages can be very costly, most motorists must carry automobile insurance in order to be able to pay for them. In fact, many states require motorists to carry insurance. There are various kinds of automobile insurance you can buy.

Liability insurance pays for bodily injury and property damage in the case of accidents for which you are responsible (liable). Although a driver can be sued for any amount in the event of a serious accident, insurance companies put limits on the amount that they will pay. For example, your insurance policy might state that the limit of liability is $100,000/$300,000. This means that the insurance company will pay a maximum of $100,000 for a bodily injury to any one individual you may have injured and a maximum total of $300,000 for *all* individuals you may have injured.

Collision insurance pays for damages to your car. If you should severely damage your car in a collision, your insurance company will pay for the damages. However, most insurance policies require the policyholder to pay for a certain amount of the damages before the company begins to pay. This is called the **deductible** amount. For example, if you have $100 deductible collision insurance and you have a minor accident that does $300 worth of damage to your car, you will have to pay the first $100, and the insurance company will pay the remaining $200. Although no state laws require motorists to carry collision insurance, banks or other lenders probably will require you to carry collision insurance as a condition for obtaining a car loan.

In addition to liability and collision insurance, there are other risks against which you have the option of insuring your car. Comprehensive physical-damage insurance provides protection against such threats as fire, theft, natural disasters, and vandalism. Medical insurance covers medical expenses of the policyholder and his or her family resulting from an automobile accident. Uninsured-motorist insurance protects you in case you are injured in an accident in which the other driver is at fault but has no insurance to cover the damages.

In recent years, several states have enacted no-fault insurance laws. In these states, when there is an automobile accident, each driver's insurance company pays for his or her damages and medical bills regardless of who is at fault. The intent of no-fault insurance laws is to eliminate the costly procedure of having lawyers and courts determine who should pay for the damages and injuries resulting from automobile accidents.

Like anything else, it usually pays to compare the policies and rates of different insurance companies. Studies have shown that although most people believe that the rates of all insurance companies are about the same, in actuality many people could save a substantial amount by shopping for the best deal. No matter where you buy your automobile insurance, however, if you are a single male between the ages of 16 and 25, you will pay a higher insurance rate than any other group. This is because insurance companies classify drivers into different groups based on age, sex, and marital status; and then base the insurance rate on the average accident rate for each group. Because single males 16 to 25 years of age have the highest accident rate, they pay the highest insurance premiums.

Homeowner's Insurance

For most homeowners, their home represents the biggest investment they will ever make. It may take as long as 30 years to pay for a home, yet that home can be destroyed in 30 minutes by a fire or in 30 seconds by a tornado. Because most homeowners could not otherwise afford to replace their home if it were destroyed, they carry insurance to cover the value of the home and its contents. A homeowner's insurance policy is a comprehensive policy covering such hazards as fire, lightning, windstorms, explosions, theft, and liability. In the event of a loss, a homeowner's policy will pay either the value of the loss or the amount of the policy, whichever is lower. In other words, it doesn't do any good to carry more insurance on a home than the home is worth. For example, if you carry $75,000 in insurance on a home that is valued at $60,000, the insurance company will pay a maximum of only $60,000 in the event of a total loss. On the other hand, if you carry only $50,000 in insurance, that will be the maximum payment, even if you have a loss of $60,000. During periods of inflation, the value of most homes increases. Therefore, it is important for homeowners to increase their insurance coverage to keep pace with inflation. Some policies have a provision that automatically increases coverage and premiums during inflationary periods.

Health Insurance

Perhaps the greatest threat to the financial security of most families is the risk of a severe illness or injury. Even a short stay in a hospital can cost thousands of dollars, and an extended illness can wipe out a family's savings and result in enormous debts. Because, on the average, about one out of every six Americans is hospitalized each year, most Americans feel that they cannot afford to take the risk of having an illness or injury wipe them out financially. To protect themselves, they carry health insurance that will help to pay for medical bills. In 1981, nearly 90 percent of all Americans had some form of private health insurance. Although there are many insurance companies and various types of health insurance coverage, there are three basic categories of health-care coverage.

Basic-coverage insurance covers the costs of ordinary short-term hospital care, including a daily room allowance, routine nursing care, x-rays, laboratory tests, and drugs and other medicines. It also covers the cost of surgery and other doctors' services associated with an illness. Usually, the patient must pay the first $100 or $200 (the deductible amount) of the bill and may have to pay a percentage of the remaining costs, depending on the specific coverage. Because there is usually a stipulated maximum amount that will be paid for a single illness, basic coverage benefits may not be sufficient to cover a severe, prolonged illness.

Major medical-expense insurance is designed to supplement basic-coverage insurance in order to protect the policyholder from large, unpredictable medical expenses. It usually covers a broader number of accidents and illnesses than basic coverage, including mental illness. The policyholder usually must pay an initial deductible amount plus a small percentage (often 15 or 20 percent) of total costs beyond the deductible. The major purpose of major medical-expense insurance is to protect the policyholder against catastrophic illness. Some policies stipulate a limited maximum coverage ranging from $100,000 to $1,000,000. However, many policies provide unlimited benefits.

Payment of medical bills alone is not sufficient to prevent financial disaster during a prolonged illness. There is also a need for an alternative source of income. A third kind of healthcare coverage—**disability income insurance**—provides cash benefits to the policyholder for living expenses if the policyholder is unable to work. Although the cash benefits are usually only about one half to two thirds of the policyholder's normal income, the money is nontaxable and thus the net income is a substantial portion of the policyholder's normal take-home pay.

Life Insurance

Life insurance is purchased to protect dependents of the policyholder in the event of his or her death. For example, if a parent with small children should die suddenly, his or her family might suffer substantial financial hardship. Life insurance provides a means of reducing this risk. Some types of life insurance also can enable the policyholder to accumulate some savings while at the same time protecting dependents. There are four basic types of life insurance.

Term insurance, which is the simplest form of life insurance, insures the life of the policyholder for a specific period of time, usually for one to five years. If the policyholder should die during that period, the insurance company would pay his or her beneficiaries, or heirs, the full amount of the policy in one lump sum. If the policyholder does not die during the period,

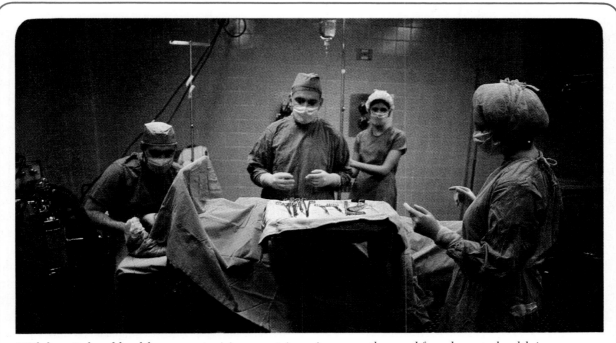

With hospital and health care costs rising, most Americans see the need for adequate health insurance. The cost of surgery, for example, mounts up when the patient receives bills for the hospital operating room, surgeon, anesthesiologist, nurses, medication, and post-operative care.

the insurance company pays nothing. Many term-insurance policies guarantee the policy-holder the right to renew the policy at the end of each term without a physical examination. Thus, a person can carry term insurance for many years by simply renewing the policy each time it expires. Of course, the premium rises as the policyholder becomes older.

The greatest advantage of term life insurance is that it offers inexpensive coverage. During the early years of a person's life, he or she can carry enough term insurance to pay off the home mortgage and leave some money for living expenses for dependents in the event of death. As the policyholder becomes older and has fewer financial obligations, some or all of the term insurance can be allowed to expire. Many experts recommend term insurance because most people cannot afford to buy enough of other types of life insurance to protect their families adequately.

Whole life insurance offers a combination of protection plus savings. Unlike term insurance, whole life insurance builds up a cash surrender value over the years. The policyholder can obtain this cash surrender value by canceling the policy. He or she also can borrow an amount equal to the cash surrender value at an interest rate that is usually much lower than is available at banks. The premium for whole life insurance is much higher than for term insurance but the premium does not rise as the policyholder becomes older. The advantage of whole life insurance is that it provides both protection and savings.

Limited payment life insurance is similar to whole life insurance except that the policyholder pays premiums for only a limited number of years. In other words, the policy is fully paid up after a certain number of years and then remains in force without any additional premium payments until the death of the insured person. The advantage of limited-payment life insurance is that a policyholder can pay all the premiums during his or her working years but still have continued coverage after retirement.

However, the annual premiums are higher than for whole life insurance.

Endowment life insurance provides both protection and savings, with most of the emphasis on savings. Although this type of insurance policy will pay the face value if the insured should die, its primary purpose is to build up savings for some future purpose such as supplementary income during retirement. For example, if a person takes out a 20-year endowment life insurance policy, at the end of the 20-year period the full face value, or endowment, is payable to the insured. He or she then can elect to take the full endowment in one lump sum or in annual installments over a period of many years. Although many financial analysts believe that other types of savings programs can provide the same cash values at lower costs, many people use an endowment life insurance policy to ensure adequate income during their retirement years.

Check Your Understanding

1. List and describe the various kinds of automobile insurance. Who pays a higher auto insurance rate than any other group? Why?

2. What kinds of hazards are covered by homeowner's insurance?

3. Describe three basic kinds of health insurance coverage.

4. Describe four basic types of life insurance.

CAREERS: Insurance Agent

Insurance agents sell insurance policies to individuals and businesses. They have contracts with specific insurance companies, and in this way they differ from insurance brokers. Insurance brokers are independent business persons who sell for many insurance companies. Insurance agents sell one or more of three basic types of insurance: life insurance, casualty insurance, and health insurance. Life insurance agents offer policies that pay survivors when a policyholder dies and, in some cases, provide retirement income. Casualty insurance agents sell policies that protect individuals and businesses from financial losses as a result of autombile accidents, fire or theft, or other losses. Many life and casualty agents also sell health insurance policies covering the cost of hospital and medical care or loss of income that result from illness or injury.

Insurance agents must do a considerable amount of local travel to meet with clients. They usually arrange their own hours of work and often schedule evening and weekend appointments for the convenience of clients. In addition to selling insurance, agents maintain records, prepare reports, and help policyholders settle insurance claims.

Although many insurance companies prefer college graduates as their agents, most will hire high school graduates with potential or proven sales ability, or people who have been successful in other types of work. Many colleges and universities offer courses in insurance, and some offer a bachelor's degree in insurance. College courses in finance, accounting, economics, business

law, and business administration help the insurance agent relate insurance to other personal financial problems and to economic conditions. In addition, courses in psychology, sociology, and public speaking can be useful in improving sales techniques.

All insurance agents must obtain a license in the state where they plan to sell insurance. To obtain a license, agents must pass written examinations covering insurance fundamentals and the state insurance laws. New agents usually receive training at the agencies where they work. In addition, many new agents receive training at the insurance company's home office and accompany experienced agents when they call on prospective clients.

Chapter Highlights

1 Using a budget to plan spending helps individuals and families increase the satisfaction they get from their limited incomes. A budget helps you get what you want most, prevents you from spending beyond your income, helps reduce conflicts, helps you keep track of expenditures, and puts you in control of your money and your life.

2 To prepare a budget, you need to determine how you are currently spending your money and then to make adjustments so you can match your spending to your income. In addition to a monthly budget, you should prepare an annual budget and also give some thought to long-term goals.

3 The five basic types of housing are single-family homes, rental apartments, cooperatives, condominiums, and mobile homes. The advantages of renting housing include a minimal cash outlay, flexibility with regard to moving, and freedom from home-repair and maintenance chores. The disadvantages of renting housing include the lack of property rights, the possibility that the owner may refuse to make prompt repairs, the possibility of rent increases, and the lack of financial breaks for tenants.

4 The advantages of buying housing include tax breaks, the building up of equity in the home, rising real estate values during periods of high inflation, and the feeling of pride and independence that results from home ownership. The disadvantages of buying housing include the high cost, restricted mobility, and the time and money required for general maintenance.

5 In selecting a rental unit, you will want to consider such factors as the size of the unit, how close it is to your job and shopping facilities, what kinds of security measures are available, whether there are any major fire hazards, and the policies regarding children and pets. You also will want to examine the lease carefully before signing it to make sure you are willing and able to comply with all of its provisions.

6 In selecting a home for purchase, you'll want to make sure that it will adequately meet your needs and that the location is convenient.

7 In order to buy a home, you usually will need a down payment of 10 to 20 percent of the purchase price and you will have to obtain a mortgage loan to finance the balance. The four most common types of home mortgage loans are fixed-rate mortgages, adjustable-rate mortgages, graduated-payment mortgages, and flexible loan insurance programs.

8   Owning a car is a considerable expense because of the many costs involved. You should obtain as much information as possible and do a lot of comparison shopping before making a commitment to buy either a new or a used car.

9   Shopping for appliances and furniture is often difficult for many consumers. Because these items can be quite expensive and are supposed to last for many years, it is important for consumers to obtain as much information as possible before making a purchase.

10   The three basic types of food stores are food supermarkets, discount food stores, and convenience stores. Supermarkets carry a wide selection of most food items but prices are usually higher than those of discount food stores. However, discount food stores do not always carry a wide selection of all food items, and some sell merchandise only by the case. Prices in convenience stores are usually much higher than in supermarkets and discount stores, and consumers should avoid making major food purchases in such stores.

11   Consumers often can save money by purchasing regional or generic brands. They also can save money by using manufacturers' coupons and by comparing the unit prices of food items as the basis for making choices.

12   Clothing serves both physical and psychological needs for most people, and your needs will determine the kind and amount of clothing you will buy.

13   Most people buy several different kinds of insurance during their lifetimes. Types of automobile insurance coverage include liability insurance, collision insurance, and comprehensive physical damage insurance. Homeowner's insurance covers such hazards as fire, lightning, windstorms, explosions, theft, and liability.

14   Because the risk of severe illness or injury poses a serious threat to their financial security, most Americans carry some form of private health insurance. The three basic categories of health insurance are basic-coverage insurance, major medical-expense insurance, and disability income insurance.

15   Life insurance is purchased to protect dependents of the policyholder in the event of his or her death. The four basic types of life insurance are term life insurance, whole life insurance, limited-payment insurance, and endowment life insurance.

Important Terms

Match each of the following terms with the correct definition:

durable consumer goods
nondurable consumer goods
budget
impulse buying
cooperative
budgeting

graduated-payment mortgage
standard fixed-rate mortgage
flexible loan insurance program
adjustable-rate mortgage
condominium
food co-ops

1. A type of mortgage in which the interest rate for the loan can rise and fall with interest rates in general.

2. A spending plan based on expected income.

3. An apartment building or group of dwellings in which each individual housing unit is privately owned.

4. Nonprofit organizations that offer their members lower food prices.

5. Unplanned buying resulting from a sudden urge to have something.

6. A type of mortgage with a fixed interest rate but variable monthly payments that start out low but gradually increase over a period of years.

7. Consumer goods, such as food and clothing, that usually do not last very long.

8. A type of mortgage in which the monthly payment and interest rate remain at one level for the lifetime of the loan.

9. Using a spending plan based on expected income.

10. An apartment building or group of dwellings that is owned by a nonprofit corporation.

11. A type of mortgage in which all or part of the down payment is deposited in an interest-earning account from which some money is withdrawn each month during the early years of the loan to supplement the borrower's low payment.

12. Consumer goods, such as appliances and furniture, that usually last for several years.

Extending Your Understanding

1. What advice would you give someone who is planning to go shopping for a car? For furniture and appliances?

2. If you were buying a house in the near future, which kind of mortgage loan would you want to obtain? Explain your answer.

3. If you were planning to buy life insurance at the end of this year, which kind do you think you would buy? Why? Would your answer be the same if you were 50 years old? Explain your answer.

Activities

1. On your next trip to the supermarket, compare the prices for several comparable national brand, local or regional brand, and generic brand items. Make a chart that shows how these prices compare.

Item	Actual Monthly Expenditure	Proposed Adjustments	Proposed Budget Allotment
CLOTHING			
New Purchases	_____	_____	_____
Dry Cleaning/Laundry	_____	_____	_____
TRANSPORTATION			
Auto Payments and Insurance	_____	_____	_____
Auto Maintenance/Gas and Oil	_____	_____	_____
Public Transportation	_____	_____	_____
EDUCATION			
School Supplies	_____	_____	_____
School Trips	_____	_____	_____
RECREATION			
Trips	_____	_____	_____
Tickets	_____	_____	_____
Records/Tapes	_____	_____	_____
Eating Out	_____	_____	_____
TOTAL MONTHLY EXPENDITURES	_____	_____	_____
TOTAL MONTHLY SAVINGS	+ _____	+ _____	+ _____
TOTAL MONTHLY INCOME	_____	_____	_____

2. Based on your current income (from working, your allowance, gifts, and so forth), design a personal budget for the coming month. In general, you should follow the steps discussed earlier in this chapter on designing a family budget. The first step involves keeping a detailed record of your expenditures for a typical month. Consider such expenditures as clothing, recreation, and school-related expenses. Record all expenditures on a worksheet like the one on page 391, but in the first column include only those items that reflect your particular needs. Then compare these expenditures with your expected monthly income. If you are spending more than you will be earning, you will have to find ways of cutting your spending. Consider what adjustments you can make and record them in Column 3. After you have made the necessary adjustments, record your new budget allotment for each item in Column 4. Be sure to allow for monthly savings since you probably will need to save money for college and for items, such as gifts, school trips, and so forth. Keep a copy of your budget for yourself only. If you can, do one for each upcoming month to help you spend your money wisely.

Building Skills in Economics: Understanding Warranties

One of the ways of getting the most for your money is to make sure that you understand the warranty that comes with a product. A **warranty** is a written guarantee that covers repairs or replacement in case something goes wrong with the product during a specified time period. Warranties may be either full or limited. A **full warranty** covers the total cost of repair, regardless of the problem. If a product turns out to be defective, the company will totally repair or replace it at no cost to the consumer. In contrast, a **limited warranty** has some restrictions. It may cover only certain kinds of repairs or state certain conditions under which the repairs will be made.

In addition, all products carry an **implied warranty,** whether or not they carry a written warranty. This means that a product should do what it is supposed to do. For example, if a microwave oven is supposed to defrost food, the consumer can return it for a complete refund if it fails to perform this function.

The warranty that follows covers an electric typewriter. The questions will help you understand it.

Applying Economics Skills

1. Is this a full or limited warranty? Explain your answer.
2. What is the specified time period covered by this warranty?
3. What kinds of repairs are covered? What kinds are not included?
4. Are there any charges involved? Explain.

WARRANTY

90-Day Warranty

Typefast Corporation warrants this typewriter against defects in parts for a period of 90 days from the date of purchase. During this period, Typefast will replace any defective part at no charge. There will be a standard charge for labor and the cost of transportation.

This warranty does not cover damage resulting from accident or from misuse of the unit, including any modification or alteration of the unit, or from attaching the unit to other than the recommended receptacle or voltage. This warranty does not cover ribbon replacement or cleaning of the unit.

This warranty is void when service or repairs are performed by a nonauthorized service location. This warranty does not cover shipping expenses to and from a service location. To determine the location of the nearest authorized service center, consult the attached card.*

*Warranties generally are accompanied by a list of service centers.

CHAPTER 18

BORROWING AND INVESTING

Kathy and Stanley Kirkpatrick were all smiles as they left the bank. Their loan application had been approved and they were finally going to be able to buy a home of their own. They were so excited that they didn't even notice Philip Schultz leave the bank right ahead of them. Philip, who lives in the same apartment building as the Kirkpatricks, also was happy because the bank had just lent him the money to buy a new car.

Like the Kirkpatricks and Philip Schultz, you, too, will probably borrow money in the future. Most people have to borrow money for major purchases like automobiles and homes, and many people borrow money to finance such things as a college education, a vacation trip, or the purchase of furniture and appliances. In this chapter, we will examine the various aspects of borrowing money, including the different types of loans and lenders. We will look also at various investment options. Let us begin with a look at credit and the importance of establishing and maintaining a good credit rating.

Credit and Credit Ratings

Credit is the lending of money, either directly or indirectly, to enable a person to buy goods and services now but pay for them at a later date. It can take the form of a loan from a bank or other lender or the use of a credit card to make a purchase. In either case, you are borrowing money with the promise to repay it at some time in the future.

At one time or another most Americans use credit. Otherwise, they would be unable to buy such expensive items as a home or a car. Credit enables people to buy things and enjoy them sooner than if they had to save and pay cash for them. However, using credit also means going into debt. A bank, a store, or a company is lending you money so that you can buy an item without having to pay for it at the time of purchase. In return, you usually will have to pay interest or a fee for the privilege of buying on credit.

Every month, or other set period, you will have to pay a portion of your debt. It is very important to pay your debts on time to avoid obtaining a bad credit rating. A **credit rating** is an estimate of the probability that a potential borrower will repay a loan with interest when due. The higher your credit rating, the easier it will be for you to obtain credit. A bad credit rating can make it difficult for you to obtain credit in the future.

For purposes of illustration, let us suppose that ten years from now you apply for a loan at a bank. How will the bank decide whether or not to approve your loan application? It will determine your credit rating, which will be based primarily on three factors: (1) your ability to repay the loan; (2) your past credit history; and (3) the amount of collateral that you have to offer as security for the loan.

Your ability to repay the loan will depend on both your income and how many other debts you have. The bank will want to know where you are employed, how long you have held your present job, and how much you earn. If you have a record of steady employment, the bank will view that as a good indication that you will continue to have a steady income in the future. However, if you have held several different jobs in the past two years, the bank probably will have doubts about your income stability. In addition to your income, the bank also will want to know how much money you owe to other lenders. Even with a good income, you may not be able to repay the loan if you have too many other debt obligations.

The second factor that will affect your credit rating is your past credit history. The bank will view your credit history as a good indication of your trustworthiness. If in the past you have always paid your debts on time, the bank probably will assume that you will continue to do so in the future. If, on the other hand, you have had a poor repayment record over the past few years, the bank may deny you credit on that basis.

In order to borrow money from a bank or obtain a credit card, an individual has to fill out a loan application. The application requests personal information about employment, earnings, and past credit history.

A lender can obtain information about a person's past and present credit status from the local credit bureau. **A credit bureau** is a private business firm that collects credit information about consumers and sells this information to lenders for a fee. There are more than 2,500 credit bureaus in the United States, and they process an average of 150 million credit reports a year. A credit bureau has credit information on almost all individuals who use any form of credit, and it can provide a lender with a list of an individual's current debts as well as a record of the individual's credit history. Furthermore, through a system of computer networks, the credit bureau can find out about any debts, including overdue ones, that an individual has anywhere in the country. Thus, an individual cannot move to another city or state and start with a clean credit slate.

The third factor that will affect your credit rating is collateral. **Collateral** is something of value that a borrower pledges as assurance that a loan will be repaid. For example, suppose that you want to borrow money from the bank to pay an unexpected hospital bill. The bank may ask you to use your car, your home, or some other item as collateral before approving your loan. You will sign an agreement that allows the bank to seize and sell the collateral to obtain repayment of the loan if you fail to repay it.

Check Your Understanding

1. What is credit? How does a person's past credit history affect that person's credit rating? What other factors are involved?

2. What is collateral? Why do lending institutions often require collateral when making loans?

Types and Sources of Credit

Credit is available in several different forms and from many sources. We will examine the most common types and sources.

Home Mortgage Loans

We discussed the various types of home mortgage loans in the previous chapter. Savings and loan associations, savings banks, and commercial banks are the primary sources of home mortgage loans. Usually, the borrower must have a down payment of 10 to 20 percent and will repay the loan in monthly installments over a period of 25 to 30 years. That is, the borrower will pay a fixed amount each month for the period of the loan. Part of the monthly payment goes for interest on the loan. The balance goes toward repaying the principal, the amount that was originally borrowed.

Home-Improvement Loans

Commercial banks, savings and loan associations, savings banks, and some credit unions make a type of loan that is usually called a home-improvement loan. As collateral for this type of loan, the lender accepts a second mortgage on the borrower's home. This means that if the borrower should fail to repay his or her debts, the lender who holds the first mortgage could seize and sell the house to obtain repayment, and the lender who holds the *second* mortgage would have second claim on any funds obtained from the sale of that house. In other words, any funds left over after the first mortgage holder obtains full repayment of its loan will be available for repaying the holder of the second mortgage. In order to obtain such a loan, the borrower must have enough equity in his or her home so that the market value of the home is high enough to cover both the first mortgage and the second mortgage.

Homeowners may take out a second mortgage to finance major improvements, such as adding on a room or finishing a basement. Such improvements will usually add to the value of the property.

As the name implies, home-improvement loans often are used to make improvements on a home, such as remodeling or adding a garage. However, the funds do not have to be used for this purpose. Some borrowers use the funds for such purposes as paying off other bills or financing a vacation trip. Home-improvement loans usually are made for periods ranging from five to ten years and are repaid in monthly installments.

Auto and Other Consumer Goods Loans

Loans for the purchase of new automobiles usually are made for periods of three to five years, with a required down payment of at least 20 percent. Loans for used automobiles usually are made for periods of two to three years, with a required down payment of at least 30 percent. In both cases, the loans are repaid in monthly installments. It often pays to shop around for an auto loan—at least for a new car—because there is usually intense competition among lenders. Auto loans are made by automobile manufacturers, commercial banks, savings and loan associations, savings banks, and credit unions. When shopping for an auto loan, however, be aware of any hidden charges that the lender is including. These may include extra insurance charges, extra maintenance policies, and additional fees.

Loans for other types of consumer goods, such as appliances and furniture, are similar to those for automobiles, with the length of the loan usually ranging from one to three years. Financing for such items is often available directly from the sellers as well as from commercial banks, savings and loan associations, savings banks, and credit unions.

Even when taking out a short-term personal loan, the consumer needs to find out the interest rate as well as the amount of time he or she has in which to repay the loan.

Personal Loans

Consumers often need to borrow cash to pay for unexpected expenses, to finance a vacation, to pay off other loans, and for other reasons. The availability of such loans and the interest rate that will have to be paid will depend largely on the financial circumstances of the individual borrower. A person with a good credit rating may be able to go to his or her local bank and obtain a short-term loan of $500 to $1,000 at a reasonable interest rate and without having to provide collateral for the loan. In some instances, the amount of a short-term loan may be much higher. At the other extreme, a person with a poor credit rating may be able to borrow the money only at a consumer finance company. Consumer finance companies are financial institutions that specialize in small consumer loans at high interest rates, sometimes as high as 36 percent. These lending institutions do business mainly with consumers who have such a poor credit rating that they cannot get loans from other lending institutions. In addition to commercial banks and consumer finance companies, savings and loan associations, savings banks, and credit unions also make personal loans.

Charge Accounts

Charge accounts are a form of credit that is extended directly to the consumer. This means that consumers do not have to obtain loans before making purchases. Instead, a store or a business allows consumers to charge purchases up to a certain amount with the provision that the consumers will pay for their purchases at a later date. There are three basic types of charge accounts: regular charge accounts, revolving charge accounts, and installment charge accounts.

A **regular charge account,** also known as a 30-day charge, allows an individual or family to charge purchases at a business up to an established credit limit. At the end of each 30-day period, the business mails the customer a bill for the entire amount, which the customer is expected to pay promptly. If the customer does not pay the bill on time, interest is added on. If this new balance is not paid by the next billing period, the customer may lose his or her credit privileges with that business.

With a **revolving charge account,** the customer receives a bill each month and can either pay the entire amount without interest or pay a portion of the bill with interest added to the unpaid balance. The unpaid balance then is carried over to the following month. At that time, the customer again is given the choice of paying the bill in full or paying a portion and carrying over the unpaid balance to which interest has been added. Regardless of what the customer decides to do, however, he or she can continue to charge purchases so long as the total balance of the account does not exceed the credit limit.

Most major items, such as home appliances, that are purchased on credit are charged to an **installment charge account.** Installment charge accounts are similar to the installment loans for automobiles and other consumer goods discussed earlier. Often the customer must make a down payment and then monthly installment payments, part of which are interest, for a specified time period.

Credit Cards

Many charge account purchases are made with credit cards. **Credit cards** are plastic, wallet-size cards that are imprinted with a customer's name, his or her account number, and the expiration date. To use a credit card, the customer presents the card at the time of purchase and the salesclerk checks the card and records the purchase with it. The customer receives a receipt and will receive a bill at the end of the company's billing period.

Some credit cards can be used only at the store or company that issues them. This is usually true with department store or oil company credit cards. Some credit cards, however, are acceptable at thousands of business establishments throughout the nation and in many foreign countries. The most popular credit cards of this type are Visa, Mastercard, American Express, Diners Club, and Carte Blanche. These cards are widely accepted by stores, hotels and motels, travel services, and many other places of business.

Although you don't pay any interest charges if you pay your entire bill each month, credit cards are not free. Businesses must pay a certain percentage of credit purchases to the credit card company or bank that issues the credit card. Businesses pass this cost on to customers in the form of higher prices. In addition, many credit card users must pay an annual fee for the privilege of having their cards, whether they use them or not.

Many businesses list what credit cards they accept on their doors or windows. Consumers find credit cards a convenient way to shop because they do not have to carry cash and they will receive a monthly statement that itemizes their purchases. However, consumers pay for this convenience in the form of higher prices.

The Costs of Credit

As we mentioned earlier, by using credit people are able to buy and enjoy things sooner than they would if they had to save and pay cash for them. That is the benefit of credit. The cost of credit is the additional money that people must pay in order to have things sooner. Let us look at some of the specifics of the cost of credit.

Finance Charges and Interest Rates

When shopping for a loan or for an item that will be purchased on credit, it is important to understand just how much the credit will cost you. Since various lenders offer different combinations of down payment, length of loan, and size of monthly payments, it is often difficult for consumers to determine the comparative costs of the various loans. For example, a larger down payment usually will mean smaller monthly payments. However, the size of the monthly payments will depend also on the length of the loan. Two concepts that are very useful in making comparisons among loans are the finance charges and the annual percentage rates (APR) of interest.

The **finance charge** is the exact total cost of credit expressed in dollars and cents. The **annual percentage rate (APR)** is the percentage cost of credit per year. The Truth in Lending provisions of the Consumer Protection Act of 1968 require a creditor to tell the borrower in writing before any agreement is signed the exact amount of the finance charge in dollars and cents. This law also requires the lender to convert the finance charge to an annual percentage rate. The higher the APR, the greater the cost of the loan. For example, a loan with an APR of 16 percent is more expensive than one with an APR of 15 percent. By comparing the finance charges and APRs of the various lenders, the consumer should be able to determine which loan will cost the least.

Methods of Calculating Finance Charges

By simply comparing the finance charges and the APRs, as discussed above, the consumer can get a fairly accurate picture of the relative costs of installment loans that involve fixed monthly payments for a fixed number of months. However, it is not as easy to determine the relative costs of open-end credit. Open-end credit, also called revolving credit, includes department-store revolving charge accounts and credit cards. With open-end credit, the method of calculating finance charges can affect the cost of credit to the consumer. The three most common methods of calculating finance charges are adjusted balance, previous balance, and average daily balance.

With the **adjusted balance method,** creditors add finance charges only after subtracting all payments made during the payment period. If the total amount is paid off at any time before the end of the period, there will not be any interest charge. If the total amount is not paid off during the period, interest will be charged on only the remaining unpaid balance at the end of the period.

Under the **previous balance method,** the finance charge is based on the payment period's opening balance. Thus, no credit is given to the consumer for any payments made during the payment period. Even if the total amount is paid off during the first week of the billing period, interest will be charged on the entire amount for the full payment period. With this method of calculating finance charges, there is no advantage in paying off a debt early.

The **average daily balance method** requires creditors to compute the outstanding balance each day during the billing period. The finance charge is then based on the average daily balance for the period. Under this method, payments made early in the period will reduce the average daily balance and thus the finance charges for the period.

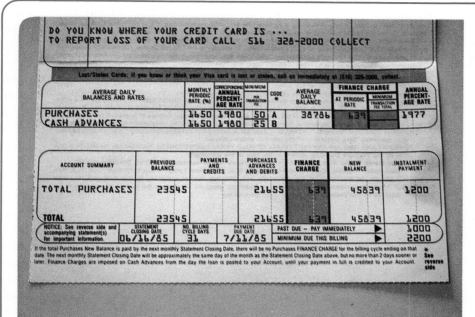

This monthly statement from a credit card company shows how the company calculates the finance charges.

Check Your Understanding

1. What are the various types of loans available to consumers? Where are these loans obtained?

2. What is a consumer finance company? Why do some people use them?

3. Describe the three basic types of charge accounts.

4. What are credit cards? What costs are involved with their use?

5. Describe two concepts that are very useful in comparing the costs of different loans.

6. Describe three methods of calculating finance charges.

Saving and Investing

In addition to borrowing money, most people also save and invest money. There is a significant difference between the two concepts. You save money when you give up the opportunity to spend it now so that it can be used later. You invest money by using it in a way that will earn additional money. You may not have much money to save or invest right now, but you probably will at some time in the future.

Reasons for Saving

There are many reasons for saving. As you learned in the previous chapter, one reason for saving is to be able to cover such unexpected expenses as a major auto repair bill or a large hospital bill. Another reason for saving is to accumulate a fund for some planned major expenditure in the future. People save for such things as a down payment on a home, the purchase of a new car, an expensive vacation trip, or a college education for their children. By saving a small amount each week or each month, it is possible to accumulate a substantial amount of money over a period of a few years.

Still another reason for saving is to build up a retirement fund. Because Social Security benefits are too small to allow most people to live comfortably on them, many people set aside a certain proportion of their income each year to build up a fund that can be used to supplement Social Security when they retire. By saving in this way, they are able to spread their spending more evenly over their entire lifetime.

Investment Concepts and Terms

Regardless of the reasons for saving, most people want to invest their savings so that they can earn additional money. As a first step in understanding investment, let us look at some of the most common investment concepts and terms used by financial experts. They include yield, risk, capital gains, capital loss, and liquidity.

The term **yield** refers to the return on an investment. The yield from an investment is the amount of money that the investment earns. This amount often is expressed as a percentage of the original investment. For example, if you put $100 in a savings account for one year and receive $6 interest at the end of the year, the yield on your investment is six percent.

Risk is the possibility that a financial investment will lose money. Risk can mean a lower yield on an investment than expected, or it can mean loss of part or all of the actual investment. There is a strong relationship between risk and yield: generally, the higher the potential yield, the higher the risk. For example, suppose you invest your money in the drilling of an oil well. If you strike oil, you may reap an enormous yield. However, there is a high risk that you will not strike oil and that you will lose part or all of your investment.

The value of some investments, such as stocks and real estate, changes. When the value of an investment rises so that an investor is able to sell it for more money than he or she paid, the investor experiences a **capital gain.** However, if an investment must be sold for less than its original cost, the investor experiences a **capital loss.** For example, suppose you purchased some land five years ago for $20,000. If you are now able to sell it for $30,000, you have experienced a capital gain of $10,000. On the other hand, if you must now sell it for $15,000, you have experienced a capital loss of $5,000.

As you learned in Chapter 11, the term "liquidity" refers to the ease with which an asset can be converted into cash quickly without loss of value in terms of money. In this case, asset refers to an investment. Investors like their investments to be liquid, but they are often faced with a dilemma. Very liquid investments usually have a low yield. Money in a passbook savings account at a bank, for example, is very liquid because it usually can be withdrawn at any time. However, it earns a relatively low interest rate, and there is no possibility for a capital gain. In contrast, an investment in real estate offers the possibility of a high yield in the form of a substantial capital gain. This investment is not very liquid, however, because it sometimes takes months, or even years, to sell real estate.

Alternative Investment Options

There are many ways in which people can invest their money, and it is often difficult to determine which investment option is best. Investors are torn between the desire to earn a high yield on their investments and the desire for low risk and high liquidity. Generally, in order to get the maximum potential yield on an investment, the investor must accept increased risk and reduced liquidity. Let us examine some specific investment options.

Bank deposits Depositing money in government-insured accounts at banks and other financial institutions is one of the safest of all possible investments. As long as you do not deposit more than $100,000 (the maximum amount covered by the FDIC and the FSLIC) in any one account, there is virtually no risk. However, in return for the low risk, you must make some sacrifice in terms of yield and/or liquidity. Deposits in NOW accounts and passbook savings accounts have the advantage of high liquidity in addition to low risk, but they have a relatively low yield. An investor can obtain a higher yield while retaining high liquidity and low risk by depositing his or her money in a special type of savings account called a **money market account.** In such accounts, however, a substantial minimum balance may have to be maintained in order to obtain the higher yield.

A **certificate of deposit (CD)** has the highest yield of any investment offered by banks and other financial institutions. This form of investment pays a guaranteed rate of interest over a specific time period. However, in order to obtain this high yield, the depositor must agree to leave the money on deposit for the specified time period. This involves a sacrifice in terms of liquidity. There are various types of CDs. Some CDs require a minimum deposit of $10,000 for a period of six months. Others are available with a minimum deposit of as little as $250 but they require that the money be deposited for 30 months. Withdrawal of money from a CD before the designated time period usually involves a substantial cash penalty.

Corporate bonds As you learned in Chapter 4, corporations borrow money by selling bonds. A corporate bond is a certificate issued by a company in exchange for borrowed money. When an investor buys a corporate bond, he or she is lending money to the corporation at a stipulated interest rate for a specific time period. Corporate bonds can be a good investment. The investor is guaranteed a specific interest rate, and interest must always be paid whether the corporation makes a profit or not. Furthermore, if a corporation should encounter financial problems, the obligations to bondholders must be met before any claims of stockholders can be considered.

Government securities In addition to corporate bonds, investors have the option of buying several different types of government bonds and other securities. When investors buy government securities, they are lending money to the government in exchange for interest payments. Interest earned on bonds sold by state and local governments is exempt from federal income taxes. Also, interest earned on bonds issued by the investor's own city or state is exempt from city and state income taxes. These tax-exempt bonds are a good investment for people who would have to pay a high income tax on interest earned from other investments.

The federal government offers various types of government securities, the most common being the United States Savings Bond. One of the greatest attractions of this type of security is its availability in low denominations. The lowest denomination currently being sold is a $50 bond, which sells for $25 and becomes worth $50 after seven years and ten months. This means that people with very limited incomes can invest in this type of bond. United States Savings Bonds also have some tax advantages. Interest earned on such bonds is exempt from state and local income taxes, and federal income tax on the interest does not have to be paid until the bonds are cashed in.

The federal government sells other types of securities that pay substantially higher interest rates than savings bonds. These include Treasury bills, Treasury notes, and Treasury bonds. The major difference among these three types of securities is the size of the minimum purchase and the maturity period, or the length of time before they can be cashed in. The minimum denomination of Treasury bills is $10,000, and the length of maturity ranges from 30 days to one year. Treasury notes mature in one to ten years and can be bought in denominations of $1,000 or $5,000, depending on the length of maturity. Treasury bonds run for more than ten years and can be bought in minimum denominations of $1,000. Interest earned on Treasury bills, notes, and bonds is exempt from state and local income taxes but not from the federal income tax.

Corporate stocks Stocks are one of the most popular forms of investment, with millions of Americans owning shares of stock. As you learned in Chapter 4, a corporation sells shares of stock in order to raise money for expanding its business. Unlike corporate bonds which represent a loan to the corporation, shares of stock represent partial ownership of the corporation and entitle the investor to share in the profits of the corporation by receiving dividends.

People buy stocks for various reasons. Some are interested in the long-term growth of their investment. In this case, they may buy either low-priced stock in a new company in the hopes that the stock will grow substantially over the next few years or stock in one of the large well-established firms with the idea that growth will at least be steady over the long run. Other investors, however, are more interested in short-term gains. They attempt to buy stock when the price is low with the hope that the price will rise substantially in the near future so that they can sell it and earn a profit. Buying and selling stocks for the purpose of making short-term capital gains is called speculation. Speculators sometimes earn large profits, but they also stand the risk of experiencing heavy losses.

In addition to the risk factor, frequent buying and selling of stocks can be costly in terms of the fees that must be paid to stockbrokers each time stock is bought and sold. A **stockbroker** is a person who is employed by a brokerage firm and serves as a go-between for buyers and sellers of stock. There are thousands of brokerage firms throughout the United States that buy and sell stocks for investors.

Mutual funds A type of investment that often appeals to investors with only a small amount of money to invest is called a mutual fund. A **mutual fund** is an investment company that pools the money of many investors and uses it to buy stocks and other securities. In exchange for their money, the investors receive shares of the mutual fund. Since most mutual funds own a variety of stocks and bonds, the chance of a major loss is minimized. Mutual funds make diversification possible for the small investor.

One very popular form of mutual fund is the **money market mutual fund.** In this form of investment, the investors' money is used to buy large bank certificates of deposit, high-yield government securities, and high-yield bonds of

Individuals and institutions buy stocks, hoping to earn a profit in the short or long term.

On the floor of the New York Stock Exchange, millions of shares of stock are bought and sold each day. The most current prices are posted on television monitors so that brokers can find out instantly what any stock is worth at any given time.

major corporations. Although these money market funds (unlike money market accounts in financial institutions) are not insured by the government, they are generally low-risk investments because of the types of securities they hold. These funds are also almost as liquid as a checking account because most of them allow investors to write checks against their money in the fund subject to a minimum amount, usually $500.

Real estate Real estate sometimes can be a good investment, but it is often a high-risk investment and one that is not very liquid. Investors often dream of buying a piece of barren land and seeing the value of the land soar as the surrounding area is developed. It may take years, however, for the value of the land to increase significantly, if it ever does. In the meantime, the investor must pay taxes on the land, and unless it can be farmed or used in some other way, the person will have no income from the investment. Furthermore, if the investor should want to turn the investment into cash, it could take months, or even years, to sell the land.

Investing in housing or other buildings is usually less risky than investing in barren land. Buying your own home can be a very good investment, and some investors experience high yields from investments in rental properties. However, because of the liquidity problem, you must be very careful when making investments in real estate.

Borrowing money for a college education is a long-term investment because people with college degrees generally earn more than those without.

Savings, Investments, and You

Now that we've examined the various investment options, you should have a better understanding of the opportunities that will be available to you when you have money to invest. Right now you may think that you'll never have any money to invest, and you may not have very much for quite some time. In your early adult years, you are more likely to be borrowing money than investing it. Even borrowed money, however, can sometimes represent an investment. The money you spend for a college education, even if it is borrowed money, is an investment in your future that should increase your future earning power as well as your job security and self-satisfaction.

Furthermore, when you have completed your formal education and have a good job, you will find that with the proper management of your money, you can set aside a small amount of savings on a regular basis. When you do, you will want to put those savings to work by investing them. If you save regularly and invest your savings wisely, you'll be surprised at how much you can accumulate in a few years' time. Moreover, by saving and investing, you not only will be helping yourself, you also will be playing a vital role in the American economy by making funds available for those who need to borrow.

Check Your Understanding

1. What are some of the reasons people save?

2. Describe the different types of bank deposits. What are the advantages and disadvantages of each?

3. Describe corporate bonds and government securities as investment options.

4. Why do people invest in corporate stock?

5. How do mutual funds compare with real estate in terms of risk?

CAREERS: Securities Sales Worker

Securities sales workers—also called brokers and account executives—buy and sell stocks, bonds, and other financial securities for clients. They also explain the meaning of stock market terms and trading practices, offer financial counseling, and offer advice on the purchase of a particular security. Before purchasing securities for clients, sales workers furnish information about the advantages and disadvantages of an investment based on each client's objectives. In addition, they supply the latest price quotations on any security in which a client is interested, as well as information on the activities and financial condition of the corporation issuing the security.

Securities sales workers usually work in offices where there is much activity. They have access to computer terminals that continually provide information on the prices of securities, and at times the pace can become very hectic. Although established workers usually work the same hours as other business people, beginners who are seeking clients may work much longer hours. In addition, most sales workers accommodate clients by meeting with them on weekends or evenings. Securities sales workers are employed by brokerage and investment firms in all parts of the country. However, most are employed by a small number of large firms with main offices in New York and other large cities.

Because securities sales workers must be well informed about economic conditions and trends, a college education is usually essential. Courses in business administration, economics, and finance are especially useful, although many employers consider personal qualities and skills more important than specific academic training. Employers seek applicants with good communication skills and a strong desire to succeed. Because maturity and the ability to work independently are important qualifications, many employers prefer to hire applicants who have achieved success in other jobs, such as selling insurance or real estate.

Chapter Highlights

1   Credit enables people to buy things and enjoy them sooner than they could if they had to pay cash for them. Credit, however, also means going into debt, and failure to repay your debts on time can result in a bad credit rating.

2   A credit rating is an estimate of the probability that a potential borrower will repay a loan with interest when due. Your credit rating is based primarily on your ability to repay the loan, your past credit history, and the amount of collateral that you have.

3   Credit is available in several different forms, including home mortgage loans, home-improvement loans, auto and other consumer goods loans, personal loans, charge accounts, and credit cards.

4   The finance charge on a loan is the exact total cost of credit expressed in dollars and cents. The annual percentage rate (APR) is the percentage cost of credit per year. The three most common methods of calculating finance charges are the adjusted balance method, the previous balance method, and the average daily balance method.

5   People save money for such reasons as being able to meet unexpected expenses, accumulating a fund for some planned future expenditure, and building up a retirement fund.

6   Depositing money in government-insured accounts at banks and other financial institutions is one of the safest of all possible investments. Types of bank deposits include NOW accounts and passbook savings accounts, money market accounts, and CDs. These vary in terms of yield and liquidity.

7   Corporate bonds represent a loan from the investor to the corporation. The investor in corporate bonds is guaranteed a specific interest rate, and interest must always be paid whether the corporation makes a profit or not.

8   Types of government securities include state and local government bonds, United States Savings Bonds, Treasury bills, Treasury notes, and Treasury bonds.

9   Stocks are one of the most popular forms of investment. Shares of stock represent partial ownership of the corporation and entitle the investor to share in the profits of the corporation.

10 A mutual fund is an investment company that pools the money of many investors and uses it to buy stocks and other securities. Mutual funds make diversification possible for the small investor.

11 Real estate can sometimes be a good investment, but it is often a high-risk investment that is not very liquid.

Important Terms

Match each of the following terms with the correct definition:

capital gain	money market account	mutual fund
collateral	annual percentage rate	yield
capital loss	certificate of deposit	stockbroker
credit rating	finance charge	liquidity
credit bureau	charge account	risk
credit cards	credit	

1. Something of value that a borrower pledges as assurance that a loan will be repaid.

2. The lending of money, either directly or indirectly, to enable a person to buy goods and services now but pay for them at a later date.

3. Plastic, wallet-size cards enabling a customer to charge purchases.

4. An estimate of the probability that a potential borrower will repay a loan with interest when due.

5. A form of credit that is extended directly to the consumer by a business.

6. The possibility that a financial investment will lose money.

7. The ease with which an investment can be converted into cash without risk of loss.

8. The percentage cost of credit per year.

9. The return on an investment.

10. A private business firm that collects credit information about consumers and sells this information to lenders for a fee.

11. The exact total cost of credit expressed in dollars and cents.

12. A high-yielding bank deposit that can be withdrawn at any time but which may require a substantial minimum balance in order to earn the high rate of interest.

13. A person who serves as a go-between for buyers and sellers of stock.

14. An investment company that pools the money of many investors and uses it to buy stocks and other securities.

15. A high-yielding type of investment offered by banks and other financial institutions that requires the investor to leave the money on deposit for a specified time period.

16. An increase in the value of an investment.

17. A decrease in the value of an investment.

Extending Your Understanding

1. If you had $10,000 to invest, how would you invest it? Give reasons for your answer.

2. Would you rather save or invest? Why?

3. Review some of the advantages and disadvantages of using credit. If you had enough money to pay for a major purchase with cash, why might you still use credit?

Activities

1. Call or visit various commercial banks, savings and loan associations, savings banks, and credit unions in your community to find out how interest rates compare for automobile loans. Present your findings in a table.

2. Visit a local bank or other financial institution, such as a stock brokerage firm, and ask about the various kinds of investment accounts or opportunities it offers. Prepare a brief description of the types of investment options available and, where appropriate, a chart showing minimum deposit requirements, time period requirements, and the estimated yields of different accounts or options.

Building Skills in Economics: Understanding the Financial Pages

One of the ways in which people who invest in stocks follow their investment is by reading the financial pages of a major newspaper. Newspapers often contain daily listings of stock transactions on the major stock exchanges. These listings contain the annual high and low of each stock stated as a fraction (e.g., 20¼ means $20.25); code letters for each company's name; the annual dividend per share; the yield; the PE ratio (the number of times by which the company's annual earnings must be multiplied to obtain the current stock prices); the daily sales (in hundreds); the daily high and low; the closing price; and the net change in the closing price from the previous day's closing price. By following a stock's record, investors can keep track of how well a stock is doing. Based on what they conclude, they might decide to buy more of a stock, sell all or part of what they already own, or hold onto the stock for future growth.

The brief table that follows shows how stocks are listed in a daily newspaper. The questions will help you interpret the table.

Applying Economics Skills

1. What was the yearly high for the XYZ Company? The yearly low? The daily high? The daily low? Was the closing price higher or lower than the daily high?
2. Did LMZ Company close higher or lower than XYZ? By how much?
3. What were the sales for ZZZ? Was ZZZ up or down from the previous day's closing? Was YYY up or down from the previous day's closing?

52-Week High	Low	Stock	Div	Yld %	PE Ratio	Sales 100s	High	Low	Last	Chg.
23½	16⅛	LMZ	.48	2.5	15	256	19¼	18½	19¼	+½
30¼	9⅜	LTT	....	....	13	206	17⅜	16⅞	17	+⅛
21	12⅞	LUW	1.00	7.6	....	3	13⅛	13⅛	13⅛	+⅛
17⅞	13⅛	Xit	.50	3.2	8	441	16⅛	15⅜	35¾	−¼
38⅝	24¼	XMN	....	....	81	3840	36	35⅝	35¾	+¾
23	19	XYZ pf	2.12	10.8	....	2	19⅝	19⅝	19⅝	−⅛
14¼	8½	YAO	....	....	3	9	10¾	10⅝	10⅝	−¼
69¾	44¾	Ybt	3.00	6.1	....	2100	50⅜	49¼	49½	−1
26⅛	16	YYY	.32	1.7	11	1524	18⅜	17⅛	18½	+½
48¾	36¾	ZOO	1.20	2.7	13	6181	45¾	44¼	44½	−⅜
23⅜	16½	Zmt	.44	1.9	19	1195	23⅝	22½	23⅜	+1⅛
25¼	22⅞	ZZZ pf	2.67	11.1	....	2	24	24	24	....

Glossary

A

ability-to-pay principle   principle of taxation based on the assumption that those most able to pay taxes should pay the most taxes

absolute advantage   the ability of one nation to produce a product with fewer resources than another nation

acid rain   rainfall that contains a high concentration of harmful acids produced by sulfur and nitrogen oxides emitted during the combustion of fossil fuels

adjustable-rate mortgage   a type of mortgage loan in which the interest rate for the loan can rise or fall with interest rates in general throughout the period of the loan

adjusted balance method   a method of calculating finance charges in which creditors add finance charges only after subtracting all payments made during the payment period

advisory arbitration   a process in which a neutral third party's recommended settlement for a labor–management dispute can be refused by either party

agency shop   an arrangement under which employees are not required to join a union but are required to pay union dues

aggregate demand   the total of consumption spending plus investment spending plus government spending

Aid to Families with Dependent Children (AFDC)   a government program under which a family in need because of death, absence from home, disability, or unemployment of a parent can receive cash payments

annual percentage rate (APR)   the percentage cost of credit per year

annually balanced budget   a budget policy under which the government would attempt to have a balanced budget each and every year

antitrust law   law designed to promote and maintain competition by prohibiting practices that tend to lead to the creation of monopoly power

assets   properties, possessions, and anything else of value that a person, organization, or institution owns

authoritarian socialism   a type of socialism in which the government controls most of the means of production and the people have little or no say in the decision-making process; also called *Marxian socialism*

automatic fiscal stabilizers   built-in features of the economy that tend to automatically change government spending and taxes in the desired direction during the various phases of the business cycle

average daily balance method   a method of calculating finance charges in which creditors compute the outstanding balance each day during the billing period

average total cost   the cost that is calculated by dividing the total cost at each output level by the number of units being produced

B

balance of payments   an accounting record of all of a nation's monetary transactions with other countries

balance of trade   the difference in the dollar value of exports and imports

bar graph   a graph that is used for making comparisons in which the indicators are vertical or horizontal bars

barter   a form of trade in which people directly trade goods and services for other types of goods and services without using money

basic-coverage insurance   the type of health insurance that covers the costs of ordinary short-term hospital care, including a daily room allowance, routine nursing care, x-rays, laboratory tests, and drugs and other medicines

benefit principle   the principle that those who benefit from a government program should pay the taxes to finance the program

binding arbitration   a process under which grievances are submitted to a neutral third party, acceptable to both the union and management, who issues a decision that is binding on both parties

Board of Governors   the central policy-making body of the Federal Reserve System

bonds   certificates that are issued by a corporation (or by government) in exchange for borrowed money and that bind the corporation (or government) to pay a fixed sum of money when the bonds reach maturity

boycott   a campaign by workers to discourage people from buying an employer's product in an effort to put economic pressure on the employer

budget   a spending plan based on expected income

budgeting   using a spending plan based on expected income

business cycles   recurrent but irregular fluctuations in economic activity

business firm   an organization that brings together the factors of production for the purpose of producing and/or distributing goods and services

C

capital gain   an increase in the value of an investment

capital goods   human-made productive resources—such as factories, tools, and machines—that are necessary for the production of other goods and services; one of the three factors of production

capital loss   a decrease in the value of an investment

capitalism   an economic system in which businesses are privately owned and operated for profit and where free markets coordinate most economic activity

certificate of deposit (CD) the type of bank deposit that offers the highest yield but requires the depositor to leave the money on deposit for a specific time period

charge account a form of credit that is extended directly to the consumer

circle graph *see* **pie graph**

classical economics the ideas that were formulated by Adam Smith in *The Wealth of Nations* and refined by his followers

closed shop an agreement under which employers hire only union members

collateral something of value that a borrower pledges as assurance that a loan will be repaid

collective bargaining the process by which a union negotiates with management in an attempt to reach a mutually acceptable agreement with regard to wages, hours, and other terms and conditions of employment

collective farms farms in the Soviet Union that are made up of large numbers of peasant families who combine their resources and talents to operate on a collective basis

collective goods and services items that tend to benefit large numbers of people collectively and that would not be available to everyone if each individual had to provide them; also called *public goods and services*

collision insurance a type of automobile insurance that pays for damages to the policyholder's car if it is severely damaged in a collision

command economy an economy in which the basic economic questions are answered by government officials, with individuals having little control over economic decisions; also called *planned economy*

commercial banks financial institutions that have been chartered by the federal government or a state government to receive deposits and make loans

common stock a type of corporate stock that gives stockholders voting privileges but no prior claim on dividends

commune the predominant form of agricultural organization in China that is similar to the collective farm in the Soviet Union

communism a theoretical system characterized by a classless society

comparative advantage a situation in which a country has a greater absolute advantage or less of an "absolute disadvantage" in the production of one of two products

competition the economic rivalry that controls a market economy

conciliation *see* **mediation**

condominium an apartment building or group of dwellings in which each individual housing unit is privately owned

conspiracy doctrine the common law doctrine that the organization of workers for the purpose of obtaining higher wages was a violation of property rights and thus illegal

consumer cooperative a cooperative formed for the purpose of collectively buying consumer products in large quantities at low prices to enable its members to enjoy the savings

consumer goods finished products sold to consumers for their own personal use

consumer price index the measure most often used to determine the inflation rate

consumer protection the process of protecting consumers from unsafe products, unsafe working conditions, and an unsafe environment

consumer sovereignty the process of allowing the people to decide what shall be produced by voting with their dollars for the goods and services they want most

consumption spending the purchase of consumer goods and services by consumers for their own personal use

convenience store a type of food store that is often open 24 hours a day but that carries a limited selection and charges higher prices than supermarkets

cooperative   a voluntary association of people formed for the purpose of providing economic benefits for its members; an apartment building or group of dwellings that is owned by a nonprofit corporation and managed by a board of directors elected by the residents

corporate charter   a legal document granted by a state government that gives a business the authority to operate in that state

corporate income taxes   taxes based on the net profits of corporations

corporation   a form of business organization that is collectively owned by a number of individuals but has the legal status to act as a single fictitious person

cost-push inflation   inflation caused by rising production costs

Council for Mutual Economic Assistance (COMECON)   an economic organization that was established in 1949 to promote trade within countries politically influenced by the Soviet Union

coupon payment   *see* interest

court injunction   a court order issued by a judge requiring a party to do, or cease doing, specific activities

craft union   a union composed of workers in a particular trade, such as carpenters, electricians, or plumbers

credit   the lending of money, either directly or indirectly, to enable a person to buy goods now but pay for them at a later date

credit bureau   a private business firm that collects credit information about consumers and sells this information to lenders for a fee

credit cards   plastic, wallet-size cards enabling a customer to charge purchases

credit rating   an estimate of the probability that a potential borrower will repay a loan with interest when due

credit unions   cooperative associations often organized among the employees of large companies or the members of large labor unions in order to offer high interest savings accounts and low-interest loans

Cultural Revolution   a political drive designed to free the Chinese from their traditional customs

customs duties   taxes on goods brought into the United States from other countries

cyclical unemployment   unemployment caused by insufficient aggregate demand

cyclically balanced budget   a budget policy under which the government would attempt to balance its budget over the course of the business cycle

D

deductible   in an insurance policy, the amount of damages you must pay for before the insurance company begins to pay

demand   the ability and willingness of people to buy things

demand curve   a graphical representation of a demand schedule

demand deposits   checkbook money

demand-pull inflation   inflation caused by too much aggregate demand

demand schedule   a listing showing the various amounts of an item that buyers are willing and able to buy at various prices during some stated time period

democratic socialism   a type of socialism under which the people take part in the decision-making process by electing government leaders

depreciation   the wear and tear of the nation's factories, tools, and machines that results from producing the GNP

depression   a prolonged period of little or no growth in the GNP accompanied by high unemployment

devaluation   the lowering of a currency's value in relation to other currencies by government order

disability income insurance   a type of health insurance that provides cash payments to the policyholder for living expenses if the policy holder is unable to work because of a prolonged illness

discount rate   the rate of interest that Federal Reserve Banks charge banks and other financial institutions for loans

diseconomies of scale   the reduction of efficiency and increased cost per unit that sometimes result from a firm becoming too large

disposable personal income   the amount of money that individuals have available for spending after personal taxes are paid

dividends   cash payments made to stockholders out of a corporation's profits

double coincidence of wants   a situation where two people each want exactly what the other person has

double taxation   refers to the fact that corporations have to pay taxes on their profits even though stockholders later pay taxes on some of these profits when they are distributed as dividends

durable consumer goods   consumer goods, such as appliances and furniture, that usually last for several years

E

easy-money policy   a policy of expanding the money supply and reducing interest rates

economic efficiency   the process of producing the maximum amount and proper combination of goods and services from the nation's limited productive resources

economic goods   things of value that can be seen, touched, and shown to others

economic growth   an increase in the economy's capacity to produce goods and services

economic models   simplified representations of the real world that help economists analyze complex problems

economic services   intangible things that have value but cannot be seen, touched, or shown to others

economic system   the organized set of procedures for answering the basic economic questions, What? How? For whom?

economics   the study of how individuals and society choose to use limited resources in an effort to satisfy unlimited wants

economies of scale   the increased efficiency resulting from specialization and the division of labor that makes possible the production of a large volume of output at a lower cost per unit than a small volume of output

elasticity of demand   a measure of the responsiveness of quantity demanded to a change in price

elasticity of supply   a measure of the responsiveness of quantity supplied to a change in price

embargo   a total ban by the government on the import or export of a particular product

endowment life insurance   a form of life insurance whose primary purpose is to build up savings for the policyholder for some future payment

entrepreneur   a person who organizes, manages, and assumes the risks and responsibility for a business

entrepreneurship   the function of combining and organizing natural resources, capital goods, and labor; assuming the risks of business failure; and providing the creativity and managerial skills necessary for production to take place

environment   the resources, forces, and conditions that surround and influence living things

Environmental Protection Agency (EPA)   an independent federal agency created in 1970 to deal with the problems of pollution

equilibrium GNP   that level of GNP at which the total supply of goods and services is exactly equal to total spending

equilibrium price   the price at which the quantity demanded is exactly equal to the quantity supplied

equity   the process of making sure that all people get the same opportunity to obtain goods and services regardless of their ability to pay for them

estate taxes taxes levied on the estates, or property, of people who have died

excess reserves the difference between actual reserves and required reserves

excise taxes taxes levied on the production or sale of specific goods or services

explicit costs those costs that involve an actual payment of money to "outsiders" who supply labor, raw materials, fuel, and so forth to a firm

export to sell a product to another nation

F

factors of production the basic resources needed for the production of goods and services; sometimes called *productive resources*

Federal Advisory Council the 12 commercial bankers who advise the Board of Governors on banking policy

Federal Deposit Insurance Corporation (FDIC) a government agency established by Congress in 1933 to insure bank depositors against bank failures

Federal Open Market Committee Federal Reserve Committee made up of the Board of Governors and five presidents of Federal Reserve Banks that is responsible for directing the buying and selling of government securities

Federal Reserve Banks the 12 banks established by the Federal Reserve Act of 1913

Federal Reserve System the nation's central monetary authority, or "central bank"

fiat money money that is declared legal tender by government decree

finance charge the exact total cost of credit expressed in dollars and cents

fiscal policy the deliberate use of the government's spending and taxing powers to influence economic activity in order to establish desired economic objectives

fixed costs costs—such as rent, insurance premiums, and property taxes—that do not vary with changes in output; sometimes called *overhead costs*

fixed exchange rates an exchange rate system under which the price of one currency is fixed in terms of other currencies so that the rate does not change

flexible exchange rates an exchange rate system under which the forces of supply and demand determine the value of a country's currency in terms of the value of other currencies

flexible loan insurance program a type of mortgage loan in which all or part of the down payment is deposited in an interest-earning account from which some money is withdrawn each month during the early years of the loan to supplement the borrower's low payment

food co-ops nonprofit organizations that offer their members lower food prices

food stamps government-issued coupons that are given or sold for a fraction of their value to eligible low-income persons in an effort to improve their diets

foreign exchange foreign currencies

foreign exchange markets markets that deal in the buying and selling of foreign currencies

foreign exchange rate the price of one currency in terms of another

fossil fuels fuels—including petroleum, natural gas, and coal—that were formed millions of years ago from the remains of plants and animals

fractional reserve banking a banking system based on the provision that only a fraction of a bank's deposits must be held as reserves

frictional unemployment unemployment that involves people who are temporarily between jobs

full-employment balanced budget a budget policy under which the federal budget would be balanced when, and only when, the economy is operating at the full-employment level

full warranty a warranty that covers the total cost of repairing a product, regardless of the problem

G

generic brand brand of merchandise that has only the name of the product on the package

geographic monopoly monopoly that occurs because of a seller's location

gift taxes taxes on gifts of money or other forms of wealth

GNP deflator a special price index used to compensate for distortions in the GNP caused by inflation

Gosplan the central planning agency of the Soviet Union

government monopoly monopoly in which the government itself is the sole producer of a product and serves as the barrier to entry

government securities IOUs issued by the United States Treasury, various agencies of the federal government, and state and local governments

government spending the total spending by all levels of government

graduated-payment mortgage a type of mortgage loan with a fixed interest rate but variable monthly payments that start out low but gradually increase over a period of years

Great Leap Forward a policy designed to drive China's economy forward at a very fast pace

grievance formal complaint accusing either labor or management of violating a collective bargaining agreement

grievance procedure a procedure for settling disagreements over the implementation of a collective bargaining contract without strikes

gross national product (GNP) the total dollar value of all goods and services produced in a year's time measured in terms of their market prices

H

horizontal axis the bottom line of a line or bar graph that always presents units of time

human resources *see* **labor**

I

implicit costs the opportunity costs resulting from a firm's use of resources that it owns

implied warranty a warranty, not necessarily written, guaranteeing that a product will do what it is supposed to do

import to buy a product from another nation

import quota a government policy that places a precise legal limit on the number of units of a particular product that can be imported into a country during a specified time period

impulse buying unplanned buying that results from a sudden urge to have something

income-earning assets assets that earn money for a bank or other institution

income effect the ability to purchase more or less of an item with a given amount of money because of a change in the price

independent union a union that does not belong to the AFL–CIO, the federation of American unions

indirect business taxes a variety of sales taxes that go directly to the government

individual income taxes taxes paid by individuals based on how much they earn

individual proprietorship a form of business organization that is owned by a single individual who makes all the business decisions, receives all the profits, and is responsible for any losses of the firm

industrial union a union composed of workers from a particular industry, regardless of the kinds of jobs they hold

industry a group of firms producing the same or similar products

inflation a general rise in the price level or a decline in the purchasing power of the dollar

installment charge account a type of charge account in which the customer must make a down payment and then must make monthly installments to which interest has been added

interest the fixed sum of money paid to bond-holders annually until the maturity date (also called *coupon payment*); the cost of a loan

investment spending business spending for capital goods: factories, tools, and machines

"invisible-hand" principle the concept that in a market economy if individuals were allowed to pursue their own self-interests without interference by government, their actions would lead to what is best for society

K

Keynesian economics a body of economic theory based on the ideas of John Maynard Keynes, who argued that the government should play an active role in maintaining the proper level of aggregate demand

L

labor any form of human effort exerted in production; one of the three factors of production; also called *human resources*

labor productivity the amount of output produced by a given quantity of labor

labor spy a person hired by management to infiltrate unions and provide management with the names of union members and supporters

law of demand a law stating that as the price of an item rises and other factors remain unchanged, the quantity demanded by buyers will fall; as the price of an item falls and other factors remain unchanged, the quantity demanded by buyers will rise

law of diminishing returns a law stating that increasing the quantity of one factor of production while quantities of the other factors of production remain fixed will eventually result in smaller and smaller increases in total output

law of supply a law stating that as the price of an item rises and other factors remain unchanged, the quantity supplied by suppliers will rise; as the price of an item falls and other factors remain unchanged, the quantity supplied by suppliers will fall

liabilities the debts and obligations of an individual, an organization, or an institution

liability insurance a type of automobile insurance that pays for bodily injury and property damage in the case of accidents for which the policy holder is responsible (liable)

legal tender the fact that money must be accepted for all debts, public and private

less developed countries (LDCs) those nations that share a common set of characteristics, including poverty levels of income, predominantly agricultural economies, rapid population growth, unequal income distribution, and poor health care and educational facilities; also called *developing nations*

lifetime employment commitment a relationship between many employees and employers in Japan where after a brief probationary period, employees are guaranteed continued employment until retirement age

limited payment life insurance a form of life insurance in which the policyholder pays premiums for only a limited number of years although the policy remains in force until the death of the insured person

limited warranty a warranty with restrictions

line graph a graph that is useful for making comparisons and for seeing how a particular item changes over a period of time

liquidity the ease with which an asset can be converted into cash quickly without loss of value in terms of money

lockout the temporary closing of a place of employment by management in an effort to pressure unions to agree to management's terms

long run a time period long enough to allow a firm to vary all of its factors of production, including the size of its plant

M

major medical-expense insurance a type of health insurance designed to supplement basic coverage insurance in order to protect the policyholder from large, unpredictable medical expenses

marginal cost the additional cost of producing one more unit of output

marginal product increased output resulting from an additional unit of labor or other input

marginal revenue the additional revenue that results from producing and selling one more unit of output

market an arrangement through which potential buyers and sellers come together to exchange goods and services

market economy an economy in which the basic economic questions are answered by households and businesses through a system of freely operating markets

markets for consumer products markets in which households are the buyers and businesses are the sellers of many consumer goods and services

markets for productive resources markets in which businesses are the buyers and, to a large extent, households are the sellers of productive resources

Marxian socialism *see* **authoritarian socialism**

mean the average that is computed by adding all the pieces of data together and dividing by the number of pieces

median the piece of data that falls in the middle of a series when the entries are arranged from lowest to highest

mediation a process under which a neutral third party tries to keep the union and management talking in an effort to reach a peaceful settlement to a labor–management dispute; also called *conciliation*

Medicaid a joint federal–state medical insurance program designed to provide health care for the poor

member banks commercial banks that are members of the Federal Reserve System

minimum wage laws laws that set a lower limit on the wage that can be paid to most workers

mixed economy an economy that has characteristics of both a command and a market economy

mode the term that appears most often in any given list

monetarism a school of economic thought that takes the position that the money supply is the key factor determining the economic health of the nation

monetary policy the actions taken by the Federal Reserve System to control the nation's money supply and interest rates in order to achieve desired economic objectives

money anything that is generally accepted and generally used as a medium of payment

money market account a high-yielding bank deposit that requires a substantial minimum balance in order to obtain the higher yield

money market mutual fund a form of mutual fund in which the investors' money is used to buy large certificates of deposit, high-yield government securities, and high-yield bonds of major corporations

money supply the total amount of money in circulation

monopolistic competition   a market structure that is characterized by many sellers, differentiated products, nonprice competition, and relatively easy entry and exit

monopoly   a market structure characterized by a single seller, a product for which there are no close substitutes, and strong barriers to entry that prevent potential competitors from entering the market

mortgage loan   a long-term loan that will be paid in many installments and that gives the lender a claim (mortgage) against the borrower's home

mutual fund   an investment company that pools the money of many investors and uses it to buy stocks and other securities

mutual savings banks   financial institutions totally owned by their depositors, with the purpose of pooling the savings of many small depositors so they can be profitably invested

N

national banks   banks chartered by the federal government

national income   an estimate of the total income earned in the economy in a year's time; net national product minus indirect business taxes

natural monopoly   a monopoly that is formed because competition is not practical

natural resources   productive resources that are provided by nature—such as land, air, water, forests, coal, iron ore, oil, and minerals; one of the three factors of production

near-money   savings accounts and time deposits that are not payable on demand but that can easily be converted into currency

negative income tax   a proposed alternative to current welfare programs under which people who earn less than a certain income would receive cash payments from the government

net national product   a refined measure of the gross national product that is calculated by subtracting from the GNP the total value of the depreciation of all the nation's capital goods during the year

New Economic Policy (NEP)   Lenin's economic policy characterized by the introduction of some capitalist methods

nondurable consumer goods   consumer goods such as food and clothing that usually do not last very long

nonprofit organization   an organization that provides a service and whose revenue is used to further the purposes of the organization

nuclear energy   energy created by fission, or splitting the atoms of uranium

O

oligopoly   a market structure characterized by a few sellers, substantial barriers to entry, standardized or differentiated products, and substantial nonprice competition

open-market operations   the buying and selling by the Fed of government securities in the open market

open shop   an arrangment in which union membership is optional and nonunion members need not pay union dues

opportunity cost   the next best alternative use of a resource that is given up when a decision is made to use resources in a particular way

overhead costs   *see* **fixed costs**

P

particulates   tiny particles of dust, ash, or liquids emitted into the air

partnership   a form of business organization that is collectively owned by two or more people who jointly make the business decisions, share the profits, and bear the financial responsibility for any losses

peak   the highest phase of the business cycle characterized by prosperity and low unemployment

personal economics areas of economics that deal with consumer issues and topics

personal income the total income received by all persons in the nation before personal taxes are paid

picketing standing or walking in front of an employer's place of business with signs that spell out the workers' complaints against the employer

pie graph a circular graph that shows the relationship of the parts of a structure to the whole structure; also called *circle graph*

planned economy *see* **command economy**

pollution the contamination of air, water, and soil

poverty level that level of income at or below which the government officially classifies individuals and families as poor

preferred stock a type of corporate stock that gives the stockholder a prior claim on dividends but no voting privileges

previous balance method a method of calculating finance charges in which the finance charge is based on the payment period's opening balance

price ceiling a government-imposed upper price limit that prevents market forces from establishing a price above this limit

price floor a government-imposed lower price limit that prevents market forces from establishing a price below this limit

price system the coordination and communication system of a market economy based on the principle that everything bought and sold has a price

prime rate the rate of interest that large banks charge their best business customers

principle of diminishing marginal utility the tendency for individuals to receive less and less additional satisfaction from an item as they obtain more and more units of the item during a specific time period

private costs the costs borne by an individual or a business firm as a result of a particular act, such as producing a product

private plots the tiny plots of land in the Soviet Union that each collective farm household and state farm worker is allowed to farm

private sector areas of economic activity in which economic decisions are made primarily by individual households and businesses

producer cooperative a voluntary association of producers of certain products that attempts to obtain higher prices than the members could get by selling individually

productive resources *see* **factors of production**

profit the money a business has left over after all costs are paid; also refers to the financial gain or benefit received by an individual or business as a result of work activity

profit motive the desire to maximize financial gains

progressive tax a tax that takes an increasing percentage of income as income rises

proletariat the term Karl Marx used to refer to the workers or the working class

property taxes taxes levied primarily on land and buildings

proportional tax a tax that takes a constant percentage of income as income rises

proxy signing over voting privileges to the current management of a corporation or to some other group

public finance the study of government expenditures and revenues at all levels of government

public goods and services *see* **collective goods and services**

public sector areas of economic activity in which economic decisions are made primarily by the government

pure competition a market structure characterized by many sellers, standardized products, easy entry and exit, and no artificial restrictions on the free movement of prices and wages up and down

Q

quantity demanded   a specific quantity that will be demanded at a specific price

quantity supplied   a specific quantity that will be supplied at a specific price

R

rate of return   the percentage of the total investment that a business gets back each year from the investment

recession   the downward phase of the business cycle characterized by a decline in GNP and rising unemployment

recovery   the upward phase of the business cycle characterized by decreasing unemployment and increasing business activity

regressive tax   a tax that takes a decreasing percentage of income as income rises

regular charge account   a type of charge account that allows an individual or family to charge purchases at a business up to an established credit limit; also known as a *30-day charge*

required reserves   the amount of reserves that a bank is required to hold as backing for money that has been deposited with it

reserve requirement   a rule that stipulates the percentage of deposits that must be kept as reserves to back up those deposits

revenue   the money a firm receives for the products it sells

revenue per unit   the selling price of a product

revolving charge account   a type of charge account in which the customer can either pay the entire amount each month without interest or pay a portion of the bill with interest added to the unpaid balance

right-to-work laws   state laws that make it illegal to require workers to join a union as a condition of employment

ripple effect   the tendency for a change in one market to cause changes in many other markets

risk   the possibility that a financial investment will lose money

S

sales taxes   taxes levied on the sale of a wide range of goods and services instead of just specific items

savings and loan associations   financial institutions owned and operated by savers that historically made mostly long-term loans for the purpose of buying or building homes

scarcity   the problem of limited resources and unlimited wants

seasonal unemployment   temporary unemployment caused by seasonal factors

seniority rights   certain rights given to employees on the basis of length of service with the company

short run   a time period too short to allow a firm to alter the size of its plant yet long enough to allow the firm to change the level at which the fixed plant is used

Social Security taxes   payroll taxes, half of which are paid by employers and half of which are paid by employees

socialism   an economic system in which most businesses are owned and operated by the government

solar energy   energy that comes from the sun

Solidarity   a union formed by Polish workers in 1980 to combat extensive government control and high food prices and outlawed by the Polish government in 1981

spillover costs   the costs borne by other members of society as a result of an act by an individual or business firm

standard fixed-rate mortgage   a type of mortgage loan in which the monthly payment and the interest rate remain at one level for the lifetime of the loan

standard of living   the quality of life based on the amount of goods and services, leisure time, and so forth that a population has

state banks   banks chartered by state governments

state farms large farms in the Soviet Union that are owned by the government and operated just like industrial firms

statistics numerical facts or data that are assembled, classified, and tabulated

stock shares of ownership in a corporation

stockbroker a person who serves as a go-between for buyers and sellers of stock

stockholders people who buy stock in a corporation

strike a mutual agreement by employees to stop working until their demands are met

structural unemployment unemployment caused by a mismatch between job seekers and job openings

substitution effect the tendency for consumers to substitute lower priced items for more expensive items

Supplemental Security Income for the Aged, Blind, and Disabled (SSI) a federal government program that, based on need, guarantees a minimum income for persons who are at least 65 years old, blind, or disabled

supply the ability and willingness of suppliers to make things available for sale

supply curve a graphical representation of a supply schedule

supply schedule a listing showing the various amounts of an item that sellers are willing to sell at various possible prices

supply-side economics a body of economic ideas based on tax cuts that became a part of national economic policy during the early 1980s under President Ronald Reagan

surplus a situation that results when the quantity supplied exceeds the quantity demanded

synthetic fuels potential substitutes for petroleum that can be made from oil shale, coal, and various forms of plant life

T

table a compact arrangement of related facts and figures, arranged sequentially in horizontal rows and vertical columns

tariff a tax imposed by the government on imported products

technological monopoly a monopoly that is formed as the result of patents

technological unemployment a form of structural unemployment characterized by the extensive use of technology in many industries

term insurance a form of life insurance that insures the life of the policyholder for a specific period of time, usually for one to five years

thermal inversion a condition under which a layer of warm air settles over a layer of cooler air and holds it near the ground

tight-money policy a policy of restricting the availability of credit and forcing interest rates up

total cost the sum of fixed and variable costs at each level of output

total revenue the selling price of an item times the quantity sold

trade deficit a situation in which a country's imports exceed its exports

trade surplus a situation in which a country's exports exceed its imports

traditional economy an economy in which the basic economic questions are answered directly by the people involved, with the answers usually based on how things were done in the past

transfer payments all sources of income to individuals that do not represent current income earned by them for producing goods and services

trend the general movement or course of an event over a substantial period of time

trough the lowest phase of the business cycle characterized by high unemployment and decreased business activity

trust a device that for all practical purposes converts a group of firms into a single monopoly

U

union security arrangement an agreement between a union and an employer that requires employees to join a union or at least pay union dues

union shop an arrangement under which employers are free to hire nonunion workers but the new employees are required to join the union within a specified time period as a condition of continued employment

unlimited liability the potential for a business owner to incur and have to pay unlimited business debts

urban renewal a government program designed to rehabilitate cities

V

variable costs costs—such as labor, raw materials, and power to operate machines—that change as the level of output changes

vertical axis the line on the side of a line graph or bar graph that always presents numerical data

W

wage-push inflation cost-push inflation that is caused by rising wages

warranty a written guarantee that covers repairs or replacement in case something goes wrong with a product during a specified time period

welfare programs programs that attempt to alleviate poverty by providing direct economic assistance to the poor

whole life insurance a form of life insurance that builds up a cash surrender value over the years

World Bank the International Bank for Reconstruction and Development, which provides foreign aid to the less developed countries

Y

yellow-dog contract an agreement under which employees promise not to join a union as a condition of employment

yield the return on an investment

Index

E

PHOTO CREDITS

1, © Larry Nicholson / Photo Researchers, Inc.; 2, NCR Corporation; 4, Giant Supermarkets; 6, Weyerhaeuser Co.; 7, © Stan-Pak / International Stock Photo; 8, United Nations / Photo by B. Wolff; 9, UPI; 11, Gregg Mancuso, Black Star © 1982; 16, Randy O'Rourke / The Stock Market; 18, NCR Corporation; 19, Library of Congress; 20, Wide World Photos; 22, Frost Publishing Group, Ltd.; 25, Wide World Photos; 27, Frost Publishing Group, Ltd.; 28, Library of Congress; 30, Wide World Photos; 33, Helena Frost; 38, © Robert Frererck, 1984 / Woodfin Camp and Associates; 46, Joan Menschenfreund; 57, International Business Machines; 62, © Sepp Seitz, 1984 / Woodfin Camp and Associates; 64, Randy O'Rourke / The Stock Market; 65, Bermuda News Bureau / Photo by Leslie Todd; 67, Isaac Geib / Grant Heilman; 68, Visual Services / Burt Rush; 69, J.C. Penney; 70, American Bank Note Co.; 73, Ocean Spray Cranberries, Inc.; 77, William E. Frost; 82, John Doran; 88, Honeywell; 89, Weyerhaeuser Co.; 93, Phyllis Stevens; 95, Bill Powers; 98, William E. Frost; 100, Dick Durance II, 1980 / Woodfin Camp and Associates; 101, Firestone Tire and Rubber Co.; 106, © Roy Hankey / Photo Researchers; 108, Library of Congress; 110, Library of Congress; 116, Wide World Photos; 117, Honeywell; 119, Tony O'Brien; 121, UPI; 127, © David Burnett, 1981 / Woodfin Camp and Associates; 128, Indiana Department of Commerce; 129, Al Ruland / City of Phoenix; 132, Diamond Shamrock; 137, Giant Supermarkets; 139, (left) Tony O'Brien; (right) Helena Frost; 141, Salt River Project; 146-147, Ford Motor Co.; 148, © Palmer / Kane Inc., 1983 / The Stock Market; 149, Bell-Helicopter, Textron; 152, © Jim Anderson, 1983 / Woodfin Camp and Associates; 155, UPI; 159, Bill Farrell / Peat Marwick; 161, Wide World Photos; 164, (top) Bermuda News Bureau; (bottom) Del Monte Corporation; 166, First National Bank of Arizona; 171, Paul Shambroom, 1982 / Photo Researchers; 173, 174, UPI; 175, Wide World Photos; 178, Visual Services / Burt Rush; 179, Chrysler Corporation; 180, Wide World Photos; 181, UPI; 183, Wide World Photos; 188, Tony O'Brien; 194, © B. Ullman / Taurus Photos; 196, Wide World Photos; 200, Ankers Capitol Photographers; 202, Hill Frost; 211, © Bill Farrell; 216, © Guy Gillette, 1978 / Photo Researchers; 218, © Paul Barton / The Stock Market; 220, Julie Betts Testwuide / Chase Manhattan Bank Archives; 222, Department of the Treasury, Bureau of Engraving and Printing; 222, UPI; 223, © Palmer / Kane, 1984 / The Stock Market; 224, Marine Midland; 226, Julie Betts Testwuide / Chase Manhattan Bank Archives; 227, Arthur Lavine / Chase Manhattan Bank; 229, Wide World Photos; 230, Salt River Project; 235, R.S. Uzzell III, 1981 / Woodfin Camp and Associates; 241, Julie Betts Testwuide / Chase Manhattan Bank Archives; 248, Wide World Photos; 250, © Richard Hutchings / Photo Researchers; 251, Salt River Project; 256-257, © George Hall, 1980 / Woodfin Camp and Associates; 258, Lenore Weber / Taurus Photos; 259, Bill Powers; 261, Jerry Soalt / ILGWU; 263, United Nations / G. Palmer; 264, United Nations Photo; 266, Michal Heron; 267, 268, Wide World Photos; 271, Tony O'Brien;

273, Thomas Airviews; 274, United Nations / B. Grunzweig; 275, Bill Powers; 276, Wide World Photos; 277, BART; 279, Phoenix City Council; 284, © Larry Lee / Woodfin Camp and Associates; 287, Drake Well Museum, Courtesy of the American Petroleum Institute; 288, Internorth, Inc.; 289, United States Steel Corporation; 290, Visual Services / Burt Rush; 291, UPI; 293, Wide World Photos; 294, Owens Corning; 296, © Allen Green, 1972 / Photo Researchers; 297, UPI; 298, William E. Frost; 300, Wide World Photos; 304, Mobil Corporation; 310-311, © Thomas Braise, 1982 / The Stock Market; 312, © Timothy Eagan, 1980 / Woodfin Camp and Associates; 314, USDA; 317, Bill Powers; 318, Michal Heron, 1983; 319, Hill Frost; 321, H.J. Heinz Co.; 322, Wide World Photos; 326, United Nations Photo; 329, Hill Frost; 330, Squibb Corporation; 336, © Susan McCartney, 1979 / Photo Researchers; 337, Frost Publishing Group, Ltd.; 339, Statue of Liberty; 340, Library of Congress; 343-344, John Launos / Black Star; 345, UPI; 346, © Michal Heron, 1983; 347, Rodale Press, Inc.; 348, Michal Heron; 350, Japan Air Lines; 351, © Michal Heron, 1983; 352, Japan Air Lines; 354, United Nations Photo; 355, UPI; 356, United Nations / B. Wolff; 358, Peace Corps / Niger / Redenius; 364-365, Susan McCartney / Photo Researchers; 366, Margot Granitsas / Photo Researchers; 371, Salt River Project; 372, Gulf and Western Corporation; 377, William E. Frost; 379, Bill Powers; 380, William E. Frost; 382, © Sybil Shelton / Peter Arnold, Inc.; 385, Mottke Weissman; 387, MLI Co. Photo Bureau / Karl Nemecek; 394, © Palmer / Kane, Inc., 1983 / The Stock Market; 395, Taurus Photos; 397, Armstrong Tile; 398, First National Bank of Arizona; 401, Helena Frost; 404, Richard Laird; 405, New York Stock Exchange; 406, Maurice Sorrell / Ebony Magazine; 407, Bank of America.

CARTOON PERMISSIONS

53, Roy Doty / *The New York Times*; 80, ©1984 Herblock / *The Washington Post*; 187, Drawing by Modell, ©1973 *The New Yorker* Magazine, Inc.; 201, Hanny / *Philadelphia Enquirer*; 244, Gamble ©1983 / *Florida Times-Union*; 247, Gamble ©1980 / *Nashville Banner*; 295, ©1973 Herblock; 320, Somerville / *The Denver Post.*